Conversation Journal For

GRAVITY:

Seven Essential Truths About Influence, Leadership and Your Soul

Ronald D Kuest

SOUL MASS PRESS
www.soulmasspress.com

Published by Soul Mass Press
6612 153rd Street Court East, Puyallup, WA 98375
www.soulmasspress.com

Journals may be purchased through most retailers
or directly from Soul Mass Press online: **www.soulmasspress.com**

Cover and Interior Design: 4th Avenue Media (www.4thavenuemedia.com)
Designer: Lauren Weldy
Production Manager: Lindsie Lauzen and Cori Geiger
Editor: Annie Roberts

ISBN: 978-1-944858-05-6
1. Spirituality 2. Leadership 3. Business

Printed in the United States of America
First Edition

ABOUT THE AUTHOR

Ron brings to GRAVITY diverse life experience. Trained as a pharmacist, he served 14 years as an executive in Washington State government. He then formed his own consulting group, MBG Management Services, Inc. For 36 years, MBG served major employers throughout the U.S., providing a wide array of cultural and organizational development services.

He formed the Institute for Spiritual Leadership Training and developed the Gravitational Leadership Traits Assessment (2017) - a 360° assessment tool for spiritual and leadership development. Ron is also the author of Embracing Conflict: Finding Peace in the Midst of Tension and Growing the Soul Through Accountability, Disclosure, and Feedback.

Ron's most recent work has included the companion to GRAVITY, A Journey of Friends Conversation Leader/Mentor/Group Member On-line Resource Library, tying the books together into a complete discipling process called The GRAVITY Experience.

Ron lives with Pat, his wife of over 50 years, in Olympia, Washington. Together they raised three children, who in turn are raising four grandchildren. Ron has served as an elder for over 30 years at Evergreen Christian Community Church.

Welcome to the *Conversation Journal* for GRAVITY

The Conversation Journal for Gravity has a distinguishing characteristic some-what different from other excellent discipling programs. The Conversation Journal is based on a transformative relational model while most other discipling programs are based on a traditional educational model.

What is the difference, you may ask? A transformative relational model focuses on the person and their journey of faith first. Foundational to the conversation are the struggles and 'ahas' in the process of growing more and more to be like Christ. In the process of that growth, deep, long-lasting friendships form. It is out of that foundation a disciple learns, understands and incorporates Scripture into their life. The book, Gravity, provides the context for a wide variety of questions about faith and influence. In this model of discipling, relationship and experience come before education and implementation. In a more traditional educational model, the growth process is based, first, on content, then on relationship. Both are valid ways to grow.

As you begin to read Gravity, you are starting an enjoyable yet challenging journey with Jason, Lew and Chelsea. To help you benefit the most from the story, this Conversation Journal has a dual purpose.

First, it will serve as a vehicle to facilitate exchange in a small group setting (three or more) as you share your thoughts and insights while you read Gravity. Second, if you meet as a mentoring pair, there are additional Drilling Deeper questions best asked and answered, one-on-one.

A Journey of Friends and Other Resources:

Whether you are a small group conversation leader or a one-on-one mentor, supplemental resources have been provided to assist you in the process of leading a conversation. Additionally, if you are a member of a discussion group or a mentor's friend, you can access Gravity journey resources that have been designed for you as well. Be sure to check out these resources for the Gravity journey at http://gravityleadershipbook.com/resources. On this webpage, you will find three links that will provide you with specific resources based on your role in the gravity journey:

Mentor & Friend

(http://gravityleadershipbook.com/resources/mentor),

Conversation Leader

(http://gravityleadershipbook.com/resources/discussionleader),

Group Member

(http://www.gravityleadershipbook.com/resources/groupmember).

Throughout this journal, resources will be referenced to help you make the most of your Gravity journey and can be found on the resource page that aligns with your role as you go through this journey (see above mentioned links).

Whether mentoring or leading a discussion group, before your first meeting read, *What You Need to Know Before You Start.* While the material is primarily directed at mentors, the tips, insights and instructions are equally applicable in leading a small group discussion as well.

GRAVITY *Small Group Conversation Guidelines:*

- As a conversation leader, be sure and visit the resource page at http://gravityleadershipbook.com/resources and click on the Conversation Leader link to get the discussion group resources. The website has a number of resources to assist you as you take your friends through the GRAVITY book. Before you start your conversation group, be sure and read What You Need to Know Before You Start and Conversation Guide at http://gravityleadship book.com/resources and then click on the Conversation Leader link.

- When you meet the expectation is that everyone has read the chapter and filled out the conversation questions.

- There is a conversation leader/facilitator for each time you meet. It can rotate or be a designated person -- your choice. It is the role of the leader/facilitator to move the conversation among members and to stimulate deeper conversation by asking further questions.

- Allow time for people to share a deep insight or a question raised through reading the chapter.

- Not every question in the Conversation Journal needs discussion. The ones you center on will depend on time, group member interest, and a sense by the conversation leader that the question is important to the entire group.

- The book borrows from physics laws of gravity and radiation and turns them into a metaphor describing our gravitational attraction and radiating influence. In our metaphor, the energy common to both gravity and radiation is love.

- The goal is for the small group discussion is to develop a trust relationship so that the discussion feels safe and is held confidential. We encourage the leader/facilitator to preface the first couple of meetings with a statement expressing the value of confidentiality within the group. Doing that assures the responses are unguardedly authentic.

GRAVITY *Soul-mentoring: Deepening the Conversation:*

This is a one-to-one mentoring friendship. The intention and the environment allows for greater intimacy in topic, depth and vulnerability. Rather than the mentor selecting or directing all the questions, it is the mentor's friend who also determines direction. The intention is for the mentor to help lead the friend into a vulnerable and authentic relationship.

If you are a mentor, be sure and visit the resources page at http://gravityleadershipbook.com/resources and click on the Mentor link. The mentor resource page has a number of resources to assist you as you take your mentoring friend through the GRAVITY book. Be sure and read:

- *What is the Purpose of Spiritual Mentoring (Soul Mentoring)*
- *Mentoring Covenant*
- *What You Need to Know Before You Start*
- *Mentoring Guide*
- *Conversation Guilde*
- *Coaching and Mentoring: What's the Difference?*

TABLE OF CONTENTS

CHAPTER 1:
Ka-boom!

CHAPTER 2:
A Fateful Encounter

CHAPTER 3:
Well, That's Life!

CHAPTER 4:
Change and Changes

CHAPTER 5:
Integration and Disintegration

CHAPTER 6:
Celebrity, Attraction and Radiating Love

CHAPTER 7:
Love Still Makes the World Go 'Round

CHAPTER 8:
Leaders and Leadership

CHAPTER 9:
Defining Leaders

CHAPTER 10:
Influence and Power

CHAPTER 11:
Influence and the Perception of Power

CHAPTER 12:
What is Soul-mass

CHAPTER 13, Part 1:
Soul-mass Woundedness

CHAPTER 13, Part 2:
Soul Qualities

CHAPTER 14:
Putting it Together

CHAPTER 15:
New Jason V 2.0

CHAPTER 16:
Trajectory

CHAPTER 1
Ka-boom!

Scripture:

Why are you like a man taken by surprise, like a warrior powerless to save? You are among us, Lord, and we bear your name; do not forsake us!

Jeremiah 14:9 Psalm 143

Lord, hear my prayer, listen to my cry for mercy; in your faithfulness and righteousness come to my relief. Answer me quickly, Lord; my spirit fails. Do not hide your face from me or I will be like those who go down to the pit. Rescue me from my enemies, Lord, for I hide myself in you. For your name's sake, Lord, preserve my life; in your righteousness, bring me out of trouble.

Psalm 143:1, 7, 9, 11.

SYNOPSIS OF THE CHAPTER:

Jason Cahill, Executive Director of New Horizons, unexpectedly has a career bomb dropped on him when he's told he is not meeting the expectations of a New Horizons Executive. He's defensive, self-justifying and angry after receiving the ultimatum to get fixed or get fired.

BIG IDEA:

We are all wired differently. As the story progresses, however, you'll see Jason's wiring is, perhaps, not too different from our own. All circumstances of living create a unique interaction between the flesh of our analytical brain, our subjective emotions, the spiritual soul-mass of mind, heart, will, soul and, as believers in Christ, the Holy Spirit. When confronted with situations like Jason just had with his board, the fears, insecurities, wants, and needs of both our natural and spiritual wiring spring into play.

Conversation Questions:

1. What was your "big idea" from the first chapter?

2. Do you know someone who behaves like Jason did? Without mentioning names, describe the impact you saw in that person's behavior on youself and others.

3. Jason seems bright. What do you think may be his problem(s)?

4. How do you think Jason handled the board meeting? If you were Jason, what would you have done in a meeting like that?

5. Have you ever been blind-sided like Jason? How did you feel? What were the issues and reasons leading up to it? Explain your thoughts.

6. Did you walk away feeling more or less trustful of others? Explain your thoughts.

7. What did you learn from the experience?

Why, my soul, are you downcast? Why so disturbed within me? Put your hope in God, for I will yet praise him, my Savior and my God.
Psalm 43:5

Drilling Deeper:

1. How did this chapter speak to you about you?

2. Are you still harboring wounds from a blindside in your life? How has that affected your trust of similar situations? How are you working through that trust issue so it doesn't create scar tissue?

3. Have you ever blind-sided someone else? What were the reasons? What's been the impact on them? What healing and restoration needs to be done?

Closing Thought:

Jason thought he had control of his world. Then wham! He's wondering, where did that come from? Faced with addressing his personal identity—a fearful or challenging thought—and forced to change a somewhat dysfunctional expression of himself, Melissa and the board give Jason a unique assignment. Instead of being told what his problems are, he must find an executive coach or mentor and discover those for himself.

We will all experience blindsides in our living. Like Jason, our most significant challenge to those blindsides is to not defensively react. Rather, it is to respond by stepping back and reflecting, How did I get to this place? and then, What is a wise response? The following chapters reveal how Jason responds by understanding and growing his interior self—his soul-mass.

Preparation for the Next Session:

Read Chapter 2 – A Fateful Encounter
Review the conversation questions before your next meeting.

Preparation for Conversation Leaders and Mentors

Read the Conversation Guide. You can find it in your resources on the Gravity Website Resources page (http://gravityleadershipbook.com/resources).

Notes

CHAPTER 2
A Fateful Encounter

Scripture:

A friend loves at all times, and a brother is born for a time of adversity.

Proverbs 17:17

Therefore encourage one another and build each other up, just as in fact you are doing.

1 Thessalonians 5:11

But encourage one another daily, as long as it is called "Today," so that none of you may be hardened by sin's deceitfulness. Hebrews 3:13
Do not let any unwholesome talk come out of your mouths, but only what is helpful for building others up according to their needs, that it may benefit those who listen.

Ephesians 4:29

For lack of guidance a nation falls, but victory is won through many advisers.

Proverbs 11:14

Synopsis of the Chapter:

Jason feels torn between resolving his tension with the board, fearing he'll lose his job, and a profound sense of being out of control. In the blindside, a part of Jason's personality comes out. He's guarded, cynical, defensive and arrogant, yet there is something tugging at his inner self saying something has to change. He wants to keep his job at New Horizons, but he feels he has few choices.

Jason approaches Lew suspiciously and yet with curiosity. Like others we may know, he covers a deep insecurity of who he is with objective control strategies, and an unwillingness to look inside. He doesn't trust Lew or the process and yet he knows he doesn't have many options. Opening up his life to a stranger is not what he wants to do, but he's intrigued by the concept of Lew being a soul-mentor—whatever that is.

Big Idea:

Lew bluntly tells Jason, "To set the record straight, Mr. Cahill, I'm working for your soul. New Horizons may write the check, but I answer to your soul." Lew goes on to say, "...I'm going to help you discover, heal and grow your soul-mass."

He sees the core of Jason's issues center around control. "Sounds to me like you're trying to control outcomes, and unintended consequences keep coming out."

Lew's premise is that until a person addresses the issues of soul-mass—the human spirit, the soul and the work of the Holy Spirit—nothing much really changes in people's lives except by the unanticipated events of being fired, confronting a divorce or some other blind-side of life. Lew goes on to inform Jason that the core composition of soul-mass is love. It is like gravity in its attractional property and it's like radiation in its influencing property. Jason is trying to get his head around the metaphor and the concept. Lew understands the issue goes deeper than comprehension. It's about Jason discovering, healing and growing his soul-mass.

Conversation Questions:

1. What was your big idea from the chapter?

2. Have you ever had a mentoring experience? Yes _______ No _______ If yes, how did it go? Do you still have a relationship? If so, why do you think that is?

3. If you were mentored, how do you feel it was helpful in your life?

4. What are a few examples of the growth you experienced as a direct result of being mentored?

5. Lew told Jason, if he wanted to have influence in another person's life, it requires they must progressively fall in love with you as their leader. Why do you think Jason pushed back on this idea?

6. Have you been around a person who you now recognize as having gravitational influence? What do you now see as the reason for the attraction and influence? How has or is that person making a difference in your life?

7. Paul had Barnabas as a source of wisdom, friendship and encouragement at the start of his ministry. The Twelve had Jesus. Who is your source of wisdom, friendship and encouragement?

For what will it profit a man if he gains the whole world and forfeits his soul?
Or what shall a man give in return for his soul?
Matthew 16:26 (ESV)

Drilling Deeper:

1. If you never had a formal mentor, how do you think your life would be different if you had?

2. What do you hope to gain from having a long-term mentoring relationship?

3. How can the Holy Spirit of Christ be your mentor?

Closing Thought:

It's becoming common for a person in a leadership position to utilize a coach. But coaching is often just for a season. What every person needs in their life is a seasoned and life-wise friend who will be a reliable and frequent point of reference for a long time, if not a life time. The Apostle Paul had several relationships like that, and Peter and James had each other as they oversaw the developing Church in Jerusalem.

Stop, look around, pray and seek out a person who cares for you as a person, and who displays the maturity of a consistent—upright—walk of life. There are Lew's (and Louise's) you never thought existed, and you probably already know them. As you conclude your time together, name the people who have poured into your life and thank God for their influence in your life.

Preparation for the Next Session:

Read Chapter 3 - Well, That's Life!
Review the conversation questions and complete the following exercise before your next meeting.

Fill out the I Am and How Do I Add Value to Life? worksheets which can also be downloaded from the Gravity Website Resources page on your Group Member, Mentor & Friend, or Group Leader resources page.

Preparation for the Conversation Leader and Mentor

Send an email to your group and remind them of the importance of filling out the I Am and How Do I Add Value to Life? Worksheets as they will become a point of reference throughout the time together.

"I AM" Worksheet

Without thinking too long about the topic complete 20 "I AM" statements about yourself. A filled in blank can describe your roles in relationships, talents and abilities, attributes, etc. For example, "I am a father, I am struggling, I am intelligent, I am good at ....

I am...

I am...

I am...

I am...

I am...

I am...

I am...

I am...

I am...

I am...

I am...

I am...

I am...

I am...

I am...

I am...

I am...

I am...

I am...

I am...

How Do I Add Value to Life Worksheet

1. If time and money were no limitation, what would you do with your time?

2. When you are feeling most empowered to add value to life and lives, what are you doing?

3. Why does this give you satisfaction?

4. What seems to be getting in the way of you achieving your goals?

5. Why are these things getting in the way?

6. Who or what empowers you?

7. Why or how do they empower you?

8. What have been the results?

9. How have those results been achieved?

10. Do you feel hard or bad stuff always seems to happen to you, or do you feel you have the potential and the capability to make a positive impact on people and issues? How does that attitude affect how you respond?

CHAPTER 3
Well, That's Life!

Gravity Truth One:

LIFE IS FIRST ABOUT *the kingdom of God*

Scripture:

So it is written: "The first man Adam became a living being"; the last Adam, a life-giving spirit. The spiritual did not come first, but the natural, and after that the spiritual. The first man was of the dust of the earth; the second man is of heaven.

1 Corinthians 15:45–47.

Jesus answered, "I am the bread of life. Whoever comes to me will never go hungry, and whoever believes in me will never be thirsty. I am the way and the truth and the life. No one comes to the Father except through me." For God so loved the world that he gave his one and only Son, that whoever believes in him shall not perish but have eternal life.

John 6:35, 14:6, 3:16.

For to me, to live is Christ and to die is gain.

Philippians 1:21

Synopsis of the Chapter:

Jason is dressed down from a person who understands the difference between having a life and going through a living.

Alisha, a former Marine Corps Captain, was seriously wounded in Afghanistan. She describes her struggle and her discovery. "For me, I realized I had to become spiritually in the same state I was physically. To be an instrument of his love, I had to realize how helpless I am without his love, saving grace and power. I had to stop proving to God that I was qualified on my own works to receive his love. He created me in love, and I'm completely helpless without it."

Jason can't shake his dependency on basing his value on his works. Chelsea is direct with him. "Oh, come on, yourself. You're smarter than that. God doesn't need our works. Our works aren't proof we're worthy. Our works are evidence the worthy One is at work in us. God so desperately wants our companionship that he was willing to sacrifice his own son." Jason leaves his meeting with Chelsea challenged, perplexed and thrown off-guard.

Big Idea:

Too often we forget to look up from our toil of living to realize that God has given us life with a purpose of an eternal relationship. Yet for most of us, we find it harder to grasp the understanding of God's promise of our purpose.

Where do we stumble? The tangible world is impatient for our presence. We have work to do if we are to survive and prosper. We have children to raise, parents to care for, and relatives and friends to support and love. We have ministries and non-profits needing our time and talent, and brief moments to enjoy recreation. No one in their hectic living has a moment, let alone an hour, to contemplate the big questions of "Who are you God?", "Why am I here?" and, "What should I do if I get the first two questions figured out?"

Who has time for thinking about a life—even a life given by God? We know, all too well, that living is about doing. What's harder to grasp hold of is that a life is about being. What good will it be for you to gain the whole world, yet forfeit your soul? Or what can you give in exchange for your soul? Matthew 16:26 (The Message)

Alisha's Notes

1. I almost died to know this truth. It's simply, all God wants from us is eternal fellowship with Him.

2. I didn't almost lose my life. That's an impossibility. I'm going to live with Christ forever. What I almost lost was my purpose for living. But strangely I had to almost die to want to really live.

3. When we forget the meaning of grace, our spiritual lives look like how we're living instead of our living looking like our life-full of grace and full of the father-heart of God.

Chelsea's Notes

1. Your identity doesn't rest in what you do. It rests in who you are and who you are is the identity of your soul.

2. The kind of relationships God desires we have with others is exactly the same relationship God desires we have with him.

Conversation Questions:

1. What is your big idea from Chapter 3?

2. Jason's scripture is Genesis 2:7. It describes the moment when God created Adam. He breathed into him life and he became a living creature. Have you ever distinguished the difference between the life you've been given and the living you're experiencing?

3. Like Alisha, when have you been confronted with an event where you realized that you may possibly die? How did you respond? How has it changed your view of life?

4. Alisha told Jason, "My purpose isn't grounded in what I do. That's my living. My purpose is grounded in who I am. That's my life." What does that statement mean to you?

5. What's your take on Chelsea's comment, "God doesn't need our works. Our works aren't proof we're worthy. Our works are evidence the worthy One is at work in us? How do you describe the difference between proof and evidence? Where do you think is the evidence in your life and the lives around you?

6. In the story, Chelsea asks Jason to fill out an "I Am" worksheet to help understand Jason's current self-identity frame of reference. Each of you has done the same. Share your top five "I am" statements. Ask for feed back: if that was all others knew about you, what does that say about you?

Jesus answered, "I am the way and the truth and the life.
No one comes to the Father except through me.
John 14:6

Drilling Deeper:

1. On a scale of 1 (near dead) and 10 (robust and healthy), what condition do you feel your soul is in? How do you know?

2. If your score is 5 or less what do you think is causing that? If it is depression, that's a brain and mind issue of the human spirit. If you're feeling tired and no energy, that could be a flesh issue due to a lack of sleep or poor diet and exercise habits. If you feel far from God and yet desiring intimacy with him, that's probably a soul issue. So, which is it?

3. Describe in your own words who you understand God to be. Why does that understanding matter to you?

4. Describe what your relationship with God looks like. How is that getting replicated in the lives you touch?

5. If you can describe who God is and what that relationship looks like, how does that make a difference in how you understand life and living it out?

Closing Thought:

Sooner or later we're all going to be confronted with our own version of an IED. It could be cancer or another significant health crisis, a death of a loved one, unplanned financial or career choices, a child predicament, or a faith crisis. How will you respond? How have you prepared in your trust, faith and belief? Like Alisha, as horrible as the event was, through her life being spared she found her living.

God will be with you. He created you as life. He cares about your living. He promised that he would never leave you or quit on you.

Preparation for the Next Conversation:

Read Chapter 4-Change and Changes
Review and make notes for the conversation questions for the next session before your next meeting.

Notes

CHAPTER 4
Change and Changes

Gravity Truth Two:

CHANGE ENLARGES *the kingdom of God*

Scripture:

For I, the Lord, do not change.
Malachi 3:6a.
Jesus Christ is the same yesterday and today and forever. Hebrews 13:8
Every good and perfect gift is from above, coming down from the Father of the heavenly lights, who does not change like shifting shadows.

James 1:17

Do not conform to the pattern of this world, but be transformed by the renewing of your mind. Then you will be able to test and approve what God's will is—his good, pleasing and perfect will. Romans 12:2
Dear friends, now we are children of God, and what we will be has not yet been made known. But we know that when Christ appears, we shall be like him, for we shall see him as he is.

1 John 3:2

Listen, I tell you a mystery: We will not all sleep, but we will all be changed—in a flash, in the twinkling of an eye, at the last trumpet. For the trumpet will sound, the dead will be raised imperishable, and we will be changed.

1 Corinthians 15:51–52

Synopsis of the Chapter:

Lew takes Jason to a surprise meeting with Bill Courtland, co-founder of C'est le Bon, a national chain of soup and sandwich restaurants. Bill explains to Jason how the chain was built on the foundation of quality and generosity, and their stewardship responsibility to build healthy and sustainable communities through footprint execution.

Bill finishes his story with this observation. "Interesting. Never realized until our crisis how much making a word plural diminishes its value. When we went from change to changes, everything changed."

Bill then leaves Jason with three cautions:

- Our first reaction to a change event is to resist.
- Second, change involves unknown risks, so we tend to avoid the moment and the need in order not to face the reality of risk.
- Finally, the reason we find change so difficult is because in resisting change we reward something in our current state for not changing, blinding us to the need for change in the first place.

Big Idea:

A clear vision and a strategic plan to achieve that vision is key to personal and organizational health. Tweaking the vision and making tactical adjustments is necessary to keep the vision relevant. But in the end, when short-term changes begin to define, and substantially alter, long-term vision, drift is the inevitable consequence. In other words, when short-term changes become more critical than evaluating long-term change, the enterprise is in trouble.

We all need advisors and supporters who understand the core purpose for what we do in our living. We need others to encourage and ask the necessary questions allowing for mid-course corrections as well as making the decisions to keep the enterprise "steady as she goes."

Bill's Notes

1. No one can put soul into an organization other than the leaders of the organization.

2. Look for the reflection of your own integrity black holes as seen in your family, your organization and even your church if you serve in a leadership position.

3. Because the vision and values came from our souls, as leaders, we lost the soul of the company as we focused on the transactional side of business management. We lost the transformational focus on enterprise leadership.

4. The healthiest organizations are ones where their leaders have clear visions of their personal life goals. The vision and mission of its leaders is bigger than the organization, and yet the organization's vision and mission is bigger than its leaders.

Conversation Questions:

1. What was your big idea from the chapter?

2. Jason was awed when he met Bill Courtland. What do you think is the "experience" people describe when they meet you? What do you think creates their response?

3. Bill said C'est le Bon has a corporate soul. Describe the "soul" of your church. Describe the collective soul of your family. Describe the collective soul of your immediate workplace. What evidences point to your conclusions?

4. Bill said he founded C'est le Bon on a foundation of (1) generosity and quality in everything—ingredients, leadership, employees, facilities. You can't be generous with something less than your best. (2) we leave a footprint in our execution. What are the pillars of your workplace? Your family? Your place of worship?

5. Describe how you see the terms quality and excellence being similar and different.

6. What kind of a "footprint" are you leaving?

7. Describe a time in your family, work, or church when you felt it lost its soul. Did you use that moment as a deep change opportunity? What did you do or not do as a result?

8. In speaking about churches and places of employment, Bill Courtland said, "The vision and mission of its leaders is bigger than the organization and yet the organization's vision and mission is bigger than its leaders." What does this mean to you and the organization where you contribute influence?

Therefore, if anyone is in Christ, the new creation has come:
The old has gone, the new is here!
2 Corinthians 5:17

Drilling Deeper:

1. Jesus said he has come to give us life; life more abundant than we've ever had. What does that "abundant life" look like for you? How is it reflected in scripture?

2. What evidences do you see of how the Holy Spirit changed you into a new creation? How do you think he does that? Why do you think it doesn't seem to last?

3. What do you find yourself doing to resurrect the "old man?" What does the "old man" look like? How does he or she act?

4. How do you kill the "old man?"

Closing Thought:

Bill concludes with this thought: "The healthiest organizations are ones where leaders have a clear vision and intention for their life goals. And, as a result, they live them out with integrity through where they work, worship and experience community. We understood the vision and mission for us is bigger than C'est le Bon, and yet C'est le Bon's vision and mission is bigger than Marge and me. Does that make sense?"

Do you believe God's mission for you is bigger than where you find yourself at this moment, yet also realizing God's mission for this world is bigger than any person, church or denomination? When you realize your significant insignificance, ministry happens.

Preparation for the Next Session:

Read Chapter 5–Integration and Disintegration
Review and make notes for the conversation questions for the next session before your next meeting.

Notes

CHAPTER 5
Integration and Disintegration

Gravity Truth Two:

CHANGE ENLARGES *the kingdom of God*

Scriptures:

Then I saw "a new heaven and a new earth," for the first heaven and the first earth had passed away, and there was no longer any sea.

Revelation 21:1

"For I know the plans I have for you," declares the LORD, "plans to prosper you and not to harm you, plans to give you hope and a future."

Jeremiah 29:11

And we all, who with unveiled faces contemplate the Lord's glory, are being transformed into his image with ever-increasing glory, which comes from the Lord, who is the Spirit.

2 Corinthians 3:18

Synopsis of the Chapter:

As Lew and Jason process their time with Bill Courtland, Lew provides a perspective on change and changes and the complexities of change. Lew also introduces Jason to the illusive concept of constancy.

Big Idea:

Change is essential for life. Change is also a consequence of the fall of Adam and Eve. Whether the change is continuous or discontinuous, our first response usually is to resist it. When we finally do react, often our first action to a change event is to make changes rather than reflecting on whether deep change or merely process changes is the next step beyond resisting.

Our spiritual life is about change too. We accept Christ and the transforming idea of salvation through Christ and the Holy Spirit's powerful presence becomes reality. Then we sin again, yet Christ provides the way to restoration. However, there will come a day when constancy, the absence of change, replaces the illusion of normal—controlled chaos. It will happen in the presence of God, the Father, as we experience eternal life.

However, as we continue to react and then hopefully respond to our living, there comes a point when the decisions we make either lead us to disintegration or integration. Integration requires a transforming idea and that's where our time and effort should be focused. Instead, too often, we remain stuck trying to overcome resistance.

Lew's Questions for Jason

- *What are some deep change issues in your life?*
- *What needs to change? Why?*
- *What needs to remain the same? Why?*
- *What do you need to do less of? Why?*
- *What do you need to do more of? Why?*
- *What are some changes you feel you need to make in your life?*

Assignment:

Complete Lew's assignment. Answer these six questions to the best of your awareness at this moment. Consider asking your spouse or adult child, your team leader and your best friend and ask them the same six questions. Write down their responses about you. What are they seeing in your life needing change and changes? Make a chart and take lots of notes.

Lew's Notes:

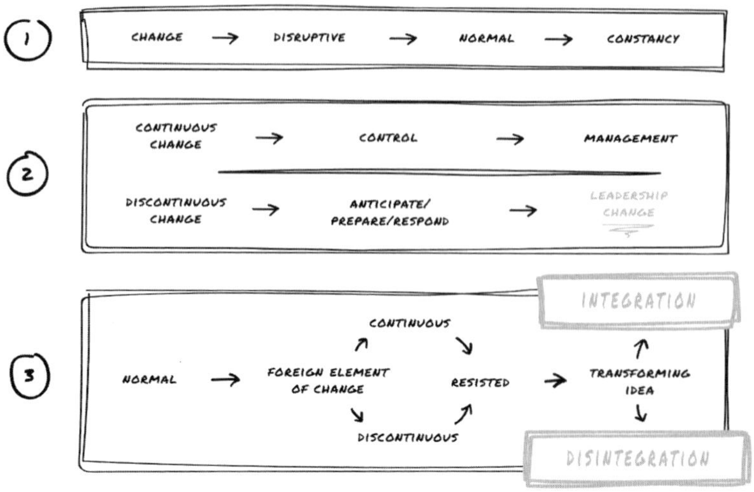

Conversation Questions:

1. Did you have a big idea after reading the chapter? If so, what was it?

2. Describe a circumstance when you applied changes. What were those changes? What were the outcomes?

3. Describe a circumstance when you applied deep change. What made it deep change and not merely changes? What were the outcomes?

4. What do you see as steps you need to take in order to regain the organizational soul of your enterprise or leadership responsibility?

5. What do you see are obstacles to your personal deep change opportunities?

6. In the story, Jason says, "The quality of my relationship with God has a lot to do with the healthiness of my soul. And, importantly, the healthiness of my soul determines the quality of my relationships with others. And, that increases the density of my core and the gravitational attraction and influence to those around me." Jason describe a circle of action and response. How is each piece of the cycle connected to the one before it? If there is not integrity in each connection, how does dysfunction occur?

7. In the story, Lew says to Jason, "You know it's a deadly temptation to confuse the little safe control dot you're standing on with greater security developed through trust." Describe a time when you found yourself stuck between the uncomfortability of the known and a lack of trust in the outcome of the unknown. How did you resolve that dilemma?

8. Lew said to Jason, "Every time you believe a lie about yourself, your soul gets punched and it withdraws. Every time you believe an indictment about yourself that's true without the covering of grace, your soul shrinks. After a time, you no longer have belief in the goodness of your soul. Yet you believe the evil lurking in your selfish human spirit. Go figure. Don't you think it is time to begin to experience trust and release the nut?" How do you "release the nut" you are holding on to?

9. Is it possible to experience constancy while still on earth? What do you think it would be like?

Therefore, if anyone is in Christ, the new creation has come:
The old has gone, the new is here!
2 Corinthians 5:17

Drilling Deeper:

1. Lew talks about the story of catching monkeys with a closed fist in a jar. What "nuts" are you holding on to that have captured your future? How are you going to release your fist?

2. What deep change have you identified that needs to happen in your life? Why is it necessary? When deep change happens, what will be different?

3. What changes must you make to assure deep change happens?

4. What are a few examples of continuous disruptive change happening in your life?

5. What are a few examples of discontinuous disruptive change happening in your life?

6. Control leads to works. Works leads to denying grace. Denying grace means denying the work of Christ on the cross. How do you distinguish your responsibilities in being an accountable person from being a control freak?

7. What personal or organizational changes have you made that you now see require deep change instead?

8. What Scriptures speak to change, changes, deep change and constancy?

9. When you accepted Jesus as Lord of your living and Savior of your life, what change did you experience? What changes did you make?

Closing Thought:

Constancy is the desire of the soul. Perhaps somewhere in the DNA of the soul is a memory of Eden where all was complete and nothing needed to change. Is it possible our souls long for a time and a place where there are no threats, no unpredictable events, no challenges to health and security? Constancy is not to be found on earth. Instead, God placed us here to be change agents. To be "instruments of righteousness" (Rom 6:13) to a world caught in the spiral of chaotic disintegration. How we respond to the changes and change events in our lives and in those we influence becomes a key role in what we do and how we experience living as Christ's stewards.

Preparation for the Next Session:

Read Chapter 6 - Celebrity, Attraction and Radiating Love
Review and make notes for the conversation questions for the next session before your next meeting.

Preparation for the Conversation Leader and Mentor

The conversation for the next chapter will involve tough topics and life-controlling dependencies. Before your session be sure and read the Tough Topics and How to Respond resource that can be found in the Journey of Friends PDF on your resource page. Anticipate where resources are in your community for support and assistance (spiritual, counselling, intervention). Hope for the best and be prepared for any surprise.

Notes

CHAPTER 6

Celebrity, Attraction, and Radiating Love

Gravity Truth Three:

LOVE IS THE FORCE *of gravitational attraction and radiating influence*

Scriptures:

In your relationships with one another, have the same mindset as Christ Jesus: Who, being in very nature God, did not consider equality with God something to be used to his own advantage; rather, he made himself nothing by taking the very nature of a servant, being made in human likeness. And being found in appearance as a man, he humbled himself by becoming obedient to death— even death on a cross!

Philippians 2:5–11

He said, "That you love the Lord your God with all your passion and prayer and muscle and intelligence—and that you love your neighbor as well as you do yourself."

Luke 10:27 (The Message)

Synopsis of the Chapter:

Jason drives out to Leaventon to reconnect with Joe Tyler. Drugs and ego fueled a full-throttle crash of Joe's professional career and ministry and took a toll on his health, almost destroying his marriage.

Joe's deficient soul-mass health took him to the inevitable crash. It was not that hard to predict. A deadly alliance was forming. Along with his emptiness and insecurity came fame and the narcotic of celebrity. Joe failed his followers.

In the clarity of sobriety Joe now sees his way back to redemption. He discovers that change only occurred when the pain of not changing becomes greater than the pain of change.

Finding his way back and responsibly influencing others, Joe realizes, "The most frightening day of my life was not the day I got outed for my addictions. It was the day I stepped back on to the platform and looked into the faces of people who were expecting me to give them something that would help them better understand scripture, the kingdom of God, Christ in their life and where they fit into community. I realized I didn't have the answers."

Joe has found a different way to minister. It's no longer about him. It is now one soul at a time. "We go on a journey of discovering, healing and growing their soul-mass. This will sound like a cliché, but we are living it out here. What's different is, we are building our faith family one soul at a time."

Big Idea:

Joe Tyler found out the hard way that celebrity attraction is a hollow substitute, on both sides, for gravitational attraction and radiating influence. Jason left their meeting with four major insights.

1. Talent ≠ the healthiness of your soul-mass

"The quality of your works is not necessarily an indication of the healthiness of your soul-mass."

2. Talent ≠ influence

Joe responds, "I think this is, perhaps, where you are at, Jason. Just because you're talented or even gifted doesn't qualify you to influence others. Try this one on for size. If you have talent, others trust you way too early in a relationship. The talent of a teacher/speaker is the most volatile of all. You can easily meet their wants instead of their needs. It's called manipulation. Talent can be a weapon, a tool or an instrument of blessing."

3. If celebrity > your soul-mass ⚠

"If celebrity is greater than your soul-mass, watch out. Collisions are coming. Like we talked about, celebrity is like a narcotic. It feeds all the wrong needs and presses all the wrong buttons."

4. Celebrity = shrunken soul-mass

"Celebrity is the reverse reflection of a shrunken soul-mass. It looks big but is simply over-inflated with the hot air of self. The core has no density."

On the drive home Jason kept thinking about these three certainties.

1. Every one of us stands in the gap between the pride of who we think we are and the shame of knowing who we fear ourselves to be.

2. We humans so desire to connect with a soul healthier than our own that we become naïve and gullible when we should be wise and discerning.

3. Radiating love is what creates the counterbalancing effect of our gravitational attraction. But the source of it all is a healthy soul

Conversation Questions:

1. In the story, Joe Tyler talks about discovering the difference between appreciation, approval and affirmation. What would be your definition of appreciation? How do you feel when you receive words of appreciation?

2. What would be your definition of approval? Words of approval sound like this. "The quality of your effort was impressive. You add so much to the value of our team." How do you feel when you hear them? Embarrassed, humbled, prideful or valued?

3. What would be your definition of affirmation? What human spirit need does affirmation feed? How does it get unbalanced in your life? How do you keep it in balance?

4. Joe said, "I knew we were making an impact on the spiritual front, yet I knew there was a big part of me who was a fake; an imposter. I walked and talked like a pastor, but no one, if they really knew the train wreck I was, should have ever wanted to follow me. I was a mess physically, emotionally and spiritually."

   This is commonly referred to as the impostor syndrome. How do you keep an honest identity? Your life is probably not as dysfunctional as Joe's. Yet, how do you keep from falling into the impostor syndrome?

A friend loves at all times, and a brother is born for a time of adversity. One who has unreliable friends soon comes to ruin, but there is a friend who sticks closer than a brother.

Proverbs 1:17; 18:24

Drilling Deeper:

1. Have you had to deal with a life-controlling dependency? Care to talk about it?

2. What did it do to you and others?

3. Have you overcome it? How did that happen? How do you deal with temptation and reversion?

4. What have you learned about God and yourself through the process?

5. What Scriptures speak to breaking free from life-controlling dependencies?

Closing Thought:

Our identities are under a continuous barrage. First are the subtle whispers of Satan and his minions, lying to us about who and whose we are, all the while condemning us for what we know is true. Then there is the self-talk. For most people, our personal view is far more negative than even our worst enemies. It is no wonder our human spirits are deformed and needy. It is no wonder our souls are wounded and shrunken. How can we be a source of radiating love when there is so little love present in our soul-mass?

Jesus said he was sending us a Comforter. For what? To tell us, "You poor boy!" or "Bless your heart!" Of course not. The Holy Spirit of God is given to us by Jesus to make our soul-mass whole and wholesome—healthy, because through the power of Christ's Spirit it is now full of love. Most importantly, through the righteousness of Christ and his sacrifice for our sins,

we are made acceptable in the presence of God, the Father.

Seems so simple—salvation. Yet a need for approval and creating a sense of celebrity is what drove Joe Tyler to self-sabotage his purpose and almost his life. Are we that different? Can we be different? Of course we can. It is God's intention.

If you are battling a life-controlling dependency, this is the time to bring it to the surface so others, in the power of God, can minister to and with you and you can reach down and draw on the redeeming and healing power of Christ made alive in you through the Holy Spirit.

Preparation for the Next Session:

Read Chapter 7 - Love Still Makes the World Go 'Round.
Review and make notes for the conversation questions for the next session before your next meeting.

Notes

CHAPTER 7
Love Still Makes the World Go 'Round

Gravity Truth Three:

LOVE IS THE FORCE
of gravitational attraction and radiating influence

Scriptures:

Therefore, as God's chosen people, holy and dearly loved, clothe yourselves with compassion, kindness, humility, gentleness and patience.

Colossians 3:12

Above all, love each other deeply, because love covers over a multitude of sins. 1 Peter 4:8
Love must be sincere. Hate what is evil; cling to what is good.

Romans 12:9

For God so loved the world that he gave his one and only Son, that whoever believes in him shall not perish but have eternal life.

John 3:16

Synopsis of the Chapter:

Jason sums up to Lew his time with Joe Tyler. "I'm realizing I have significant work to do on my soul-mass. I've spent too much energy trying to prove my worth by my works. I'm not sure how much I'd be valued if people just knew me as a friend. However, I still feel I'm unable or unwilling to trust people that much right now. I know it sounds like my admission of shallowness, but there it is."

Lew then shows Jason the interdependency between gravitational attraction and radiating love. Both of which have their source in soul-mass. He then goes on to present to Jason the progressive properties of gravitational attraction and radiating influence propelled by and leading to love—loving God, loving self and loving others.

Big Idea:

Love at first sight is perhaps one of the great misrepresentations of life. Love is more complicated than hormones, attractiveness and charm. If we miss the progressive steps of falling in love through awareness, curiosity, appeal, inspiration, encouragement and friendship, we may miss love. What we are often left with is empty attraction possibly fueled by empty celebrity. Lew concludes his time with Jason with this observation: "Jason, you are coming to realize that loving others and being loved is a wonderful burden of expectation and responsibility. Genuine gravitational attraction comes from the substance of the soul, and in the soul we find progressive forms of love. Gravitational attraction draws others into a team to accomplish mission and purpose. In return, it enriches those within our sphere of influence. These are accomplishments unattainable on our own.

Conversation Questions:

1. At this point in your life, how would you rate the influence (attraction and radiation) of your soul-mass? Insignificant? Small? Medium? or Substantial? How do you know? How much is a sense of false humility playing into your answer? How much is pride?

2. Name three people who are aware of your presence. What are you doing that they would even be aware of your existence?

3. Name three people who are curious about you. What is it about you that creates curiosity?

4. Name three people who find you appealing. Why would they have confidence in your capacity to believe and live wisely?

5. Name three people who find you a source of encouragement. What is causing them to trust you with their thoughts?

6. Name three people whose friendship is so secure you would trust them with your emotions.

7. Name three people who love you so deeply that they trust you without conditions. They know, without question, you will always act in their best interests.

8. What are you doing or not doing to increase your gravitational influence on these 18 people?

9. What is your take on the aversion Jason has with 'falling in love'? Do you feel the same way? Why or why not? Do you feel there are barriers of intimacy? If so, why?

Watch what God does, and then you do it, like children who learn proper behavior from their parents. Mostly what God does is love you. Keep company with him and learn a life of love. Observe how Christ loved us. His love was not cautious but extravagant. He didn't love in order to get something from us but to give everything of himself to us. Love like that.
Ephesians 5:1–2 (The Message)

Drilling Deeper:

1. Have you ever had difficulty accepting the truth that God loves you unconditionally? What do you think are some reasons for that?

2. Are there issues of reconciliation you need to face? Do you need to ask God through Jesus to forgive you?

3. Do you need to forgive others? For what? How will you go about that?

4. Do others need to have the opportunity to forgive you? How will you begin that process?

5. What Scriptures speak to the need and opportunity for confession, forgiveness, restoration and reconciliation?

Closing Thought:

Jason concludes his time with Lew with this observation. "Look, Lew, I get the fact that my love is not my works. My works are an expression of my love, not proof. I get that. It's merely consequence. Because if I don't get that, I don't get the humility of Jesus Paul spoke of in the letter to the Church at Philippi. I'm realizing how much of my life I've tried to prove my worth through my works. Doesn't work for God and I now realize it doesn't work for people in my life either."

This is the most vicious and subtle trick of the enemy. He wants us to believe that works validates goodness and righteousness. Everything in our tangible world confirms that point. Yet, when we believe the lie--we are who our works say we are--we unintentionally deny the eternal work of grace, accomplished through Christ on the Cross. From the Father's perspective, the Cross is the last work he sees until the end of the age.

Preparation for the next conversation:

Read Chapter 8 - Leaders and Leadership
Review and make notes for the conversation questions for the next session before your next meeting.

Notes

CHAPTER 8
Leaders and Leadership

Gravity Truth Four:

LEADERSHIP IS THE CRAFT *of a leader*

Scriptures:

When the righteous thrive, the people rejoice; when the wicked rule, the people groan.

Proverbs 29:2

But you are not to be like that. Instead, the greatest among you should be like the youngest, and the one who rules like the one who serves.

Luke 22:26

Not so with you. Instead, whoever wants to become great among you must be your servant, Matthew 20:26 Have confidence in your leaders and submit to their authority, because they keep watch over you as those who must give an account. Do this so that their work will be a joy, not a burden, for that would be of no benefit to you.

Hebrews 13:17

Synopsis of the Chapter:

Paul Ishii experienced a leadership transformation. For most of his professional career he was seen as a leader but performed like a manager. In the process of reforming how he relates to the people he's responsible to and for, Paul discovered seven dysfunctions of leadership ruled by three fears—rejection, failure and irrelevance."

Big Idea:

Managing is essential for keeping systems from chaos. Managing well keeps systems normal—a form of controlled chaos. It's about safety, stability, predictability, following rules, and accountability. All very important for a healthy organism and organization. Managing well requires control, cooperation and conformance. However, managing well, while keeping systems safe and assuring relational hygiene will never take an enterprise beyond the present.

Leading and influencing people and organizations is the only process to move to the future with a sense of purpose.

We attach to a managing group. In contrast, in a leadership team or family or tribe people form bonds of trust. Leadership requires a shared vision, mutual accountability and a loving commitment to each other.

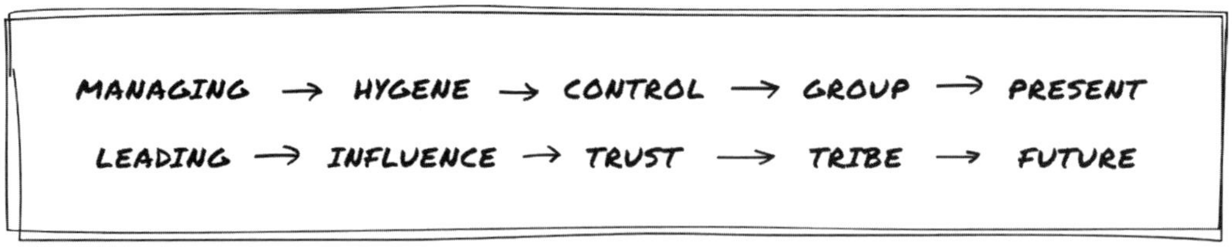

Yet leading others, even for the best of reasons, sometimes turns out to be frustrating and disappointing for the leader and the team. Some of that frustration can be explained by seven blind spots of leaders ruled by three fears.

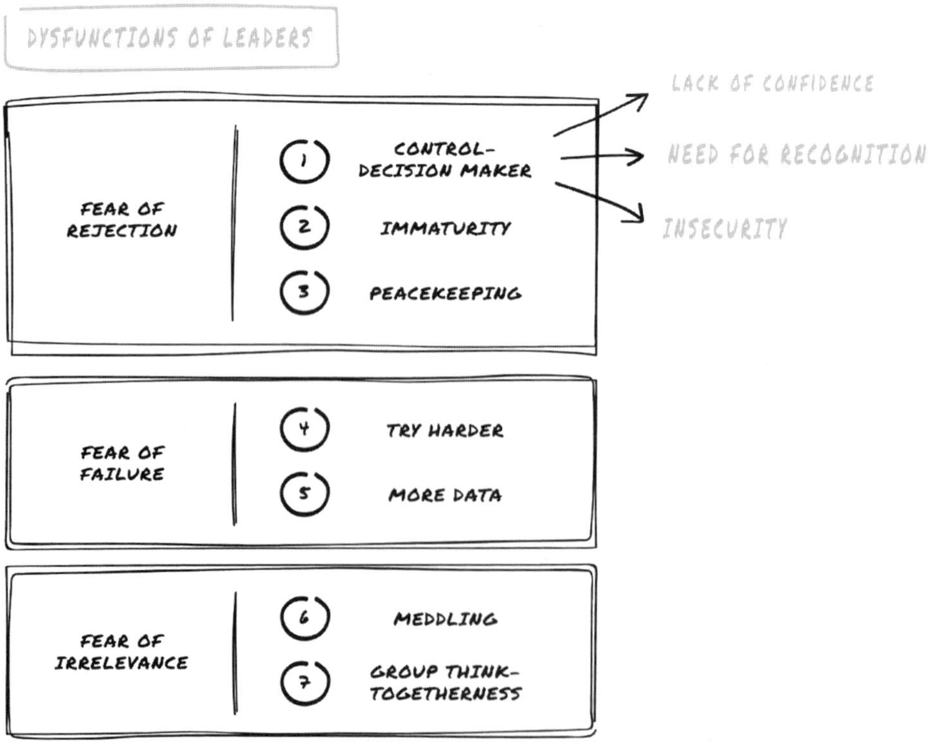

Conversation Questions:

1. In your responsibilities at work, what percent of the day are you leading and what percent are you managing? What are the percentages in your home or ministry responsibilities? Are those percentages achieving the results you want?

2. Using Abraham Wald's discovery, describe an experience where you now see you failed to focus on protecting the most vulnerable parts of a project or team. What were the consequences?

3. Paul Ishii talks about the scotomas of leader dysfunction. In his first grouping were three dysfunctions centering around the fear of rejection. In your experience, describe a time when your fear of rejection of you as a person or your ideas led to you needing to be in control. How does a lack of confidence and/or a need for recognition play into that dysfunction?

4. How does the immaturity of the team or leader feed a fear of rejection? What have you found to be the consequence of leader or team immaturity?

5. In your experience, what is an example of how fear of rejection led to peacekeeping behaviors and resulted in dysfunction?

6. When the team isn't performing well and you or your team fears failure, how has trying harder and trying to gain more data actually produced the failure you feared?

7. Describe a personal experience or an observed situation where you've seen the fear of irrelevance result in meddling or group-think.

And David shepherded them with integrity of heart; with skillful hands he led them.
Psalm 78:72

Drilling Deeper:

1. We read many times (over 100) in Scripture where God says, "Fear not." (ex. Joel 2:21) How are you able to obey that command?

2. When is fear a human mechanism to keep us safe and when does it morph into a fear of losing relationship, possessions, or our life or our enjoyment? How do you respond?

3. Tell me about your fears of failure. Who do you feel (or fear) you are failing?

4. Tell me about your fears of rejection. Why is other's approval so essential?

5. Tell me about your fears of irrelevancy. Why is doing well important?

6. What are your fears as you have the responsibility and opportunity to influence others?

Closing Thought:

Whether it's influencing a family or an enterprise, in the end, what really counts is legacy. Is anything and anyone different because you were present? Too often in trying to be conscientious we over-focus on the details of managing: majoring on the do's. Why? Because the do's are tangible reminders of how good our works are in spite of our shortcomings. Good works must mean a good person. Right? But in the process we often miss the opportunity to influence others because of who we are in spite of and because of what we do. Too often we are like Martha.

"Martha, dear Martha, you're fussing far too much and getting yourself worked up over nothing. One thing only is essential, and Mary has chosen it—it's the main course, and won't be taken from her." Luke 10:41–42 (The Message)

Preparation for the next conversation:

Read Chapter 8 - Leaders and Leadership
Review and make notes for the conversation questions for the next session before your next meeting.

Notes

CHAPTER 9
Defining Leaders

Gravity Truth Four:

LEADERSHIP IS THE CRAFT *of a leader*

Scriptures:

Remember your leaders, who spoke the word of God to you. Consider the outcome of their way of life and imitate their faith. Have confidence in your leaders and submit to their authority, because they keep watch over you as those who must give an account. Do this so that their work will be a joy, not a burden, for that would be of no benefit to you.

Hebrews 13:7, 17

God blessed them: "Prosper! Reproduce! Fill Earth! Take charge! Be responsible for fish in the sea and birds in the air, for every living thing that moves on the face of Earth."

Genesis 1:28 (The Message)

No one will be able to stand against you all the days of your life. As I was with Moses, so I will be with you; I will never leave you nor forsake you. Be strong and courageous, because you will lead these people to inherit the land I swore to their ancestors to give them. Be strong and very courageous. Be careful to obey all the law my servant Moses gave you; do not turn from it to the right or to the left, that you may be successful wherever you go.

Joshua 1:5–7

Do nothing out of selfish ambition or vain conceit. Rather, in humility value others above yourselves,

Philippians 2:3

Kings detest wrongdoing, for a throne is established through righteousness.

Proverbs 16:12

Synopsis of the Chapter:

Lew first points out to Jason that to be an effective leader it requires three mindsets: being a slave to righteousness, a servant to all, and a steward of the process. He then goes on to give a definition of leadership having five nested parts with the last part having a set of interdependencies.

Big Idea:

Leadership is a personal calling. It is a commitment to goodness and personal growth. An effective leader cultivates a shared vision leading to a shared sense of destiny and intentional effort. An effective leader invests in loving relationships knowing the profit from that relationship may take years to mature. All the while, the effective leader is creating and maintaining optimum environments where competency, growth, trust, flexibility and authentic openness is leading to healthy tension. All the best practices of a dynamic leader are wrapped in virtuous practices reflecting the mind of Christ.

When those elements are in harmony, teams are able to successfully tolerate, embrace, navigate, and arbitrate surprise tension and paradox.

Conversation Questions:

1. What are evidences in your life of a commitment to goodness and personal growth, both internally and externally?

2. What are ways to cultivate a shared vision? How does it form? How do you know it is truly shared? As a leader and influencer (parent, manager, minister), do you understand the shared vision? What is it?

3. How can you be a committed friend when you supervise or are responsible for the behaviors of another?

4. Describe some examples of optimum environments. What makes them optimum?

5. How do you foster virtuous practices in a secular setting?

6. Looking at the chart, describe in one sentence an example of each couplet. What would tolerating surprise look like?

Tolerate	*Surprise*	
	Tension	
	Paradox	
Embrace	*Surprise*	
	Tension	
	Paradox	
Navigate	*Surprise*	
	Tension	
	Paradox	
Arbitrate	*Surprise*	
	Tension	
	Paradox	

I myself am convinced, my brothers and sisters, that you yourselves are full of goodness, filled with knowledge and competent to instruct one another.
Romans 15:14

Drilling Deeper:

1. Thinking about the three mindsets of slave, servant, and steward, describe when your leading looks like the work of a slave to righteousness. What does it look like when you are a servant to all? How would you describe the differences? What are you doing in your steward identity to be a steward of the process?

2. Describe how leadership becomes a personal calling. Describe your current sphere of influence. In what ways are you pleased with the impact of your radiating love?

Closing Thought:

Effective influence is hard. Too often it's made to appear to be simple by focusing on one aspect instead of the whole. Yet, with God's help, we are able to focus on allowing the Holy Spirit to empower our soul-mass with the goodness of God to be an inspirational influence in others. It is an awesome and fearful responsibility to think that who we are affects those around us. Yet nothing could be closer to the truth. We are influencers. With Christ we become agents of light, not darkness.

Preparation for Next Conversation:

Read Chapter 10 - Influence and Power
Review and make notes for the conversation questions for the next session before your next meeting.

Notes

CHAPTER 10
Influence and Power

Gravity Truth Five:

LEADERS BECOME DEFINED *by their gravitational attraction and radiating influence*

Scripture:

Those who walk righteously and speak what is right, who reject gain from extortion and keep their hands from accepting bribes, who stop their ears against plots of murder and shut their eyes against contemplating evil— they are the ones who will dwell on the heights, whose refuge will be the mountain fortress. Their bread will be supplied, and water will not fail them.

Isaiah 33:15–16

Be shepherds of God's flock that is under your care, watching over them—not because you must, but because you are willing, as God wants you to be; not pursuing dishonest gain, but eager to serve.

1 Peter 5:2

Now the overseer is to be above reproach, faithful to his wife, temperate, self-controlled, respectable, hospitable, able to teach,

1 Timothy 3:2

Then he said to them, "For whoever is least among you all is the greatest. The greatest among you will be your servant."

Matthew 23:11

Synopsis of the Chapter:

Jason has the unique opportunity to meet Wilson Barlow, Governor of the state, and his chief of staff, Jim Oliver. Jim catches Jason off-guard. "Feel the power?" Jim continues, "Coming up the steps to the capitol building, you see the massive dome, the ornate brass doors, the marble steps and walls, the massive artwork, the ornamental ostentation—all designed for a single purpose. To show you, the little people, and the state's enemies, how powerful we are."

Wilson Barlow has brought a new style of leadership to governing the state: influence. He gives Jason a brief overview. "This is how it works. If I am able to anticipate your objective need, and then work with you to freely give it to you, it empowers you to be more free, more prosperous, more healthy.

"Power always leaks, and I must constantly find ways to replenish the supply. On the other hand, influence grows without direct action by me. The more I give away, the more I have. The more I focus my concerns on you, the more influence I gain."

Big Idea:

Power is tangible and is based on what you own. Power is contained in land, monetary wealth, information, technology or weapons. It costs something to acquire and it costs even more to maintain. The very power you presently own can, in an instant, be flipped and become a weapon against you.

Influence, on the other hand, is intangible and rooted in the hearts and minds of those who choose to let it hold sway over them. An essential element of influence is trust—trust in the goodness, benevolence, and integrity of the person possessing the influence. Influence is truly a derivative of the size and density (the mass) of the soul. And the soul contains the substance and essence of pure love.

Governor Barlow's Notes

1. To rule from power means you have to possess something other people want or need.

2. Power is an alliance of dependency.

3. The leader's genius is in being able to re-interpret and reform those wants into more selfless needs.

4. Influence grows without direct action by me. The more I give away, the more I have. The more I focus my concerns on you, the more influence I gain.
5. I believe the true mark of influence is not in what gets accomplished. Rather it is in whether greater virtue and integrity is demonstrated by those who identify with the organization, the cause or the constituency.

6. My influence is a radiating force of love and is the root, the origin of trust. You have

influence when you have trust. And when people trust you, you've got influence.

7. If you want to make a difference in this world, allow people to fall under your influence. Let them fall in love with the goodness of your soul.

8. If you really want to understand the nature of influence, you must determine to understand the nature of God.

Power:

- Transactional
- Requires currency
- Delivers/satisfies wants
- Creates an alliance of dependency
- Requires an opponent who must become weaker

Influence:

- Transformational
- Mutually exchangeable
- Anticipates needs
- Creates freedom and empowerment
- Origin is love
- Product is trust

Conversation Questions:

1. Governor Barlow said, "To rule from power means you have to possess something other people want or need." How would you distinguish a want from a need? How does exercising power to meet needs create influence?

2. What is an example you've seen of the use of influence instead of power?

3. Describe examples where you've experienced the consequence of OPM addiction.

4. Make a list of the 'power chips' you own as it relates to your family, your ministry and your work. Next list how those 'power chips' can be turned into influence by anticipating needs.

5. Seriously, how realistic is Governor Barlow's theory of influence in real life? What makes it realistic? What makes it unrealistic?

6. How do you, personally, find balance between the power you possess and the influence you can exert?

He who forms the mountains, who creates the wind, and who reveals his thoughts to mankind, who turns dawn to darkness, and treads on the heights of the earth — the LORD God Almighty is his name.
Amos 4:13

Drilling Deeper:

1. Wilson said to Jason, "If you really want to understand the nature of influence, you must determine to understand the nature of God." What do you think he meant by that?

2. How do you lead from your soul?

Closing Thought:

Wilson's parting words to Jason summed up the meeting. "Here's the bottom line. My influence does not reside in my title. It resides in my soul. Not in my willful spirit or the power of this office. My influence is a radiating force of love and is the root, the origin, of trust. You have influence when you have trust. And when people trust you, you've got influence." It is in Christ we find power, simply in his name.

Preparation for the next conversation:

Read Chapter 11 - Leaders and Leadership
Review and make notes for the conversation questions for the next session before your next meeting.

Notes

CHAPTER 11

Influence and the Perception of Power

Gravity Truth Five:

LEADERS BECOME DEFINED *by their gravitational attraction and radiating influence*

Scripture:

The God of Israel spoke, the Rock of Israel said to me: "When one rules over people in righteousness, when he rules in the fear of God, he is like the light of morning at sunrise on a cloudless morning, like the brightness after rain that brings grass from the earth."

2 Samuel 23:3–4

Do nothing out of selfish ambition or vain conceit. Rather, in humility value others above yourselves,

Philippians 2:3

Here is a trustworthy saying: Whoever aspires to be an overseer desires a noble task. John 13:12-15 But select capable men from all the people—men who fear God, trustworthy men who hate dishonest gain—and appoint them as officials over thousands, hundreds, fifties and tens.

Exodus 18:21

Choose some wise, understanding and respected men from each of your tribes, and I will set them over you."

Deuteronomy 1:13

"I am the good shepherd. The good shepherd lays down his life for the sheep.

John 10:11

Synopsis of the Chapter:

Like so many citizens, Jason was cynical of politics and the politicians who make the responsibility of governing like a blood sport. And with good reason. Power, like water, seeks its lowest level of resistance. It is the most seductive narcotic on earth. The Governor possesses great power and Jim's role is to be the arbiter of that power, forming and reforming it into influence.

Lew explained to Jason, "Jim, the steward of the governor's estate, preserves the assets of power. And let's bring this analogy back into this century. For Jim, as the governor's steward, what is the fruit and grain produced from the land?"

"Influence?"

"Exactly."

Lew then drills down to Jason's core issue. "Let's stop here for a moment and survey the field. Right now you're looking back at all your trust issues, and you have little foundation for going forward. I get that. But your leader effectiveness—as a person of influence with a tribe of followers—will only increase in proportion to the size of your soul-mass. You can't trust others if you aren't able to trust God through your soul. And people won't trust you until and unless your trust of them radiates out from your soul. In other words, you've got to start finding a way to trust God, trust others and become a trustworthy person. The key to that, I think, is learning to trust yourself through your soul, which is your window to God."

The simple truth of power doesn't take you to relationships of trust. The only vehicle on the highway is influence.

Big Idea:

Lew chooses this meeting to make a simple point. We are stewards of the health of our soul-mass. That stewarding—caring for the possessions of the owner—is what we are to do. God gave us life in our flesh and in our souls. How we care for that life is called our living. As leaders, we have a steward's responsibility for the souls of others as well. As we learn to be good stewards of our souls, we gain the influence to be stewards of influence in the lives of others.

However, without Christ in our life and the Holy Spirit empowering our living, our selfish human spirit seeks to find stability by controlling the world around us. We become tyrants. Our human spirits are too small, the world is too big, and the task as God intentioned it is impossible. But the more controlling we are and the harder we try, the smaller and harder our spirits become. We have a stiff-necked mind and a hardened heart. Who can save us from such a seemingly endless spiral of futility? As the Apostle Paul said, "Thanks be to God, who delivers me through Jesus Christ our Lord!"

Conversation Questions:

1. What is your big idea from reading the chapter?

2. Think of a person in your life experiences whom you'd now describe as a tyrant. This isn't a judgmental label. Rather a description of their style of getting other people to follow them. What behaviors made them appear to be a tyrant?

3. Think of a person in your life experiences whom you'd now describe as an influencer. What behaviors made them appear to be an influencer?

4. Jason said, "Lew, I think that's what I've been running from. I've believed in what I can do, but I'm really uncomfortable with people believing in me simply for who I am." Can you identify with Jason? In what ways? How do you change your 'value proposition' from doing to being?

Drilling Deeper:

1. How does your doing provide a substitute for your need to trust others?

2. How much integrity would be found if someone drilled into your soul-mass? How hard is it to be pure when no one is looking?

3. Integrity doesn't come from the flesh. Most integrity found in the human spirit is of a self-serving variety. How do you find your integrity in your soul?

Closing Thought:

Jason sums up his meeting with Lew. "Here's where I've got more work to do. I realize my identity is not defined by how much power I possess. I am realizing that is a false sense of security. It's elusive. Rather, it comes from the health of my soul and radiates out through the influence I cast or spread or whatever. It's just that old habits die slowly. The area I'm struggling with is coming to grips with owning the reality that my influence is found in the integrity of my being, not in the quality or effectiveness of my doing. I get it, but I don't yet own it."

Preparation for Next Conversation:

Read Chapter 12 - What is Our Soul Mass?
Review and make notes for the conversation questions for the next session before your next meeting.

Preparation for the Conversation Leader and Mentor

Before the next session read What is Our Soul Mass? You can find this in the Journey of Friends PDF on the Conversation Leader or Mentor resources page of the Gravity website.

Notes

CHAPTER 12
What is Soul-Mass?

Gravity Truth Six:

SOUL-MASS AND THE SPIRIT OF GOD DETERMINE *gravitational attraction and radiating influence*

Scripture:

And Mary said: "My soul glorifies the Lord.

Luke 1:46

Praise the LORD, my soul; all my inmost being, praise his holy name. Praise the LORD, my soul, and forget not all his benefits— Praise the LORD, my soul. LORD my God, you are very great; you are clothed with splendor and majesty.

Psalm 103:1–2; 104:1

I delight greatly in the LORD; my soul rejoices in my God. Isaiah 61:10 We have this hope as an anchor for the soul, firm and secure. It enters the inner sanctuary behind the curtain,

Hebrews 6:19

What good is it for you to gain the whole world, yet forfeit your soul? Or what can you give in exchange for your soul?

Mark 8:36–37

Jesus replied: "'Love the Lord your God with all your heart and with all your soul and with all your mind.'

Matthew 22:37 (Mark 12:30; Luke 10:27)

For "you were like sheep going astray," but now you have returned to the Shepherd and Overseer of your souls.

1 Peter 2:25

Synopsis of the Chapter:

Lew and Chelsea take Jason on a deep drill into the core of spirituality—our soul mass. Lew lays out their assignment.

1. **Define soul-mass components.** In that part of the conversation Chelsea delineates that the human spirit is made up of the will, the heart, and the mind, and connects to our conscious awareness. Jason has an 'aha', and labels the container for the spirit and soul and filled with the Holy Spirit as the new wineskin.

2. **Define their purpose.** Jason sees that this "new wineskin", as he calls it, is the place of shalom. The purpose of the human spirit is to be the connecting point of our spirituality to our flesh—what we touch. This is where transformation occurs. The soul is the connecting point with God through the Holy Spirit, and while not God, it contains the essence of God.

3. **Define how soul-mass relates to influence and leadership.** Lew starts the conversation by saying, "I think you now realize our human spirits are hopelessly addicted to self. The additional problem is, your human spirit desires to be in control of your living, and therein we find the enigma. We've got a dysfunctional, addicted human spirit trying to still be in control."

Jason sums up what he's heard. "I'm not ready for my final exam, but it seems to me this is the core of your principle of gravitational attraction and influence. The size, density and health of our soul-mass combined with the empowering work of the Holy Spirit determines our impact on others."

Big Idea:

Soul-mass is the core of our identity. We live in the flesh but we relate to God in the spiritual realm. Perhaps the simplest way to keep flesh and soul-mass straight is to ask the question, "Who's talking here?" The flesh is oriented to survival, raw passion and conscious awareness. As a result, the voice of the flesh is strongest in meeting immediate wants and needs. The intangible, mortal human spirit contains the mind, the heart and the will. It is oriented to control and selfishness. The voice of the human spirit sounds like an immature child. Finally, the intangible and immortal soul contains the essential goodness of God since it came from and will return to God for reckoning. Its purpose is to glorify the Father. The voice of the soul sounds like praise and worship. (Luke 1:46)

Lew's Notes

SOUL-MASS / WINESKIN PROPERTIES

SOUL	HUMAN SPIRIT / WILL	HOLY SPIRIT
• Immortal • About life • Needs a protector • Tender, wounded but restorable, naively innocent • Filled with the character of God.	• Immaterial/Mortal • About living • Wild yet tamable • Selfish by its nature • Obsessed by survival	• Eternal • About experiencing God • Patient, gentle, kind, powerful • Fully of the nature, expression and embodiment of God, the Father, and Christ, the Son

SOUL-MASS / WINESKIN INVENTORY

DISCOVER ✓		HEAL		GROW	
WILL/HEART-MIND/SPIRIT	SOUL	WILL/HEART-MIND/SPIRIT	SOUL	WILL/HEART-MIND/SPIRIT	SOUL

Conversation Questions:

1. Have you discovered the voice of your soul? If so, what does it sound like to you?

2. How do you distinguish between the voice of your soul and your flesh's self-voice of conscious awareness that blends in with your human spirit? How do you know who's talking?

3. Lew describes the flesh as being like a bear—mostly focused on survival. Would you agree or disagree? Why?

4. The human spirit in Lew's view is like a Siamese cat—self-centered and focused on control. How do you see yourself in that view? Where do you see selfish, self-centeredness residing? Why do you think we have this nature?

5. The soul, as Lew points out, is like a Golden Retriever. Faithful, ever-present, even-tempered, and devoted, regardless of how it is treated. What do you think is God's intention for us having a soul?

Whoever wants to be my disciple must deny themselves and take up their cross and follow me. For whoever wants to save their life will lose it, but whoever loses their life for me will find it. What good will it be for someone to gain the whole world, yet forfeit their soul? Or what can anyone give in exchange for their soul?

Matthew 16:24–26

Drilling Deeper:

1. How is the voice of your soul different and the same as the voice of God?

2. How do you see the Holy Spirit changing, growing, and/or enlarging the properties of your soul-mass?

3. In looking at the soul qualities list, what one(s) do you feel is most necessary to start your focus? Why have you chosen this one?

Closing Thought:

We focus, as we should, on the source of righteousness that comes through Christ. But how often do we also reflect on the receptacle for that righteousness? For many of us, when we do, our thoughts are often limited to the agenda of sin management. We forget that the Apostle Paul referred to us as "instruments of righteousness." And how is that instrument played? By subduing the wild flesh, taming the rebellious human spirit and releasing our wounded and shrunken soul to glorify God as it was made to do.

Preparation for Next Conversation:

Read Chapter 13 - Soul-mass Woundedness
Review and make notes for the conversation questions for the next session before your next meeting.

Preparation for the Conversation Leader and Mentor

Read Heal and Restore -- Helping to Restore the Sick and Wounded Soul-mass. You can find this in your Conversation Leader or Mentor resources on the Gravity Website Resources page.

Notes

CHAPTER 13, Part 1

Soul-Mass Woundedness

Gravity Truth Six:

SOUL-MASS AND THE SPIRIT OF GOD DETERMINE
gravitational attraction and radiating influence

Scripture:

My soul yearns for you in the night; in the morning my spirit longs for you. When your judgments come upon the earth, the people of the world learn righteousness. Isaiah 26:9
My soul yearns, even faints, for the courts of the LORD; my heart and my flesh cry out for the living God.

Psalm 84:2

I cried out to God for help; I cried out to God to hear me. I cry out to God Most High, to God, who vindicates me.

Psalm 77:1; 57:2

He refreshes my soul. He guides me along the right paths for his name's sake.

Psalm 23:3

Synopsis of the Chapter:

Chelsea revealed a traumatic violation in her past. Jason asked how she was getting through that experience. "For me—and I think everyone has to find their own route to restoration—it was a dual process of healing and growing at the same time."

The shattering of trust can, and often does, last a lifetime, affecting relationships with others and perhaps even God. For many who have had devastating violations of trust, as Chelsea did, serious questions arise, such as How could God, creator of heaven and earth, who knows all, sees all, and works all, allow that to happen? Jason finds some of the answers from Chelsea as they explore Lew's fourth point of meeting on the topic of soul-mass—Show how the nature of soul-mass, leadership and influence relate to Jason's life.

Big Idea:

One of the great mysteries of life is why some humans have to experience so much pain--particularly if they are an innocent victim of sin and evil from others. Perhaps it's not so great a mystery. Pain and the consequences of sin are the expected outcomes of living in a world so desperately in need of redemption. Our role as agents of redemption -- Christ-ones -- is to bring the source of healing, restoration, hope, eternity and power to people who are deeply trust-wounded in their flesh and in their soul-mass. As instruments for the Grace of God, we courageously stand up for the weak and speak and act against the forces of evil while finding a seemingly contradictory countenance of humility. We bring good news at a time when it desperately needs to be heard. We bring hope as is evidenced in our own lives. We offer a message of eternity through Christ as Savior. Most importantly, as believers in Christ, we also bring the Holy Spirit with us. It is the Holy Spirit who completes our new wineskin, as Jason discovered, and makes our soul-mass whole.

The reality is that all of us have soul-mass woundedness. The assault of Satan and his minions, the unintentional jabs of friends and associates, and the planned attacks of our enemies leave our soul-mass in need of restoration before scar tissue forms.

It is difficult for a physician to heal herself. Likewise, it is often difficult to heal the woundedness of our soul-mass without the prayers, compassion and simple presence of a caring friend.

Conversation Questions:

This is not the time or place to have any more conversation about soul-mass woundedness. It is a time and a place to ask God, through his powerful Holy Spirit, made available by a loving Jesus, to do the work of restoration.

Go around the gathering and ask each person how others in the room can pray to help restore a wounded soul, a broken heart and a weary mind? Ask, "will you, like each of us as well, set aside our prideful will and allow others who deeply care for us to pray for you? Will you set aside your cautious or even skeptical trust of God and allow him to demonstrate his love for you?"

Then do. Pray for each other.

Preparation for Next Conversation:

Read Chapter 13 Soul-Mass Woundedness Pt. 2 Soul Qualities
Review and make notes for the conversation questions for the next session before your next meeting.

Notes

CHAPTER 13, Part 2
Soul Qualities

Gravity Truth Six:

SOUL-MASS AND THE SPIRIT OF GOD DETERMINE *gravitational attraction and radiating influence*

Scriptures:

My soul yearns for you in the night; in the morning my spirit longs for you. When your judgments come upon the earth, the people of the world learn righteousness.

Isaiah 26:9

Who has known the mind of the Lord so as to instruct him? But we have the mind of Christ.

1 Corinthians 2:16

Through these he has given us his very great and precious promises, so that through them you may participate in the divine nature, having escaped the corruption in the world caused by evil desires.

2 Peter 1:4

The king stood by the pillar and renewed the covenant in the presence of the LORD—to follow the LORD and keep his commands, statutes and decrees with all his heart and all his soul, thus confirming the words of the covenant written in this book. Then all the people pledged themselves to the covenant.

2 Kings 23:3

But be very careful to keep the commandment and the law that Moses the servant of the LORD gave you: to love the LORD your God, to walk in obedience to him, to keep his commands, to hold fast to him and to serve him with all your heart and with all your soul."

Joshua 22:5

Synopsis of the Chapter:

Chelsea and Lew take Jason through the process of discovering, healing and growing his soul. Jason shares, "I'm coming to realize a—okay, my—deformed identity can't protect my soul and may even become the assailant. I vividly know I'm not always good, caring, full of integrity, pure or disciplined. Not only do I act poorly toward others, but I betray myself as well. And I believe this is true for everyone; we all remind ourselves of our failings. Of course those reminders are egged on by Satan, speaking lies and ridiculing us for who we aren't while at the same time, prosecuting us for who we are. Therein lies shame, which is truly out of the pit of hell."

The growing part of soul care comes through consuming the nutritious bread of life contained in 1 John 1:9. At their last meeting, Chelsea gave Jason a list of seven categories of soul qualities to meditate on and through.

Big Idea:

By design, the soul has no way to protect itself. Between the taunts, lies and truths spewed out by Satan and his minions, the soul is under continuous attack. Beat the soul down and the light of Christ shining through dims. The selfish human spirit can protect the soul by only one simple action. By stepping aside and allowing the Holy Spirit to do his transformative work infusing the love of Christ into every shrunken and scared nook and cranny of the soul. Jason's soul is wounded, as is ours. Like Jason, if we are to make forward progress beyond this point, we must be willing to admit our soul is wounded and in need of loving restoration. Once healed, it is finally ready for sustainable growth.

Are these truly soul qualities. We don't really know since they aren't specifically identified as such in scripture. However, what makes these qualities unique is that if you meditate on them they will not take you to sin. How much more pure can you get than that?

Conversation Questions:

1. The Soul Qualities list is not another checklist to see how pathetically inadequate you are at consistently maintaining spiritual goodness. So what is the list to you?

2. What has been your experience with the Soul Qualities list? Have you been able to start making this a discipline of the soul? Share your experiences by picking a category or a quality and discuss how that has made a difference. Did you use the worksheet? Discuss how it was helpful.

3. In focusing on the Soul Qualities, are you becoming more aware of your human and spiritual thought-life? In what ways?

In your relationships with one another, have the same attitude of mind Christ Jesus had. Whatever is true, whatever is noble, whatever is right, whatever is pure, whatever is lovely, whatever is admirable—if anything is excellent or praiseworthy—think about such things.
Philippians 2:5; 4:8

Drilling Deeper:

1. If you could write down your thoughts of the day, what would the transcript look like? What do some of the thoughts, emotions, conclusions, fears, hopes, joys, suspicions, prayers and expressions look like in the hours before we met?

2. What are some thoughts that take you to sin?

Soul Qualities		
Caring/Loving (agape, - philos, -eros)	**Full of Integrity**	**Wise**
Brave	*Courageous*	*Discerning*
Compassionate (gracious)	*Faithful*	*Knowledgeable / Information (What)*
Concerned	*True / Straight / Upright / Genuine*	*Understanding / Aware (How)*
Generous / Benevolent	*Honest*	*Wise (Why)*
Gentle	*Just*	**Disciplined**
Hospitable	*Above Reproach*	*Enduring / Perserverant*
Kind	**Pure**	*Patient / Long-suffering / Forbearing*
Merciful	*Innocent*	*Temperate / Self-controlled*
Peace loving-making / Peaceful	*Chaste*	*Sober (serious-minded)*
Grateful / Thankful (Indebted)	*Godly*	*Steadfast*
Forgiving	**Spiritually Centered**	*Self-Controlled*
Selfless	*Holy/Godly (Imputed)*	*Alert / Watchful / Vigilant*
Humble	*Righteous (Man and God-imputed)*	*Diligent*
Meek	*Good (Full of)*	*Frugal / Resourceful*
Servant-hearted	*Pure Heart (of a)*	*Obedient*
Tolerant	*Faith (Full of)*	
	Worshipful / Devout	
	Content	
	Joyful	

An Experiment in the Disciplines of the Soul

Finally, brothers and sisters, whatever is true, whatever is noble, whatever is right, whatever is pure, whatever is lovely, whatever is admirable—if anything is excellent or praiseworthy—think about such things. (Philippians 4:8, NIV)

On the following pages is a list of what I believe are qualities of our soul—our spirituality. They are called that because they are the exhortations of how to BE as found throughout New Testament scripture. The qualities are not about behaving, rather, they are about being. They are qualities of the soul because if we become them and then do them, they will not lead us to sin. It is as simple as that.

Suggestions/Instructions:

I've grouped the soul qualities into seven categories. Caring/Loving, Selfless, Full of Integrity, Spiritually Centered, Pure, Wise and Disciplined. Start by meditating on a category and asking God to reveal a prayer or statement about that category. Write it down. Start with any category you want. None is more important than another. Take as much time as appropriate (at least a day) to experience awareness and/or evidence of that soul quality in your life. Write down the evidence(s) of the quality you experienced. As a part of your devotional discipline, meditate on the scripture references or look up a scripture reference or illustration of that soul quality brought to your remembrance.

Next, look at the soul qualities within a category. What is your soul saying about that quality? In your life? What is your prayer? Listen for the voice of your soul. It is quiet, gentle, pure and always brings glory to God.

As you go through the list, do not make this a forced march. Take as much time as you feel is necessary to hear from God through your soul about each quality. From time to time would you please report to me, rdkuest@comcast.net, of your progress, your insights and whether this has been a helpful process to become more aware of the qualities of your soul. I would love to see a copy of your worksheet to celebrate your insights as well.

PLEASE feel free to share this project with others. In doing so, please encourage them to assist me in this wonderful experiment by sharing with me their progress of discovering the qualities of their soul as well.

Closing Thought:

Who really knows where the pure ethos of who we are is contained. We know all too well where memories, fears, suspicions, and imaginations are found. It can't be the soul. Could it be that the soul contains the memory of Eden and possesses the essential goodness of God himself? Not out perfection and certainly not our righteousness, but an essence of His pure righteousness? Peter tells us we can participate in the divine nature, the essential mind of God as we "think on these things..." So, meditate on these Soul Qualities and allow the Holy Spirit to bring to life in our living an awareness of the awe, majesty, depth and richness of the wisdom of God.

Preparation for Next Conversation:

Read Chapter 14. Putting it Together
Download a hard copy or an electronic copy of the Soul Qualities Worksheet and go through the following exercise. You can find this under the Group Member, Conversation Leader or Mentor & Friend link on the Gravity website.

- *First, focus on a soul category such as, Caring/Loving or a soul-quality such as Compassionate.*
- *Next, under My Ownership, write your own one sentence definition of what that soul-quality means to you—your personal definition. Consider putting in form of a prayer.*
- *Next, begin to pray for and anticipate opportunities where that soul-quality can show itself. Record those evidences.*
- *Finally, look up Scriptures illustrating how God wants that quality to live out in you.*

During the time between meeting again, meditate on the content. Find one major category to focus prayer or meditate on and pray through the qualities within the category. Ask God to reveal to you how to grow in the depth and richness of each quality.

Preparation for the Conversation Leader and Mentor

In preparation for Chapter 14, download and review the Group Coaching Exercise for the next meeting. You can find this under the Group Member, Mentor & Friend, or Group Leader resources page on the GRAVITY Website. The next two chapters may take several additional sessions. Take your time.

CHAPTER 14
Putting it Together

Gravity Truth Six:

SOUL-MASS AND THE SPIRIT OF GOD DETERMINE *gravitational attraction and radiating influence*

Scripture:

I am the true vine, and my Father is the vinedresser. Every branch in me that does not bear fruit he takes away, and every branch that does bear fruit he prunes, that it may bear more fruit. Already you are clean because of the word that I have spoken to you. Abide in me, and I in you. As the branch cannot bear fruit by itself, unless it abides in the vine, neither can you, unless you abide in me. I am the vine; you are the branches. Whoever abides in me and I in him, he it is that bears much fruit, for apart from me you can do nothing.

John 15:1–17

Praise the LORD, my soul; all my inmost being, praise his holy name.

Psalm 103:1

My soul is consumed with longing for your laws at all times. Psalm 119:20 And now, Israel, what does the LORD your God ask of you but to fear the LORD your God, to walk in obedience to him, to love him, to serve the LORD your God with all your heart and with all your soul,

Deuteronomy 10:12

Jesus replied: Love the Lord your God with all your heart and with all your soul and with all your mind.

Matthew 22:37

Dear friends, I urge you, as foreigners and exiles, to abstain from sinful desires, which war against your soul.

1 Peter 2:11

Synopsis of the Chapter:

Jason is finally at a state of self-clarity and soul-mass health that he's now ready to receive feedback in a way he can process in a mature manner. Lew gives him this sentence to unpack: "The State of my human spirit and soul determines the foundation of my belief and behavior values. And my fears and desires strongly influence my motives for my actions and behaviors. In the end, our actions and behaviors are what others experience."

Jason and Lew spend a rich time peeling the onion, perhaps not without some tears in the process. In the process of maturing and focusing the gravitational attraction and radiating love, Lew points out that Jason must become courageously vulnerable.

Big Idea:

Jason has spent many hours with Lew, and for what? To get fixed? And if so, is "fixed" what God intends for his life or just for selfish purposes? Isn't there more? Yet, to find the more we must understand the cause and consequence of our dysfunctional habits, routines, mindsets and triggers. Perhaps, too often, after we unwind our story, we just rewind it back the same way.

How do we rewind our life's narrative? We all understand it starts with the salvation of Christ which allows the Holy Spirit, Christ's Spirit, to take up transformative residence within us. It's that simple and that hard. Unless we invite Jesus to take up residence in us, and to rule this world as His instrument of righteousness, life is about as futile and meaningless as Jason feared it could be.

Conversation Questions:

If we name our temptations we have a better chance of overcoming them.

- **Preservation:** What are your temptations of preservation? Money, health, pride and/or reputation? How can you trust God for your protection?

- **Control:** What are you (dysfunctionally) trying to control? Your way, your version of the world, your relationships? How does worshiping God and serving only Him bring this temptation under God's realm?

- **Gratification:** What are you experiencing that is giving you temporary pleasure yet taking you away from a whole and holy relationship with God? Food, drugs, alcohol, sex, TV, entertainment, recreation? How does the Word of God provide you with the gratification your body and brain and mind demands?

1. The actions and behaviors of Old Jason V1.0 is what created his crisis. Looking back at his story and seeing what Lew has identified as the issues (i.e. control, limited trust, driven by works, etc.) was he unfairly treated by the board? Explain your thoughts.

2. Be ready in conversation to fill out the Old_YourName_V1.0 worksheet. You can use the worksheet in the book or you can use the Old_YourName e-worksheet. You can find this under the Group Member, Conversation Leader or Mentor link on the Gravity website Resource page.

You have searched me, LORD, and you know me. You know when I sit and when I rise; you perceive my thoughts from afar. You discern my going out and my lying down; you are familiar with all my ways. Before a word is on my tongue you, LORD, know it completely ... Search me, God, and know my heart; test me and know my anxious thoughts. See if there is any offensive way in me, and lead me in the way everlasting.

Psalm 139: 1-4, 23-24

Closing Thought:

What a blessing to have a friend like Lew. One who will, in love and wisdom, help a friend see how to grow in God, to become more Christ-like. Sadly, this is a rare blessing, yet this is how the Body of Christ on earth should be. The church is built as two, then multiplied. Perhaps we allow the business model to distort our effort. We don't reach out to crowds hoping to snag a few. We have to be more intentional. No one can walk the narrow road of Christ as a lonely sojourner. It's not safe to merely walk it in a crowd as well. Two-by-two, multiplied, is the equation of ecclesia.

Preparation for Next Conversation:

Read Chapter 15 - New Jason V 2.0
Complete the New You worksheet before your next meeting. You can use the worksheet on the following page or download it from the Conversation Leader or Mentor resources found on the Gravity website.

Review and make notes for the conversation questions for the next session before your next meeting.

Old Man (Your Name) V.1

Actions and Behaviors	Fears and Desires	Motives	Belief and Behavior Values	State of My Human Spirit and My Soul
Surface		*Core*		
				State of my human spirit. On a scale of 1-10 with 1 being whiney, possessive, insecure, and attention seeking, and 10 is a completely subordinated and humble human spirit who has given rule over to the Holy Spirit, where would you rank the state of your human spirit? __________ **State of my soul.** On a scale of 1-10 with 1 being a beaten, buised, shrunken ball and 10 being robust, healthy, and worshipping God in all you see, say, and do, where would you rank the state of your soul? __________

New You (Your Name) V. 2

State of the Human Spirit and Soul	Belief and Behavior Values	Motives	Fears and Desires	State of My Human Spirit and My Soul
Core		*Surface*		

Notes

CHAPTER 15
New Jason V 2.0

Gravity Truth Six:

SOUL-MASS AND THE SPIRIT OF GOD DETERMINE *gravitational attraction and radiating influence*

Scripture:

Remember not the former things, nor consider the things of old. Behold, I am doing a new thing; now it springs forth, do you not perceive it? I will make a way in the wilderness and rivers in the desert.

Isaiah 43:18-19 (ESV)

For I know the plans I have for you, declares the Lord, plans for welfare and not for evil, to give you a future and a hope.

Jeremiah 29:11 (ESV)

And we know that for those who love God all things work together for good, for those who are called according to his purpose.

Romans 8:28 (ESV)

In him we have redemption through his blood, the forgiveness of our trespasses, according to the riches of his grace,

Ephesians 3:7

The Lord will fulfill his purpose for me; your steadfast love, O Lord, endures forever. Do not forsake the work of your hands.

Psalm 38:8 (ESV)

If you know these things, blessed are you if you do them.

John 13:17 (ESV)

"Before I formed you in the womb I knew you, and before you were born I consecrated you; I appointed you a prophet to the nations."

Jeremiah 1:5 (ESV)

Synopsis of the Chapter:

Jason comes to Lew a changing man. Not changed and not just making changes. He is a work in progress. His rediscovered and wounded soul is healing. With the scar tissue of betrayed trust sloughing off as he meditates on the soul qualities, his soul is growing again. He is experiencing self-clarity and is now aware that he is able to take risks and trust. "For me, this is the biggest 'aha' of our whole process. I'm learning I can trust God, others, and myself, and in the process become a person worthy of trust in the lives of others. As long as I held what I thought was the control lever, there was very little trust given or received. Saw no need for it. To get to where I was is a scary, hard and slippery slope, so now I must continually dig in so I don't slip back into my old ways."

Big Idea:

The state of our human spirit and soul is determined by our belief and behavior values. They are propelled by motives and influenced by fears and desires. That is where and when actions and behaviors impact others.

Conversation Questions:

1. Describe your experience in filling out the NewYourNameV2.0 worksheet. Was it hard? Why? Was it meaningful? In what ways? How will this exercise help you in the future?

2. What do you have for your sentence-chart—the chart narrating the new you, V2.0? Share with your conversation partners what you've put in your chart and why that is important to you. (Break in to pairs to share your work)

3. Lew tells Jason, "You are the most significant and influential person in your life. Not anyone else." Do you believe that about you as well? If your answer is 'yes,' why? If your answer is 'no,' why is that?

4. The Principle of Gravitational Attraction and Influence starts by stating that love, like gravity, influences through attraction. It causes objects to fall. To be an effective leader requires others to fall in love with you. How are you doing with the "falling in love with you" part?

5. Response to Jason's four "big ideas" that came out of his soul-mentoring experience.

   1. Let God be God.

   Seems cliché but how do you relinquish control to trust?

   2. Become a serial killer.

   A little grotesque in imagery, but how do you kill the "old man" in you?

   3. Become piercingly vulnerable—be authentic.

   What does that look like? How is that different from being too open and too much "what you see is what you get?"

   4. Tame my will through spiritual disciplines.

   How do discipline exercises tame the will?

6. Are you engaged in any of these ideas? If so, how so?

7. As you begin to put it all together, describe some strategies, thoughts and actions you now own related to each of the first six truths.

LIFE IS FIRST ABOUT
the kingdom of God

CHANGE ENLARGES
the kingdom of God

LOVE IS THE FORCE
of gravitational attraction and radiating influence

LEADERSHIP IS THE CRAFT
of a leader

LEADERS BECOME DEFINED
by their gravitational attraction
and radiating influence

SOUL-MASS AND THE SPIRIT OF GOD DETERMINE
gravitational attraction and radiating influence

Closing Thought:

It's amazing the loops we find ourselves in. Most of them are illogical and oftentimes dangerous. At best, they waste our time. At worst, they spiral us into frenzied rituals of uselessness. What are loops? One of Jason's loops was that works were the proof of our goodness before God and man. Another loop many of us find ourselves in is being relentlessly unforgiving of our self while trying to be graciously forgiving to others. Instead, how about trying to love others as we love ourselves and then completing this loop by loving ourselves the way God loves us and then we are able to truly love others. Jason shares a final "aha" that may be useful for all of us when he says, "It's not my power, my celebrity or even my competence that causes others to fall in love with me. Maybe that's the clue I've been looking for."

CHAPTER 16
Trajectory

Gravity Truth Seven:

TRAJECTORY IS *the leader's legacy*

Scripture:

A new command I give you: Love one another. As I have loved you, so you must love one another.

John 13:34, 15:12, 17

For this is the message you heard from the beginning: We should love one another.

1 John 3:11

And this is his command: to believe in the name of his Son, Jesus Christ, and to love one another as he commanded us.

1 John 3:23

Dear friends, since God so loved us, we also ought to love one another.

1 John 4:11

Do not be like Cain, who belonged to the evil one and murdered his brother. And why did he murder him? Because his own actions were evil and his brother's were righteous.

1 John 3:12

And now, dear lady, I am not writing you a new command but one we have had from the beginning. I ask that we love one another.

2 John 5

Let no debt remain outstanding, except the continuing debt to love one another, for whoever loves others has fulfilled the law.

Romans 13:8

Above all, love each other deeply, because love covers over a multitude of sins.

1 Peter 4:8

Synopsis of the Chapter:

As he promised the board, when he completed his coaching, Jason would come back and explain to them what he found to be his problems and, more importantly, his solutions for moving beyond his self-imposed crisis. Jason chooses to invite his staff to the "celebration" as well.

Jason explains in a nutshell what everyone knows and has seen as well – that he's a changed person. "I think I can make this fairly brief. Lew has taken me through a process of growing my gravitational influence by becoming more aware of the need for health in my soul-mass.

However, there is a caution. Here's a brief physics lesson and a life lesson as well. An object under the influence of gravity continually accelerates until it impacts with the mass of a larger object. Collisions aren't good for celestial objects or for followers attracted by the gravitational pull of leaders. To avoid collision, we possess the capacity, the force, to alter a follower's course of movement. Our radiating influence causes objects to veer into their own trajectory. And this is a key point Jason missed as the old Jason V1.0. The key point: Gravitational attraction without a corresponding radiating influence is neither safe for the leader or the follower.

Big Idea:

You aren't discipling unless you can see the trail of a trajectory.

Conversation Questions:

1. The seventh truth of Gravitational Attraction and Influence says that the forces propelling a trajectory are attractional gravity and radiating influence expressed through the love of a leader. What are some practical examples of radiating love producing a trajectory?

2. What are some of the challenges you face in keeping a consistent effort of trajectory at work as well as at home?

3. What effort of trajectory between work and home seems to be harder? Why?

4. Describe the journey and transformation that occurred in Jason.

5. Do you think Jason's path was realistic? Why or why not?

6. If you were Jason, describe how the story would have turned out.

7. Do you know a Lew in your life? Describe him or her.

8. As you conclude the conversation time with Gravity, ask each person what they have gained from the conversation. What in them was like Jason? What else happened? Pray over each person as they conclude their thoughts.

Closing Thought:

Gravitational attraction without a counterbalancing force can result in a collision. It's the nature of gravity. In influence and leadership, it is not about the leader, no matter how large the size and density of their soul. Leaders must always work to make sure the reason others gather around is not due to a misguided sense of celebrity.

Rather, discipling ALWAYS means the person being discipled is being helped to form their own trajectory of influence. Discipleship is the process of becoming more Christ-like and occurs inside of the disciple. Discipling is not just the mirror-image of the discipler. Instead, discipling is an intentional effort to help the disciple find their own identity in Christ. As that happens, they will begin to develop their own attractiveness and a progression of filial love that begins with others.

Jesus said, "Love the Lord your God with all your passion and prayer and intelligence." This is the most important, the first on any list. But there is a second to set alongside it: "Love others as well as you love yourself." These two commands are pegs; everything in God's Law and the Prophets hangs from them: to love the world with a whole heart a whole soul and a whole mind. By this all men will know that you are My disciples, if you have love for one another."
Matt 22:37–40; John 13:35 (The Message)

Garden Projects

WINDWARD

Picture Credits

A-Z Collection: 21(b), 27(t), 28(t,b), 28/9, 177, 178, 181(t). Brigitte Baert: 27(b), 68/9 Michel Nahimias. Barnaby's Picture Library: 21(t), 42(r), 178/9, 183, 217. Steve Bicknell: 113(t). Michael Boys/Susan Griggs: 90/1(t), 114(b). Pat Brindley: 16(bl). Jon Butcher: 124-129. Simon Butcher: 228-235. Camera Press: 30, 88, 90/1(b), 91, 114(t), 115 Bjorn Linberg, 151. Bruce Coleman Ltd: 17(b) Eric Crichton. John Daws: 166. Peter Dazeley: 211-215. Ray Duns: 34/5, 46-51, 56-61, 83-87, 93, 98, 103, 104, 119-122, 130-134, 142, 159-165, 171, 193-197, 198-205, 206-210, 218-233. Brecht Einzig: 11. Iris Hardwick Library: 73. Nelson Hargreaves: 78-82. Clive Helm: 45. James Johnson: 188-192. Larch Lap: 182. Marley Building Ltd: 184/5(b). S&O Mathews: 19(b). Bill McLaughlin: 13, 135, 184/5(t), 227. Tania Midgley: 18(b). The Picture Library: 36/7. Rotoflex Home Lighting: 42(l), 44(b). Kim Sayer: 32(r). Alan Smith: 74(r). Donald Smith: 18(t), 19(t). Harry Smith Horticultural Collection: 9, 225. Spectrum Colour Library: 89(b), 92. Jessica Strang: 10(b), 20/1, 31, 64/5, 90. Sunstor Ltd: 38/9, 40/1(b). Syndication International: 113(b). Transworld: 12/13, 14, 67, 70/1, 72. John Ward: 236-242. Michael Warren: 6, 7(t), 8, 10(t), 15, 16(t), 22/3, 23,24(t), 26, 32(tl), 74(l), 75(b), 146, 147, 180, 181(b), 244/5, 226/7. Elizabeth Whiting: 12, 32(bl) Jerry Tubby, 33 Michael Nicholson, 34 Michael Nicholson, 37, 38, 40/1(t,b), 44(t), 62(l) Clive Helm, 62(r) Jerry Tubby, 64(l) Anne Kelly, 66 Jerry Tubby, 69, 71, 75(t), 76(t,b) 77(t,b), 94, 95, 116(t,b) Michael Nicholson, 152, 179 Ann Kelly, 180 Michael Nicholson, 185, 186, 224, 226, 243, 253. Zefa: 19(b).

Editor: Keith Faulkener
Art Editor: Eddie Pitcher

Published by Windward,
an imprint owned by
W. H. Smith & Son Limited
Registered No. 237811 England
Trading as WHS Distributors,
St John's House, East Street,
Leicester LE1 6NE

ISBN 0–7112–0408 X

Printed and bound in Hong Kong by
Dai Nippon Printing Company

INTRODUCTION

A garden is a place for enjoyment and relaxation. Throughout the year it provides a variety of colour and texture, and in the summer months it becomes an extension of your home. Most people have small gardens and may think that their scope for improvement is limited, yet with thought and planning any small garden can fulfil all your family's growing needs.

Garden Projects is not a book about plant choice and care, but a practical guide to planning and construction. Whether you want to build a patio, erect a fence, or create a play area for your children, *Garden Projects* is packed with all the ideas and techniques you will need.

There are projects to suit everyone, from making simple garden furniture to constructing your own luxurious swimming pool. Each project is illustrated with photographs and explained in an easy-to-follow step-by-step approach.

Any garden can benefit from the ideas in *Garden Projects,* and provide you and your family with even more pleasure and enjoyment throughout the seasons.

CONTENTS

Chapter 1
OUTSIDE IMPROVEMENTS
Planning your garden 6
Making the most of small gardens 11
Water gardens 15
Designing rock gardens 20
Sloping gardens 26
Garden storage 31
Awnings and sunshades 36
Lighting outdoors 42
Outdoor electrics 46
Returfing 52
Garden drainage 56
Disguising unsightly walls 62

Chapter 2
PATHS AND PATIOS
Patios 67
Decorative paving 74
Lay a brick path 78
Repairing paths 83

Chapter 3
FUN AND RELAXATION
Outdoor play areas 88
A sandpit in the garden 94
A children's climbing frame 98
A garden swing 103
Rustic garden furniture 108
Garden furniture 113

Chapter 4
BUILDING IN THE GARDEN
Which concrete? 119
Concreting tools 124
Laying raft foundations 130
Turning a corner 136
A brick terraced planter 142
Planning a swimming pool 146
Pool construction 152
Filtration and circulation 159
Heating your pool 166
Front garden facelift 171

Chapter 5
FENCES AND WALLS
Walls and hedges 177
Fences and gates 182
Repairing fences 188
Repairing gates 193
Erecting a close-boarded fence 198
Chain link fencing 206
Basic blockbuilding 211
Drystone walling 218

Chapter 6
GARDEN CONSTRUCTION
Greenhouses and conservatories 224
Building a garden shed 228
Building a greenhouse 236
Build a carport 243
Octagonal greenhouse 248
A garden pergola 253

INDEX 256

Chapter 1
OUTSIDE IMPROVEMENTS

Planning your garden

Because a garden is a practical and visual extension of the house, it is logical to give its style and layout extremely careful consideration. The demands of a garden change with the family life cycle and at some time or another it will probably have to cater for a wide range of activities each requiring an allotted space and a particular design. If you want to include flowers, vegetables, shrubs, trees, a lawn, a terrace, and have privacy as well as children in your garden, achieving a balance is not entirely straightforward.

Of the various outside factors which affect the way you set about planning or replanning your garden, the most important is what exists there already. You may find you have to deal with a garden which has been totally neglected by former owners and you must decide how much effort you are willing to put in to changing it—a general overhaul is quite different from a new landscaping plan.

Another point to bear in mind is that climatic conditions, the location and the soil in your garden will influence the type and style of garden with which you end up. Certain flowers, plants and shrubs will be more suited to your particular conditions than others; if in doubt consult your local garden centre.

Finally there is the immediate environment of your garden. If you live in a town and are surrounded by houses or ugly industrial buildings it will probably be important to establish privacy and to try and blot out the worst of the views—high hedges, trees, fences and plant screens being the principal ways of doing this. With all these factors in mind, you can move on to establish the basics of style and layout. After this, there is no end to the visual interest and ornamentation you can achieve; and no space, however small or irregular in shape, need be a restriction.

Determining the style

The visual and practical link between the house and outside is of great importance in determining the style of the garden.

Your first task is to recognize the style of your house. Take careful note of the building materials used: if concrete and bricks are the main elements, you can establish a sense of unity by incorporating these materials in the garden for walls, terraces and paths. On the other hand a cottage or rustic-styled house looks wrong with a predominance of brick or concrete in the garden, however cheap or available these materials may be. A house with a good deal of timber in the structure looks better with timber fences and a timber-framed greenhouse or shed.

The style of the garden depends also on its surroundings and in a residential area, it pays to blend in your garden to some extent with those around you. Shock-tactic contrasts are seldom successful.

The interior of the house is another major consideration: as the garden is a physical extension of the house, it should in some measure harmonize with it. An English country cottage with small rooms and picturesque furniture does not look right with large terraces and a geometric layout; instead it demands a more ornamental approach with natural stone and perhaps an area of rockery.

By the same rule, asbestos plant pots look out of place in the garden of a brick-faced house. And the more modern interior is better complemented by a streamlined type of garden with the architectural use of plant materials, terraces and paths.

But whatever the style, remember that it will be influenced also by any long-established features such as a break in the level of the plot or a group of trees. Such features tend to serve as indicators of the way a garden will be laid out. They point to whether it requires an open, spacious aspect with a sweeping lawn and herbaceous borders or whether it is more suited to intricacy, cobbles, shrubs and ornamentation. A heavily featured garden might even look in style completely paved over with raised beds and trees highlighted in the artificial surroundings.

Below: *A pergola with a variety of climbing plants provides a peaceful shady nook for hot summer days.*

Design and layout

Taking style and outside factors into account, the design and layout is going to depend on what you want your garden for—growing flowers, growing vegetables, relaxing, sunbathing, an outside dining area, a children's play area, or a combination of all these.

You must consider also how much terrace you need, how much of the garden you require for vegetables and herbs, how much lawn you want in relation to flower beds and where to site such service areas as sheds, greenhouses and water taps—not to mention special requirements like an enclosed play area, a sandpit, pond or colourful rockery.

Careful planning with the aid of squared paper is essential for roughing out your ideas to get a guideline for shaping and proportioning the plot. But before doing this consider the various possibilities that concern each type of garden and some of the many types of materials and plants you may require to keep it at its best.

Above: *Make the front garden a showpiece for your home with splashes of colourful flowers and let one colour dominate for extra effect. For instance, these brilliant red salvias provide a dramatic display*

The front garden

This needs particular attention in terms of the overall style of the house. Front gardens tend to be showpieces or, at the very least, areas which introduce the visitor or passer-by to the individuality of the house. Most front gardens are too small to use as anything more than a decorative frontage. Nothing looks worse than a bare, shabby area or one that clashes in style with the house itself.

In small, terraced houses the front area often comprises a single brick wall hiding a place to keep dustbins. But even this can be made attractive: you can place window boxes on the front window sills, establish creepers such as clematis, ivy, virginia creeper and honeysuckle on the walls and set a run of flower boxes along the front wall. To increase the exterior greenery still further, plant hardy shrubs—many of which are colourful and need little attention—in one corner. Altogether, these effects give an urban terraced house a very pleasant cottage-like appeal.

Larger front gardens can be used as children's play areas if you want to use the main garden for your own purposes. In this case, you must pay particular attention to the safety factor of the enclosed area: make walls and hedges high enough to keep in children and fit a secure gate.

Another possibility is to pave the area completely and use it as a place to tinker with cars and motorcycles, or for other practical outdoor activities such as carpentry or the odd painting job the handyman might embark upon.

On more conventional lines, the front garden can go a long way towards setting up the atmosphere of privacy—with high hedges or young saplings on the front border. And, for the green-fingered, the area can greatly enhance the look of the house if it includes a rose bed or two or a bed of colourful flowers.

Below: *This elegant leisure garden with its secluded pond has been given extra privacy with a border of tall shrubs.*

The flower garden

The garden given over solely to attractive plants and flowers is not for those who dislike gardening. But it is a good choice for the keen horticulturist who has only a small garden area; a restricted space does not deny the effect of a profusion of flowers if the garden is properly planned. A few beds asymmetrically or geometrically arranged around a small lawn is both practical and attractive, because the flowers and plants themselves make the layout unique.

Planning your garden

A flower garden should not normally have a large terraced area but there ought to be some hard surface—such as a path or a narrow terrace—at the back of the house next to an outside tap for use as a solid base on wet days. If there is room, a squared island terrace jutting out from the back of the house will give you a base to sit on warm summer days to enjoy the view of the flowers.

If the design of the garden is to be wholly successful the planting should be worked out as carefully as the layout. There are three basic levels for planting design. The first is the sculptured level with larger plants and shrubs taking up dominant positions; the second level provides the bulk of garden planting including grass and small shrubs against which the third level, the decorative element, is set.

It is particularly important in the flower garden to remember the background effect created by such plants as evergreen shrubs.

But try not to overburden the borders of the garden with high hedges and greenery, as this detracts from the decorative effect of the flowers and restricts the amount of light coming into the garden.

Try to find room for a garden tool shed and possibly a greenhouse within the design. Sheds are best tucked away into corners and made accessible by means of natural stone pathways, paved or even cobbled paths.

The site of the greenhouse will depend to some extent on what you use it for. If you intend growing attractive hot plants such as orchids you might want to bring the greenhouse forward into the visual scheme of things. But if you use it for raising seeds or keeping the odd garden tool in, then a site at the end of the garden might be more suitable.

Above: *Shrubs and borders of varying heights give a most effective, sculptured look when used together.* **Right:** *Small gardens come to life with short and tall plants in many colours*

The vegetable garden

Even in a small garden it is possible to be self-sufficient in flowers and fruit to a fairly large degree. The emphasis should be on practicality and accessibility: allowing yourself enough beds or plot space to work a seasonal rota of growing.

The traditional area for vegetables is at the end of the garden, screened off by a trellis. But nowadays the high price of fruit and vegetables often makes the vegetable garden the central part of the garden layout. In this case, their conspicuous position demands that you grow them in as neat and attractive a form as possible. Give the visual appearance of the garden as much consideration as the productivity of what you are growing.

In a small square, or average-sized rectangular garden, a good functional layout is to have three vegetable areas intersected by pathways with the fourth quarter given over to a terrace for a timber-frame garden shed housing essential tools.

You can then plant espaliered fruit trees such as plum, apple and pear around the borders and turn over spare areas at the back of the house to potted strawberries. In Britain, plants such as gooseberries and currants grown fan-like on walls take up little room and are both attractive and productive.

In terms of visual appeal, a combination of herbs and vegetables provides interest throughout the year. Remember that many of these can be grown intensively in containers or raised brick boxes which serve to ornament the garden. Fruit trees also double as decorative plants—especially if you consider the merits of apple and cherry blossom, or grape vines draped around a pergola.

As with flowers, light is important to the appearance and productivity of vegetables so keep their plot as much to the centre as possible.

The leisure garden

Designing purely for peace, privacy and leisure—with space to sunbathe, eat and give the children free rein—allows a great deal of scope. For a start, it is a good idea to incorporate a large area of terrace—which need not be in one block—especially now that the range of stone flooring, concrete paving and brickwork is so wide and varied.

A combination of terrace, lawn and herbaceous borders with a good deal of shrubbery and the odd tree, is ideal for the leisure garden. But the prime consideration should be the bordering hedges, fences or walls. For extra privacy you can build up small neighbouring walls, either with more of the same brick or by adding a stretch of louvred or interwoven wooden fence to the top of them.

Plenty of shrub and tree foliage is the natural way to increase the sense of isolation and privacy, but a wooden-framed pergola extending over the terrace at the back of the house goes even further. Such a framework should be distinct and simple, and the wood need not necessarily be of the highest quality to be adequate. With a profusion of climbing plants around it, blossoming overhead in spring, a pergola provides an attractive, shady sitting area, a place to eat out of doors or leave a pram on warm, sunny days.

If you are thinking in terms of a play area for the children, a terraced area surrounding a central lawn with a built-up sandpit situated accessibly on one side is a practical answer. This gives the children a circuit for riding tricycles while you have the lawn to yourself for sunbathing.

On more geometric lines, you could extend the terrace down one side of the garden and inset a shallow paddling pool and a sandpit with the rest made over to a lawn and attractive flower border.

The leisure and play garden tends to be one which requires little maintenance, but you could lessen the amount of work even more by concentrating less on flowers for decoration and more on shrubs and trees. There are several hardy, attractive shrubs—rhododendrons, camellias, azaleas, bush roses, lilacs and tree peonies, to mention but a few—which look ideal in eye-catching positions. And once planted, they can be left largely to themselves.

Likewise, trees are most obliging plants: they live longer and grow larger than other plants, they give shade, screen you from neighbours, provide fruit to eat, flowers for decoration and grow while you sleep—sometimes surprisingly quickly. Trees in a new plot, if you choose the right kind, can give the appearance of maturity within only a year or two.

The all-purpose garden

This type of garden, which incorporates something of all the other types, requires a very carefully worked-out balance. To start with, it is probably best to relegate the vegetable garden to its traditional place at the end of the garden and grow a small hedge or build a fence to screen it from the rest. Remember, too, that the garden lawn is usually the dominant feature and that it must be in proportion to the other areas: a small lawn will be incongruously overwhelmed by a large terrace—it is far better the other way round.

In long, narrow plots or awkward L-shaped gardens the shapes lend themselves to the division of the garden into separate areas—often a necessity in the all-purpose garden. It is even possible to accentuate the

Above: *A monochrome garden using a variety of interesting shapes and textures is an effective alternative to the colourful flower garden.* **Left**: *Add charm and character to a town house entrance with a selection of plants in pots and window boxes to simulate a garden*

individual areas by dividing them off with hedges, bamboo thickets or saplings so that each can be given its own particular style.

But a more flowing layout could be adopted in a small square garden, perhaps by having a central lawn surrounded by flowers, shrubs, trees and vegetables with the vegetable area occupying a slightly elevated section.

If you have room for a lily pond or fish pond you will find the effects particularly worthwhile: plants and flowers grow in profusion around ponds because they benefit from the reflected sunlight. And like a sandpit, a statue or a tree, a pond provides a highlight for the garden and leads the eye in a particular direction.

Remember that the most important unifying factors in the all-purpose garden are the materials used for partitioning and paving. Get these right and even the most varied garden can be prevented from looking too 'patchy' and untidy.

Terraces and fences

When you terrace an area it is best to use a stone, concrete slab or brick that suits your house and its location. Local stone in country areas is worth searching for despite its comparative expense. Brick houses can often take a warm-coloured local stone or brick placed side-on as a terrace and even rather bland concrete can sometimes look good.

Concrete for walls and paving is probably most suited to the garden of a modern house while for a house with delicate features, internal hedges and wooden fences are a good choice—and wooden fences are by far the easiest to erect yourself. You can even carry a bordering palisade fence into the garden to form a wrap-around compost heap.

Brick walls can be matched with brick paths and terraces, arranged in herringbone, diagonal or circular patterns. In the same way, concrete or stone slabs can unify an area if you inset them in the border of the lawn as a path or a pattern. All these materials should be used with three important purposes in mind: to establish the different sections, to lead the eye, and to give continuity of theme to the garden.

Making a plan

Once you have weighed up all the various factors and decided exactly where your needs lie, it is a good idea to make a scale plan of the proposed layout on graph paper.

Start by measuring up the garden and marking this in outline. Follow with the positions of all the immovable objects such as trees, humps, and depressions.

After this, you can start to plot in your proposed features—flower beds, the lawn, paths, terraces. As you make each addition, stop for a moment and think carefully whether it fits in with the rest of the house.

For example, a sunbathing patio will be of no use if it is overshadowed for most of the day. Nor will the children's play area be very safe if you cannot see it from the kitchen or living room window.

Finally, remember that if you try at every turn to make your garden both a physical and practical extension of your home, you can be sure of the very best results.

Making the most of small gardens

Getting the most from a small garden requires very careful planning. The trick is to keep it simple and easy to maintain, by choosing the right plants, and making sure they can all be seen from the house

Perhaps the biggest difference between planning for inside and outside is that much of what you put in the garden will rapidly change—plants are seasonal and their appearance alters dramatically from month to month. But this can work to your advantage and with careful planning, you can create a garden that is a delight throughout the year because it is never the same.

Unlike a house interior, it is rarely desirable to start completely from scratch, without a single tree, flower bed, scrap of lawn or vegetable patch. So, whatever the present layout, it should form the basis for your new garden design.

Your first thoughts should be to the type of garden you want. You might want a garden that is first and foremost productive, where you can grow fruit for jam-making, and vegetables to last through much of the year. Or you may want a garden that is primarily for show, where the flowers come first and the garden is a wealth of colour through all the seasons. Or perhaps you prefer a garden that is easy to maintain—a place where you can entertain friends during the warm summer evenings.

Although the style of your garden will depend mainly on what you want to do in it, the shape of the plot and the style of the house—even the materials used in its construction—should also be taken into consideration. A cottage garden might be ideal for a small country cottage but not so good for a modern, semi-detached house—rustic brick or random stone walls and paths can look completely out of place in a setting dominated by glass and concrete. Harmonizing existing buildings and materials with the garden always achieves a more satisfying result.

Making a plan

Before you consider moving or adding anything to the garden make a detailed plan of the area on graph paper. Indicate the extent of any lawn, the position of flower beds and other notable features such as a tree, path or steps. Then add in your house, taking

Below: *Japanese-style simplicity is particularly suited to a small space, and provides a peaceful outlook from within the house*

special account of doorways and windows that open out on to the garden. You might find that the garden consists of too many straight lines—a rectanguiar lawn and flower beds in narrow strips to one side and a concrete path on the other. There may be an old shed in full view of your living room window, a tree may be casting shadows over the very spot you thought ideal for sunbathing.

Look for areas which can be improved upon. For example, you might have good or bad views within and beyond the garden that can be emphasized or disguised. A change of level might be put to good use or made into an interesting feature.

Privacy is an important consideration for many people, though if you are fortunate enough to have substantial walls or fences already bordering your plot this will not be a problem. Both can be decorated with fast-growing vines, creepers or ivy for added attraction. If your garden is badly overlooked you might consider building a wall, installing a fence or using screens to section off part of the area..

Below: *The classic solution to space problems in a garden. A small paved area surrounded by hoards of colourful plants and shrubs*

Patios and lawns

Patios and lawns are like the open spaces inside your house—areas against which fixtures, fittings and ornaments are contrasted.

On your plan, draw in the sort of proportions you would ideally like and then the shapes that complement it best. For example, a strictly rectangular plot might be nicely complemented by a circular patio leading into a gently curving lawned area. But avoid following the existing shape of the plot too closely and try instead to create more interesting lines for the eye to follow.

If there is a tree close by the house which does not cause too much shading at a time of day you are most likely to sit out, then you might even build a patio around this. If there are walls on either side, match the building style and materials to harmonize new with old. Changes of levels—whether requiring steps up into the rest of the garden or down—are ideal for extending the patio further with steps or enclosed plant terraces, low retaining walls or rockeries.

While a geometrically-shaped lawn is easy to design, it is rarely the best shape for a small garden. Surrounded by plants and shrubs, a circular lawn creates a focus of interest that keeps the eye away from the limited — and often claustrophobic—boundaries. It is a diversionary tactic which also enables you to create interesting shapes for flower beds and vegetable patches, with a sweeping path leading the eye around the garden rather than straight across it.

Nevertheless, the lawn does not have to be circular, kidney-shaped or curving in any way if you can find other shapes that do just as well in creating interest. A courtyard-style garden can be designed with paved areas which extend across the lawn—breaking it up into smaller squares and rectangles—and linked perhaps by a brick planter set alongside a path. A lawn can also be broken with shrubs or small trees that visually interrupt the clean lines of the grass and yet lead the eye on to the rest of the garden.

Of course, in a very small garden you might want to do away with the lawn altogether. For ease of maintenance, a paved area using random sandstone slabs or even gravel between some flower beds and shrubs can be

Below: *Add interest and life to a flat, paved area by building a barbecue pit. Brick paving goes very well with low brick walls*

just as effective in creating interest—and it is a style that is ideal for most modern houses.

Steps and paths

The materials you choose for steps and paths should harmonize with those used for your patio, or at least with the brick of the house or the surrounding walls. Their style should also blend with the shapes you create in the garden itself. Paving slabs work well on steps and paths leading through the garden, and in less formal arrangements, crazy paving, brick paths in various patterns from herringbone to straight lines, or even pebbles set into concrete create that bit of extra interest.

Just as paths need not run in straight lines, steps need not be simply squared off. Curved steps add to the grace of a sweeping pathway, and you can create beds on each side for flowers or shrubs that step up into the garden from the patio.

In a garden with a fairly dramatic change of level, it might be worth exploiting this further by creating several levels of part-paved, part-planted areas so that you can neither walk in a straight line through the garden, nor follow a particular visual line to the boundary. Such an arrangement could easily incorporate a built-in bench seat, a barbecue, and even raised planters. Again, you can build around existing trees and leave occasional gaps in the paving for different kinds of plants.

Above: *Very small backyards can be given that Mediterranean touch by whitewashing the walls and covering them with plenty of colourful hanging plants and pots*

Pools and rockeries

In gardens without any significant change of level, pools and rockeries can add the elusive extra dimension. Although relatively easy to build from scratch, they are often inherited from the previous owner, and are ideal features around which to plan a layout for maximum use of space.

In this case it is often a good idea to link them with a path—and unless there is an overriding style of material used in the house, patio or in the garden walls, it is a good opportunity to mix materials. A garden pool might be surrounded by random stone slabs in an informal style; and if you want to introduce a geometric order, square shapes will contrast well with a round pool.

Enclosures

From fences to pergolas, enclosures can be used for anything from major screening to creating a delicate flower display. The variety offered by simple wooden structures is enormous, and most are easy to erect yourself.

Against the house, a pergola can create an open-roofed extension on which climbing plants quickly wind their way upwards; against a wall, it makes a colourful focus of interest. Simple screens can be built of anything from slats of wood to trellis-work on a simple frame.

Half screens of all kinds in the garden are very effective in diverting attention away from unsightly features, unattractive views or neighbouring buildings and can also be used as wind-breaks. Here again, there is a wide choice of materials including all varieties of brick, which can be laid in different ways to create a half-open effect and stone of all kinds, from flint or bushrock to random squared blocks to give a more rustic look.

In a wall built without mortar, the joints can be filled with soil to form a rooting place for lichens and creeping plants that quickly lend the appearance of age and permanence. Of course, if you already have walls in the garden which need a bit of extra interest, you can add trellis work for climbing plants, or even paint a wall white to create a stark background for the delicate foliage of a newly-planted tree.

Vegetable and herb gardens

A kitchen plot can be easily incorporated into a small garden and just because it provides a ready supply of vegetables and herbs there is no reason why it should not also look attractive. Neat rows of plants can be divided by narrow paths to combine an attractive visual appearance with productivity, albeit on a small scale.

In very small gardens you can also use containers and even proprietary grow bags for vegetables, tomatoes and even strawberries. Just ensure that each variety has sufficient space to grow to its full potential.

Take advantage of the sunniest spots, and plant the tallest groups at the back with rows of ground-hugging plants at the front of the beds. Fruiting trees and vines, gooseberries or redcurrants can be grown against a wall or fence where they will do double-duty as decorative plants.

Above: *Stacked planters allow all the foliage to be seen and make the most efficient use of available space*

Flowers and shrubs

A garden planted with flowers and shrubs that bloom in different seasons, and with at least a certain number of evergreens and perennials, achieves the best compromise between colour and ease of maintenance. Which plants you choose will depend on the local soil and your own taste, but always think ahead when planting anything. For example, if you want a climber to disguise an old shed, you will need a variety that does the job throughout the year and not die off in the winter. And if you plan to use shrubs to create a screen for privacy or to hide an unattractive view, go for a fast-growing variety otherwise you will be waiting years for relief.

Similarly, if you are planning to plant trees to add extra variety to a rather open garden, do not choose a type that will eventually shade the entire area. Before you plant anything, find out what its soil requirements are, its growing potential and its preferred location—then you can allow nature to do the rest.

Water gardens

A water garden can provide a restful and relaxing focal point. Whether your garden is large or small, formal or informal, incorporating a stream, waterfall or fountain into its design makes a most attractive feature

Your garden needs a visual point of interest in just the same way as your lounge or dining room. And the temptation is often to rely upon a group of shrubs, flowering trees or a rockery to provide this focal point.

However, an alternative which offers endless decorative possibilities is a water feature. There are many types of water garden—pools, streams, waterfalls—and an equal amount of decorative accessories like ornaments and fountains. And, of course, as well as a wide variety of waterplants from which to choose, you can also introduce fish into the pool.

Ponds can be constructed from glass fibre, concrete or pool liners. The size and shape to choose will, to a large extent, be dictated by the nature of your garden layout and also where the pool is to be located. The important point to remember, is to choose a design that fits in well with the overall appearance of the garden.

Pools can be roughly divided into two categories—formal and informal. A fine example of an informal pond is shown **left,** stocked with a wide variety of plants—water lilies, marginals (a form of grass), and suitable border vegetation.

Other effective marginal plants ideal for an informal pond include those from the reed family—probably the most popular being the bullrush. Marginal plants should be potted just below the surface of the water—most proprietary garden pools have ledging incorporated into their design for just this purpose.

If you want to introduce fish into the water, then you will also need to have a sufficient supply of oxygenating plants in the pond. Bear in mind, however, that these tend to grow profusely and will need constant thinning.

A semi-formal pond is shown **overleaf,** and here clever use has been made of York stone walling and greystone paving. The neutral stone colours are offset by flowing marginals and the colourful potted plants on the pool's edge. The characteristic style of the L-shaped pond makes it ideal for the smaller garden or even a patio.

The pool **bottom left, overleaf** is an example of a formal pond—normally a rectangle or a square, with paving around its periphery. But here, some of the formality has been removed by the random placement of shrubs on the lawn around the edge.

The cluster of tall reeds at the far end tends to lead the eye along the length of the pond and the pool layout adds artificial perspective to the small garden, giving the effect of a longer dimension.

Another example of the formal pool is the circular layout—again formality relies on symmetry. This type of pool is ideally suited to small gardens or where there is a natural junction in the garden—such as the meeting place of two paths.

The example **below** clearly illustrates this effect. Symmetry has been further emphasized here by the clever use of border brickwork and the ornate, multi-jet fountain located in the middle of the pool. A circular pond can also look very attractive with a stock of flowering water lilies floating on the surface.

In total contrast, the remarkable informal pond shown on the **right,** is highlighted by the border plants and the nature of the pool construction itself. The unusual waterfalls, constructed from water butts, adds an interesting touch of eccentricity.

This type of raised pool is reasonably easy to build yourself, and again, is particularly suitable for very small —or even paved—gardens.

If you have a very large garden and are prepared to spend time and money on a water feature, it is quite possible

to combine modern ideas with formality as shown in the pool **below**.

Here the overall construction relies on the use of hexagons—both for the pools themselves and for the paved stepping stones. The use of massive surrounding shrubs and marginals prevents the whole pool appearing too flat or from being overshadowed by the extensive paving around the perimeter.

On the other hand, if you have a very small garden, it is possible to make your pool seem larger by digging it down rather than raising it. This arrangement gives you another opportunity to create a visually dramatic effect, especially if you incorporate a series of steps leading down to the pool in your design.

The pool shown **overleaf** uses an unusual formation of flint stones for the surrounding wall and steps, and is stocked with both fish and plants. Although the actual space occupied by the pool and its immediate surrounds is very small, the depth of wall and steps gives it a rather unusual perspective. And clever use of rough flint stone adds drama to the effect.

Using border plants is probably the easiest way of introducing colour, but some types of marginal and water plants have brightly flowering blooms.

For example, water lilies like these shown **overleaf,** need very little

care and will last for many years. Generally water lilies can be obtained with flower colours of red, white and yellow but do not expect them to bloom in the first year, During this time, however, it is a good idea to place 'feeding blocks' into their bedding pots and under the roots to encourage growth. These can be readily purchased at most garden centres.

Ornaments, too, can be used to highlight your garden pool or fishpond. These are available in a wide variety of shapes and styles to suit both formal and informal layouts. A combined statue and fountain like the one shown **right** can be particularly attractive in a formal setting.

Where the pool is stocked with fish, fountains are vitally important— especially during hot weather when the intake of oxygen into the water is limited. The constant flow of water picks up oxygen and introduces it into the body of the pool water. It also has the added advantage of helping to stabilize water temperature and prevent stagnation.

The same effect can be achieved with waterfalls. The example shown **below,** which is probably best suited to a larger garden, is unusual as well as attractive, because the supply head is yet another, smaller pool. Both pools have been adequately stocked with immersed and marginal plants.

Designing rock gardens

A rock garden doesn't have to be enormous to be attractive. If a bit of thought is given to its design and construction, and to the selection of suitable plants, a small rockery can be a source of beauty all year round

In nature, rock plants grow where small pockets of soil and stone chippings collect at the base of large outcrops of crumbling stone. What makes these 'natural rock gardens' so attractive is the contrast between the enormous scale of the rocks, some of which weigh several tonnes, and the delicacy of the tiny, bright or pale coloured, alpine plants.

While botanic gardens and large parks can successfully recreate natural looking rock gardens on this grand scale—covering acres of land at vast expense—a rockery for your own front or back garden is likely to be a much smaller proposition. A miniature rock garden can be just as beautiful, though, and give as much year-round pleasure, provided you give a bit of thought to its design and construction.

Choosing a site

Because a rock garden should ideally look like a natural occurrence, the more lawn or open space it is surrounded by, the better. Try to keep it well away from such formal features as flower beds, geometrically-shaped pools or paths—although if you have enough space, a large rock garden with a path running through it, or an informal pool incorporated within it, can be most attractive. If space is very limited, you can build up a rock garden against a garden wall, or wedge one in the corner between two walls, although the result will never look quite natural.

A sloping bit of ground makes the best site for a rock garden, and steeper level changes can be terraced with rocks to give an almost retaining wall effect. But if your garden is dead level, you can still construct an attractive rock feature by building up a slight angle within the rockery.

Because most alpine plants prefer full sun, choose a site which gets most sunshine. Although some alpine

Left: *An ideal way to find out which rock garden plants you like is to visit a local botanical garden* **Above:** *On a smaller scale, steep level changes are enhanced by a rockery*

plants will tolerate light shade, dense shade is unsuitable. Keep your rock garden well away from overhanging trees, as they will shade the rockery, and their leaf fall in autumn can smother the plants. Trees with greedy root systems can also rob the soil in the rockery of moisture in summer, with disastrous results. A background of trees in the distance is quite another matter, however, and the overall effect can be stunning.

Above right: *A drystone wall offers much the same growing conditions as a free-standing rockery* **Right:** *Gravel or grit edging adds an authentic finishing touch to a rockery*

Lastly, if your rock garden is visible from your living room window, then the pleasure you derive from it will be greatly enhanced—changes in weather need not prevent you from enjoying its beauty through all the seasons.

Size and shape

Very little space is actually needed for a small rock garden—an area of $4m^2$ is plenty—and a modest-sized but well thought out rockery is much more effective than a large, rambling mass of rubble.

The shape is a matter of taste and depends on the layout and levels of your own garden, but as a general rule, avoid rigidly geometric plans, such as circles and rectangles, because they look unnatural. A blunt, wedge-shaped or roughly L-shaped plan can be a good starting point. But keep the shape simple.

Where many rockeries go wrong is in the build-up of height. While enormous, hill-like rockeries, meant to be walked around and viewed from all sides, work in the large scale, when miniaturized they tend to look like rubble tips.

Rock gardens should be built in a series of increasingly smaller diameter layers, rather like a tiered wedding cake—it makes good design sense and the result will be structurally sound. A small free-standing rock garden is best confined to one or two layers only, facing in one direction, with a flat, rather than a rounded, top surface. A shapeless heap of hardcore or soil, into which rocks have been studded, may be quick to erect, but the result will be short lived—it will quickly settle and erode—and the appearance will be haphazard.

Selecting rocks

If you provide your own labour, then most of the expense in building a rock garden is in the cost of the stone. This is largely made up of the cost of transporting the stone to your garden, so it pays to buy it locally. Besides being less expensive, local stone looks more natural, particularly if your house or nearby garden walls make use of similar stone.

Some of the larger garden centres may have rock in stock, but a better bet is to try local quarries, stone merchants, builders' merchants and demolition sites.

Besides considering which stones you find attractive, you should consider the plants' needs as well. Because their roots like to penetrate rock, both for stability and in search of moisture, porous rock, such as sandstone or limestone, is much better than very hard rock like granite. The latter never weathers well, and discourages plant life. Be wary of very soft sandstone, though, as this very quickly crumbles in poor weather.

Right: *Two large-scale rock gardens in open sun, but with a background of trees* **Far right:** *Level changes make ideal sites for rockeries, and steps can be successfully incorporated*

DO

- Clear the area to be built on of all weeds before starting, paying particular attention to pernicious perennials such as couch grass. Apply a residual weedkiller, such as dichlobenil, to the cleared site.
- Check roots of pot-grown plants for bits of crock or other drainage material before planting, and extract any you find.
- Consult keen local gardeners or good local garden centres before purchasing plants. They will be able to help you select the plants most suited to your soil type, growing conditions and your own particular design scheme.
- Keep an eye on the plants for their first season, until they become established. This is important if they are planted during the growing season, or if the summer is particularly dry; frequent watering will be needed.

DO NOT

- Use the rockery as a dumping ground for builder's rubble. While a layer of hardcore in the excavated area can improve the drainage on heavy soil, and lime mortar is appreciated by lime-loving plants, the central bulk should be of good quality soil.
- Attempt to build a rockery out of several different types of rock, because it will look disorganized and shoddy.
- Build a rockery up against a house wall, as it is liable to cause trouble with damp.
- Leave a rock in position which looks awkward or unstable. It is much easier to reposition a rock immediately, rather than try to do so after the rockery is finished.
- Start the second tier of a two-layer rockery until the first tier is absolutely firm and solid, and you are satisfied with its overall shape.

Constructing a rock garden

Once you have decided on your rockery's size, shape and location, some preliminary work is necessary before the creative work of positioning the rocks begins.

First, carefully mark out the area to be built on with strings and pegs. Allow an additional 300mm all the way round for a grit edging strip. As well as recreating the appearance of the gritty scree, found in nature near the base of rock outcrops, this strip enables you to use a lawn mower close up to the rockery. You can usually buy grit—ranging in size from coarse sand to 10mm chippings—from the same source as the rocks.

Next remove the turf and excavate

1 After initial soil preparation, shape the soil or special compost for the bottom layer. Angle the top surface slightly, facing the sun

5 If the rocks do not fit tightly against each other, fill any gaps with wedges of smaller stone. This prevents the soil seeping through

6 Work your way towards the back, using progressively smaller rocks. Make some stones jut out and others recede slightly for a jagged effect

7 After the first layer is complete, start the second by putting the largest rock in position first. Proceed as before, checking for stability

to a depth of 150mm, removing any weed roots as you find them. If your topsoil is free draining and fertile, put it to one side, as you can use it to build up the central bulk of the rockery. If your soil is very heavy or otherwise unsuitable, cart it away and use instead a mixture of three parts good loam, or proprietary loam-based compost, to two parts of leafmould or peat and one and a half parts of sharp sand or grit. All parts are by volume, not weight. Once this is mixed, add bonemeal at the rate of 1kg per cubic metre of soil mixture.

A word of advice—it is far better to mix more than you need of this prepared soil, as it stores well, rather than to mix too little and run out part-way through the exercise. When calculating how much you will need, remember that a 75mm thick layer of this special mixture will be needed as a top-dressing for all the exposed soil surfaces in the finished rockery.

The step-by-step instructions and photographs show you how to proceed once you have prepared the ground, but a few general points need special emphasis. Disturbed soil is always subject to settlement, and unless you compact each layer of soil thoroughly as you build up your rockery, very soon after it is finished you will find the levels sinking. And, of course, the plants will sink along with them.

Do not rest each rock on the soil; bury it about one quarter of its height into the soil, for greater stability. Try to get the upper surface of each rock tilted towards the soil pockets, so rain water is directed back towards the plants, rather than away from them.

The larger the rocks, the more impressive the result, but your own strength must be a guide here—after all you will have to lift and position them on the rockery.

However, each rock should be large enough to retain the central core of earth, and the smallest should be no less that half the size of the largest. For a two-layer, 4m/ rockery, you will need about 1m³ of rock.

2 Put the largest rock in place first, angled 15° backwards, and ram soil around and under the base. Each rock must be firm enough to stand on

3 Many rocks have obvious strata lines. Ensure these lines run parallel to each other and roughly parallel to the ground as well

4 Select a slightly smaller rock and push it hard up against the first rock, so that the join between them is as tight as possible

8 When the soil is roughly level, and all the stones in place, spread the special topsoil mixture, 75mm thick, over the soil surface

9 When planting, make the hole large enough to take the roots comfortably. After planting, firm the soil hard up against each plant

10 Finally, cover all the exposed soil with a 25mm layer of grit. This keeps weeds down and keeps the soil from drying out in summer

Sloping gardens

A sloping garden lends itself well to creative planting and offers immense scope for more unusual decorative effects. With just a little thought and careful planning, you can bring a whole new dimension to your garden design

Below: *The profusion of differently coloured heathers covering the entire slope of this small front garden presents a most welcoming sight for visitors. Slow growing dwarf conifers complement the design and make an attractive border for the pathway*

Above: *This large garden makes good use of its sloping terrain. Drystone walling adds a decorative touch to the lawns and colourful flower beds*

Below: *A rockery is the perfect answer for a sloping garden. This one provides plenty of colour and interest and even incorporates a delightful water pool*

Gardens come in all shapes and sizes but whether large or small, any sort of slope – however gentle – seems to offer the gardener the promise of a more interesting effect than a perfectly level site can produce. And this is true even in a comparatively small garden, because a slope brings a third dimension to whatever plans you have in store. This section looks at some of the ways you can turn a sloping plot to your advantage.

The starting point

The hardest thing in the world in gardening is to start from scratch, with the sort of refuse dump of a back garden that many modern developers leave the new homeowner to deal with. New houses always seem to be provided with a front garden that is half concrete and half hastily laid turf; but at least some effort has been made to tidy things up a bit. At the back of the house things are usually very different. At best the soil will have been 'tidied up', meaning that it is at least fairly level (or is a fairly uniform slope on hilly terrain).

At worst, the topsoil will all have been removed as work began on clearing the site. Spoil from excavations will have been dumped behind the house, mixed with broken bricks, sand, ballast and cement then left to mature its own special crop of weeds. Such a plot needs a tremendous amount of work to turn it into a garden.

Above: *Large stone slabs set into the natural slope of the garden provide a highly decorative pathway and add a dramatic touch to surrounding foliage*

Below: *A formal yet attractive arrangement for a gentle slope. Semicircular steps with rockery plants complement the circular stone patio*

Left: *An effective way of exploiting a partially sloping garden. The slightly curved stone steps bordered by a decorative rockery on either side form an extremely pleasant and colourful pathway up to the garden lawn*

Easier in practice to tackle is the established garden, either in your present home or in another house that you have recently purchased. Here you will at least have certain features in existence that can be incorporated in your new plan, and it is likely that the slope of the garden will have been developed to some extent, even if not to your total satisfaction.

Up or down

The sloping garden is usually level across its width, with a lengthways slope up or downhill when viewed from the house. A few gardens may also slope widthways, creating a terrain with more possibilities, but such a slope is hardly noticeable in all except the comparatively wide garden.

The degree of the slope is an important factor when you are trying to decide on your plans for the plot. In a very small garden – less than 10m long – the slope is unlikely to be extreme. But where it is larger than this you can best judge the slope for yourself by walking down (or up) it and lining up features of the house by eye. For example, on a downslope you may find your eye level with the back door step when you are half-way down the garden, indicating a drop of around 2m over that distance.

What you can judge from this is whether your garden is best treated as a uniform slope away from the house or whether it could be terraced to create a series of 'steps', each of which would contain part of the garden and be level – or at least less steeply banked than the present slope.

A gentle slope – less than about 2m over the length of the garden – is best left as it is. The lawn will not be difficult to mow on such a gentle gradient, and in any case the rise or fall does not really lend itself to any worthwhile special treatment. If the fall is steeper than this, some form of terracing will alter the perspective of the garden dramatically and will also make it easier to tend.

Such an approach works particularly well in a long and narrow garden, which might tend to look more like a green-carpeted corridor unless broken up in this way. This is particularly so where the boundary on either side is a fence rather than a hedge.

Creating terracing

If you decide to break up the slope of your garden by creating terracing, you will have to consider retaining walls and steps. Most people like to have a paved area immediately behind the house and this can be pleasant to sit on, useful in providing somewhere for children to play and washing to hang, and practical as a 'buffer zone' between the house and garden. It is at the far side of this area that your first change of level will probably occur.

If your garden slopes downhill from the house, a low wall here with steps down to the next level will make the patio seem a more dramatic viewpoint. If the slope is up from the house, a retaining wall will provide shelter for the patio and the chance to create natural shade by planting trees and shrubs immediately above this.

The area beyond the first wall can then be brought right up to the wall, or the steps can lead through flower beds or shrubberies to the lawn further away from the house. This latter idea can be extremely effective where a steep slope (which would be awkward to mow if turfed) is involved since a series of steps can be used to cross a relatively steep bed on a rockery.

The technique can be continued along the length of the garden. Depending on the degree of slope, you can either go for dramatic (if infrequent) changes of level or have shallower steps – perhaps only two or three courses in height made from natural brick or stone.

Remember that retaining walls do not have to be at right-angles to the plot's boundaries, nor do they have to be straight lines – in fact they will look much more interesting if they are angled, curved or broken in line. The positions of flights of steps, too, can be altered from level to level to break up the appearance of the garden, and the flights can even be set at different angles to the wall.

Above: *Water makes a very attractive addition to the sloping garden. Here an unusual arrangement of pebbles and stones effectively creates a dam to form two separate water pools. When the upper pond is full, water trickles over the pebbles to form a waterfall*

Each retaining wall will have to be built on a concrete strip foundation. Low walls need only be one brick deep, but any wall over about 600mm in height should be of double bonded brick or stonework. In the case of high walls – over about 1200mm in height – steel reinforced piers should be provided at 2.5m intervals otherwise there could be a very real danger of collapse.

Remember that by creating shallow steps you will have less earth moving to do than if you go for dramatic changes in level, as well as less wall building. But in either case you must allow for drainage from one 'level' to the next by incorporating weep holes in the retaining wall masonry. If you do not do this, water might build up behind the walls and cause them to collapse.

Planting the sloping garden

One advantage of a sloping garden over a level one is that you can use the changing levels to display plants, shrubs and trees to better effect. For example, a row of conifers across the downhill end of a slope could be high enough to screen the bottom of the garden from neighbour's eyes without interfering with the view from the patio or the house itself. If the garden slopes up from the house, you can concentrate on low-growing species that help to disguise the steepness of the plot.

Of one thing you can be certain: with a sloping garden you are unlikely to be troubled with standing water every time there is a downpour. But if the garden slopes down to the house, make sure there is adequate drainage from the patio or you could soon find yourself with serious damp problems inside the house.

Water in the sloping garden

The crowning glory of the sloping plot is the scope it offers for the use of running water. Of course, any garden can (and frequently does) have its ornamental pond; but in a flat garden you can create moving water only by artificial means, with pumps powering fountains or small waterfalls down man-made rockeries. In the sloping garden you can experiment far more, and perhaps even create a complete water garden with a series of small ponds at different levels spilling into each other via waterfalls and watercourses. This not only gives you the chance to relax with the sound of water tinkling gently down the slope; you can also grow a wide range of aquatic and semi-aquatic plants along the waterway.

You will of course have to use an electric pump to recycle water from the lowest level to the highest, but this (and the associated pipework) is easy to conceal. It is best to site the pump near the house to simplify wiring.

Garden storage

Given time, even the smallest garden can land you with a mountain of things to store – be they pot plants and tools or outdoor furniture. A shed usually provides the answer, but there's plenty to think about before making a choice

Whatever size garden you have, you are sure to need some form of storage out of doors for 'garden equipment' – whether for the tools you need to keep the garden from turning into an overgrown and unattractive wilderness, or for furniture and other accoutrements, indispensible if you are to enjoy the garden to the full.

Before deciding on the type of storage facilities to instal, however, it is important to evaluate the extent of your requirements and assess just how much storage space you really need.

Basic considerations

Of course you may already have firm ideas about just how big your garden storage problem is, especially if you have nowhere to store anything. On the other hand, you may be struggling along with thoroughly inadequate facilities, and wondering how to cope.

If your garden tools consist of nothing more than a fork, spade, pair of shears and a small lawn mower, then they could probably all be stored on shelves or hooks on the garage wall. On the other hand, if you have a large garden, with a vegetable plot as well, your garden tool inventory might well encompass two lawn mowers, a cultivator, a number of other power garden tools, plus a full range of hand tools and all the garden chemicals and equipment vital to the keen gardener.

Then there is the question of garden furniture and leisure equipment to consider. Unless you are in the habit of carrying a chair out from the house every time you want to sit in the sun, you will need somewhere to store at least a couple of deckchairs or sunloungers, and perhaps a table as well.

Quite often it makes sense to combine a garden storage zone with space for a workshop or other activities. For example, the vegetable gardener may also need somewhere to store crops – potatoes, apples and so on – after harvesting, and also a potting shed for springtime planting activities. The home handyman could combine garden storage with a workshop where he can also store tools and materials. And the family may simply want additional leisure space – an outdoor playroom or sun lounge.

The garden shed

If you decide that your needs are for storage only, your choice of facilities is

Left: *A garden shed for a keen grower: the pitched roof with rafters provides plenty of hanging space while shelving and racks take care of everything else*

fairly straightforward – a traditional garden shed. This can be little bigger than a cupboard, to hold a few garden tools and provide room for a couple of chairs. Or it can be big enough to store mowers and cultivators, wheelbarrows and sacks of potatoes.

In either case, there is a wide choice of styles, shapes and materials from which to choose. The simplest garden shed consists of a wooden rectangle or square, with a floor area of $0.5m^2$ to $1.5m^2$, plus a pent (sloping) roof, a door and no windows – although the roof may be of translucent plastic to let in some light. Larger wooden sheds come with either pent or ridge roofs and probably incorporate at least one window. Those with ridge roofs offer more headroom and provide useful storage space for longer items such as beanpoles.

Alternatively, there are concrete sheds – consisting of prefabricated panels that are bolted together to make up a square or rectangular structure, with windows and doors – and easy-to-erect panelled buildings with a simple framework clad with weatherproof panels. Again, there is a wide range of shapes and sizes available to suit your requirements.

Apart from size and style, there are one or two practical points to bear in mind when choosing a storage shed. Firstly, it must have a lock: many burglaries are committed with the aid of tools taken from unlocked garden sheds; and as well as being extremely expensive, it might prove impossible to replace many of the tools that have been collected over a number of years.

Secondly, it must be totally dry – not just weatherproof – so that tools do not rust and stores do not rot. This means providing a suspended timber floor, rather than a concrete base or a few paving slabs. Ideally, the inner walls of the shed should be lined with some form of insulating board. Such improvements are well worthwhile in the long run, even if they do add to the initial cost and effort of building the shed.

Storage/workroom

If you have decided that you need a workroom as well as a storeroom, then you will want a somewhat larger building. The actual size will, of course, depend on your requirements and the space you have available, but the minimum size you should consider for the purpose is about 1.8 × 3m, with good headroom over the entire floor area. So choose a ridge rather than a pent roof.

One end of the building can then be designated for storage (and will therefore

Above: *Garden sheds quickly become chaotic unless tools and implements are well organized. Hang large tools on nails and fit shelves to take smaller items*

Left and above left: *Before and after shots of an ugly storage bunker cleverly disguised with a fast growing creeper – the same can be done to a shed*

Right: *A redundant doorway adapted for garden storage: a window replaces the original door and the bunker below has access from both inside and out*

not need a window), while the other end can be used as a potting shed or workshop with a window at waist-level to admit adequate light. This arrangement also ensures that you have plenty of wall space for shelves and other storage arrangements.

Comfort will be important if you are going to work for long periods in the shed. A suspended timber floor will again be an asset here, although you may need to consider ways of setting workbench legs on a concrete screed below the floor level to provide a firm work surface for carpentry and similar jobs. Bear in mind too that a concrete shed will be warmer than a timber one in cold weather, unless the latter is lined on the inside.

Storage/summerhouse

You may feel that your additional requirements are not so much for space to work in as for space in which to relax – somewhere to sit in a comfortable chair out of the wind on bright, but chilly days. In this case what you need is a summer-house, which can also double as an outdoor playroom for the children as well as providing storage space for gardening equipment. Do take care, however, to place any garden chemicals or sharp implements on shelves well out of the reach of children's inquiring hands.

There is a choice of timber outbuildings ranging in style from modern and rustic to the 'Swiss chalet' look. The biggest choice is in cedar or other softwoods and especially useful are those types with casement windows and glazed panelled doors. In fine weather these can all be opened up to admit plenty of fresh air to provide the perfect environment where you can just sit and relax and enjoy the peace and quiet of the garden.

Siting the building

Apart from the obvious practical aspects of size and style, it is important to consider the appearance of the building in the garden – whether you want to make it a feature of the garden or disguise it to blend in with its immediate surroundings.

Although it is mainly a question of personal taste, it is well worth looking at as many different types and styles as possible and considering all the options before committing yourself to spending money on a building that might look totally out of character with your garden once it is erected.

Timber outbuildings, especially cedar ones, look very attractive when new but need regular applications of wood preservative or paint, and also occasional re-roofing with new roofing felt. Concrete buildings, on the other hand, need virtually no maintenance, and those with a simulated brick and stone finish can look extremely effective.

Sheds that are intended purely for storage are best sited where they are most needed. For example, a storage shed for garden tools and equipment might be most practically positioned at the bottom of the garden, while one used mainly for storing garden furniture could go near the back of the house – to one side of the patio or backing on to the garage.

A combined storage/workshop will obviously be of most use near the house and a storage potting shed near to the flower beds or the vegetable garden. A summer house on the other hand should be positioned according to the geography of the garden to catch the maximum sunlight for the longest part of the day.

It is worth remembering that a building used for any kind of garden storage must be easily accessible, and it might be worth laying a permanent path leading to it which will be passable in wet, as well as in dry, weather.

Give some thought too to whether you will need a supply of electricity to the shed. If it is to be used as a workshop, this will probably be vital for driving power tools and for providing light and warmth. Remember that an outbuilding should be supplied via a permanent and separate

electrical circuit taken from the house's main fuseboard, and that the cables should either be buried in the ground or carried overhead to the building out of harm's way.

If you do not want to make a feature of your garden shed, it can be tucked away to one side or placed at the bottom of the garden, and screened from the house with quick-growing conifers, fencing or a screen block wall. Alternatively, it can be stained or painted to blend in with its surroundings, or covered with climbing plants such as ivy.

Storage alternatives

If you feel that a separate outbuilding is not the solution to your garden storage problems, there are one or two other ideas you could consider.

The first is to build a simple lean-to structure against the back wall of the house to provide lockable storage space for a few garden tools or a small selection of fold-away garden furniture. Such a structure need be only about 600mm deep with a sloping roof and a hinged door. The inside walls can be lined with polyethylene, stapled to the woodwork to help keep the damp out, and the junction between the new structure and the house sealed to prevent water penetration.

Another idea is to construct a small porch or conservatory outside the back door of the house – again a lean-to building, but this time mainly glazed to admit optimum light – to provide not only the necessary storage space, but also somewhere to raise houseplants, keep muddy shoes and even dry the washing on wet days. This type of structure would have the added bonus of cutting down on draughts inside the house and heat loss through the back door.

Below: *Hoses often cause more clutter than anything else. The answer is a capstan with its own water supply*

A vegetable rack

Build this simple low-cost rack to help you make the best use of the space available in your garden shed. Use it either for garden produce or for storing bulbs over the winter.

It is based on a timber frame which forms trays on five levels. The tray bases are made from wire mesh. Although the timber sizes specified are ideal, you can use any available offcuts if they are of approximately the same dimensions. You could, for example, use thicker timber for the tray sides. Note however that the tray front rails are designed to be lower than the sides or the backs, so that you can reach in easily.

Cut out all the timber parts to the appropriate lengths. Finish is not critical, so it does not matter if you are using slightly sub-standard wood, but you should remove any splinters. Assemble with glue and nails, checking the alignment with a square. Start by making up the front and back, joining the uprights with the cross rails, then join these two together with th side rails.

When the assembly is complete turn upside down and fix the bases in place working from the lowest one up. Make th bases from chicken wire mesh (the plastic coated variety resists corrosion better held to the frame with small nettin staples. Cut the mesh oversize and pull tight. Trim after fixing and bend any shar ends under to ensure that they will nc damage the fruit or bulbs.

There is no need to seal or paint any c the timber, although you can if you prefe so long as you choose a non-toxic variety

Use the rack for storing vegetable crop before they are brought into the house, c for keeping them through the winter. Yc should only do this, however, if your shed frost proof. Crops such as apples, whic should be kept separate, can be stored divided apple trays which are ofte discarded by greengrocers or mark traders.

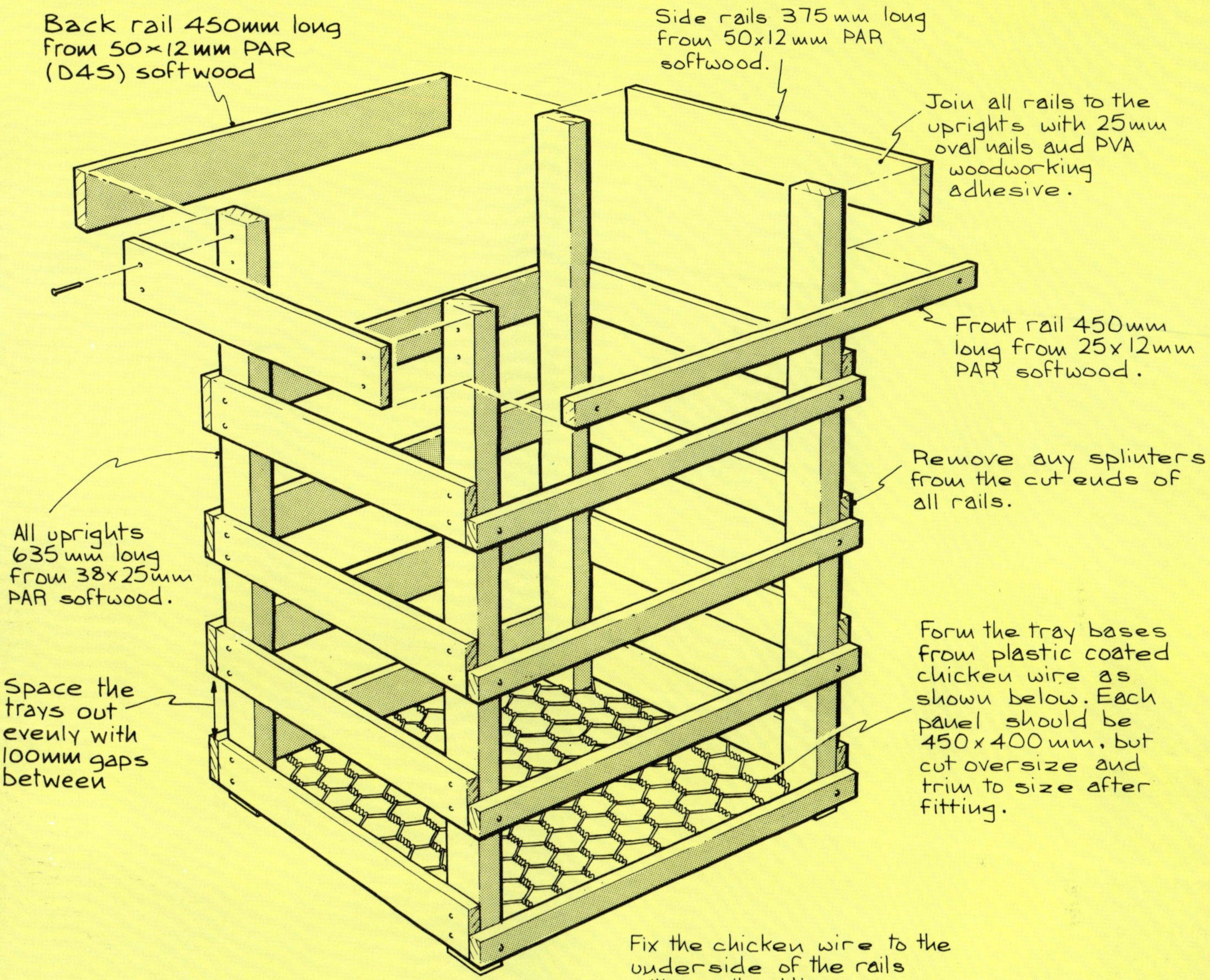

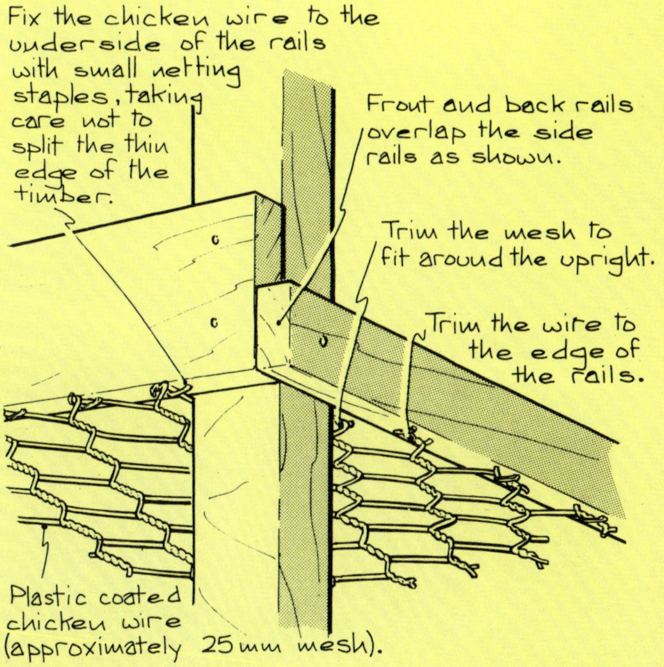

Cutting list
All sizes are in millimetres. All timber is planed all round, PAR (dressed four sides, D4S).

Part	Material	No.	Size
uprights	38 × 25mm softwood (PAR)	4	635mm
back rails	50 × 12mm softwood (PAR)	5	450mm
front rails	25 × 12mm softwood (PAR)	5	450mm
side rails	50 × 25mm softwood (PAR)	10	375mm
tray bases	chicken wire mesh	5	450 × 400mm

Additional materials: 25mm oval nails, PVA woodworking adhesive, netting staples

Awnings and sunshades

Sunshine can be great in the right place at the right time, but when you want a rest from it in the heat of the day there is nothing like a pretty awning or sunshade for keeping the inside of your house cool and fresh

Although they are attractive to look at, sunshades are primarily intended as functional items. In hot countries they protect interiors against the full strength of the sun's rays. Even in cooler countries there is usually one face of a house which catches the sun and where shading is a practical addition.

Left: *On a garden window, an awning can add a touch of colour to the outside decorations of a house and prevent the room getting overheated from too much sun.* **Below:** *An umbrella-style sunshade provides excellent shade for reading or simply relaxing on the patio*

Modern carpets and fabrics are much more resistant to sun than they used to be, but prolonged sunlight still eventually causes fading and, unfortunately, this rarely happens evenly. One half of a carpet often becomes lighter than the other, or the edges of a curtain fade while the centre retains its colour.

Worst of all, polished furniture may be damaged by the sun to a point where it cannot be restored. Pictures can also suffer, especially delicate watercolours, so it makes sense to protect them by some other means than hanging them in a dark corner where they will be difficult to view.

External sunshades have another

benefit—they can be used to enhance interiors by cutting off an unattractive or dull view, or by reducing the size of windows that seem too large in full daylight.

Fitting sunshades

In hot countries, such as Australia, many homes have sunshade fittings built into them; but in the UK you are probably going to have to fit them yourself.

Some of the houses built in Victorian or Edwardian times had roll-down shades as a fixture to protect the dark atmosphere and pale complexions of the people who lived in them. However, even if you own one of these houses you will almost certainly have to replace the sunshade fabric—although the pulley mechanism should work with a little attention and perhaps a new set of cords.

If you are adding sunshades to your house, you must first choose between the fixed type and the ones which roll away for storage. In hot climates, fixed shades have the advantage of always being in position when the sun strikes a particular window. But in countries where the weather is changeable, the sunshade material will not benefit from being alternately scorched and soaked.

Right: *This large blue awning with decorative scalloped valance protects the window and provides a shaded area for picnicking—even in the heat of the day.* **Below:** *An awning over a basement patio makes an attractive feature and gives protection against sun or wind for a secluded barbecue party*

Fixed shades can also make interiors rather dark at certain times of day. Choose them only if you know that the sun will shine every day and are prepared to completely dismantle the shades in winter to prevent damage.

The simplest type of rolling shade goes up and down in the same way as an ordinary interior blind. This is also the cheapest type, requiring a minimum of fabric and mechanism. However, these shades do not look particularly attractive from the outside, particularly if they are installed on all the windows on one face where they give the house a closed-up look. They also tend to make interiors excessively dark.

There again, if you want to protect a particular room, perhaps a living room with antique furniture or a bedroom with delicate furnishings, this type of sunshade is a convenient and cost-conscious solution.

Roll-out awnings or blinds are perhaps the most attractive. When not in use they can be rolled up neatly and fairly unobtrusively against the top edge of the window, and when rolled out they will protect the room from sunlight without spoiling the view.

While the roller blind type of shade can be bought fairly easily, the roll-out type is not so easy to obtain. A good department store may stock them, but if you are looking for a special individual effect consult an interior designer or a retailer of shop style fittings.

Colour and design

When making your choice of colour and design remember that the fabrics used for outdoor blinds and awnings need to be tough and weatherproof.

Keep the exterior style of your house in mind and look for something that enhances it. Most outdoor canvas designs tend to be bright and bold.

Since your blinds will be seen from the outside in the context of the whole face of the house, it is important that they should look like a positive decorative feature. Consider adding to their appearance with unusually shaped edging or fringing.

It is also important to avoid light colours if you live near heavy traffic or in an otherwise polluted environment since they will soon soil.

Patios and terraces

It is often desirable to be able to provide protection from the sun for people sitting on a terrace or patio. While a beach umbrella, placed on its own stand or through the centre of an outdoor table, serves some purpose, its protection is limited and is usually only extended to one or two people as the sun moves around.

A patio or terrace adjoining a house can be protected by an awning which rolls down from the main wall. If the awning is only a couple of metres long, it can be supported by cantilevered arm brackets. But if it is to stretch over a wider area, it will need supporting legs like a tent flap.

A natural and attractive sunshade can be provided by suspending trellis work across the area to be shaded. Fix the trellis to sturdy supports and grow climbing vines—or other fast

Above: *Translucent curtains are an excellent way of enclosing a covered patio and can be adjusted to give shade at all times of the day.* **Right**: *These decorative, striped awnings blend perfectly with the colouring of the house and also make a most attractive exterior feature*

Above: *Even an open porch can be given a touch of colour simply by adding a small, roller-type sunshade over the front door*

growing plants—over it. The sun will shine through the chinks, leaving the area underneath attractively shaded. The only maintenance required will be to prune the plant occasionally.

Winter storage

It is important to protect sunshades when storing them away for the winter. Wait until the sunshades are absolutely dry before taking them down, then roll them out open and brush off any dust or dirt. An aerosol stain remover can be used on any bad stains, but check the instructions to make sure it is suitable for the particular fabric you are treating.

Once the shades have been removed from their fittings, roll them up, cover them in well-fitting polythene film to protect them against dirt and damp, and store them away in a safe, dry place for the winter.

It is also a good idea to retexturize the shades each year with a tent canvas protective spray. Spray the material evenly, and allow it to dry thoroughly before putting the shades back in position.

Lighting outdoors

Outdoor lighting—strategically placed to pick out the best features in your house and garden—adds that touch of glamour that may be missing during the day and creates the ideal atmosphere for dining by moonlight

Well-designed exterior lighting can turn your patio or garden into a night time wonderland. On warm summer evenings, garden lights enable you to extend your living space outside. And even in colder climates, when there is frost or snow in the air, exterior lighting adds a sparkling new dimension to the view from your windows.

But exterior lights serve more than just a decorative purpose. You can use them to light up a porch and front door; or to illuminate drives and pathways so that visitors can see the way in. And if street lighting is inadequate, as it often is in rural districts, they will light up your street number or house name.

Left: *Add drama and mystery to your garden by spotlighting statues or ornamental features such as pools and rockeries*

Choosing exterior lights

The variety of exterior lights and lamps almost equals that of interior lighting. Long gone are the days when you could buy only rather crude floodlights which made the garden resemble a football pitch. Modern exterior lights range in function from spotlamps to hanging lanterns, and in style from old-fashioned brass to ultra-modern bulbous glass.

Wall-mounted lamps which cast a soft, diffused light are suitable for lighting a porch, a patio or even a gate in a garden wall. Many shops sell beautiful old brass lanterns converted for this purpose, and replicas are just as easily available. Cast-iron, cottage-style lamps have a similar function and with frosted glass windows, lend a Dickensian glow to the porch. More suited to modern-style houses are the cylindrical, circular and oval designs with frosted or clouded glass.

Floodlights and spotlamps, casting a swathe of light through the darkness, can pick out anything from trees to the whole front or rear elevation of the house. You can buy them hooded to restrict the light path, or fully exposed to cast a broader beam.

Mounted in the ground they can be pointed in any direction, in trees they appear as a secret source of light and on a sweeping driveway they can illuminate the house as though it were day. But in a small garden avoid anything powerful since the effect might be to dazzle.

For lighting paths and driveways—and for any part of the garden, patio or terrace which would benefit from general illumination—there are many kinds of pole-mounted downlighters which cast a diffused light over a fairly wide area. The styles vary from miniature street lights to elegant bowl-shaped lamps perched on tall poles.

Finally there are underwater lights, which you may want to consider if you have a swimming pool or a garden pond worthy of illumination. These lights come in two basic forms—spotlamps/floodlights or glowing lamps—and as on the ground, the effects are very different. The former tend to light up areas in a beam of light and can be used to pick out features which are remote from the light source. The latter create a diffused, glowing light. Directed underwater, the effects of both are spectacular.

Above: *For a rustic look use old coach lamps or street lights mounted on poles or hung from trees*

Wiring up

Any exterior light fitting, unless it is sheltered in a porch, must be fully sealed and insulated because it will always be exposed to the elements—even if it is not always switched on. Porch lights and lamps mounted on exterior walls can generally be connected directly into the interior lighting circuit. But with lights fitted some distance from the house, this is not always possible.

Installing an exterior lighting circuit is a job that requires great care—the results must remain safe even after years of exposure to the weather. If you have any doubts about your skills, let a professional do the job; in Canada, your local codes may in any case prevent you from doing the job yourself: check before you start.

Use only fittings—lights, sockets, bulbs and so on—that are designed for

Positioning lights

Choosing what to illuminate and where to place the lights is almost as critical as selecting the lights themselves. At all times bear in mind that once you have positioned a light outside and buried the cable, it can be a lengthy job repositioning it. Always experiment with different locations before you make any final decisions—the extra effort will be well worthwhile.

If you simply want to illuminate a drive or pathway, the kind of lights you choose and where you position them will depend mostly on the surroundings. If you have trees lining a sweeping drive or even a narrow path, the lights should be positioned to offer a clear line to the house.

Placing spotlamps up in the trees might add to the interest, but not to the effectiveness of the illumination. And too many lights might also give the drive or path the appearance of an airport runway—it is usually better to keep to as few lights as possible.

A long drive is often adequately served by just one pole-mounted downlighter near the entrance and another closer to the house. Casting a glow over a wide area, these lamps will create a welcoming atmosphere without being excessively obtrusive.

Remember that a powerful single lamp close to the house can also serve to illuminate the house itself, so here you might consider a spot or floodlamp more effective. Positioned behind a shrub or rockery and pointing upwards to the house, the secret source of light can have a most entrancing and mysterious effect.

Left: *Upward pointing spotlights below trees and bushes create large areas of dramatic colour overhead*
Below: *A candlelit dinner on the patio takes on a romantic air with illumination from hidden spotlights*

outdoor use. Unless your lighting circuit is very simple, wire it to a separate fuse on the fuseboard—the circuit should have its own isolating switch as well. In the UK, you could wire a lighting circuit via a fused switched connection unit, fitted to a spur on the ring main. Use suitable cable—in the UK, mineral insulated or armoured PVC sheathed, buried at least 450mm below ground, or ordinary PVC cable protected by heavy-gauge conduit and buried at the same depth, to avoid possible damage.

It is sensible to have the circuit checked by a professional before connecting it (or having it connected for you) to the mains.

Lighting outdoors

Many families now enjoy barbecue parties on warm evenings and some kind of lighting is essential to make the most of the occasion. In a well-appointed patio, there may be separate eating and cooking areas which would best be served by individual lighting of different types.

Powerful spotlamps pointing up towards the house would undoubtedly create too much glare: softer, glowing lamps which cast a more diffused, softer illumination over a wider area would be a better choice. Position one close to the barbecue as this is where you will need the biggest concentration of light.

If there are surrounding walls, they might be the ideal places on which to mount the lights—and spotlamps can be used here sparingly as long as they do not dazzle.

It can be very disconcerting to be confronted by a black gloom just a few feet beyond the patio, so consider adding one or more lights some distance away in the garden. A single lantern in a tree will probably not be enough, particularly in a large area, so experiment carefully with other lights until you achieve a satisfactory compromise for both patio and garden.

Left: *Why not give your visitors a double welcome and spotlight your house number on an outside wall as well as on the front door*

Drawing the eye to one or more points of interest in the garden not only relieves the gloom lying beyond the house, it also enables you to make fuller use of the garden when you are entertaining. Just as lighting a driveway introduces a welcoming atmosphere at the front, so lights in the back garden make it a friendlier place.

The shape and texture of many natural features in the garden take on quite a different aspect when illuminated at night. A lamp mounted in the trees creates moving patterns of shadows in the slightest breeze, while spotlamps pick out the delicate tracery of the leaves. Patches of rocks and bricks, shrubs and flowers are all enhanced by illumination: try lighting them from spotlamps hidden away in a tree or bush.

Even from inside the house, especially during the colder months of winter when the trees sparkle with frost or are covered by fingers of snow, the garden itself can become a picture in a window frame.

Illuminated from below by spotlamps, a pergola can be transformed into a night time roof of greenery; because of the effects of shadows, any foliage thickens and becomes glossy—the very shape and proportion of the garden is often altered beyond recognition at night.

But of all the features in a garden that are transformed by exterior lighting, the most spectacular are pools of water. A fountain or even a pond will sparkle when lit from above by spotlamps. Plants and ornaments in water become more distinctive, goldfish shimmer and the contrast with surrounding shadows is striking.

Lighting the house

The house itself can benefit from some illumination and again spotlamps work best at picking out the most attractive and decorative features.

Lamps mounted on the walls are not generally very effective in this respect because they tend to cast shadows which distort the exterior features.

It is better to position a pair of spotlamps centrally, some distance from the front of the house, so that they can be angled to either side. This ensures that the entire front elevation is evenly illuminated.

Alternatively, individual spotlamps can be placed at the sides pointing inwards. In both cases, the lights should be positioned at ground level pointing upwards. Take care not to buy excessively powerful lamps (unless you have a very large house) since even the low-powered variety create some glare.

Left: *Spotlights are invaluable for garden lighting. They help create a romantic, gentle atmosphere, perfect for a quiet drink or evening meal in the moonlight*

Light up your patio

To bring your patio to life at night with a brilliant display of outdoor lighting, use spotlights to pick out features, or diffusers for a gentle background glow.

It is essential to use only special waterproof light fittings designed to be safe outdoors such as those types of outdoor lights shown on the right. Many such fittings have adjustable brackets designed for mounting on a wall or post. Alternatively, you can buy a light mounted on a spike or post which is driven into the ground. Most lights can be easily fitted with a choice of coloured bulbs for different visual effects.

Outdoor wiring needs special care. If in doubt, consult a qualified electrician. You should use an armoured, insulated cable laid along a wall (not a fence) or buried at least 450mm and preferably covered as shown below, to protect the cable from spades and forks.

Outdoor electrics

The uses of an outdoor supply ● Methods of installing a supply ● Overhead cables ● Underground cables ● Wall-mounted cables ● Types of armoured cable ● Making the connections ● Outdoor lighting ● Garden sockets

A. Below: *An electricity supply to an outhouse or garage – or even to a garden socket – can be very useful. Installation need not be difficult and the connections can be made according to normal practice providing you take special care to weatherproof them*

If you have a detached garage or greenhouse with no power supply, you will know how frustrating it can be to have to work occasionally in conditions of poor light and with a cobbled-up supply for your tools and appliances.

An electricity supply to a detached building – or even to a socket outlet in the garden – can be a boon if you intend to use an outhouse as a part-time workshop or if you use electrical garden tools. The installation work is not difficult; what is important is that you know how to make an outdoor supply safe.

Warning

The descriptions of outdoor electrics installation following refer primarily to the systems used in the UK. Wiring practice in Canada is different, and cable colour coding and types also differ from those in the UK.

In some areas of Canada, you may not be allowed to do your own outdoor electrical work: check your local electrical code to find out what regulations apply in your area.

Whatever country you live in, electricity must be treated with respect. **Never** work on a circuit until you are certain that it is not live.

Preliminary considerations

Unlike a lean-to garage or greenhouse, which you can supply off a ring main spur, detached buildings must have their own fused supply from the consumer unit.

The cables can be run in the normal way from the consumer unit to the point where they leave the house and the same applied once they get to the outhouse. In between, however, you have a choice of three possible cable routes: overhead; underground; or along an outside wall (but not a wooden or wire fence).

An overhead cable must be fitted at a height of at least 3.5m–5.2m if there is access for vehicles underneath.

Underground cables must be buried in a trench at least 500mm deep and should be heavily protected—which applies also to cables run along a wall. Where the cable enters the house, drill a hole in the wall above the damp-proof course to accommodate it.

Materials

For overhead wiring you will need one or more lengths of 100m × 50mm treated timber to support the cable at the required height (allow at least a metre extra for posts that are to be sunk into the ground). At the same time buy wall bolts to secure the posts, lengths of stout galvanized steel fencing wire to support them, and tensioning devices for the wire and a supply of twin core and earth PVC sheathed cable.

For underground cables you can use either armoured PVC insulated and sheathed cable, or PVC covered mineral insulated copper sheathed (MICS) cable, sold in the UK under the trade name 'Pyrotenax'. It is also possible to use ordinary PVC twin and earth cable if protected by high impact plastic conduit. Protect them by laying paving stones over the cable trench.

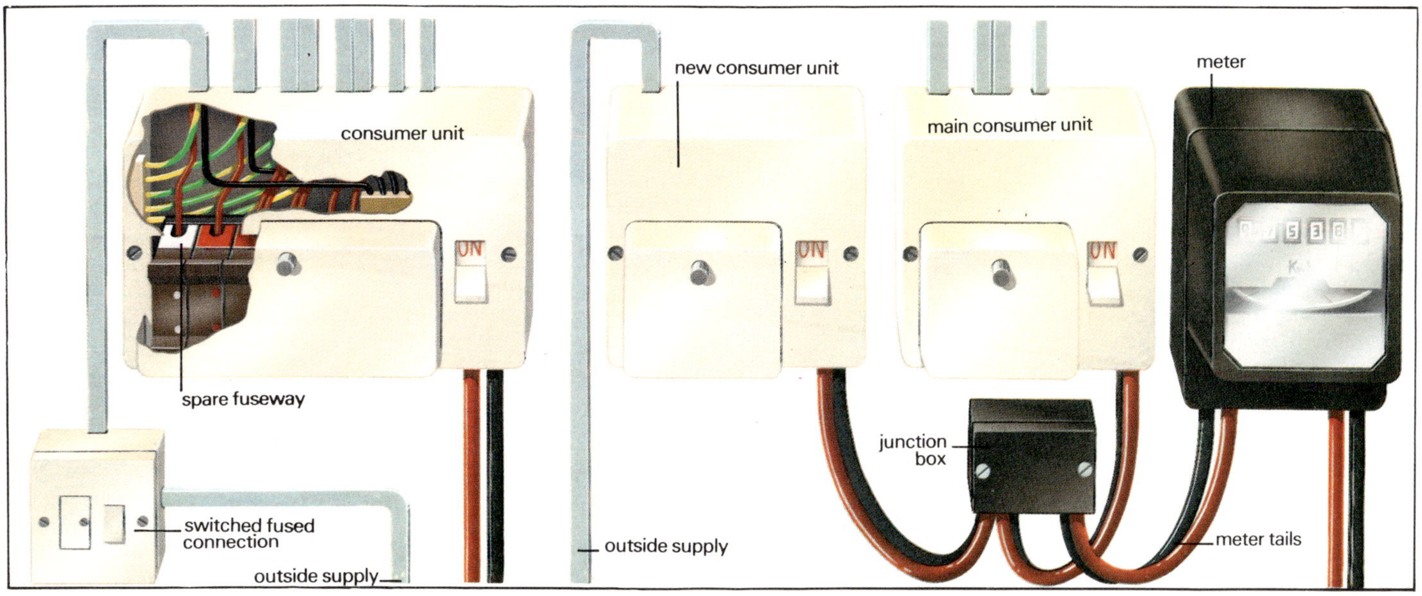

B. *Two methods of supplying the outside electric circuit. If you already have a spare fuseway in the consumer unit then you can use this (left); if not, you will need to install a new consumer unit next to the original one and get the electricity board to connect it to the supply from their meter via a junction box (right) or directly from the meter*

To connect the armoured cables to the house and outbuilding circuits you will need special compression joints for connection to a steel junction box. **Size of cable:** For a 20 amp supply over a distance greater than 20m, use $4mm^2$ cable. You can also use $4mm^2$ cable for 30 amp runs of less than 20m, but on longer runs you will need $6mm^2$ cable to prevent excessive voltage drop.

Overhead cable installation

Drill a hole for the cable through an outside wall, so that the cable will lie beneath the upstairs floorboards. If that position does not give you enough height, go into the roof space and drill a hole through the wall above ceiling level or through the fascia board or soffit at the eaves. You can then begin to feed the required length of cable through the hole and let it drop to the ground while you erect the post at the outbuilding end. Seal the hole with a non-hardening mastic. Mark off the end of the post which will be buried and then drill holes to take the expanding wall bolts that will secure it to the wall of the outbuilding. Dig a 1m deep hole next to the wall and drop the post into it. Then align it vertically and mark the positions of the bolt holes.

Lower the post, drill the holes in the

1 When running a cable along an outside wall, use armoured cable of the correct size for its length and then fasten it with stout clips

2 Drill and plug holes in the brickwork for the clips and secure them with wood screws. Do not drill into mortar as this may cause it to crumble

3 Drill through house walls below the DPC, making sure you do not damage services inside the house. Use a long masonry bit for cavity walls

4 Allow enough length of cable for connection inside the house before feeding it through the wall and sealing the hole with non-hardening mastic

wall, and then screw an eye-bolt securely into the top of the post. Attach one end of the support wire to this, cut it to the correct length and then securely fix a wire tensioner to the other end.

The support wire must be bonded to earth for safety reasons. Connect one end of a length of $2.5mm^2$ green and yellow PVC insulated cable to the eye-bolt and clip this to the post using cable clips. Allow enough length for the cable to be attached to the switched fused connection unit inside the outbuilding with the supply cable. Route the wires side by side.

Next run the power cable from the house to the outbuilding and lay it alongside the support wire. Allow enough extra length to reach the inside of the building from the top of the post and then clip it to the support wire using stout cable ties every 1m or so. Raise the post again, fit it into its hole and bolt it to the wall. Fill in the hole and compact the earth around the post as hard as you can by stamping on it.

Returning to the house, get up on a ladder and drill and plug a hole in the wall or the eaves for another eye-bolt as close as possible to the cable entry point. Screw in the eye and then pull the free end of the cable support wire up to it. Fix the wire securely and take up the slack with the tensioning device. Inside the house take up the slack on the cable and either run the wire directly back to the consumer unit, or cut it off and be sure to leave about 3m of the cable inside the house for connection.

Underground cables

Decide first where the cable will enter the house – you will have to drill a hole for the cable through one of the walls above the DPC or through a corner of an air brick. If you cannot do this without going through the wall above the floorboards, or if you have a solid floor, choose a room where the sight of exposed cable does not matter too much – a laundry room is ideal.

Once you have finalized the route of the trench, mark it out with string and pegs and start digging. The trench should be 500mm deep and about 300mm wide. When you have finished, remove any flints or sharp stones from the base and cover it with a 50mm layer of fine sand or sifted soil to act as a cushion.

Armoured cable can be laid directly into the trench, but if you are using PVC sheathed cable and conduit assemble the conduit first to make sure it fits before dismantling it again and threading the cable through. Allow about 1m of cable inside each building for connection.

Secure the conduit or cable to the walls with saddle fasteners and lay slabs of concrete over the cable in the trench to protect it from spades and forks at a later date. Fill in the trench compacting the earth as you do so.

Outside walls

Where the cable can be run along the outside wall of the house or along a garden wall, use the same cable types as for underground installations. Pass the cable through the house wall in the same way as for underground or overhead installations, depending on how high off the ground you intend to route it. Secure the cable to the walls using saddle fasteners.

Supply and connections

Once you have installed the outside cables, you can lay the supply cables inside the house. If you have a spare fuseway inside the consumer unit, use this for the supply, through a junction box. If not, ask the electricity board to cut off the power and connect a supply from the meter to a new consumer unit once you have completed the rest of the installation.

Start by screwing a fixed appliance outlet or new consumer unit to the wall next to the consumer unit – this will allow you to isolate the entire cable and out-building circuit without having to fiddle with the fuses in the unit (fig. B).

Connect to the outlet a length of twin and earth cable of the same cross-sectional area as the cable outside. Run the outer end of the cable to the consumer unit and leave it there. Now run more of the same cable from the switched fused unit to the outside cable entry point – follow normal house wiring practice in routing and fixing it.

If the outside cable is twin and earth PVC sheathed, connect the two using a junction box screwed to the inside wall, to a floor joist below the floorboards, or to a ceiling joist in the roof space. If the outside

5 *Remove any turf on the route of an underground cable before digging a trench 500mm deep and about 300mm wide in which to bury it. This will avoid risk of damage when gardening*

6 *Unroll the cable into the trench, making sure that it is not kinked. For a garden socket, allow 1m of cable at the end of the trench for connection to the household supply*

7 *Cover the cable with fine sand or soil before laying slabs of concrete or concrete cable tiles to protect it from garden spades and forks*

8 *Prepare Pyrotenax for connection by stripping off the outer PVC sheathing for about 150mm and slipping the rubber boot over the end*

cable is MICS or armoured, cut it off inside the house at a suitable mounting point for a junction box. Screw a steel knockout switch box directly to the inside wall or a joist at this point and remove a knockout on two opposite sides.

Prepare the outside cable by stripping off about 150mm of the outer PVC and armoured sheathing to expose the wires. The compression fittings which join the cable to the switch box are exactly the same as those for copper pipe and are fitted in the same way. Slip the capnut over the PVC sheathing and then fit and tighten the threaded gland. Insert the fitting into one of the holes in the box and secure it with a back nut. Fit a PVC grommet over the other hole in the box, slip the PVC sheathed cable through and connect the two cables using a three-way terminal block. Use a blanking plate to seal the box.

Repeat the connection procedure at the outbuilding end then run twin and earth cable of the correct cross-sectional area to a switched fused connection unit mounted on the wall near the door. From this point, run the cable neatly and directly to all the lights, switches and socket outlets in the building.

Outside lighting

Outside lighting takes many forms, ranging from floodlights mounted on the house walls, or concealed in the garden, to courtesy lights mounted at the end of the drive on the gate posts. A wide range of weatherproof lights is available, most of which operate on mains voltage. Some—based on motor car sealed-beam headlamp units—operate at a lower voltage and require a transformer.

Power supplies to outside lights are run

9 *Slip the compression fittings over the end of the exposed copper sheathing and slide them well down the cable out of the way*

10 *Now strip back about 70mm of the copper sheathing. As you do this the mineral insulation will crumble away to expose the cable cores*

11 *Screw the pot on to the exposed copper sheathing using a pair of pliers—making sure that it goes on absolutely straight*

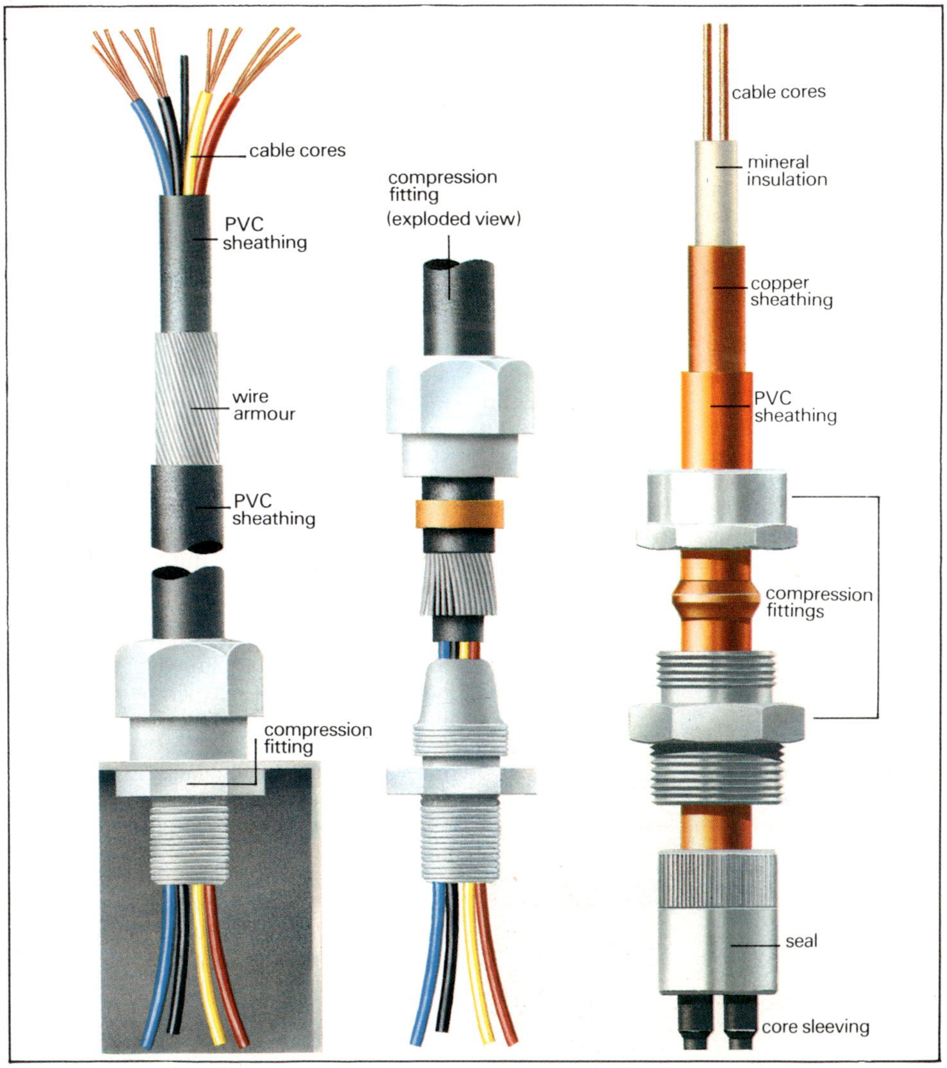

C. *The two main types of armoured cable: PVC sheathed wire-armoured cable (left and centre) shown with its compression fittings exploded and fitted to a switch box. Pyrotenax armoured cable (right) is shown with its slightly different compression fittings and watertight seals in place*

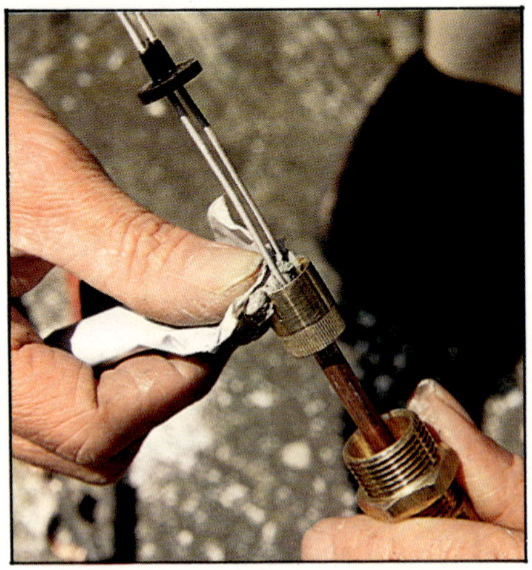

12 *Slip the watertight seal over the ends of the cores and then press sealing compound firmly into the pot to separate them*

13 *Press the seal down hard to compress the compound and then slip sleeving over the cores, leaving about 20mm exposed for connection*

14 *Mark one of the cores with a piece of red tape to identify it as the live wire and use a meter or test bulb to identify the other end*

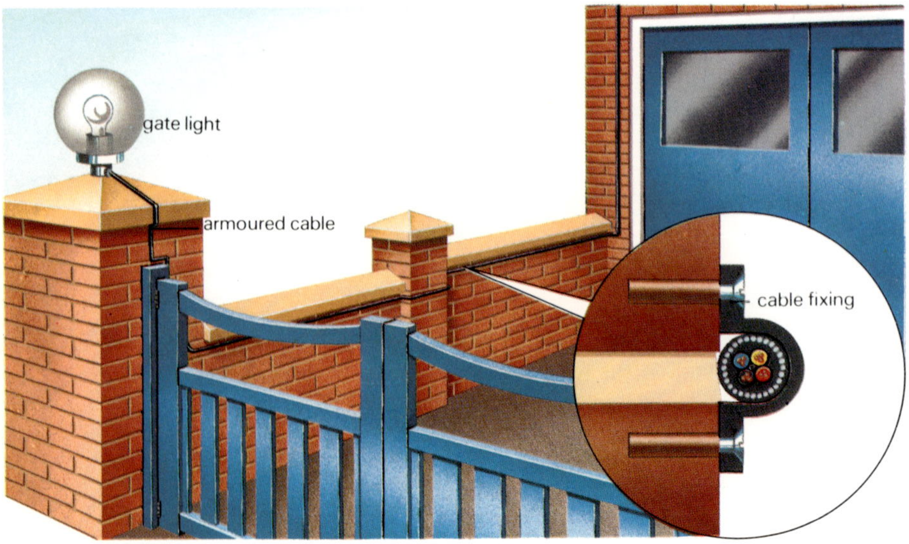

in exactly the same way—and using the same materials—as the supply to an outbuilding. The only exception is where a light is fixed directly to the outside wall of the house: here you can supply the unit through a hole drilled in the wall with the switch inside the house.

Gate lights can be supplied with either an underground or a wall-mounted cable, MICS and armoured cable being run directly to the light fitting itself. If you wish to install an outside switch as well, use a weatherproof lockable key switch to prevent tampering by vandals and children. These are fitted and connected in exactly the same way as their domestic counterparts indoors.

Transformers should ideally be located inside the house or an outbuilding but many are weatherproof and can be located discreetly in the garden. Make sure, however, that all the cable entry points are protected by weatherproof seals.

15 *Attach Pyrotenax to a switch or junction box by slipping the compression gland into a knockout hole and securing it with a back nut*

D. Above: *An outside gate light with a wall-mounted power supply. This kind of supply can be used for other types of light and also for garden sockets*

Fairy lights: There are a number of units ideal for fairy lights. These have two steel pins projecting from the lampholder which are protected by a weatherproof screw-on cover and are called Festoon lampholders (fig. E).

To connect the lampholders run a twin and earth $4mm^2$ seven-strand cable from a 13 amp socket in the house or the garden (see below) and lay it out on a lawn or similar flat surface. Unscrew the cover on the pins, press the cable on to them so that one pin pierces each core, and screw the cap firmly back in place.

Use a maximum of 10 lampholders per circuit with a bulb rating of 40 watts. The last lampholder on the circuit should conceal the cut end of the cable.

When you hang the lights—whether in a tree or from a support wire slung between two poles, trees or buildings—make sure that the cables are not under tension and that the bulbs cannot get blown against branches or walls; if this happens, the bulb may break and expose the filaments which could be dangerous in wet weather.

Once you have made up a set of fairy lights in this way, do not remove any of the lampholders or you will expose holes in the wire which, in wet weather, could cause a short circuit.

Garden socket outlets

Because so many garden tools are now electrically powered, a socket outlet in the garden can be very useful. And if your garden is quite small you may be able to fit the socket on the outside wall of the house or outbuilding.

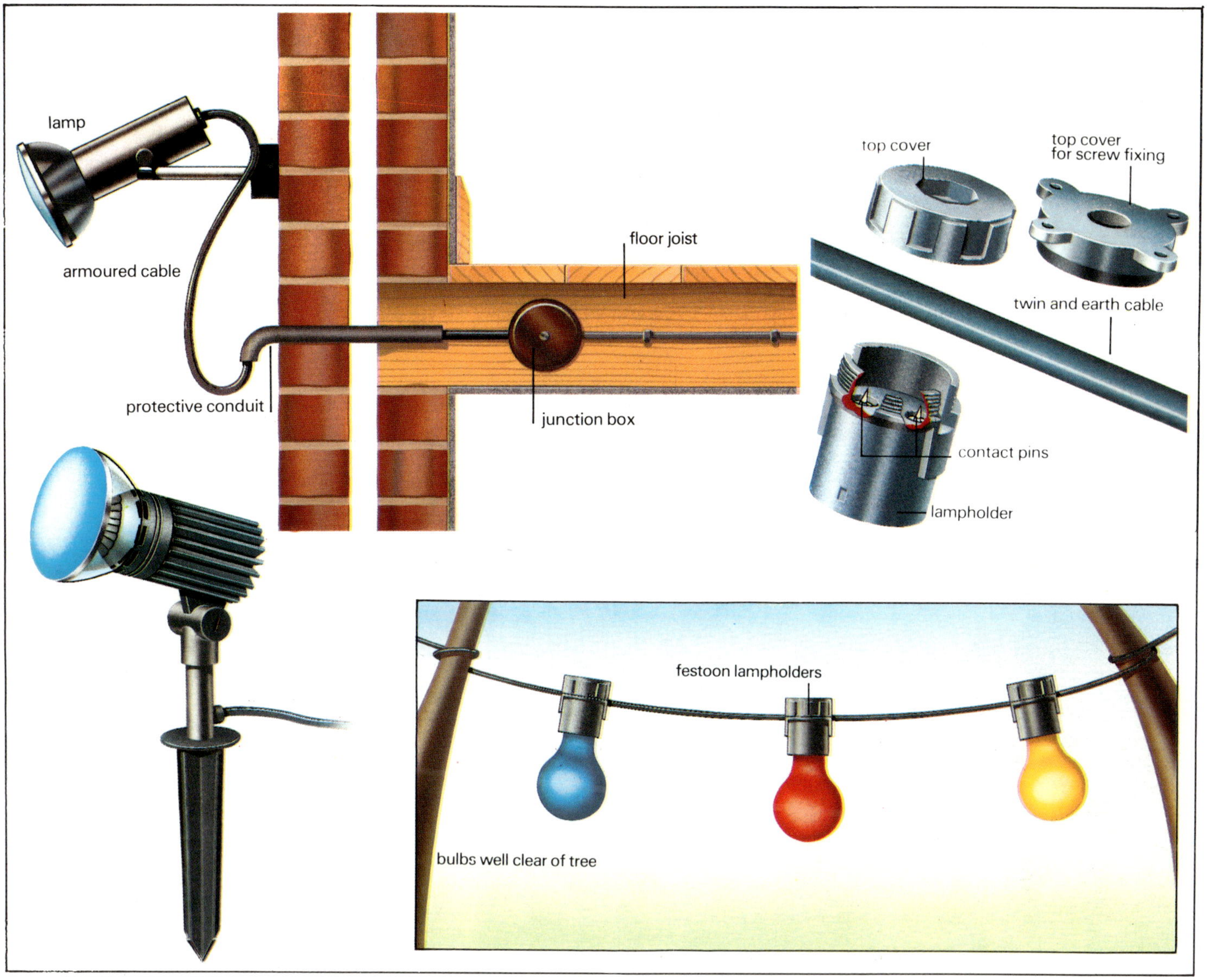

E. *Clockwise from top left: wall-mounted spotlight; festoon lampholder; fairy lights between trees; garden spotlight*

Buy either a heavy duty weatherproof unit or use a standard surface-mounted socket with a proprietary weatherproof plastic cover. Make sure, however, that the cable entry and the pin holes are protected with a weatherproof seal.

The supply for an outside socket can be taken from a ring main spur, which makes installation inside the house a little easier. If the unit is to be wall-mounted, run the cable inside the house to the socket position and drill a hole in the outside wall at the socket height. Remove one of the knockouts in the back of the mounting box, feed the cable through the wall and the box to the socket plate, and screw the box down so that it conceals the hole in the wall. Seal the joint between the box and the wall with mastic, connect up the socket and screw the plate to the box.

A socket in the garden itself should be screwed to a treated timber post securely sunk into the ground. The socket should be high enough off the ground to prevent inadvertent damage from lawn mowers and boots while you are working.

Supply the socket through an underground armoured or MICS cable that connects directly with the surface mounting box.

Extension leads: These are extremely useful for temporary outside work, but they must not be used as a permanent supply to an outbuilding or power tool, and they should not be used in wet weather in any circumstances.

Always disconnect the extension lead (at the mains end) when you are not using it, as a spade or rake could pierce the sheathing and cause a serious and possibly fatal shock.

Fountain pumps

There are several designs for these on the market–some are intended for total immersion in a garden pond and others for use alongside it. As the majority are 12 or 24 volt units you will need to use a transformer to supply them (see above).

Read any wiring instructions carefully–especially those concerning safety. There should be no way in which water can reach and short-circuit any of the electrical connections.

Cables from the transformer to the pump should be run underground in plastic conduit and then looped over the edge of the pool–for a submersible pump–where it can be hidden by rocks and pond plants. Pumps by the side of the pool can have the power supply coming from directly underneath them so that there is no exposed wiring at all. Plumb them in to the pond following the manufacturer's instructions.

Returfing

● Why returf? ● Types of turf ● Checking the state of your lawn ● Planning the job ● Lifting turf ● Storing turf ● How to buy turf ● Preparing the soil ● Levelling the soil ● Laying turf

A. Above: *Returfing your lawn is not difficult, but it requires careful planning*
B. Right: *A workplan showing how to lay out a lawn for returfing, and the area around a house extension which should only be returfed after it is complete*

Almost certainly, a major home improvements project such as building a house extension or demolishing an outhouse will involve you in some kind of gardening work. This may mean nothing more than digging up a couple of flower beds or a patch of lawn to make room for the extension. But equally you might wish to alter the layout of your garden—either by lifting whole areas of turf and laying them elsewhere, or by buying turf from a nursery and laying it on a recently-cleared part of the garden.

For this reason it is useful to know how to deal with turf: how to raise it; how to store it; how and when to lay it; and how to buy it. There is nothing particularly complicated about this, and doing the work yourself cuts costs considerably.

Turf

Turf is the name given to the layer of grass and roots that grows on your lawn. There are two basic types of grass; high-growing, which is the 'wilder' type; and low-growing, which is the more 'cultivated' type. High-growing grass has deeper roots that tend not to be very densely packed, whereas low-growing grasses have what is called a 'prostrate' growth: their shoots lie low on the ground and their roots form a tight, dense and fairly shallow mat. It is this mat that makes the raising and laying of turf possible because it binds the squares of grass (known as turves or sods) together when they are lifted. When you lift the turves, they come away very much like floppy floor tiles.

Most lawns are a mixture of the two types of grass, and are fairly easily handled. But lawns which have been allowed to run wild have a higher proportion of wilder grasses which, in time, make it almost impossible to raise good turves because the roots do not bind well and the turves fall apart.

To check the state of your lawn, try lifting a well-watered patch in an inconspicuous spot. Take a sharp long-bladed knife or a straight-edged spade and cut around a section about 300mm square. Then try to ease a flat, broad garden spade into the cut along one side of the square, about 30mm deep. Working the spade from side to side and keeping the depth fairly constant, try to lift the square in one complete piece. If the square falls apart because there is only a thin and weak root mat, you have a high proportion of wild grass and you must (if you are intending to buy extra turves from a local nursery) take the sod along with you when you order the turves so that it can be properly matched.

Planning

When raising or laying turf consider the seasons carefully: early autumn and spring are the best times of the year for all turfing operations and give you the best chance of achieving good subsequent growth. Do not lift turf immediately after a frost, or if frost is expected within the next few weeks. Extreme heat and drought are also bad for grass as they cause turves to contract and make accurate laying difficult.

When ordering new turves, allow your supplier at least ten days for delivery as turves have to be specially cut and should not be stored for longer than is absolutely necessary to lay them.

It helps to have a sketch plan of the entire working area. Obviously, if you are building a house extension some of the turf that you lift will never be replaced, but you may wish to extend turf into what was previously a path or flowerbed close to the house. Remember that any grass within about 2m of the building work is likely to be trampled or damaged by building materials so do not lay turf in these areas until the building

1 When lifting turf, divide the lawn into rectangles with pegs and string and subdivide these into squares or rectangles of the desired sod size

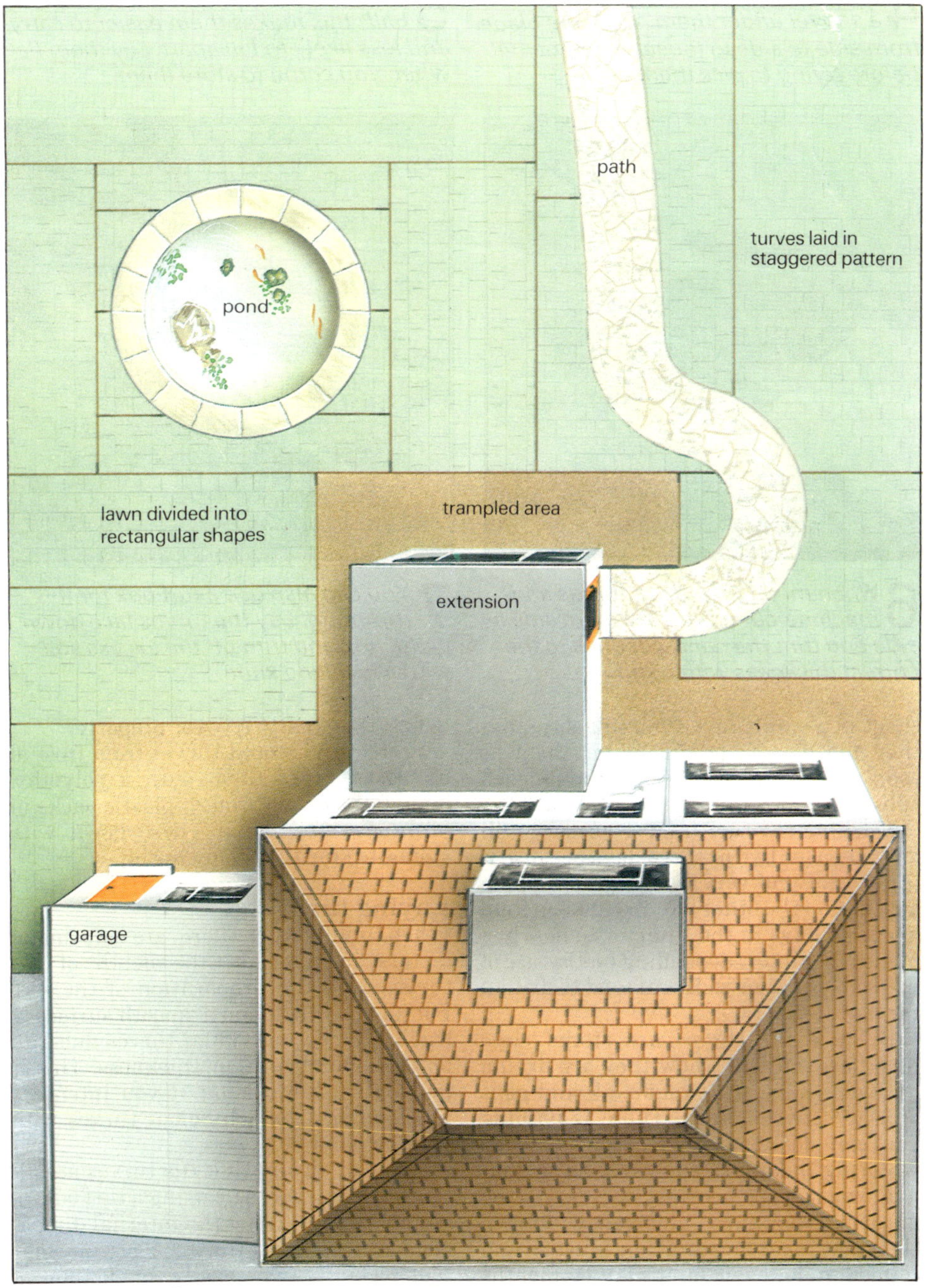

2 Mark out the lawn with pegs and string and make a cut 30mm deep along the opposite edges of six sods, using a spade or a half moon cutter

3 Now make similar cuts between each sod. If you are mixing these with machine-cut turves, cut them to match the turves you are buying

work is finished. Draw a plan of the entire area and mark the sections of turf to be removed or laid, setting aside an area where the turf can be stored for a day or two while the building work is completed.

When you actually come to raise or lay the turf, mark off the ground into large rectangular areas with pegs and string, making sure that the corners are square. If you intend only to raise and transplant the turf you can then subdivide the rectangles into 300mm strips thus ensuring that each sod is the same width and more or less interchangeable.

If you are planning to buy turves from a nursery, however, you must mark the ground out in rectangles compatible with the machine-cut turves that are supplied. These are usually 330mm × 1m, or 400mm × 2m but you should check the measurements with your supplier in advance. If you intend to mix machine-cut turves with sods you have dug yourself, cut your own sods into multiples of these dimensions.

Lifting turves

The essential considerations here are cutting equal-sized sods and trying to get their depth as shallow – and as even – as possible. If the lawn is bumpy, however, you may have to dig down quite deep so that no part of any sod is less than 15-20mm deep.

When you have marked out the ground, start lifting the turves along one side of the rectangle you have drawn. Use a spade to make a long cut about 30mm deep along the edge of the first strip you have marked out, then along the opposite edge, and finally between each turf. Lift the sods as described above, making sure that whatever mixture of grasses you have in your lawn, the sods are thick enough to come away cleanly but light enough to be manageable.

You can make the cutting slightly easier by making a square of sod size out of 12mm plywood. Lay this over the sod you are cutting and stand on it; the edges of the sod will be compressed, making the cuts cleaner, and guaranteeing that each sod is exactly the same size.

When you have raised all the turves in the marked out rectangular area, start raising the turves in the irregular areas abounding it. Where possible, cut them to the same size and shape as the others.

Storing turf

You will certainly have to store the turves after they have been raised or delivered, pending actual laying. If they have to be stored for more than a day or so, find a shaded spot and cover it with polyethylene sheet or a layer of overlapping plastic binliners or fertilizer bags. Lay the sods grass side up on the sheet in a single layer, making sure that they touch each other. Water them as soon as they are in storage, and on each subsequent day so that they stay moist.

Machine-cut turf from a nursery will only keep for two or three days because it is generally cut very thin. Heavier, hand-cut turf, on the other hand, will keep from about 10 days in the summer to nearly a month in winter, depending on the size of the sod—smaller sods will tend to dry out far more quickly.

Because the turves are stored close together, you will know they are drying out when they start to shrink and gaps appear between them. There is nothing you can do about this except to keep watering them and allow for the shrinkage when you lay the turves in the garden. If they start going yellowy-brown then they are dying and they must be laid immediately; even so, it may be months before they really recover properly.

Protect the stored turves from frost at all costs: cover them with a polyethylene sheet or with more plastic sacks or binliners, and weigh these down with stones to stop them blowing off.

Laying turf

When laying turf there are two major factors to consider: the depth of the turves; and the preparation of the soil. For a good finish and a smooth surface to the lawn, the individual turves must all be the same depth, or thickness. This is particularly important if you intend to mix bought-in machine-cut turves with your own hand-cut ones.

You can ensure that the turves are all the same thickness by using a turf box – a simple timber frame the internal dimensions of which are the same size as your sods. The box is easily made out of

4 Lift the turves by easing the blade of a shovel under them. Work the blade from side to side to loosen the root mat before trying to pick them up

5 As you dig them, fold the turves in half: this makes them easier to carry and less likely to fall apart. Lay them flat when you come to store them

6 When mixing hand-cut turves and machine-cut turves, lay them side by side and trim the hand-cut ones to the correct thickness with a knife

7 You can also use a turf box for this trimming. Lay the turves face down in the box and trim off the excess soil with a levelling knife

8 *Before laying turves, prepare the soil carefully. Rake it over and try to remove any stones and large lumps before levelling it off*

9 *Run the straight edge of a timber batten or plank across the soil in both directions, filling any hollows and levelling any bumps as they appear*

10 *Lay the turf in rows, standing on a plank to protect turves laid already. Stagger the rows and cut off any excess with a spade or half moon*

11 *How the finished job should look. The turves are staggered, flat, and laid shoulder to shoulder so that they will knit together in a few weeks*

softwood screwed or nailed together and its timbers should be the same thickness as the thinnest turves (fig. 7). To use it, simply lay it on a flat piece of ground and lay a turf grass side down inside it. If the turf is too thick, simply cut it down to the correct thickness by scraping a long knife or the back of an old saw across it. But make sure that the turf is fairly moist when you do this or it may simply crumble and disintegrate.

Turf boxes have the additional advantage that they can be used to square off turves that have been cut slightly askew.

Soil preparation: Level the ground by digging it over to redistribute the earth. When the earth is well broken up and more or less flat, check it with the aid of an assistant: lay a long straight timber batten at one end of the area to be turved and, taking one end of it each, draw it slowly across the ground looking for hollows and high spots. Where you find any, fill them in or flatten them as necessary then repeat the operation going across the area at right-angles to the first pass.

Work the ground with the back of a rake to remove any stones and weeds that could spoil the effect of the lawn once it is laid, and while it is exposed to the elements make sure that it receives enough water—either from rain or from a garden sprinkler—to sustain growth when the turves are laid.

Immediately before laying the turves, water the ground again and sprinkle some proprietary grass fertilizer over the soil. Follow the manufacturer's recommendations on how much should be used on each square metre. This will give the turf the nourishment it needs during the first few vital days of growth while it knits together and takes root.

Laying the turves: Because the turves are (or should be) in neat, identical shapes like tiles, laying them is simplicity itself. Start by marking out a clean rectangular shape on the ground with string and pegs, but do not bother subdividing it into small squares.

Lay the first turf in one corner of the rectangle and tamp it down by laying a sheet of plywood over it and stepping on it gently. The turf should stand about 5mm proud of any surrounding grass, and will bed in over the next few weeks. If the turf does not stand proud then you must lift it again and raise the level of the marked area slightly with some light sandy soil that has been levelled and gently tamped down. Err on the side of generosity when doing this; you can always roll the lawn flat later.

Lay turves along one side of the rectangle, pulling each one with a garden fork until it closely borders its neighbour before laying the next. When the first row is complete, lay a plank on the grass so that you can stand on it and lay the second row without damaging the first. Lay the second row in exactly the same way as the first, but stagger the joints as if you were laying a second course of bricks. When you get to the ends of the row where the turves overlap the marked area, cut them to size with a flat spade and use the left-over pieces in a later row or to fill in irregular shapes.

Where the shape of the lawn is irregular, first fill in the marked-out rectangles, then start laying the odd-shaped pieces around it. Where possible lay the smallest pieces near the centre of the area and the largest on the outside so that the smaller ones do not lose too much moisture. Again, trim any pieces that overlap the edges—or each other—with a flat spade.

To allow for settlement the entire surface should stand proud of any surrounding grass even though the plank supporting your weight has compressed it. Also, you should ensure that the level of the turves are well above any paths, so that a lawn mower can be used right up to the edge of the grassed area.

You can now sprinkle the lawn with a very thin top dressing of light sandy soil. If there are any gaps, fill them with a mixture of lawn seed and soil.

Keep the lawn well-watered at this stage to encourage growth and do not use weedkiller until the new turf is well-established. Over the next few weeks, the root mat will take hold and spread and the individual sods will knit together because of the staggered pattern. The grass will spread into the joints and the proudness of the new turf will eventually disappear—especially if you encourage it with a little light rolling.

Garden drainage

● The basics of garden drainage ● Drainage in a small garden ● Planters ● Retaining walls ● Constructing a field drain ● Disposing of the surplus water ● How to build a soakaway ● Discharge downpipes ● Driveways and paths

A. Below: *Where garden drainage is inhibited by a topsoil with a high proportion of clay, and where a planned structure or patio is in danger of flooding, the construction of an underground soakaway is an ideal solution and very simple to build*

Good drainage is essential for successful gardening. Poorly drained soils are sour and acid, requiring frequent applications of lime. And a wet soil is also a cold soil, retarding the growth of shrubs and plants. In extreme cases, the heave and shrinkage of clay sub-soils as they absorb and lose water can cause cracking in the fabric of the house. Less damaging, but still annoying, poor drainage causes doors and windows to jam at certain times of the year as the weather varies.

In temperate climates where the rainfall is moderate (about 500mm to 750mm per annum) and well spread thoughout the year many drainage problems can be solved by gardening, rather than constructional, methods. Raising the level of flower beds above the adjacent lawn or paving and adding peat, sand or compost to 'sticky' soils is often sufficient.

If pools of water form on an old lawn, it may merely be that the soil has compacted from years of traffic. This can be cured very easily by lifting the lawn, double-digging the soil underneath (adding new soil if necessary) and then re-sowing or returfing.

But in areas where the topsoil contains a high proportion of clay, or where the rainfall is exceptionally heavy, more drastic measures are needed. In all cases you should aim to have the water table (the level of water permanently in the ground) at least as low as the bottom of your house foundations—unless, that is, you have a below-ground basement, when you will have to settle for something less.

To establish the depth of the water table, simply dig a narrow hole the same depth as the foundations (about 1m in the UK) then cover it over and leave it for two or three non-rainy days. If it starts to fill with water, your water table is too high.

Drainage basics

There are three basic methods of laying garden drains, whether they are to be below ground or behind a retaining wall.

The cheapest, but the one with the shortest life, is to dig a trench about 600mm deep by one spade's width, and half fill it with bundles of brushwood.

The next best method is to fill a similar trench with about 225mm of rubble. Use bits of bricks, broken concrete or large stones, but do not use old gypsum plaster which will only disintegrate and clog the bottom of the trench. If you have no rubble left over from other jobs, the cheapest source is a demolition site.

The best method is to fill a trench with a 50mm layer of coarse gravel, then lay a row of 75mm or 100mm diameter pipes surrounded by—and covered to a depth of about 100mm with—rubble. Pipes come in a wide range of materials and can be either perforated or unperforated. Perforated pipes are available in plastic, concrete and pitch fibre, the latter being especially easy to use because they are light in weight and fit together with snap connectors. If you use perforated pipes, lay them with the perforations towards the bottom of the trench so that the water seeping into them takes a minimum of sediment with it.

Unperforated pipes come in plastic, concrete, and the traditional and inexpensive clay (field pipes). If you use unperforated pipes, leave a space of about 10mm between each pair, with a 'roof' over the gap made from broken roof-ridge tiles, pieces of slate or heavy polyethylene sheets of the type used by builders.

Whichever type of drain you choose, four things are important:

- The slope must be consistent. If part of

1 *When calculating the size of the hole remember that it is difficult to dig a very small hole. Use a fork to shift a sticky soil such as clay*

2 *To create straight, square sides you must dig them with a spade; to help the soil slip off, dip the spade in water before you dig each clod*

3 *Once the hole is completed and the soil has been well tamped down, mix up a stiff batch of cement and 18mm all-in ballast and lay it thinly on the base*

4 *Next, mix up a sharp sand and cement mortar with a little plasticizer added to stop the mortar drying too rapidly and cracking as a result*

5 *Start laying the bricks so that there is a small gap between each one. For speed, leave the centre of the base bare then complete it after the walls*

6 *Continue to build the walls of the soakaway in a honeycomb pattern until you reach the height of the hole, then allow the mortar to set*

the drain is steeper than the rest, sediment will lodge where the drain 'flattens out' or stops altogether.

- Only a gentle slope – anything from 1:60 to 1:100 – is needed. If you lay a steep slope, the water will rush along it leaving a rim of sediment to cause problems later. Where a sharp fall is unavoidable – for example to enter a stream or sewer – lay the bulk of your pipes in a gentle slope and finish with a vertical drop so that silt cannot accumulate.
- Always start laying at the lowest point and work your way uphill. This is the only way of getting a consistent fall.
- Above the brushwood or rubble you must place a layer of finer material to filter out the soil which otherwise would clog the drainage system. Use 150mm or so of cinders, coarse sand or very fine gravel. Then you can fill the rest of the trench with topsoil.

Planters and retaining walls

The most effective method of draining a small garden is to divide it into naturally self-draining areas. On a sloping plot you could make a series of terraces between 1m and 1.5m high, depending on the slope. On flat ground you might divide the area into planter boxes with paving or lawn strips between. Either way you improve the appearance of the garden, as well as its drainage.

Retaining walls at the feet of terraces (fig. C) need to be strong because a large weight of soil is bearing against them. Dig the foundation trench 450mm wide × 300mm deep. Use pegs driven into the ground and a spirit level on a long straight-edged board to ensure that the top of the foundation will be level; otherwise the masonry will slope and look odd. If the ground slopes across the width of the wall, you may have to step the foundation to keep it below ground level.

In the bottom of the trench pour a concrete foundation 150mm thick by the full width of the trench. Use a mix of one part cement to four of 18mm all-in ballast

B. *The best way to drain a large area is to instal a field drain. The most efficient shape is a herringbone, and for very large areas this can be repeated. The cheapest drains are of brushwood, next best is rubble, and the best are of perforated or unperforated pipes*

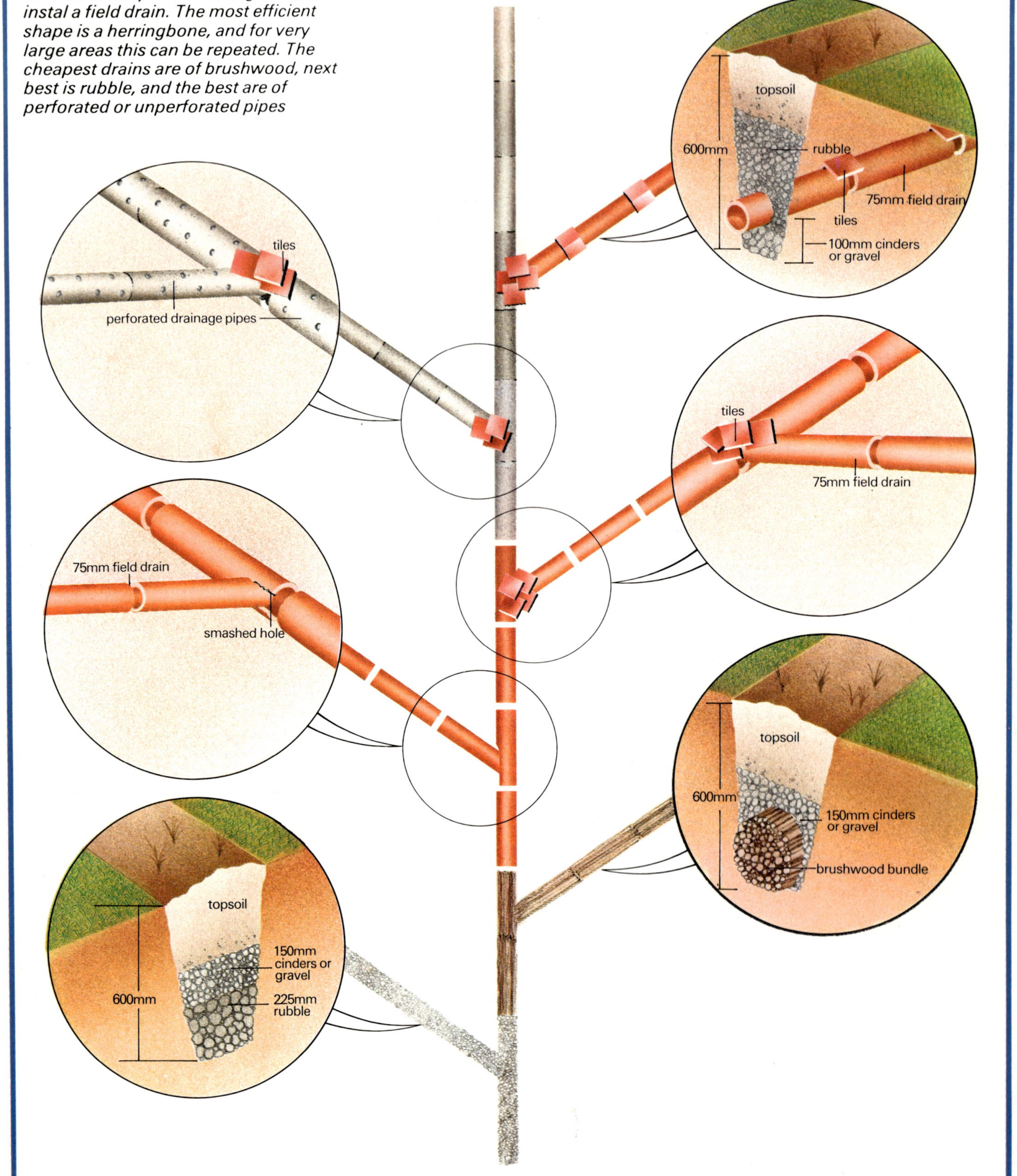

(shingle). Up to about 1m high, the masonry can be vertical. Above that, it should slope backwards by about 15°, and the foundation should be sloped to suit (see below).

Lay the first two courses of brickwork – or an equivalent depth in other materials – below ground level so that the concrete foundation will not show should the surrounding earth settle or subside. Brickwork should be laid in English bond (see page 136) for maximum strength, and in a long wall should be further reinforced by 330mm (one and a half brick) piers at 2.5m intervals, the piers being bonded into the wall.

As you go along, provide weep holes every 2m or so – one row just above ground level and a second row about four brick courses higher. To do this, you reduce the wall thickness to half a brick at the point concerned, leave the mortar out of a vertical joint, and fill the area behind with rubble.

Remember also to leave an outlet hole for the drain which will run behind the wall. This can be laid by any of the methods described above.

Pre-cast concrete blocks are also suitable for retaining walls, and are somewhat cheaper than bricks. Buy the sort that is made from cement and dense aggregate, not the lightweight blocks used for interior work. A handy type for retaining walls is the 450mm × 225mm × 225mm hollow block.

In a long wall, or one retaining a large garden, blocks need reinforcing at intervals corresponding with the piers used in brickwork. So every 2.5m or so, drop two 12mm steel reinforcing rods down the holes in the middle of the blocks and fill the holes with concrete, well tamped down. Concrete coping slabs along the top of the wall will hide this reinforcement and keep water away from the steel, as well as giving a neat finish.

Planters can be of brick, stone, pre-cast concrete blocks, plain or coloured dry walling stones or even heavy timber – for example old railway sleepers, which are sometimes available cheaply.

Planters of up to five brick courses high can be of loose-laid materials, although the joints will require constant weeding and maintenance. Up to about ten brick courses, single-skin (half-brick thick) brickwork or blockwork is strong enough, provided that you lay them in stretcher bond pattern. Above that height, double-skin (one whole brick thick) masonry is the bare minimum needed.

Single-skin planters are easily drained by providing weep holes in the bottom course of bricks. Over 1.5m or so, you simply omit the mortar between adjoining bricks. Fill the bottom of the planter with rubble to about 100mm deep, then use a finer material as described above before filling with topsoil.

Weep holes alone will also serve to drain double-skinned planters up to about 3m square. Above that, planters should be drained in the same way as retaining walls (see above).

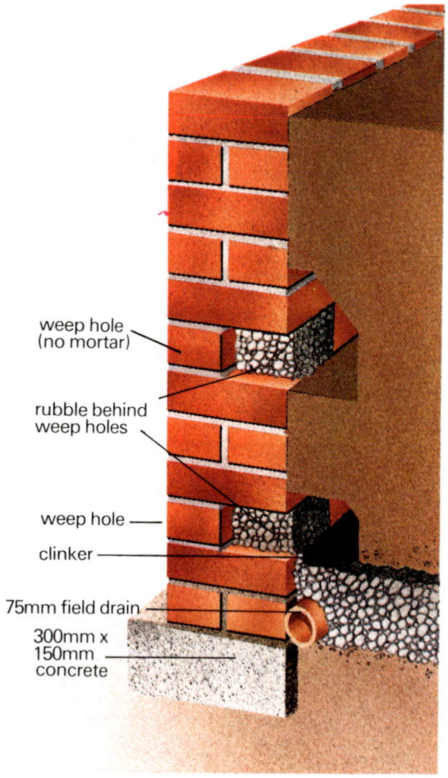

C. Above: *Small gardens can be divided into self-draining terraces. The retaining walls need to be between 1m and 1.5m high, with weep holes every 2m or so*

Field drains

In large flat gardens converting the garden into a series of terraces or planters is a back-breaking job, involving moving tons of soil. Unless you have cheap secondhand bricks it is also extremely expensive.

A simpler method is to instal a field drain system under the whole garden as shown in fig. B. It should if possible slope away from the house, and the subsidiary drains should meet the central one at an angle of about 45°.

There are several ways of laying out such a system. In slightly uneven sloping

7 *To insert a drainage pipe into the soakaway, remove a brick from the wall then position the pipe and finish the wall with half bricks as necessary*

8 *To support the concrete roof of the soakaway, start by cutting some corrugated sheet steel to size then lay it over the tops of the bricks*

9 *Next construct a timber formwork around the top of the soakaway, relying on bricks and battens rather than nails to hold the structure*

ground the subsidiary drains can follow the natural 'dips' in the ground. In flat ground a herringbone pattern, as shown, is effective. In really heavy soil, or a huge garden, two herringbones can be laid side by side with their central drains turned to meet each other near the outfall.

To establish a consistent fall in your drains, equip yourself with a long and reasonably straight batten. Give this its own 'fall' by fixing a small wooden block to the underside at one end only. A batten 3m long with a 38mm block, for example, will give a fall of 1:80.

With the gravel bed spread in the bottom of the trench, lay the lowest pipe first. Then lay a second pipe one batten's length away. With the block on the first pipe and the other end of the batten on the second, the batten should be level. Check this with a spirit level.

Once you are satisfied that the two pipes are correctly placed you can use a builder's line stretched taut over them to align the pipes in between. Afterwards transfer the block end of the batten to pipe number two and work uphill over the next section.

With the central drain laid you can start on the branches. If these are to be narrower – for example, 75mm instead of 100mm – the first branch pipe will have to be aligned by eye, but after that you can proceed as before.

Outlets

The simplest method of disposing of the surplus water is to run the drain into a nearby ditch or stream. If the outfall pipe is much higher than the stream, you can prevent scouring by pouring a short concrete channel, starting below the outfall pipe and sloping down to the stream, for the water to splash on.

Another method is to dig a soakaway, as described below.

A third method is to connect the outfall pipe to the domestic sewage or rainfall/sewage system, which in the UK is about 1m below ground level. This method should be used, however, only if your garden is tiny. The average domestic

10 *Mix a large quantity of cement and 18mm all-in ballast with a little plasticizer and shovel it carefully into the formwork until it is full*

11 *When you have half filled the formwork, place a suitably sized piece of steel reinforcing grid on top of the concrete mix*

12 *Next, continue to fill up the formwork with the concrete and use a shovel to dig out all the pockets of air which would weaken the roof*

13 *Using a sufficiently long piece of timber, spread and tamp the concrete until the surface is level and fill up any gaps before the mix goes off*

14 *After 24 hours the concrete should have set hard enough for you to be able to remove the formwork. Jar it free and carefully remove the timber*

15 *Before you bury the soakaway, place stones around the edge in the gap between the walls and the bricks to stop the gap becoming filled with earth*

sewer line is only about 100mm diameter, and the volume of water coming from even a medium-sized garden in a heavy downpour could make the system back up and overflow, with messy and unhygienic results. Check with your local authority before using this method; in the UK you will need permission, and it is illegal in many other countries.

Soakaways

Failing a simpler method you can dispose of the surplus water by running it into a soakaway from which it will permeate the surrounding ground.

Soakaways work well in soils containing a high proportion of gravel, sand, chalk, limestone and some types of crumbling clay, but less well in tightly-packed, small-grained clays, rock and similar ground. If your land has a clay subsoil or a hard 'pan' of rock half a metre down, try breaking through it – you may find a more permeable material below. In all cases you should site a soakaway as far from the house as is practically and economically possible.

Calculating the correct size for a soakaway depends not only on the soil conditions but also on the rainfall likely in your area and over how many days it is spread. A heavy downpour will run quickly across the surface, for example, while slow persistent rain will soak in and make the soil sodden.

As a very rough guide, allow for 15mm of rain over the whole catchment area served by the soakaway. If the catchment area is 20m × 10m, the volume of water will be 20 × 10 × .015, or 3m³. This means the soakaway could be 1.3m square by 1.8m deep. This calculation, however, is for a temperate climate with 500-750mm of rain spread over 115 days; in areas of heavier rainfall, the size could well be increased by half a metre all round.

The simplest soakaway is a pit filled with pieces of rubble into which your drain is run. Dig the hole at least 300mm deeper than is needed for the rubble. Tamp the rubble down well, pour a few centimetres of concrete across it, and fill the hole with at least 250mm of topsoil – enough for grass or plants to grow.

For a more capacious soakaway dig the hole and line it with bricks, laid in a honeycomb pattern as shown in fig. 6 so the water can seep out between them. With the drain led in through one side, mortar a continuous row of bricks around the top edge of the soakaway. Then cover it with old corrugated iron or asbestos-cement sheets, supported on a couple of boards. Pour a concrete slab at least 150mm thick over the sheets and, when it is dry, replace the topsoil (fig. D). Returf or sow grass seeds to disguise the slab.

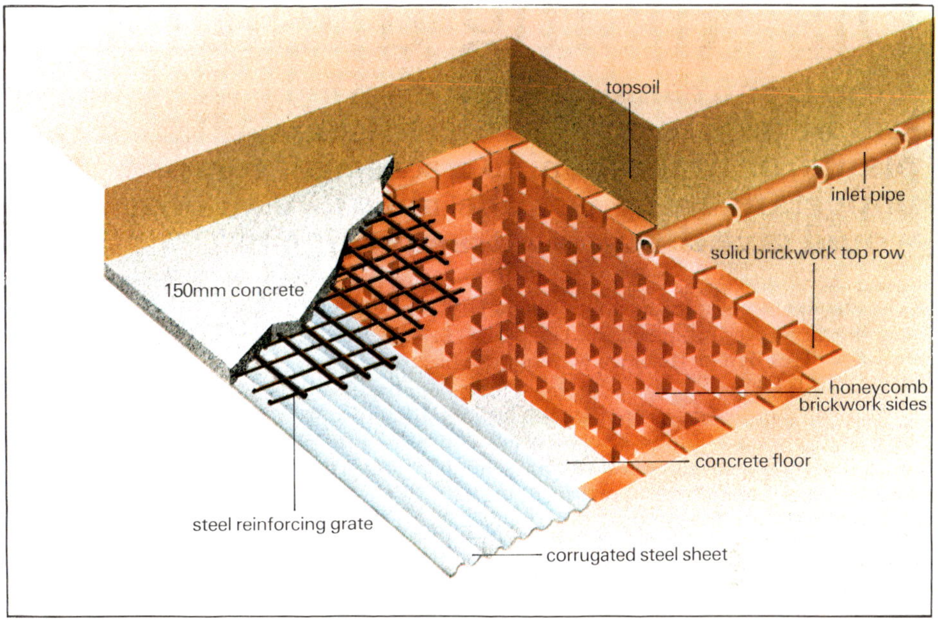

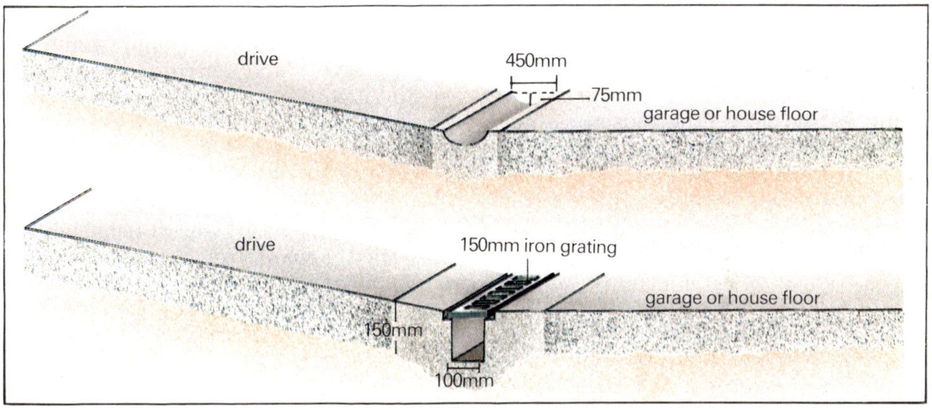

D. Top: *A soakaway provides a simple way of disposing of surplus water*
Above: *Where a large drive slopes towards the house, instal a drain*

Discharge downpipes

In some countries, though rarely in the UK, the downpipes from roof drainage systems do not run into an underground system but instead discharge on to the ground beside the house. In this case a small concrete splash block will help divert the water away from the house, and prevent splashing water from spraying the side of the house.

Driveways and paths

In the UK, driveway drainage is not usually a problem. But if you have a large driveway or other concrete area sloping towards the house, it will pay to do what is done in countries with heavier rainfall: cast a small drain across the drive at its lowest point to divert the water sideways and away from the house.

At its simplest the drain could be merely a shallow depression about 75mm deep × 450mm wide which can be driven across to enter the garage. At its most elaborate it can be a 150mm × 100mm square sided channel with a row of iron gratings inset across the top.

Small paths running beside the house should be sloped sideways to carry water away from the house. To do this you tape a 12mm offcut of wood under one end of your spirit level as you place the shuttering for the concrete, thus making one row of boards a consistent 12mm lower than the other, automatically.

Alternatively, you can slope a path (or drive) towards the gulley into which the roof drainage empties. The concrete guard around this gulley is often a one-piece concrete casting, mortared in place. It can usually be chipped free with a cold chisel, allowing you to make a small outlet underneath it for any surplus surface water.

When laying any drive or path, make sure also that your concrete does not bridge the damp-proof course in the house wall – in masonry houses it is usually about 150mm above ground level.

Disguising unsightly walls

Even if you cannot demolish an ugly wall, you may still be able to give it a facelift, camouflage it with plants, or hide it behind a screen of some sort. The important thing is to be able to visualize which would give the most attractive finish

Even the best kept garden can be spoiled by an obtrusive, unattractive slab of masonry. This can be the back wall of the house itself, boundary walls at the sides or bottom of the garden, an undistinguished outbuilding, a coal bunker or even a left-over air-raid shelter. Demolition may be the long overdue answer to any building or walls that are redundant. But more often the eyesore serves a purpose and has to remain. The options are to improve the wall itself, cover it with greenery or build a screen to block it from view.

Cosmetics for house walls

The first thing you must do is to appraise the problem carefully. If your trouble-some wall is part of the house, a cosmetic job is likely to be your only option.

If the wall is of brick or stone, consider cleaning it by hosing or sand-blasting. Done professionally, it is very quick and not necessarily expensive, but a do-it-yourself job can be long and tedious. This is also the time to attend to any minor repairs to frost-damaged bricks, and to repoint where the mortar is cracked or crumbling. The end result can be extremely attractive, with the wall looking as it was the day it was built. The only problem with this method is that you may feel tempted to have the rest of your property brought up to the same standard.

A less drastic solution is to consider painting the wall surfaces, using exterior wall paint. Preparation should be thorough – including brushing down and repointing – and you should choose your paint colour carefully to blend in with the house style and surroundings. You should also remember that once painted the wall cannot be restored to its original condition except with great difficulty and it will also need regular decoration.

An alternative to painting is rendering. In this case the finish can be trowelled smooth and marked out to resemble ashlar stonework, textured in a variety of ways or given a pebbledash or Tyrolean finish. If you have render treated in this way it need not be decorated for some years unless you live in an area of particularly severe industrial air pollution. These surface treatments are also an effective way of protecting walls with a degenerating surface or which are in need of extensive repointing.

More expensive cover-ups such as tile hanging, timber cladding or random 'crazy paving', or man-made stonework tiles are also suitable for masonry walls in bad condition. Tile hanging, usually confined to upper elevations, can be an attractive finish on most houses. Timber cladding, whether on part or all of the wall, suits only some styles.

If you choose timber cladding, ensure that the wood is treated with preservative before it is fixed in place and decorate it with preservative stains rather than paint if you want to avoid having to redecorate. If you prefer the look of brilliant white cladding, choose glass fibre types or PVC extrusions instead –

Right: *A total disguise – ivy drapes around the entire structure of the house*
Below left: *Garden walls disappear amidst a disguise of greenery and flowers*
Below: *Wisteria forms an unusual 'porch' and creates a pretty view while at the same time camouflaging a plain wall*

although expensive initially, they are then virtually maintenance free.

All these treatments can also be applied to home extensions housing kitchens, larders, bathrooms and WCs. While giving your wall its facelift, consider repainting or even replacing windows, doors, bargeboards, soffits, gutters and downpipes at the same time.

Outbuildings and garden walls

Single storey outbuildings, boundary and retaining walls pose fewer difficulties than house walls – at least in terms of scale. All can be given cosmetic treatments of the type outlined above especially buildings such as garages, sheds and coal bunkers.

Low retaining walls, whether of brick, blockwork or stone, often lose their looks because of staining or discoloration due to water percolating through the wall's structure. Although they should have been waterproofed on the inner face and perforated with drainage holes during construction, many retaining walls act as dams for all the moisture trapped in the soil behind them. Painting and rendering often fails for this reason so it is better to chip out new drainage openings in the existing wall and face the wall with a new skin of masonry. Use split stone, bricks or man-made block bonded to the old wall and incorporate new drainage openings.

Another solution to unsightly boundary walls and outbuildings is to hide them behind a wall of pierced screen blocks built just in front of the eyesore. Such walls can easily be built to a height of 2m with suitable reinforcement. They make a screen that is solid without being impenetrable and there is a wide range of block styles to choose from. You can also use materials such as larch-lap or woven timber lath fencing panels or ranch-style fencing to achieve a similar effect.

Right: *A simple façade takes on an air of distinction with a coat of paint*
Below: *Timber cladding adds a touch of character to the house and is also continued around the decorative porch*

Plant camouflage

Vegetation makes an excellent cover-up for unsightly walls and you can use a wide variety of plant life to conceal even the ugliest eyesore. Clothing a wall with vegetation encroaches very little on to the existing garden and provides an attractive backdrop for it. A boundary wall requires climbing plants but for a retaining wall you have the alternative of trailing plants too. However, it is important to think carefully about the effect you want to achieve before rushing off to your local garden centre.

Climbing plants come in all shapes, sizes and colours. The garden centre or nursery will be able to advise you on a choice to suit sandy, chalk or clay soils in sunny or shady positions. But you should first decide whether you want evergreen cover or a profusion of spring or summer blooms. The key to training the plants lies in covering the surface effectively. Creepers and cotoneasters can generally look after themselves once started in the right direction with a few strategically-placed plant ties. Other plants are best retained by a series of horizontal wires strung across the wall surface about 300mm apart so that they support the plants without interfering in any way with their growth.

You can also train plants up walls by letting them wrap their way round a wall-mounted trellis. The traditional garden trellis is a light framework of wooden laths nailed together to form a square or diamond lattice. This can cheer up the wall surface even before the plants have begun to grow up it. Plastic-coated mesh is another alternative. In either case, firm fixing is essential as established climbing plants are heavy and replacing a collapsed trellis interwoven with roses can be a very painful process.

You must make allowance for the plants to grow round and through the trelliswork by fixing it on spacer blocks which hold the lattice away from the wall surface. If the wall is painted you may want to make provision for future redecoration without damaging the plants. One way of doing this is to hinge the lower edge of the trellis to a wall batten, and to hold its upper edge in place with stout hooks and eyes. At painting time the top edge of the trellis can be unhooked and the trellis swung carefully away from the wall without causing unnecessary damage to the plants.

Tree screens

Sometimes climbing plants do not offer a solution because you cannot provide suitable planting for them at the foot of the wall, even using planting tubs: in this case a screen of vegetation planted in front of the wall is the answer. The unrivalled leader in fast screen formation is the family of quick-growing conifers and a row of saplings should grow into a very effective screen in about five years. The commonest mistake people make with conifers is to plant them too close together and then fail to trim them so that they stay within manageable proportions. So remember that when these trees are allowed to grow unchecked they take up valuable garden space, block out sunlight and prevent anything else from growing nearby.

Unless you specifically want a dense, high screen, it is better to select slower-growing species, or perhaps to concentrate on traditional hedging plants such as privet and lonicera which are easier to keep under control. Your local nursery is the best source of advice, whether you want a low flowering hedge to hide the coal bunker or a boundary screen to conceal the local highrise flats. Whatever you do, think ahead; you do not want to be tackling an eyesore of a different kind in five years because your screen of vegetation has taken over the garden.

Above: *Stone cladding in a mixture of natural colours provides an attractive finish for a modern style bungalow*

Chapter 2
PATHS AND PATIOS

Patios

A patio adds charm and character to both your home and your garden. And as well as being one of the most attractive exterior home improvement features it adds greatly to the value of your house.

A large expanse of lawn needs a great deal of care and attention to keep it looking tidy and attractive. All too often it is either too wet or too soft to take tables and chairs—just when you want to do some outdoor entertaining.

Giving over part of your garden to a patio is a practical and reasonably inexpensive answer to such problems. A lot of traditional gardening chores are cut out and you will find the hard, level surface of the patio much easier to maintain.

Siting the patio

Ideally a patio should be approachable from the living room or dining room and also have access to the kitchen or conservatory to avoid bringing muddy shoes into your living areas.

If you are planning a barbecue on the patio, easy access to the kitchen is even more important because you will need to transport food and equipment. It might even be worth installing a door which opens directly on to the patio if one does not already exist.

The aspect of the patio needs to be considered in relation to privacy, outlook and, of course, sunshine.

Below: *A planter full of soft green plants provides a stunning focal point in this covered patio. Planters of this size are almost gardens in their own right*

Below: *A novel idea for the modern patio. The large picture window divides the indoor/outdoor pond, creating continuity between the inside and the outside of the house*

Right: *Sunken patios let more light into basement rooms and create areas which can be used for outdoor dining or a play space for the children where you can keep an eye on them*

For example, if your house has a room jutting out which forms a sheltered L-shape and a natural corner, it might look like the ideal area in which to focus your activities. But if there is somewhere else which is sunnier for longer during the day, this would obviously be a more suitable spot for the patio.

So before you embark on constructing a new patio—or extending an existing one—observe the sunniest and least windy positions during the day. You may need to build a screen wall to give the area more privacy or even re-site a flower bed, but in the long term it is well worth the extra effort.

Size and shape

The size of your patio will depend to a large extent on the size of your garden, your family's needs and the activities you share. If you have a small town garden or suburban back-yard, you might consider paving it over completely.

The most important thing is to keep the patio in balance with the house and the rest of the garden. A large patio in a small garden looks totally out of proportion—it would probably be better if the whole garden were paved over.

Plan the shape of your patio on a piece of graph paper, as you would an interior room and start by choosing a focal point around which to build. Consider the outlook from your living room window—maybe there is a tree worth retaining, or a banked-up rockery to lead the eye down to the main garden area.

Whatever you choose as a feature will affect the overall shape of the patio, so aim at balance and simplicity in relation to the proportions of your house. It is so easy to start out with ideas which are too fussy and then to include too many features. You may fancy a barbecue, fountain, a free-standing sculpture and an apple tree but if there is only room for one of these, choose the feature which is best suited to the practical use of the patio.

And when making your scale drawing bear in mind the size of the slabs or bricks you are going to lay. By designing your patio in multiples of whatever materials are to be used you will save a lot of difficulty cutting later on.

Style and design

Family life usually dictates the form of a patio. Different age groups have different needs, all of which you must bear in mind at the planning stage.

Tiny tots need to be safely enclosed and should have a play area which is visible from the house—preferably in a sheltered corner. A rectangular cavity inset into the patio could initially hold a playpen and later be made into a sandpit. Later still you might even consider turning it into a paddling pool. This would be easy to include in the initial plan, and need be no more than about 1.5m square.

Older children might appreciate the addition of a swing or slide or even a simple climbing apparatus. But if you plan to let your children play ball-games or ride tricycles on the patio, ensure there are no flower borders nearby which could get damaged.

Older people look more for privacy and shelter on their patio; somewhere to eat out of doors or enjoy a coffee or glass of wine. Even on dull days, a well-sheltered patio with plenty of colourful foliage or points of interest, offers you pleasant surroundings for a bit of relaxation in the fresh air.

Remember though that toys, cycles, gardening tools and furniture all need to be stored somewhere, in easy reach for day-to-day use. Lift-up bunker-style units are a better choice than a garden shed and can be easily incorporated into the initial patio layout.

Convert that narrow passageway into an excellent storage area. Simply pave or tile the passageway in the same material as the patio, and cover it with a reinforced glass roof. Use the corridor as a workshop and potting shed as well as a store for outdoor equipment.

Choosing materials

When you come to choose a flooring material for the patio, try to find one which blends in with the exterior of the house. Precast concrete slabs—which have a non-slip, durable surface—are a popular material because they are comparatively cheap and easy to lay. Available in various sizes and thicknesses, they come in shapes which range from rectangular to hexagonal and circular. Coloured slabs are also available, though they can look rather garish; cream or stone grey looks more natural.

Bear in mind that concrete slabs look quite different when they are wet so it is a good idea, when buying them, to ask to see them wet as well as dry.

You can lay the slabs in a variety of ways to create different patterns and textures—such as square, using slabs all of the same size, for instance, or a random effect, using different-sized rectangles. A rectangular shape, with infils of another material, such as brick or granite setts, can also look very effective.

Jointing is important, as it contributes to the overall look of the finished paving. A butt-joint, with the slabs placed as closely together as possible and infilled with mortar, is less likely to allow weeds and water to penetrate. But if you want to give the paving stones a more defined look, infil with either liquid grouting or a dry mix of sand and cement.

Cutting precast paving stones into any kind of curve can be costly and is not always possible. If curved areas are called for, say around a tree or flower bed, you would be better to use granite setts or bricks.

A mixture of bricks and pre-cast paving slabs is very appealing, particularly in a small area. But as bricks are expensive, you will probably only want to use a few of them in your design. Make sure the bricks you choose are hard enough to withstand damp and frost, and have a textured surface to prevent slipping.

Bricks are not strong enough for a driveway, but are ideal for a rear patio-cum-courtyard and can be laid in various patterns.

Granite setts are a similar shape to bricks, and useful for defining large areas of paving. Like bricks, they can be set at an angle and in curves.

Cobble stones, egg-shaped in size, are ideal for decoration or for filling in awkward corners. But they are unpleasant to walk on so avoid laying them in a main thoroughfare. The stones are normally set close together in a dry bed of concrete or mortar over a prepared base, though you could also use them combined with water plants and loose-laid in a recess.

If the patio is designed to be an extension of your living area, try laying ceramic or quarry tiles. A wide range of floor tiles is now available and you could continue your choice through from indoors. However, although many ceramic floor tiles are frost-proof, it is not a good idea to lay them in an area which is entirely open to the elements.

Patio decor

A small patio needs a focus of attention. It may be a tree which you have carefully preserved in the centre, and encircled with a pattern of bricks or granite setts. Or you may choose to focus attention on a side or rear wall: a green-painted trelliswork decorated with roses or clematis looks really outstanding against a wall of white-painted bricks or concrete.

Larger patios-cum-terraces often need the addition of a screen wall either to give more privacy, act as a windbreak or simply to obscure an ugly view. Pierced screen walling is ideal for these purposes, though it needs to be used in moderation or it will become overbearing. Otherwise, there is a wide variety of wooden screen panels available from garden centres.

A pergola with trailing vines and greenery makes an excellent decorative feature which also provides partial shelter for dining outside. You can slant wooden struts of the pergola to follow the roofline of the house or square them up into a rectangle.

Much of the fun in planning a patio comes when you introduce elements of surprise. For example a stone sculpture of a small child or animal lit from behind at night; or a tree hung with fairy lights, as if for a constant party.

Consider using unusual objects for display—an old wooden wheelbarrow painted in bright colours to match the

Above: *Enclosing a patio with a pergola or series of climbing frames allows you to scatter hanging plants around and creates cool, shady spots on hot days. Painted white they bring a fresh, cool feel to your patio and provide an excellent lounging area*
Right: *This paved-brick patio has been livened up by a dramatic fence sculpture and massive climbing screens. Plants provide colourful decoration and help to disguise ugly pipes. Even the most boring patios will benefit from such imaginative treatments of fences and accessories*

flowers perhaps. Or maybe a circle of round beer barrels, cut down into different heights and painted green. You could plant a laurel tree at the highest level in the rear, softer plants in the middle sections and perhaps some herbs and lettuces nearest the ground level.

Use wooden tubs to hold bay trees or hanging baskets for ferns and ivies. Or use even more unusual containers like old chimney pots, disused hay racks, a shapely Victorian hip bath or an old-fashioned pram. Remember that the more ordinary the space, the more you can liven it up in this way.

Dining out of doors

If you plan to do a lot of outdoor cooking and entertaining, a barbecue is a must and can easily be incorporated into the patio layout.

Commercial barbecues range from the simplest of constructions to the highly elaborate canopied types or wheel-around trollies which come equipped like a portable kitchen. But you might prefer to build your own barbecue from brick—perhaps a simple H-shape inset with a rectangular metal grid for cooking. Remember to allow plenty of horizontal space for plates, foodstuff and cooking utensils to keep everything tidy and in one spot.

Furniture for a patio is available in all shapes and sizes and in materials ranging from cast-iron and aluminium to wood, PVC and canvas. You can also buy fully upholstered sun loungers, though these can be rather expensive.

When you are buying garden furniture remember that some types need to be taken indoors at night while others, like lightweight PVC, can be left out in all weathers.

Another point to bear in mind is whether the table and chairs are to be a permanent fixture or whether they need to be portable. For example, some cast-iron designs are highly decorative but also extremely heavy to move about.

The patio garden

If you want to give the patio more of a garden atmosphere—especially if you are paving over a small garden completely—try introducing new levels of interest by using vertical as well as horizontal space.

Building raised flower beds around the perimeter of the patio will give the area a new dimension, make weeding easier, and will make plants look more dramatic.

Make the planters look as unobtrusive as possible by using the same material as for the patio floor. Soften their sides with trailing greenery.

If you decide to construct raised flower beds, you can also include some built-in seating. Give one area of wall slightly less plant space and build against it a flat surface of paving stones or bricks, deep enough to sit upon in comfort. Pick a sheltered corner so that you can gravitate there when the sun gets too hot

Before choosing flowers and plants for the patio, take a look around a well-stocked garden centre and perhaps have a chat with a knowledgeable nurseryman for some ideas on suitable plants and flowers.

Confined spaces make the most of aromatic plants such as lavender while you can soften hard edges with trailing plants like members of the ivy family. Dramatic plants, such as the large-leafed philodendron, are ideal for disguising uninteresting corners.

A patio garden which uses only green and white foliage can be very arresting to the eye and has the advantage of being easy to maintain. Alternatively, you might prefer to have lots of flowers that can be cut for use inside the house.

Another good idea is to have a small vegetable garden on the patio. Tomatoes, courgettes (zucchini), cucumbers and lettuce all look attractive intermingled with each other as well as having obvious practical benefits.

Below: *A pull-back awning over the patio keeps the glare of the sun off the diners, who can be served conveniently from meals prepared on the built-in barbecue*

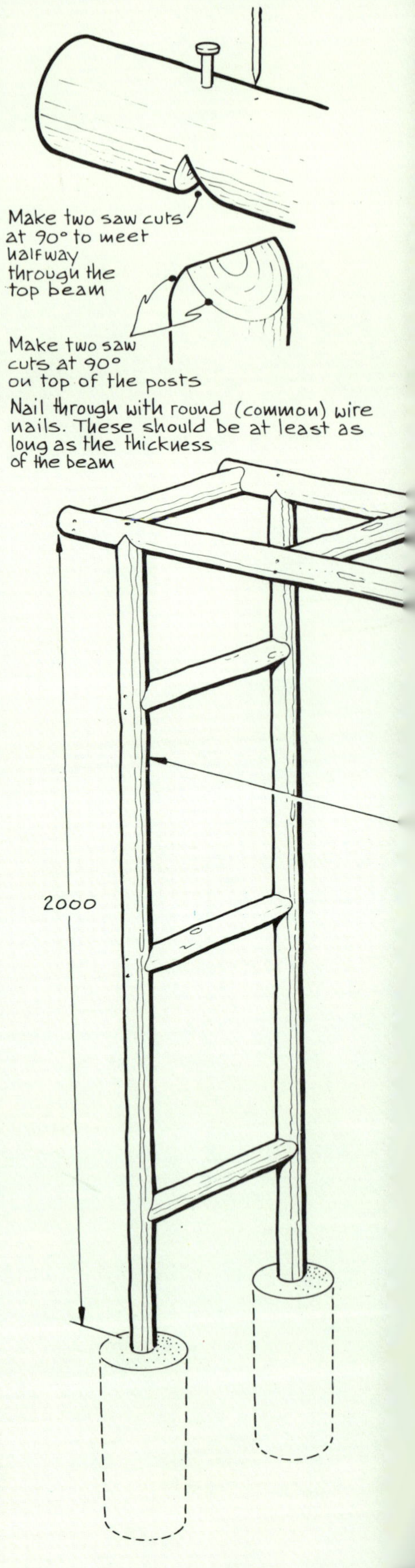

A rustic climbing frame

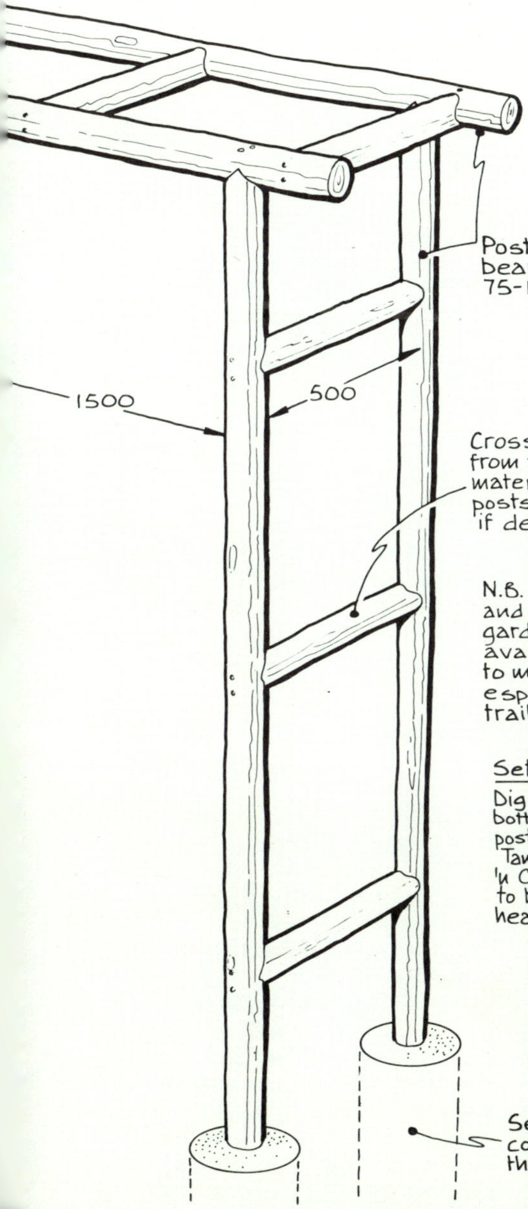

Make an interesting transition from your patio to the garden by building this rustic frame for climbing plants. Construction is very simple, and all you need is a few rustic poles which you can buy from garden centres. The arch itself is attractive from the moment you make it but when you have trained climbing plants to grow over it, like the roses in the picture, or perhaps use ivy or honeysuckle, you will have an even more charming view.

N.B. All dimensions are approximate, and can be varied to suit your garden or the poles you have available. It is inadvisable, however, to make the arch much lower, especially where plants may trail down from it.

Setting the posts

Dig a hole with a post hole borer. Fill the bottom with gravel or small stones. Set the post upright and pour concrete around it. Tamp down firmly.
In Canada, concrete (and posts) may need to be set below the frost line to prevent heaving

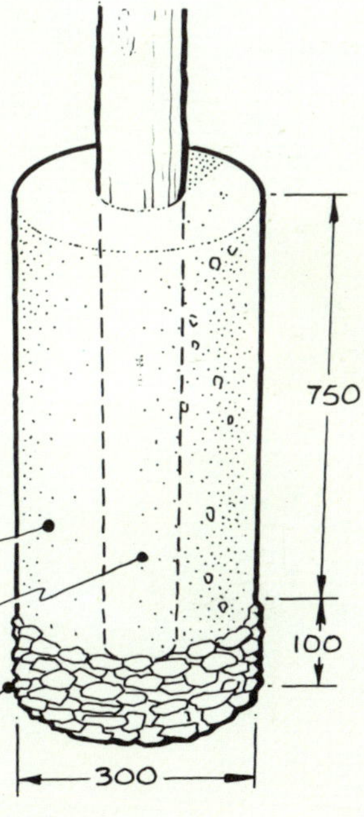

Decorative paving

Pathways are often left until last in the overall design of a garden. They end up as functional elements of the design rather than the decorative accents they could so easily become—with a little thought and planning

Your garden path need not be a simple strip of concrete. By using unusual materials which blend in naturally with the surroundings, you can create a pathway which is an attractive feature of the garden and is not purely a functional necessary.

Using bricks

Bricks are a natural alternative to concrete, being both easy to lay and very durable.

Available as special paving bricks (**see picture left**) or simply as regular building site material—such as the hard engineering bricks **above**—bricks come in so many colours and textures that they can blend in with any type of garden.

For instance, the patterned red paving bricks **left,** provide a subtle contrast to the predominantly green and woody shrubs and plants. Just imagine what a simple concrete path would have looked like. The natural texture and warmth of the red bricks adds significantly to the overall atmosphere of the garden. They are by no means

way of breaking up what might otherwise be a cold expanse of grey across the width of the patio.

The path across the lush grass lawn **below** could have been laid simply as a straight line with parallel sides; but how much better to stagger the pattern in semi-geometric steps, giving the effect of a winding pathway without elaborate curves.

Wooden paths

Usually, the first choice for paving material is some kind of stone, or other hard, rock-like covering. It is not generally realized that deep wooden beams can be just as effective. They are even simpler to lay than bricks—the best kind of wood to use being scrap or driftwood, which is cheap and easily obtainable.

As long as the wooden beams are thoroughly soaked in preservative before they are laid, a properly designed wooden pathway can take many years of wear.

But the ideal bedding material for a wooden walkway is a spread of gravel or small pebbles as in the picture, **top centre, overleaf.**

Well seasoned old wooden beams can be embedded in such material either by digging deep grooves in an existing sweep of stones or by laying the wood on the bare ground and then infilling with carefully graded pebbles to pack down the beams tightly against each other. Vary the lengths of each slat to get a ragged edge to the

a material for just another path!

Similarly the path **above left** has been laid with neutral coloured bricks to set off and enhance the bright flowers which line its length.

In this case bright red bricks would have been distracting. These bricks have been laid in mortar but most paving bricks can be laid simply on a bed of sand that has been well tamped down and compressed.

For the full techniques of laying **bricks and paving stones to make a** pathway see pages 78 to 82.

Paving stones

Unlike brick, paving stones are usually fairly neutral or pastel coloured and to make the most of their special appeal they should be laid in interesting patterns.

They are the ideal paving materials for small gardens and patios and if they are laid as in the picture **above** they can allow quite a bit of greenery to spill over into any confined space. Using grass as a filler between staggered slabs is a particularly effective

path and add that characteristically rustic, weathered look.

The pathway **below** has a bed of stones on one side, a lawn on the other and provides a natural link between two different areas of activity in the garden.

The beams have been laid lengthways to create a tidier effect than those in the picture **right** and a series of wooden steps links this section of the path to a conventional concrete type around the edge of the lawn.

Wooden paths age very differently from the brick or concrete varieties, developing a thin covering of moss and lichen. Although this can often add to their charm, such growths should be cleared from the actual trodden part of the path as they can be slippery in wet weather. Mossy borders, on the other hand, look delightful.

Pebbles, stones and mosaics

Beds of pebbles such as those in the pictures **left** and **above** are an easy way to cover large areas of ground where plants will not grow, because the ground is shady or otherwise unsuitable. Pebbles graded according to size and colour can be bought from specialist garden centres and sometimes from builders' suppliers. If you have the patience, a mosaic path made from finely graded pebbles can look very attractive, and almost Mediterranean in style (**above right**).

The small pebbles should be embedded in a screed of wet concrete and it is important to choose each stone carefully—setting it against its neighbours so that an even surface is produced overall.

A rough stone path such as that in the picture **right** is not as easy to lay

as it might at first appear. The stones are readily available from quarries and suppliers of rubble and hardcore, but you must choose each stone very carefully, looking for a flat surface which can be laid uppermost.

When they are laid, each slab must butt as closely as possible with the stones around it and the whole surface must be as level as possible. Properly laid, however, rough stone paths look very attractive and are particularly suited for gardens full of bushes and trees. They have an old-fashioned, country feel and lend an air of age and maturity to any garden, however small. Part of their charm is the weeds and plants that sprout up in the cracks but again, such growths are best cut back every so often or they will engulf the whole path and become a safety hazard in damp and wet weather.

Choosing your paving

If you are thinking of relaying one of your garden paths or even laying a completely new one, consider the varicus areas of the garden through which it will run.

There is no strict rule that says the nature of the path must be the same along its whole length. You can use one or more of the ideas discussed here to blend in the path with the surrounding aspects of the garden.

Lay a brick path

The attractive appearance of brickwork need not just be confined to house building and boundary walls—paths, drives, patios and steps all look great built in brick

The porous nature of some ordinary bricks—especially internal soft types—makes them unsuitable for paving work. Coming into direct contact with the ground, with no damp proof course to protect them, they quickly become saturated and start to crumble. For this reason you must use either engineering bricks or purpose-made paving bricks. Both are available in many different forms, all of which are extremely dense and hard—making them impervious to moisture and frost.

Paving bricks vary in size from 215 × 65mm × 33mm to 215mm × 215mm × 35mm and come in a variety of colours, allowing them to be laid in different combinations like quarry tiles. They are not as deep as ordinary bricks, and this saves time and effort when digging the trench for the path.

Best of all are the rough stock bricks which are burnt longer than other types, giving them a very red appearance and making them more resistant to bad weather conditions.

Alternatively, you might like to consider using old bricks bought from a demolition contractor: if they have withstood 50 years or more without crumbling (in the same sort of situation that they are to be used in now) they are bound to be resistant to frost and moisture—and they may be cheaper than new bricks.

Remove the old mortar on the bricks with any sharp-edged instrument or trowel. Clean a good number before you start work, so you do not have to stop half way through and risk the fresh mortar going hard. You can use the old mortar as hardcore for the foundations.

If you decide to use more expensive engineering bricks, bear in mind that you may need more of them because they may have frogs on both sides and must be laid on edge.

In Canada, use standard Type I bricks, as recommended by your dealer or brick merchant.

Brick patterns

Brick paths, drives and patios can be laid in a variety of patterns—basket-weave, herring bone, running or half bond, transverse bond (fig. B). Norfolk bond and Flemish bond look particularly good.

The running bond is easy and quick to lay, being exactly the same as the stretcher bond used for walls, and the bricks can go either across the path or lengthways. The transverse bond is thought to be stronger because it runs across the direction of traffic.

You can make the patterns even more attractive by varying the colours of the bricks. For example, in the Flemish bond, the headers and stretchers could be in an off-white brick with the half closers in red. Similarly, in the basket-weave bond, you could have one half red and the other in a very pale colour to give a chess board effect or a diagonal pattern. Use a simple run of bricks to form the borders, with either the stretcher faces or the header faces butting up the edges of the path.

For a more varied appearance you can lay a ragged brick edging (fig. B), though this uses more bricks than the simpler bonding methods. For wide areas—such as a patio or drive—it is a good idea to start by paving one or two longitudinal courses each side to act as a gutter and border. The same idea is useful for the Norfolk bond, where, to save cutting bricks, you make up the required path width with borders of longitudinal courses.

With transverse bonds, you should always start and end the alternate courses with a half brick—it is easier and saves on cutting bricks to awkward sizes.

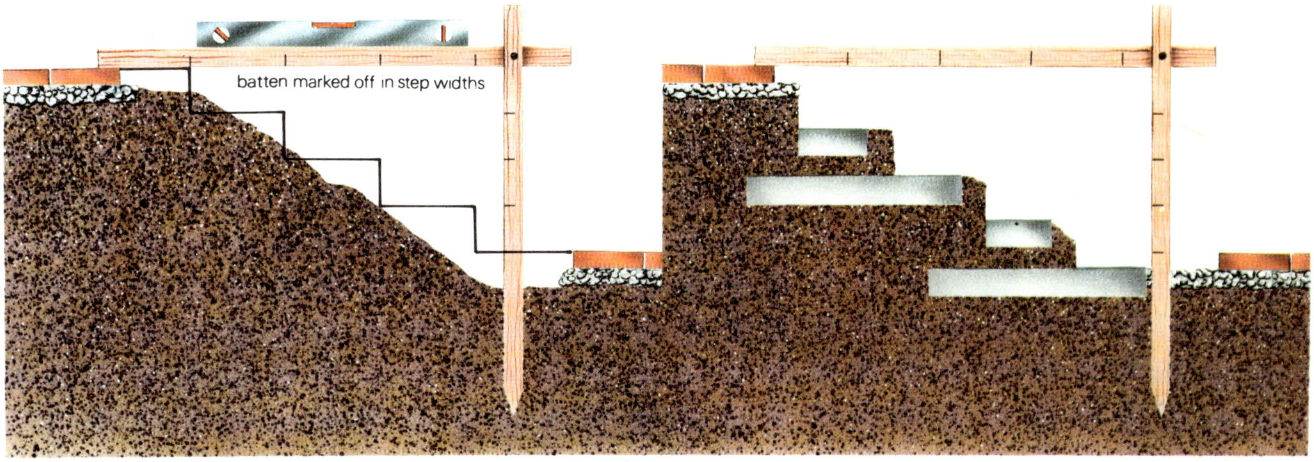

Foundations for steps

A. *The footings for brick steps should be combined with those for the side walls as shown, having first marked out the site in equal sections*

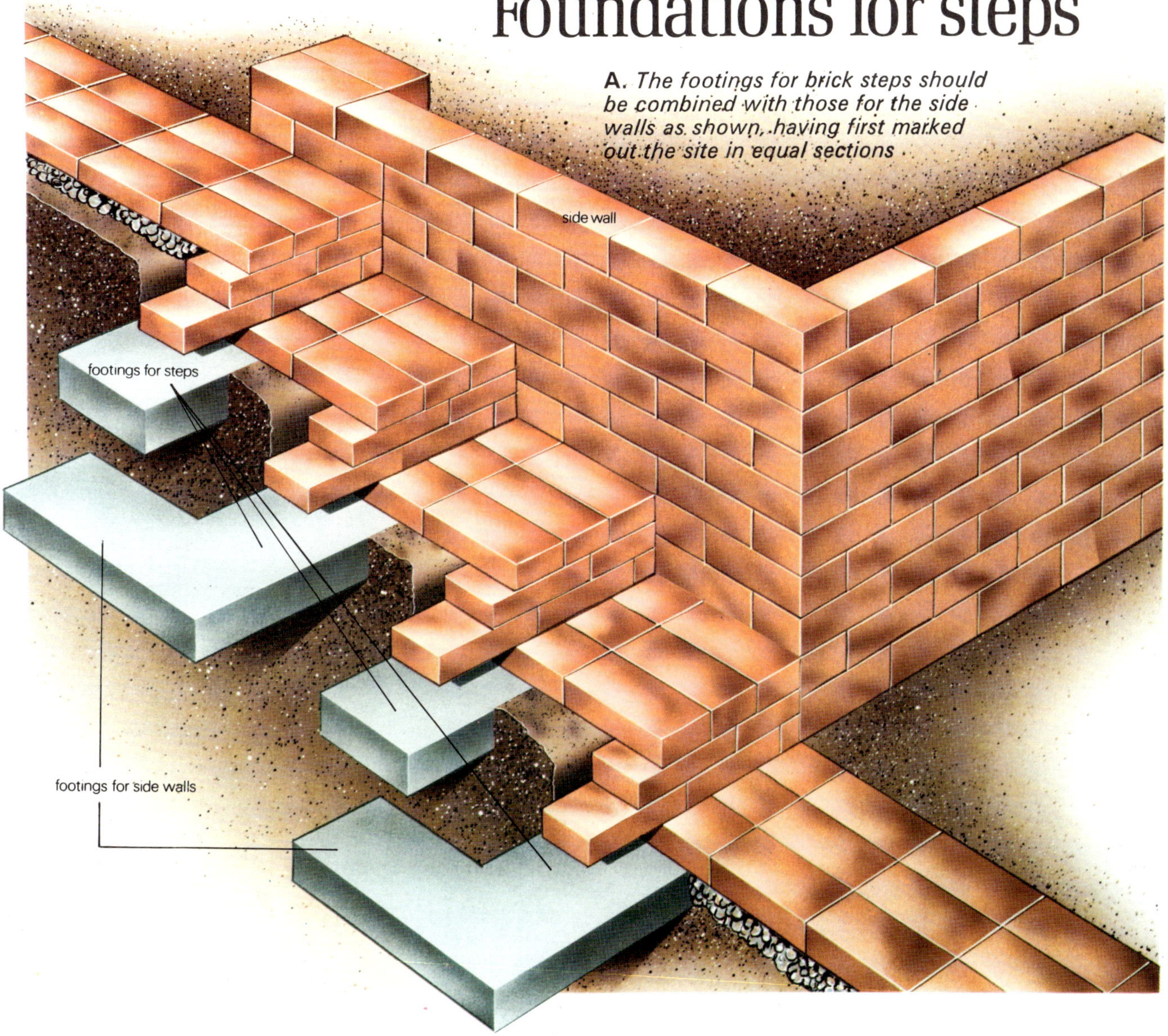

1 *If you are laying the path on firm ground fill any holes and take away bumps then roll it smooth with a heavy roller*

Preparing the site

Before starting to lay any foundations drive in pegs at each corner of the proposed path. Stretch twine taut between them, check this for level, then adjust the height of the pegs where necessary so that you have a level guide for the foundations.

Where a path is to curve, fix one peg to the middle of the site and attach a length of twine as long as you want the furthest part of the curve to extend (fig. C). Stretch this taut to another peg, level it, then move the second peg around as you dig out the foundations. Shorten the twine, and repeat for the inside edge of the path.

A patio or path is not usually expected to take great weight, so most ground can be made to suit the job. If the soil is very firm, try not to disturb it when marking out the area—simply pull out any grass or weeds and roll the ground flat.

If the ground is soft, you must lay down a layer of rubble or stones, compact it with a roller then cover it with sand. You need to remove extra soil to allow for this.

Where soft patches occur in otherwise firm ground, fill them with rubble, tramp it well down and roll it level. In extremely wet conditions, or where the site is below ground level, it is a good idea also to install a 25mm wide sub-soil drain in a bed of clinker beneath the hardcore. If possible, the drain should have a slight gradient and discharge into a ditch or soakaway. However, it is a good idea to consult your local building inspector at the planning stage.

Ideally, all paths should have a gradient of 25mm in one metre. To obtain this, check that the marking out pegs are level then adjust their heights so that the twine between them slopes away from the house. As you use the twine as a guide for digging the foundations, the gradient will eventually be transferred automatically to the bricks themselves.

A paved patio which butts up to the house must be at least 150mm below the level of the damp proof course so that rainwater cannot splash up to the wall above it. And for the same reason water should not be allowed to collect where the patio joins the house.

A gradient of 25mm every three metres is sufficient for a level patio, but a site which slopes dramatically away from the house also needs a soakaway at the far end—a shallow, gravel-filled trench will do the job.

When the patio site slopes heavily

2 *Mark out the path with twine stretched between pegs. Adjust the twine with the help of a spirit level to obtain the right slope*

towards the house, bring the adjoining edge up to ground level with hardcore and insert a vertical DPC against the wall of the house. When you lay the concrete, form a gutter in it with a length of PVC guttering arranged so that it slopes out to a soakaway.

Large, flat areas often look as if they are concave—turning up at the edges. To avoid this, introduce a slight camber of, say, 25mm every three and a half metres by gradually lowering the marking-out lines from the middle of the site outwards.

Bedding material

The site for paths and patios needs to be excavated to about 100–150mm, depending on which bricks you use. Though bricks can be laid directly onto a well-tamped bed of clay or gravel, the path is best protected against subsidence by laying a sub-foundation of concrete. Make the concrete bed from one part cement to six parts all-in ballast and with just enough water to make the mix workable.

Lay the concrete to a depth of between 50mm and 75mm and hold it in place with formwork (see pages 130 to 135). The surface need only be roughly levelled at this stage, as the mortar in which the bricks are laid will help to take up any irregularity. Hardcore is not really necessary for paths and patios, but is for loadbearing driveways or sites where the subsoil is very bad. At least 100mm should be laid—plus a layer of small chippings or stone dust and sand as the final layer. Alternatively, over the hardcore, 100–150mm of weak concrete can be laid, made up as described above.

3 *To make a sand foundation spread the sand over the site and then smooth it down so that it is about 50mm deep all over*

4 *Now lay the bricks down in the desired pattern, spacing them about 15mm apart and removing or adding sand to make them level*

Laying bricks on sand

Where the ground is naturally hard, brick paths can be laid loose on a bed of sand—although you may have to excavate to a depth of 180mm before you reach sufficiently firm and level subsoil. In this case level off as much as possible, roll out the area, then spread a layer of sand over the site. Lay down the bricks in the desired pattern, spacing them about 15mm apart and removing or adding sand as necessary to level them.

When you have laid all the bricks, spread sand over the surface and brush it well into the cracks. Then, to hold the bricks together, make up a concrete joint filler from one part cement to one of sand. Mix this with just enough water to allow it to run freely, then spread it over the path so that it fills the joints. Afterwards, clean the path quickly with sand or sawdust.

Laying bricks on mortar

Before you start to lay the bricks, prepare two lengths of board, about 2m long × 125mm wide and prop these at the side of the path as the bricks are being laid. Move the boards along as you work and lay a straight edge, with a spirit level on top, across them to act as a gauge to keep the surface level.

Use a guideline stretched taut along the length of the site to indicate their correct height; place this to the right if you are right-handed and vice versa.

Start at the lowest point of the project and lay the bricks in the usual way. Position the bricks about 5mm proud of the line to allow for slight movement when you are tapping them into place.

Press the bricks into the mortar bed and tap them gently into position with a lump hammer handle until the straightedge passes cleanly over them. It will help you to have a scaled plan of your chosen design so that there can be no confusion over the pattern.

Brick borders

Adding a border to a brick path or patio serves two purposes—it makes the work look more attractive and helps to hold the bricks together.

Always use new, purpose-made bricks—soil piled up against them will make them more vulnerable to decay.

Another sensible precaution is to build the mortar up around the outside of the border bricks, as far as you can without ruining the appearance of the path. A raised border of, say, two courses would give even more protection. Lay these in the normal way, adhering to a recognized bond.

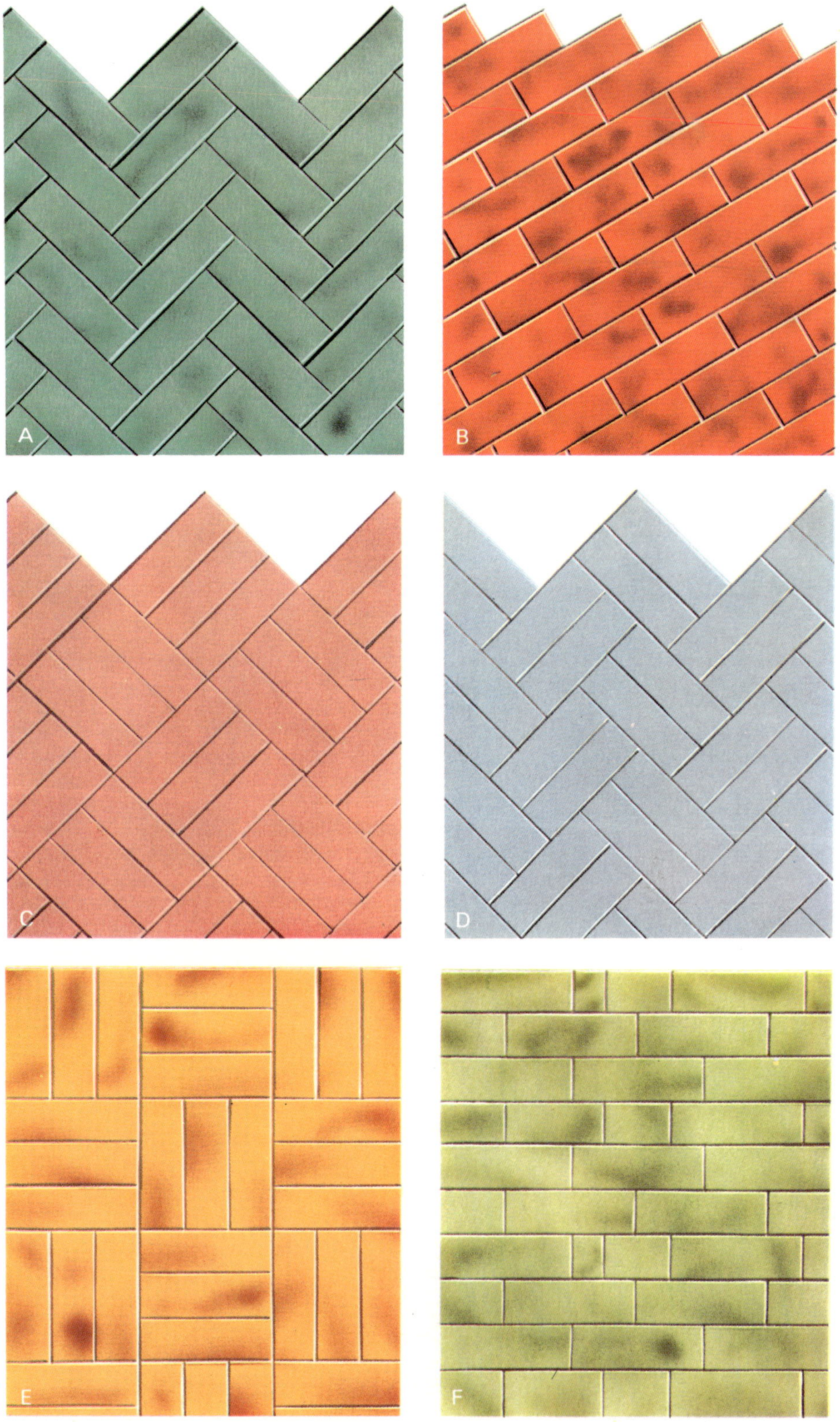

B. *Among the various patterns you can lay are (A) single herring-bone bond (B) raking bond (C) diagonal basket weave (D) double herring-bone bond (E) basket weave bond and (F) a mix of half bond and Flemish bond. You should bear in mind that the more complicated patterns will require some brick cutting which is both difficult and wasteful of material not to mention expensive*

5 *Protecting the bricks with a piece of wood, tap them with a heavy club hammer to make the surface as level as possible*

6 *Spread sand over the path and brush it well into the cracks, leaving a trough of about 30mm deep between the bricks*

7 *Finally spread a free running concrete filler over the path and clean it off the brick faces by brushing with sand*

Brick steps

All the bricks suitable for paths can be equally suitable for steps, although you must be careful to choose a type which does not become slippery when wet and therefore dangerous.

Before deciding how many steps to make, determine the height and horizontal width of the slops or incline by banging in a post—at least as high as the ground you are measuring—at the foot of the slope. Use another piece of wood to run from this to the level ground at the top of the slope (fig. A).

When you have checked that the horizontal piece is level, measure exactly the height at which the posts meet. Measure the horizontal distance between them as well, then divide the proposed number of steps into this measurement to give you the width of the treads.

Before finally deciding on the number of steps, consider your proposed number in relation to the gradient of the slope: if it is steep, the riser should not be too high and the tread should be as wide as possible—at least 300mm.

Normally, it is possible to divide the height equally into steps with risers of about 100mm. But if this leaves too narrow a tread, reduce the height of the risers slightly.

The next stage is to roughly cut out the shape and number of steps and dig a trench to form the footing of the first riser. Continue this trench around the sides of the steps in preparation for the side walls.

Next, excavate the steps to allow for a riser equivalent to the depth of two courses of the bricks you are using plus a 50mm mortar bed and two 15mm mortar joints. Excavate gradually, checking for level all the time.

When you are satisfied that the steps have been correctly cut and are level, fill in the trench with a 1: 5 mix of cement and all-in ballast. When this is set—and it will probably take at least a day—the first riser and tread can be laid. For this, you need a mortar mix of 1: 3 cement and builder's sand. Lay the first course of bricks for the riser in a stretcher bond on a 50mm bed of mortar and lay the next course on a 15mm bed.

For laying the front course of the tread, single bull-nose bricks are satisfactory, although for comfort and safety the nosing should be of a small radius. If you use conventionally-shaped bricks, adjust the level of the mortar to allow for a slight drainage gradient and stop water gathering.

Lay the front course flush with the second course of the riser and complete the tread in the normal stretcher bond (fig. A). Carry on this way until all the steps are complete, remembering to check each course for level before moving on to the next.

To prevent subsidence of the soil from the steps and to give them a more attractive appearance, you should now build a side wall. Check that the ground is level before you begin, then build the wall in a stretcher bond using the same bricks for uniformity. Mark out and build the quoin in the usual, way, cutting the bricks so that the edging is flush. The top of the wall should finish as shown in fig. A with the topmost course extended along the path above the steps and butted up to it to form a border.

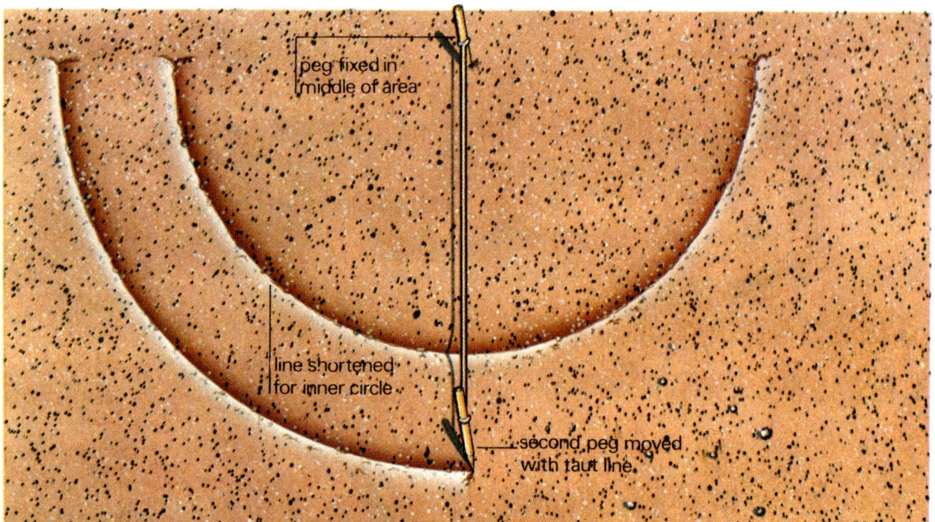

C. *To mark out a curved path, scratch the lines with this make-shift compass. Simply shorten the line to mark the inner edge*

Repairing paths

Damaged paths and drives are dangerous as well as unsightly. Yet maintenance and a few simple repairs are usually all that are necessary to make them last a lifetime

Above: *Raising a heavy paving slab can be difficult. Use two pieces of wood and form them into a lever and fulcrum to make lifting easier. Dig out the earth so that the lever can be inserted under the slab*

The most common materials used for paths and drives—concrete, tarmac and bricks—should last for years providing they have been properly laid and finished off. But even so, continuous use, frost and subsidence can all take their toll by causing surface damage. This is best put right before it becomes too extensive.

Concrete paths and drives

Structural defects in concrete can cause it to crack, chip easily or become uneven. The most common reasons for this are: an inadequate or unsuitable hardcore base which leads to subsidence, expansion of the concrete in warm weather which leads to buckling, an inadequate thickness of concrete, badly laid or poor quality concrete and badly laid or poor quality surface screed.

Not only do broken edges and cracks detract from the appearance of the path, drive and surroundings, they can also be dangerous. And if they are not repaired, the faults will spread, obliging you to break up and relay large sections. Prompt action saves both time and money.

Filling cracks

Providing there are no signs of serious subsidence, you can patch up cracks in paving concrete with a 1: 6 cement-sand mortar mix. To ensure a good bond with the original concrete, you also need a supply of PVA bonding agent, which you can buy from builders' merchants.

To provide a good key for the mortar, chip the crack out to a width of about 25mm with a hammer and bolster (fig. 1). Be sure to wear goggles to protect your eyes from flying bits of masonry. Afterwards, brush away the debris with a wire brush and paint on a coat of the bonding agent (fig. 3).

Add a little more of the bonding agent as you make up the mortar, but remember that this means you will need less water in the mix. Force the mix well into the crack using a pointing trowel and smooth it level with a flat piece of wood or a wooden float. Where a crack extends to the edge of a path or drive, take particular care that the mortar does not fall away after application. You may find that a timber former (fig. 7) helps to give the edge a clean finish.

Where cracks or chipping at the edge of the concrete are confined to a small area—possibly the result of lawnmower damage—hack away the damaged material back to firm concrete and brush it out. Check that the base below is sound, tamping it down and adding a little more hardcore if necessary—you can use the old, chipped concrete for this.

Use a timber former as shown in fig. 7 to form the new edge, paint on some bonding agent, then fill the hole with mortar as above. Leave the repair for at least a week before treading on it.

Surface chips and flakes often appear in screeded concrete or in concrete which has been laid too wet. In the latter case, the flakes are due to *laitance*—a thin layer of watery cement and fine ballast—which forms on the surface of the concrete leaving a rough aggregate surface below.

If the damage is not too extensive, you can patch it with a 1:5 mortar mix including a proprietary hardening additive. Chip away all the loose—or potentially loose—debris so that the repair mortar has a substantial hole in which to settle.

Where the screed shows signs of being too thin and badly laid, or where there is excessive laitance, you have no choice but to rescreed the entire area. Excessive laitance is a common fault in concrete laying and is mainly caused by over-trowelling with steel tools. When steel is applied to the surface of wet concrete it causes water to rise to the surface, bringing with it raw cement. It is this water-cement scum on the surface, which, when dry, becomes laitance.

Also remember that laitance means less cement in the concrete body, which of course means a weak concrete mix. Excessive laitance can be avoided by using wooden floats to level and solidify the concrete, as these keep the mixture well bound together.

Cracking and subsidence

If this becomes apparent, the most likely reasons are that the concrete is too thin or that there is something wrong with the hardcore base on which it has been laid.

The minimum recommended thicknesses for concrete are 75mm for paths and 100mm for drives, laid on a base of well-tamped hardcore. In the case of drives, it is preferable—especially on a light soil substrate—to reinforce the concrete with steel reinforcing mesh which is obtainable from builders' merchants.

The mesh should be 100mm x 100mm formed from 6mm wire and should be set 40mm above the hardcore. If your concrete does not match up to this, the only permanent solution is to relay it. However, as a temporary measure, it is well worth filling in the cracks in order to stop any water from entering the concrete and cracking it still further.

Subsidence—likely wherever the concrete cracks and sinks—will probably be confined to a localized area. The only remedy is to hack away the subsiding material back to firm concrete and relay.

Once you have removed the old concrete, inspect the base carefully. It may be that no hardcore was used, the base was not properly tamped, or that the ground is indeed slipping. Less likely, but still possible, is that the original hardcore contained plaster or rotting waste which has eaten away at the cement in the concrete.

Unless you are confident that the ground is firm, it is a good idea to dig out the old base and make a new one with fresh hardcore. Use only clean brick, aggregate or old concrete for this. *Hogging*—waste sand from gravel pits—is ideal if you can get it, being easier to compact and level than ordinary broken brick.

When you come to lay the fresh concrete, coat the edges of the existing concrete with bonding solution and make sure there are no crumbling patches left.

Cracks due to expansion

Sure signs of this are when the concrete appears to have lifted slightly around the cracks. Although concrete shrinks when it is drying out, hot weather may later cause it to expand considerably. If there is no room for movement at the edges, it forces upwards, cracking in the process.

In addition to filling in the cracks, it is necessary to provide expansion

1 Chip out cracks in concrete paths using a hammer and bolster. Clean the crack out carefully to a width of about 25mm

2 Use a wire brush to clear away any loose dust and debris. Do this thoroughly or the mortar will not take proper hold

4 Jam stones, rubble, or pieces of brick into the larger cracks. This will form a solid foundation for the application of mortar

5 Force the mortar well into the cracks using a pointing trowel. Smooth it off with a piece of wood or a wooden float

joints to allow for future movement. Do this at the edges by chipping away about 25mm all round, especially if the path butts up against a wall, then cut another 25mm groove across the width of the affected area.

Fill the joints with strips of 13mm bitumen-impregnated insulation board, then pack any gaps with pitch or a 1:6 mortar mix. Finally, trowel the filling level with the surrounding area. Any further movement will be confined to the filled joints—which can be patched up easily.

Surface damage

Superficial surface damage caused by general wear and tear can often be patched with a proprietary surface sealer. These are available from builders' merchants in polyurethane, epoxyresin and vinyl-based forms and

3 *To help the mortar to adhere well, paint a liberal coat of bonding agent all around and inside each of the cracks*

are easy to apply—just follow the manufacturer's instructions.

Before you apply a surface sealer the surface must be free of flakes, dust, vegetable growth, lichen and grease or oil. De-greasing agents are available from builders' merchants, motor spares shops and some garages. Lichen must be scrubbed off with a stiff wire brush and the concrete should then be treated with a proprietary lichen inhibitor, also available from builders' merchants.

Faded concrete and concrete slabs can be revived by washing off the dirt and then removing the surface layer of cement, which has usually decayed slightly. Use a dilute solution of hydrochloric acid—available from large builders' merchants, and apply the liquid with a stiff brush, taking care not to contaminate nearby soil.

When the surface has stopped fizzing, hose the path down thoroughly with plenty of cold water. You must wear protective rubber gloves when using acid and protect your eyes with goggles. Keep children and pets away from the area you are treating.

Brick paths and drives

Only hard bricks should be used for drives and paths, the most suitable being purpose-made paving bricks. Such bricks are only half the thickness of ordinary building bricks, but their length and breadth are the same. Commonly known as *paviours*, they are rarely kept as stock by brick merchants and may have to be specially ordered to your requirements.

Ordinary household bricks are not noted for their resistance to wear when used for paths and drives: water enters cracks in their surface, expands in cold weather and eventually causes the bricks to break up completely. For safety's sake it is a good idea to replace those bricks which have crumbled to the stage where they leave a hole.

Dig out the remains of the old brick carefully, taking care not to damage those around it. Bed in the replacement with a strong 1:3 mortar mix, slightly on the wet side to allow for adjustment. If you find that the brick is out of level with the others, remove it and start again—do not try to force it, or it is likely to split.

Fill the mortar joints around the brick—together with any other joints which have crumbled—with the usual 1:5 mortar mix. Maintaining the joints in good condition goes a long way towards stopping the bricks from breaking up and turning to dust.

Tarmac and asphalt

Drives and paths made from tarmac or asphalt, the latter containing a higher proportion of bitumen binder to aggregate, improve with age as the surface becomes more consolidated. But after a while the binder loses its adhesive properties, releasing bits of aggregate and causing the surface to break up.

If you catch it in time, you can treat this problem by applying an emulsion, or tack coat, of binder and fine grit. Both materials are available from builders' merchants who will usually deliver them to your door. Be sure to quote the area you wish to cover when ordering.

Having swept the area clean, and clear of loose chippings, brush on the tack coat as evenly as possible. Shovel the grit on top of this, adding just enough to cover the tack coat and fill any depressions.

When the tack coat starts to harden, run over the area with a garden roller dampened with water to prevent the binder sticking to it. A week or so later, brush away any surplus grit.

Repairing the edges

The edges of tarmac and asphalt drives and paths are best lined with kerb stones to stop them crumbling. The procedure for mending the edges follows closely that for repairing concrete edging, except that in this case you need a supply of ready-mixed tarmac or asphalt.

Use a hammer and bolster to cut back the edge to firm material, forming a regular, straight-sided hole (fig. A). Having brushed away the debris, and flattened and levelled the base, secure a timber former along the old edge and tap it down level with the surface

6 *Use a hammer and bolster to cut the edge of a worn path back to solid foundations. Try to get a regular, straight-edged finish*

7 *Brush away the debris and build a timber former along the edge of the path. Fill the gap with mortar and level off with a float*

8 *When replacing or laying paving slabs, clear away the ground beneath so that it is deep enough to accept the hardcore and mortar*

9 *Build up a solid foundation of hardcore and tamp it down firmly. Cover this with a thick layer of 1:3 mortar mix*

10 *Make gentle ridges in the mortar when you lay it. This allows the flagstone to be tamped down more easily when it is replaced*

A. Above: *Cut back the worn edges of a tarmac path to form a regular shape, brush away the loose debris, then flatten and level the base*

B. Below: *Secure a former against the path then fill the patch with fresh tarmac. Tamp it level with the existing surface using a punner*

of the existing tarmac (fig. B). Make sure that it is firmly fixed.

Warm the ready-mixed tarmac according to the manufacturer's instructions and shovel enough into the hole to protrude slightly above the surrounding surface—if you heat your spade beforehand, the tarmac will not stick to it. Wait until the mixture has started to harden, then roll it flat with the dampened roller. Remove the timber former when the tarmac has fully hardened.

If you do not have a roller, you can compress the tarmac using a special tool called a *punner* (fig. B). Make this from a 150mm x 150mm piece of blockboard nailed to a broom handle or other suitable length of timber.

Use the punner to press on the fresh tarmac, making sure that you cover the whole area. If small indentations

Unusual paths

Lay a new path or freshen up an old one using one of these ideas.
Left to right: *Create a natural look with broken paving slabs or irregular-shaped flagstones, surrounded by gravel and bordered by rough-stone walls. Bricks used on paths and borders create interesting effects—a herring-bone pattern is shown here. Sawn-off 'rounds' of timber can be set into concrete and surrounded by gravel with borders formed out of durable hardwood that will not easily rot or disintegrate*

11 *Position the new flagstone using wedges and tamp it down gently, checking for level with a straight edge*

are left between strokes, fill them with more tarmac and repeat.

Holes and damaged patches

Use a hammer and bolster to chip holes and damaged patches back to firm tarmac so that you are left with a larger, square or rectangular hole (fig. A). Check that the base below the tarmac is firm and level, adjusting the height where necessary, then fill and roll as above.

Flagstone paths

Cracks in flagstone paths are rarely worth patching: it is better to replace the damaged stone. Take great care when you prise this away or you will damage those around it.

Inspect the base under the stone for signs of subsidence or inadequate hardcore and correct as necessary,

12 *Fill in the surrounding joints with a pointing trowel using 1:6 mortar. Allow the mortar to dry fully before using the path*

bringing it up to the level of the hardcore under the other stones.

On top of this, lay a bed of strong, 1:3 mortar and smooth it out as level as you can. Gently position the new stone, then check it for level with a straightedge. Make small adjustments by lightly tapping the stone with a piece of heavy, but soft, timber. Finally, fill in the surrounding joints with 1:6 mortar (figs 8 to 12).

Gravel drives

Normally the only problem with these is that hollows develop, leaving 'bald patches' of the base material. Rather than try to distribute the existing gravel, it is better to enlarge the hollow to form a completely clear patch then fill it with fresh gravel. Use a garden rake to blend the old and new gravel together.

C. *Use a spade or shovel to dig out any hollows which form in gravel drives, clearing away enough material to leave a solid base*

D. *Fill the hole with fresh gravel, raking it out so that it blends well with the old material and gives a flat, smooth finish*

Chapter 3
FUN AND RELAXATION
Outdoor play areas

Above: *A tree house is great fun for children of all ages – but be sure the platform is firmly supported and the 'house' is surrounded by a sturdy fence*

Left: *A sandpit simply constructed from timber will keep a child happily entertained for hours. And you do not need vast areas of space – this one fits very nicely in a small patio area*

Children need somewhere to play out of doors, so that they can 'let off steam' without causing damage to furniture and furnishings. But even in the garden tiny feet can inflict staggering damage on a prize lawn and quickly destroy months of work spent raising flowers and plants.

At the same time a low hanging branch or a thorny rose twig can inflict nasty injuries on children deeply immersed in a game. Fishponds, paved areas and stone steps are all potential hazards.

A busy mother cannot spend her day watching the children and the garden to make sure that neither of them get unduly damaged. Equally, it is unreasonable to expect children to stay indoors when the sun is shining. The simple answer is to create a play area, designed to keep the children safe while at the same time allowing them the maximum freedom of movement.

Although this is most practical in a large garden where a play area does not seriously diminish the space for cultivation or sunbathing, it is usually possible in most gardens to set aside a small area where the children can play safely. Even so, really active ball games, like cricket and football, might best be practised in the local park.

Below: *Portable paddling pools come in a variety of sizes and are ideal on the garden lawn for tiny tots to splash about in on hot summer days*

Territory for toddlers

Children up to the age of about seven or eight need the greatest supervision. And tempting though it may be to banish all their paraphernalia and noise to the far end of the garden, it is far wiser to select a site which is clearly visible from the house – preferably an area with an uninterrupted sightline from a frequently used room, such as the kitchen.

A physical barrier of some sort will prevent children from wandering off into the main part of the garden and will also conceal the play area from the lawn or patio. From the point of view of appearance, a fairly low hedge is best and also enables you to see into the play area from other parts of the garden.

Evergreen hedges blend in well with most styles of garden and are fairly easy to maintain. Alternatively, a flowering hedge, such as lavender, is both pretty and practical. Avoid using prickly plants like holly which can easily scratch children and, of course, stay right away from any poisonous plants. Yew is particularly dangerous and even the common privet has poisonous berries.

Fences are less suitable barriers because of the danger of splinters. They are also less durable, especially if a child climbs on them or throws a ball against them. If you require a more solid barrier than a hedge, a brick wall is a better choice. A solid wall can often look obtrusive, so think about pierced screen walling or grow climbing plants on the garden side. Again, make sure that the plants are not poisonous.

If there are stone or concrete steps between the play area and the rest of the garden, then a gate is essential. More often than not, a child will unwittingly choose the most dangerous place to take a tumble. If the garden is level, then a gate is not a necessary safety factor, but would be useful to keep the children's games confined to the area intended for them.

Above: *A Wendy house built from odd pieces of timber does not need an elaborate finish – your children will enjoy it simply because it is 'theirs'*

Above: *A collection of colourful cardboard tubes screwed together with nuts and bolts creates a novel arrangement for a child's play area*

If the play area is sited on a solid surface then it is probably best to have it grassed over in case of accidents. Choose a variety of grass that is tough and resilient and which does not grow luxuriously long.

Make sure that there are no open drains in the area. Children are bound to satisfy their curiosity with an unhygenic investigation, and there is always the possibility that they could be badly scalded. If it is not possible to site the play area away from drains – outside a kitchen, for instance – then make sure the drains are securely covered and that small fingers cannot become trapped.

Organized activities

There are a number of toys and activities you can provide within the play area, depending on the number and ages of the children and, of course, the amount of available space.

A climbing frame will keep young children happily occupied for hours. You can buy ready-made metal or wooden frames or erect one yourself using your own design. Be sure the base is securely bolted down and set in concrete so that it cannot tip over, and seal or paint the frame because it will have to withstand all kinds of weather. A number of mats such as those used by gymnasts can provide further protection for budding amateur athletes and can be easily stored away during wet weather.

A swing is a firm favourite with children of all ages. Again, the frame

Below: *A child's vivid imagination can turn a simple wooden structure like this into anything from a castle to a sea-going battleship*

should be securely bolted down and set in concrete. Site it so that there is adequate clearance both behind and in front of the swing, bearing in mind the positions of doors, gates, walls and windows. Check suspension ropes or chains from time to time, and especially after bad weather. Removable ropes or rods which hook into chains are best as these can easily be detached from the main frame and stored away for the winter.

A sandpit brings the seaside to a child's own garden, especially if it is combined with a paddling pool. These can be any size and shape, with a minimum of about 900mm diameter. A depth of 300mm for the pool and 150mm for the pit is quite sufficient. Site the pool in full sunlight, not too far from a tap and drain for easy filling and emptying.

Ready-made pools are suitable only for ornament and cannot stand up to hard wear. Both paddling pools and sandpits are best made of concrete and lined with non-slip tiles to provide a smooth and easily cleaned surface. A concrete or paved area around the pit and paddling pool will be easier to keep clean than a grass verge. Choose a non-clinging, fine sand for the sandpit and use detachable covers to keep the sand and water clean.

Above: *Solid logs form a very definite barrier around this play pit to create a well-secluded hideaway which any young child would love*

Creating for juniors

In many ways, play areas for older children are much easier to plan, although they usually require rather more space. In fact, older children are generally happier in an area which has not had too much planning. They can safely be banished to the end of the garden – and if this is something of an overgrown wilderness, they will like it even better.

Make sure that the area is safe, however, and check long grass for any old and rusty tools that may still be concealed there. Check, too, that any overhanging branches of trees are solid and that fallen trunks will not roll over when climbed upon. If they are secure, leave the branches and trunks in place to provide part of an adventure playground.

Although older children will have outgrown the babyhood tendency to put colourful berries and leaves in their mouths, it is still best to remove and destroy any poisonous plants and weeds in the area, especially if it has been

neglected for any length of time. Obviously, the play area should be separated from bonfire sites, rubbish tips and compost heaps.

Grass is nicer underfoot, but the safety factor which precluded concrete or paving for young children no longer applies. Perhaps a combination is best for junior play areas, providing both soft and hard surfaces to cope with any activity.

Again, a physical demarcation of the area is advisable to at least try and deter children from straying over the rest of the garden. Walls, fences and hedges are all suitable here.

One of the things that children seem to like best is a mini version of an army-style assault course. This need not be elaborate and could include such things as a couple of old car tyres hung on a rope from a tree, a low, wooden ramp, a length of plastic 'tunnel' and an overhead rope suspended from posts or trees.

Another great favourite is a tree house, which you can create quite simply using a secure platform, a rain-proof roof and sufficiently high 'walls' to prevent

Above: *A traditional climbing frame is great fun for children of any age, but add a slide to the construction and it becomes doubly exciting*

anybody falling out. Most children will value such a simple structure as a palace, although, of course, more complex designs are possible.

The house should be built on one of the lower branches and the ladder leading up to it must be firmly fixed. Be sure too that the house itself is securely fastened to the tree and check ties at regular intervals, especially after the winter.

If a tree house is too ambitious or if there are no trees in your garden, then a play house on the ground can also be great fun. Build it in a similar way to an ordinary garden shed and paint the outside in bright colours, perhaps including the child's name on the front door. A couple of old chairs, a rug and a pair of bright curtains will furnish the interior. But make sure that the children cannot lock themselves or each other inside the house.

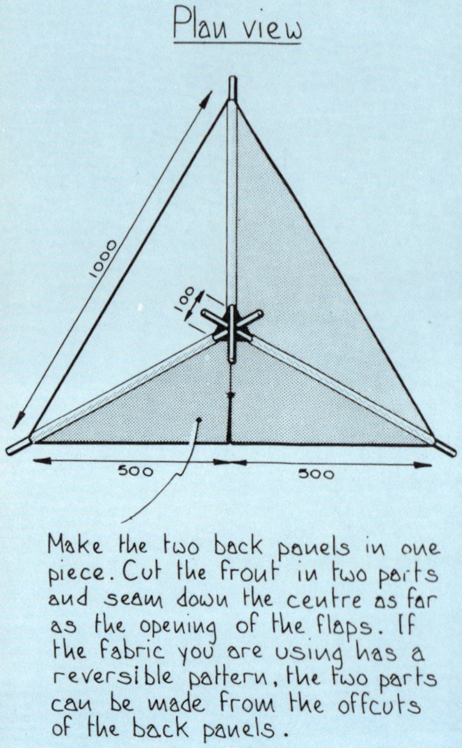

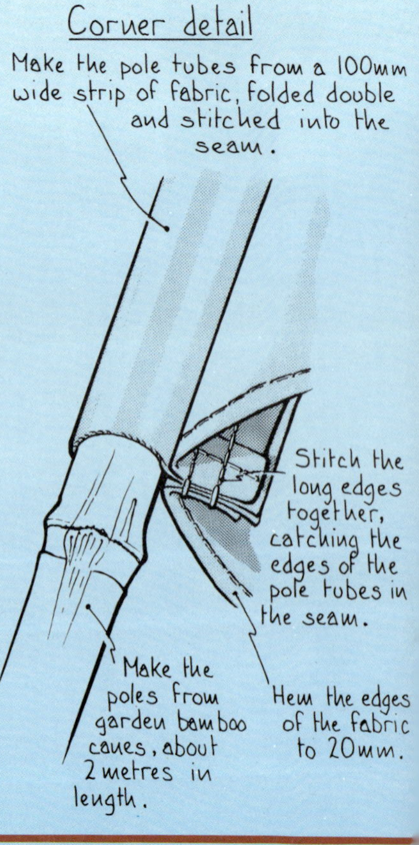

You can make the wigwam from almost any fabric 1 metre or more wide. For economy, use old curtains or sheeting. You can dye a plain fabric, or decorate with fabric paints.

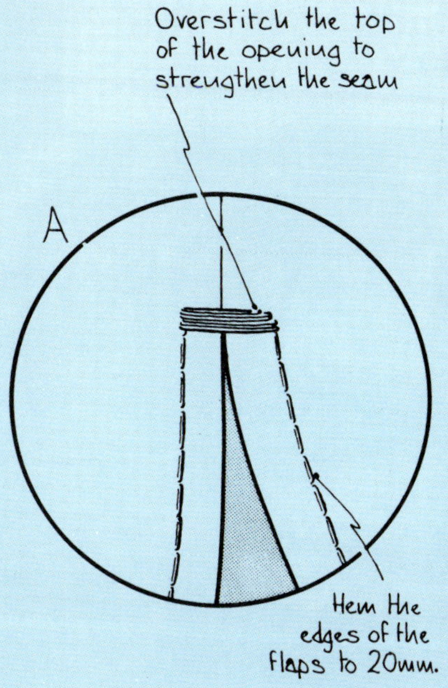

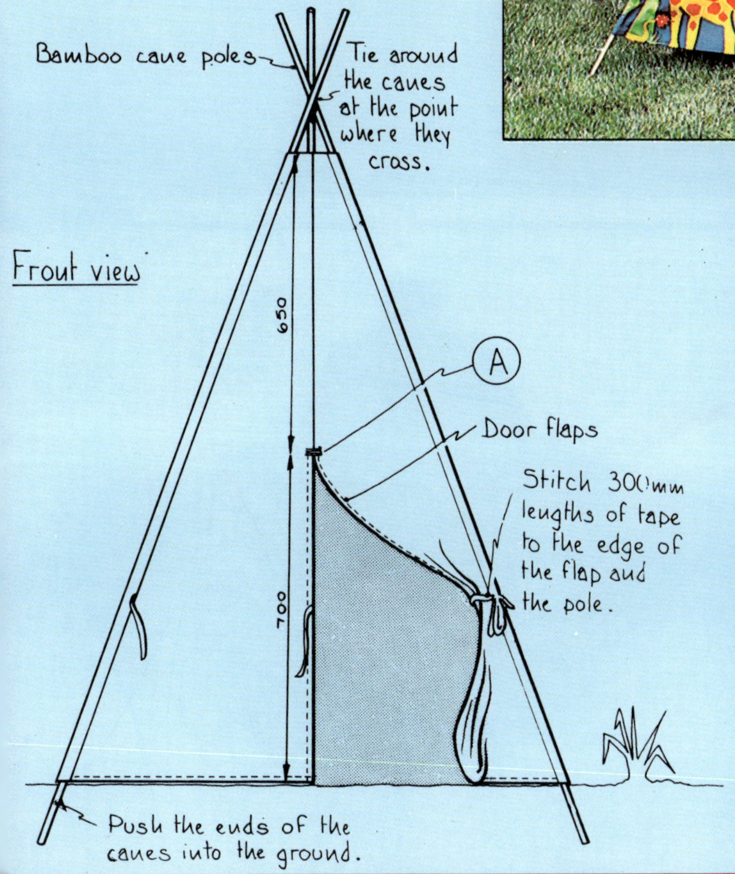

Make a wigwam

This traditional Indian wigwam design for younger children will give them hours of fun and enjoyment during the summer months. Because it takes up little room it is ideal for smaller gardens, and it can be folded up neatly.

The framework consists of three bamboo poles. Get them from a garden centre, and choose sturdy examples. Any fabric can be used for the covering, as long as it is a metre wide—you can even consider using old curtains or sheets. For a waterproof wigwam, use canvas and spray the finished article with tent waterproofer.

If you are using a plain fabric, you can decorate it with traditional Indian motifs using fabric paint and cardboard stencils—zig-zag edging around the base looks most effective and other patterns can be found in books and comics.

Make up the covering as shown on the workplan, using a single piece of fabric for the sides and another—seamed down the middle as far as the opening—for the front. Add strips of tape to form ties to close the flaps. If you prefer, you can use a zip fastener stitched to the flaps on each side.

Insert the poles and drive their feet into the ground, making sure that the sides are taut. Tie off the poles where they cross at the top of the wigwam. It is a good idea to bind the ends to avoid the risk of splinters.

A sandpit in the garden

This easy-to-build garden project combines a shady picnic spot with a child's sandpit. It is made of low cost timber, and the boarded decking has removable lids which cover the pit at one end and a small storage area at the other

Building this boarded platform is extremely simple, yet the finished result is attractive and practical. Built around a tree, it provides a shady sheltered spot for outdoor meals or just for sitting and reading a book, magazine or newspaper.

Begin by choosing a firm, level, well-drained site. If you have no tree which is suitable to build around, any other spot which meets these requirements will do. Next, set out the eight stakes which support the structure. The technique for this is described on page 130. Note that the stakes around the pit are longer to allow for the excavation. You should make the excavation at the same time as sinking the stakes which surround it.

If you are concreting the pit and lining with boards, do so at this stage. It is possible to use an unlined pit, but the sand will tend to become contaminated with soil. The alternative is to line it with a plastics sheet, which will be effective for some time but will eventually deteriorate.

Cover the frame with 150mm × 25mm boards nailed in place. Use galvanized nails to resist rust. You can use either new timber, or, as a cheaper but effective substitute, buy old floorboards from a demolition site. Whichever you choose, treat the timber thoroughly with a wood preservative. If the timber is very rough, it is advisable to give it a thorough sanding to remove most of the roughness and splinters. This is particularly important in the pit area where children will be playing.

Make the two lids to fit on each side of the fixed decking using more boards braced with battens. The lids will keep the worst of the weather from the pit and storage area, but it is as well to use a polythene sheet too.

If you are lining the pit with plastics, fit it as shown, using a batten to secure the top edge. Allow for drainage to prevent the sand from becoming soaked. Fill the pit with sugar sand, obtainable from builder's merchants. Check the walls of the sand pit particularly carefully for splinters and sand down any rough areas.

Alternative ideas

You can build these two attractive tree seats using the same method as for the sandpit.

The picture on the left shows a bench seat and backrest built up against the trunk. Make this on a framework of stakes. However make sure that you do not attach the backrest to the growing trunk or you may damage the bark.

Build the picnic table and benches shown on the right in the same way, but using longer stakes to support the table top. Set the top at about 750mm high, and the bench at around 500mm.

Workplan

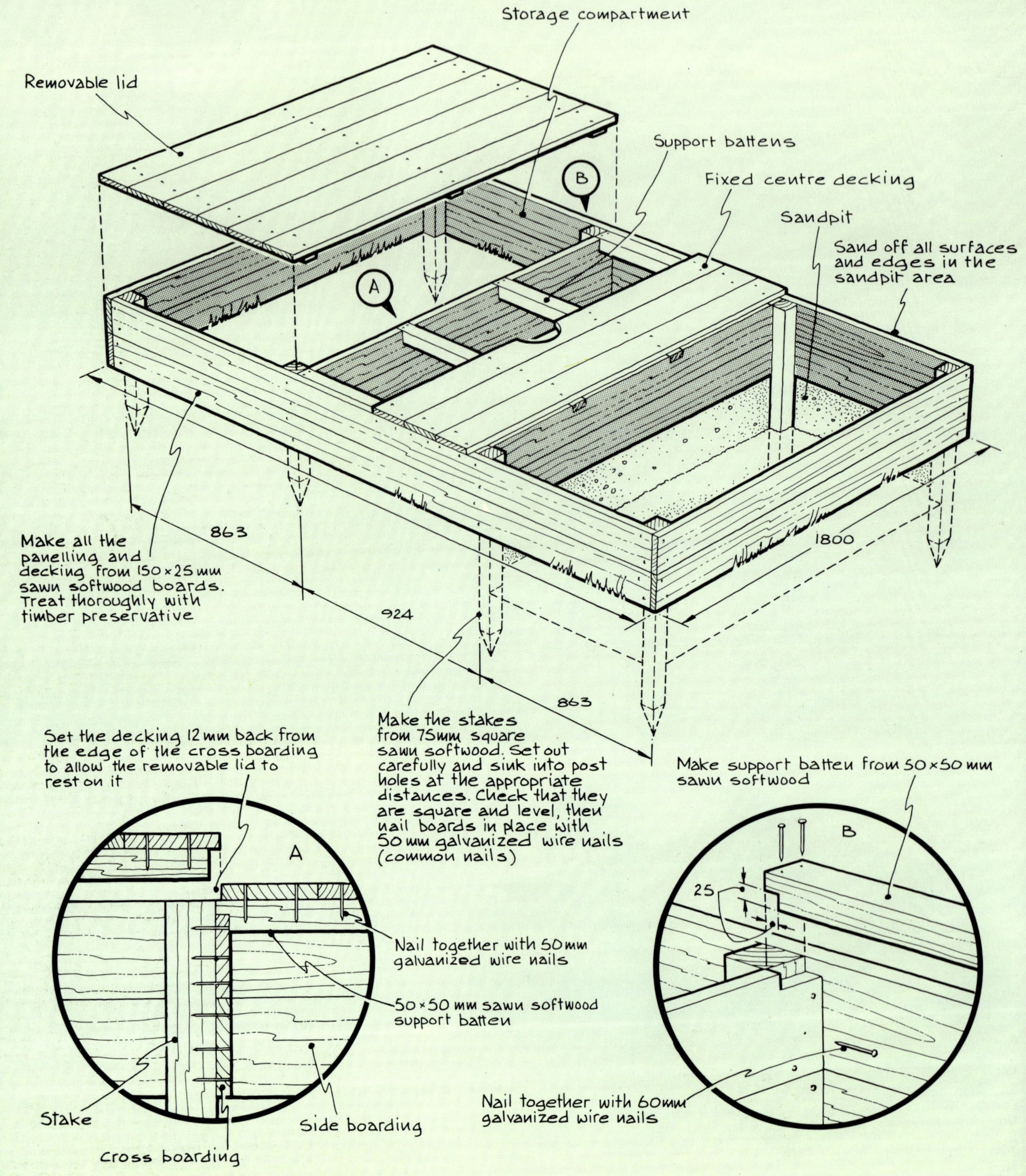

Storage compartment
Removable lid
Support battens
Fixed centre decking
Sandpit
Sand off all surfaces and edges in the sandpit area
B
A
863
1800
924
863
Make all the panelling and decking from 150×25 mm sawn softwood boards. Treat thoroughly with timber preservative
Make the stakes from 75mm square sawn softwood. Set out carefully and sink into post holes at the appropriate distances. Check that they are square and level, then nail boards in place with 50 mm galvanized wire nails (common nails)
Set the decking 12 mm back from the edge of the cross boarding to allow the removable lid to rest on it
A
Nail together with 50mm galvanized wire nails
50×50 mm sawn softwood support batten
Stake
Side boarding
Cross boarding
Make support batten from 50×50 mm sawn softwood
B
25
Nail together with 60mm galvanized wire nails

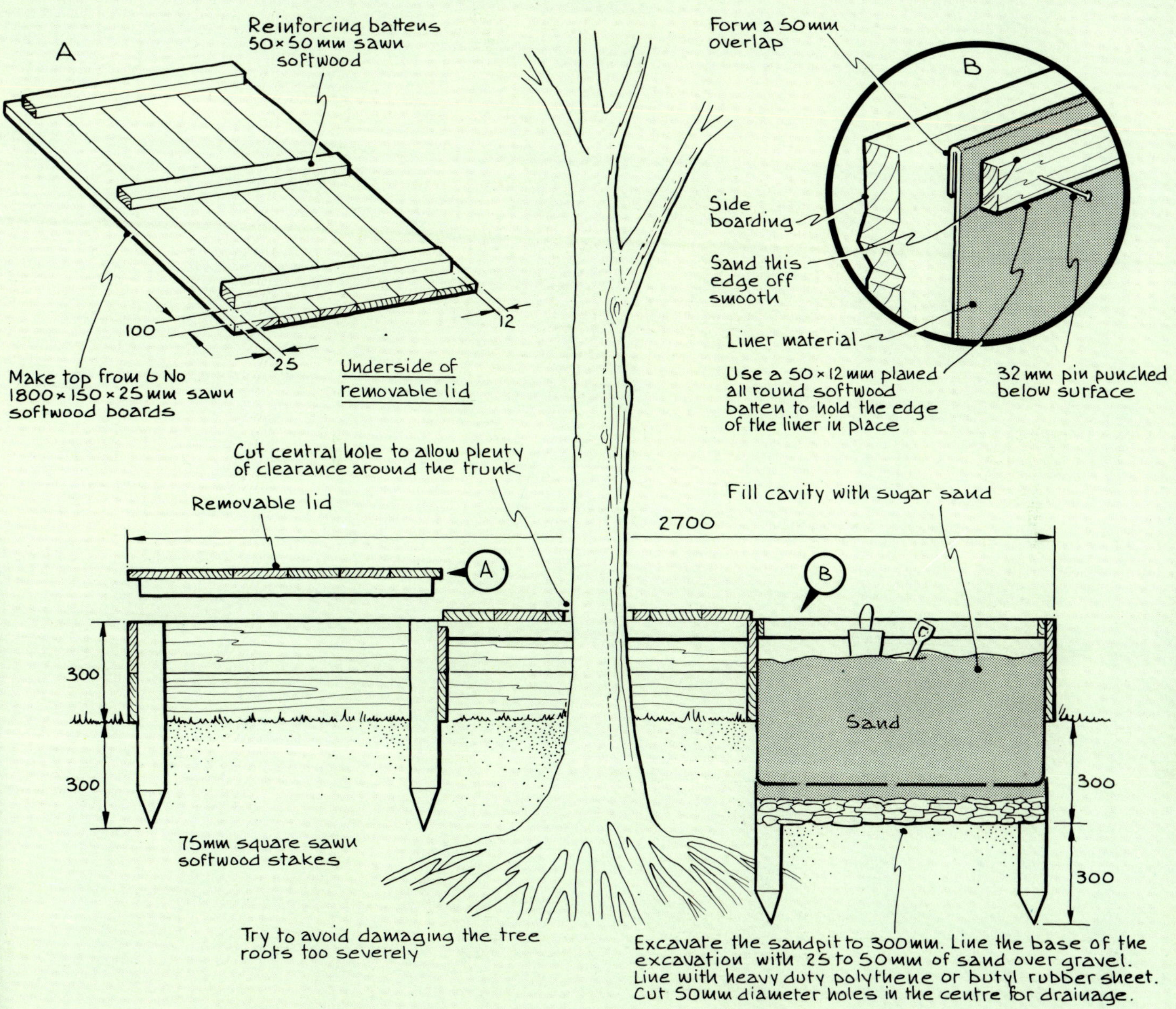

Alternatively, you can line the excavation as shown. Continue the boarding down the stakes (either nail through from the inside, or dig a larger excavation, nail then fill up to the boards. Line the base with concrete over hardcore for drainage.

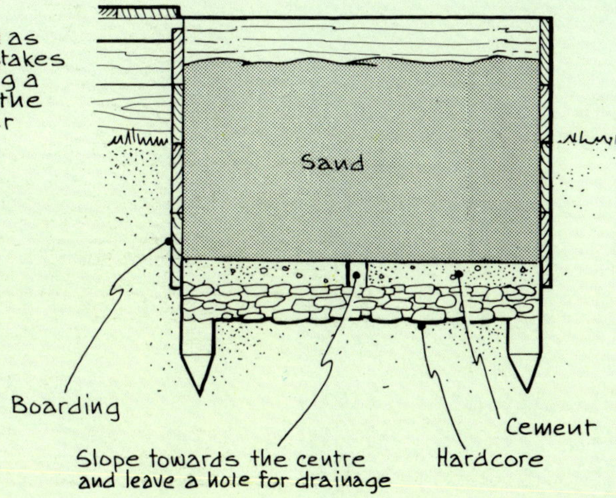

Cutting list
All sizes are in millimetres. Timber is either planed all round, PAR (dressed four sides, D4S) or sawn.

Part	Material	No.	Size
Stakes (short)	75mm × 75mm sawn softwood	4	600mm
Stakes (long)	75mm × 75mm sawn softwood	4	900mm
Side boarding	150mm × 25mm sawn softwood	4	2650mm
End boarding	150mm × 25mm sawn softwood	4	1800mm
Cross boarding	150mm × 25mm sawn softwood	4	1750mm
Support battens	50mm × 50mm sawn softwood	4	925mm
Reinforcing battens	50mm × 50mm sawn softwood	6	863mm

Additional materials: Pit lining (timber or plastic), cement, hardcore, sugar sand, 50mm galvanized wire nails, timber preservative, 50mm × 12mm batten

A children's climbing frame

This sturdy and attractive climbing frame should provide years of pleasure and exercise for growing children. It is simple to put together but if space is limited, you can just as easily pack it away for storage

Children love to climb, and can get useful exercise from their games. This traditionally constructed climbing frame provides an environment where they can play safely and under the watchful eyes of their parents. It will fit comfortably into a small garden, and can be dismantled in an hour or so to make four panels which can be easily and compactly be packed away during the winter months.

The frame is sturdily constructed in timber and is based around the four collapsible panels. These are rigidly held together when the climbing frame is assembled by fitting bolted-on cross-beams. All the joints are either screwed and glued or bolted, so construction is very simple. Only basic woodworking tools are needed, but the dowel rods which form the climbing rails are run through holes in the uprights, so you will need a large (32mm) drill. You can use a brace and bit to bore the holes, but a powerful electric drill, preferably with a drill stand, makes the work much easier.

Following the plans, cut all the timber to length then mark each piece with a letter or a number so you can identify its position. Construct the four fixed panels first. These are shown shaded on the plans. Drill all the uprights with the holes for the dowel rails running across the panel. Note that the holes on the outer uprights are stopped at 30mm depth, so fit a depth guide to the drill.

Now fit the cross dowels. These should be hardwood for maximum strength, but well selected Parana pine can be used instead. Glue the dowels in position with urea formaldehyde adhesive, which is suitable for exterior use. Fit the top and bottom rails of 75mm×25mm softwood, and glue and screw them to the uprights.

When all four panels are complete, mark them out and drill the holes for the dowels, noting which are stopped and which are through. Also, drill the holes for the bolts which hold the top and bottom rails in position.

To assemble the frame, thread the dowels through the panels. Fit the top and bottom rails in position, and secure with coach (carriage) bolts. To prevent the dowels from turning, lock them by inserting a thin cross dowel into a hole drilled through one of the uprights and into the rail.

The main assembly is now complete. You can dismantle it by unbolting the cross rails and removing these and the dowels. The panels will then pack flat for storage.

Before use you should sand all the surfaces smooth, paying particular attention to the edges—you can round these off with a plane. Treat all the timber with a timber preservative, using a non-toxic formulation; you can use paint or lacquer but if this wears off, the timber underneath will be unprotected. If you use timber preservative, retreat every two years.

Add a rope ladder and a swing made from an old tyre, using strong rope, and making sure that the knots are secure. You can also fit a movable platform made from lengths of batten as shown. This will fit between any adjacent pair of dowels and is quite secure once dropped into place.

The frame should be stable when free-standing, but on an uneven surface, you can secure it further by lashing it to stakes set into the ground.

Alternative ideas

You can easily make a useful addition to your climbing frame by adding a slide. Make it from 12mm plywood, lined with plastic laminate or highly polished. Fit hooks at the top to hold it to the frame.

A children's climbing frame

Cutting list

All sizes in millimetres. Timber is planed all round, PAR (dressed four sides, D4s)

Part	Material	No.	Size
outer uprights	50mm× 50mm softwood (PAR)	12	1800mm
centre uprights	50mm× 50mm softwood (PAR)	4	2250mm
fixed cross dowels	32mm diameter hardwood dowel	11	1768mm
fixed cross dowels	32mm diameter hardwood dowel	3	1170mm
through dowels	32mm diameter hardwood dowel	12	1170mm
fixed cross rails	75mm× 25mm softwood (PAR)	4	1800mm
fixed cross rails	75mm× 25mm softwood (PAR)	2	631mm
cross rails	75mm× 25mm softwood (PAR)	8	1995mm
cross rails	75mm× 25mm softwood (PAT)	2	677mm
ladder rungs	50mm× 25mm softwood (PAR)	5	400mm
platform sides (optional)	75mm× 25mm softwood (PAR)	2	710mm
platform deck (optional)	50mm× 25mm softwood (PAR)	10	580mm

Additional materials: Rope, old tyre, 72 No. 75mm × 10mm coach (carriage) bolts with nuts and washers, 72 No. 50mm No. 10 (4.9mm) countersunk wood-screws, urea formaldehyde adhesive, 25mm × 6mm dowels.

Finish: Timber preservative.

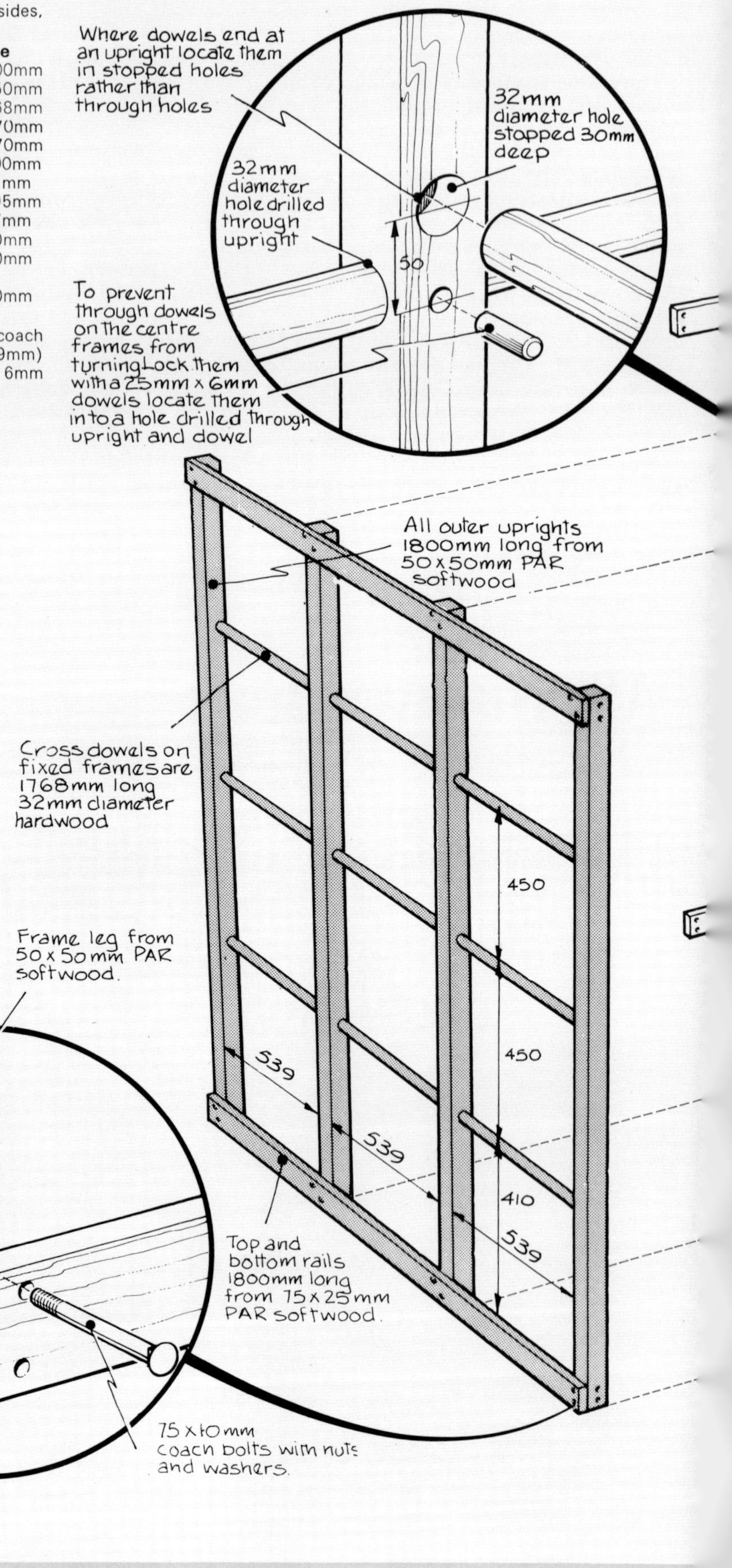

Assembling the main frame

Make up the four panels shown in grey as complete permanent assemblies. Fix the joints with screws and use urea-formaldehyde adhesive. Cut all the other rails and dowels to length and drill the holes for them in the uprights. To assemble, thread the dowels into the two central frames and bolt the top and bottom rails on to hold them in position. Now add the end frames, one at a time, fitting the end of the dowels into the holes. Finally bolt the ends of the top and bottom rails in place.

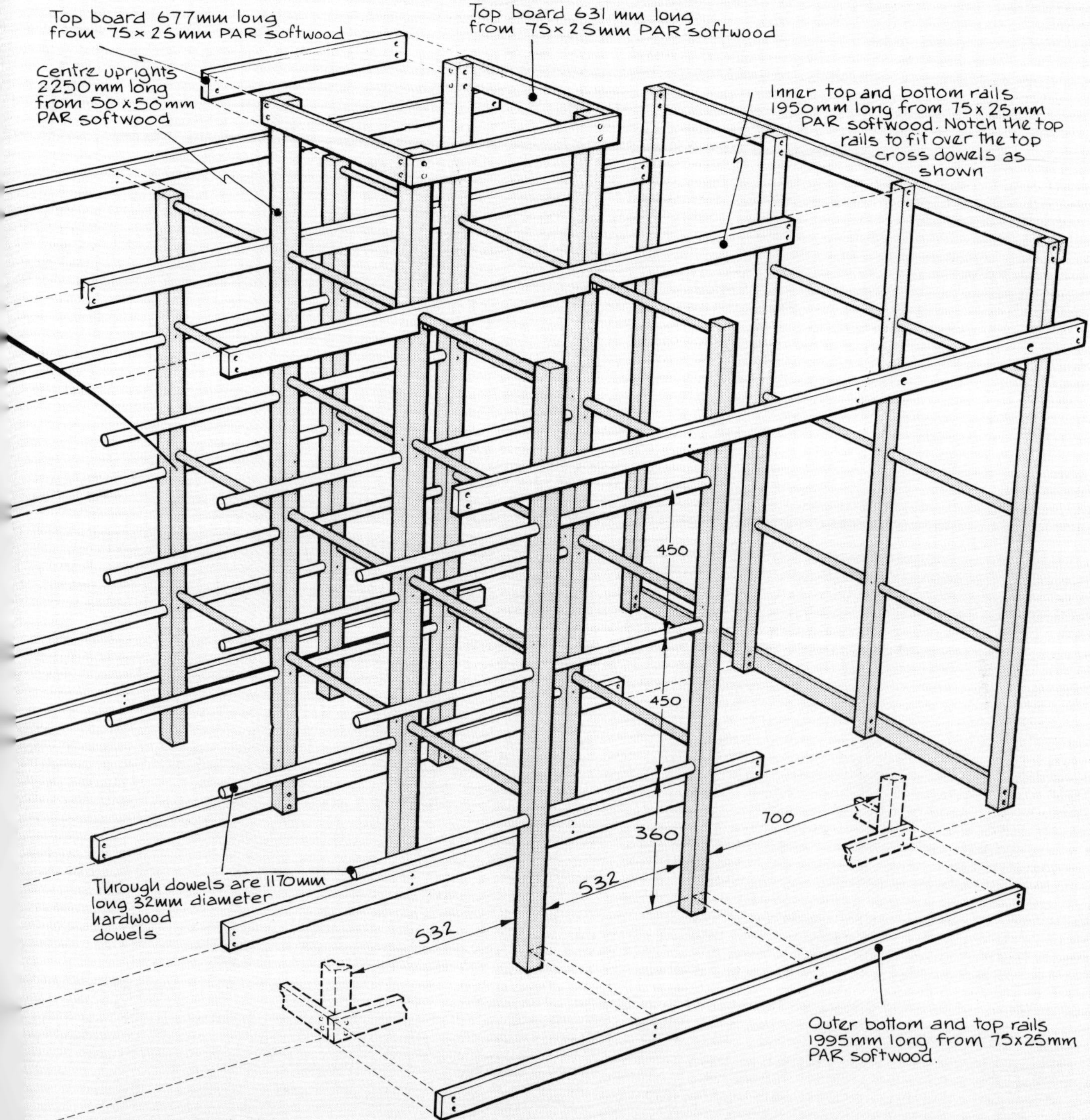

Drilling the uprights

After cutting, mark each upright with a key letter so you can identify its position on the plan. Mark out each of the drilling holes at the correct height and on the correct side. Note whether the dowel runs through the upright or stops. If it stops, stop the hole at 30mm deep so that the end of the dowel does not project. Also mark out and drill each upright for the bolt holes for the top and bottom rails.

Finish

You can paint or lacquer the frame, but if this wears through, the timber underneath will be unprotected. A better alternative is to use timber preservative but make sure that you can use a non-toxic formulation.

Making a rope ladder

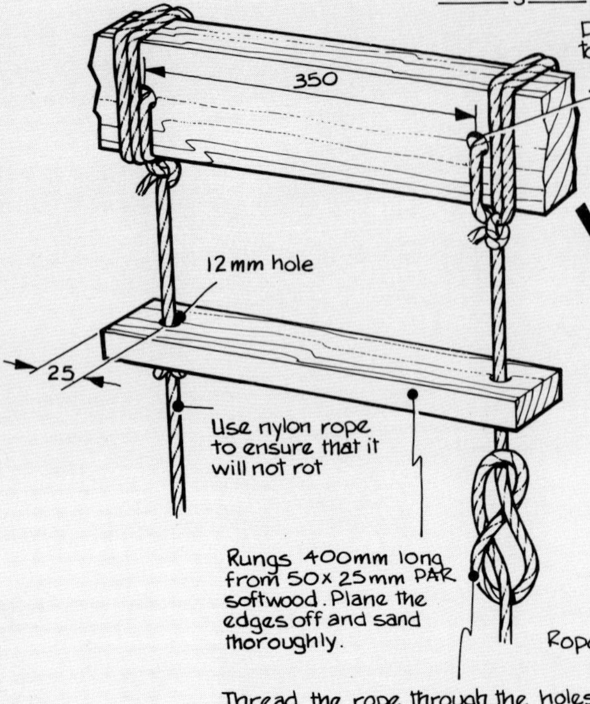

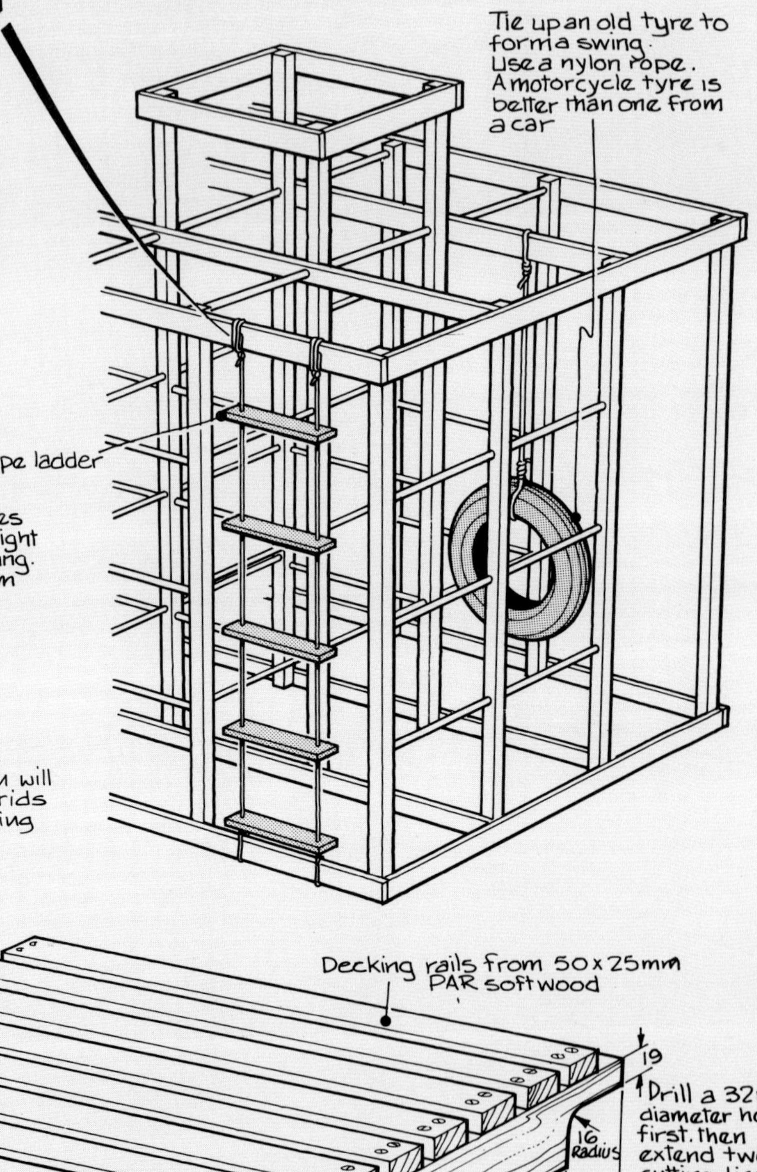

Making a platform

You can make a moveable platform which will slot between the dowels on any of the grids by lifting it into position and then dropping over the notches cut in the ends

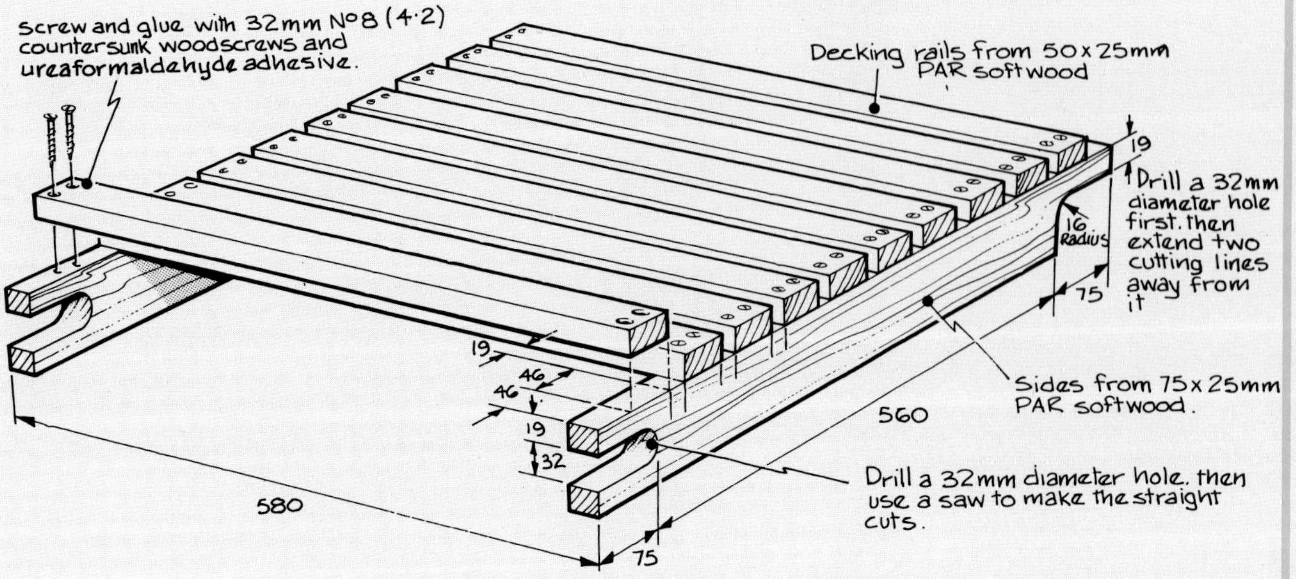

A garden swing

This sturdy but simple swing design is easy and cheap to build yet it is guaranteed to give your children hours of fun and pleasure. The swing can be made with either a cradle or bench seat so that it is easily adapted to suit youngsters of all ages

Below: *The swing, which uses treated softwood for the frame, should be stable enough to stand as a free-standing unit. But if you have to cope with a really boisterous youngster, you can peg into the lawn through the ground boards or fit additional cross-members*

Left: *For a small child, the design includes plans for a simple cradle seat in plywood. The component parts are dowel-jointed together, ready to receive a drop-in seat which is padded with foam and then covered with vinyl*

Below left: *More proficient swingers are certain to prefer a simple bench seat like this. Both types of seat are hung from eyebolts on heavy-duty galvanized steel welded-link chain*

A garden swing is one of the most traditional – and enjoyable – outdoor activities for children of all ages. This design uses a sturdy softwood frame and includes two types of seat to suit both toddlers and older children.

The frame is based on a strong crossbeam and four legs. Cut shouldered tenons on each end of the crossbeam, angling them as shown. All four legs are cut to an angle at the ends and housed to accept the tenons. The joints are secured with bolts. Make sure that you fit locking nuts on all bolts, either by using self-locking nuts with a nylon insert or adding a second nut to lock the first.

The lower ends of the legs are also cut to an angle. They are braced by being bolted to long boards which lie on the ground. If extra bracing is required, you can fix these to the ground, or add extra bracing between them.

Treat all timber thoroughly with timber preservative – or use pressure treated timber – to avoid problems with rot. Assemble the frame and erect it on a firm, level surface. If extra bracing is needed, fix the ground boards as described above. You can also add side guy ropes, fixed to the crossbeam and pegged to the ground.

Both seat designs are hung on chains hooked over swing hooks bolted to the crossbeam. Make sure you use a sturdy welded-link steel chain, and be sure to use locking nuts on the hooks.

The simpler seat is based on a softwood board. This is padded along its edges to prevent accidents, and covered in a waterproof fabric. You should still treat the timber, however, to resist damp. Fit eye bolts and attach it to the chain using shackles. You can adjust the height of the seat by raising or lowering the chain a few links on the swing hooks.

The cradle seat also has a foam and fabric covered seat, supported in a sturdy plywood frame. Additional safety can be ensured for very small children if you add a strap between the two side panels to prevent the child from slipping forward off the seat. Hang the strap on a double chain arranged as shown, and fix these to the ends of the chains attached to the swing hooks.

Workplan

General assembly

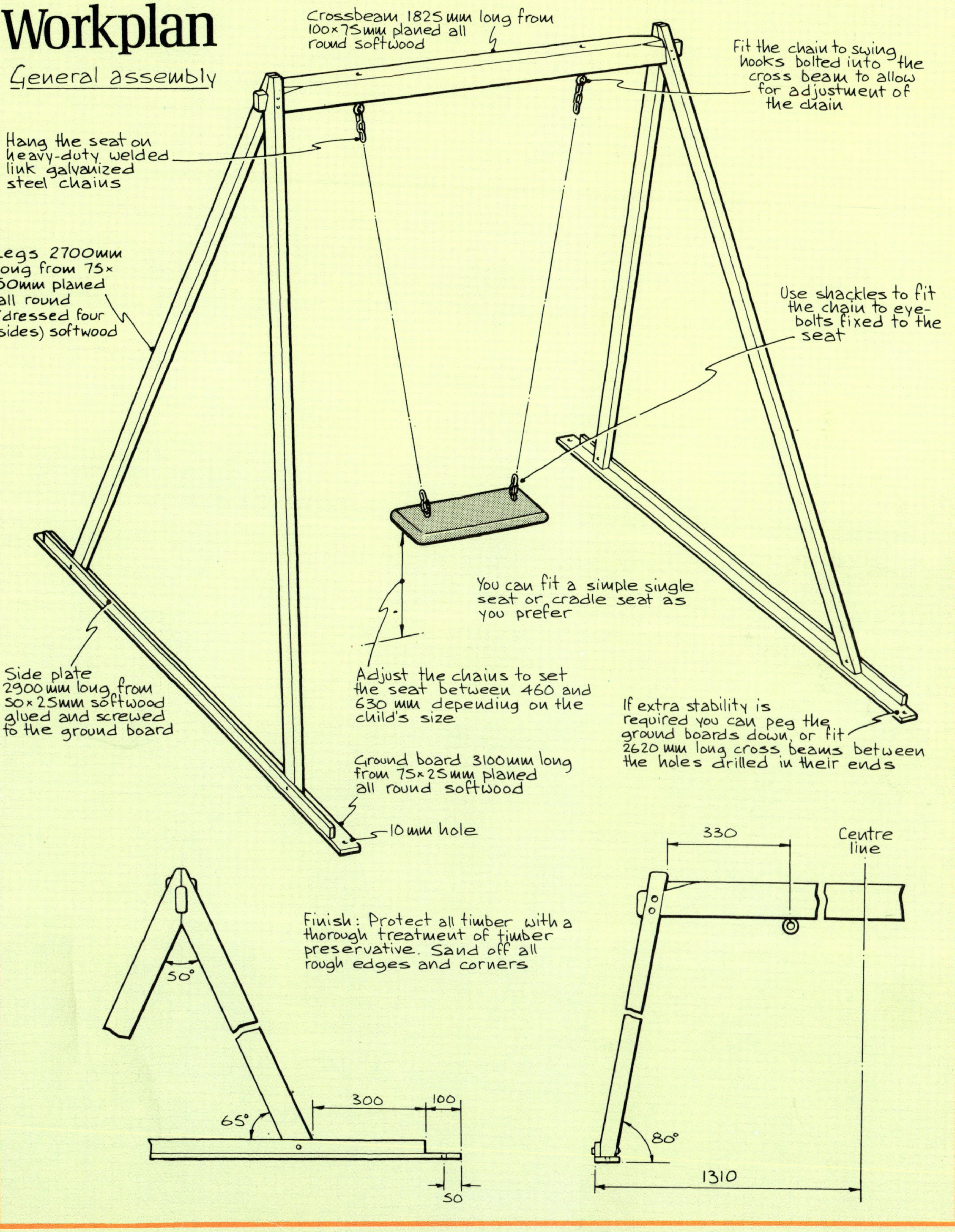

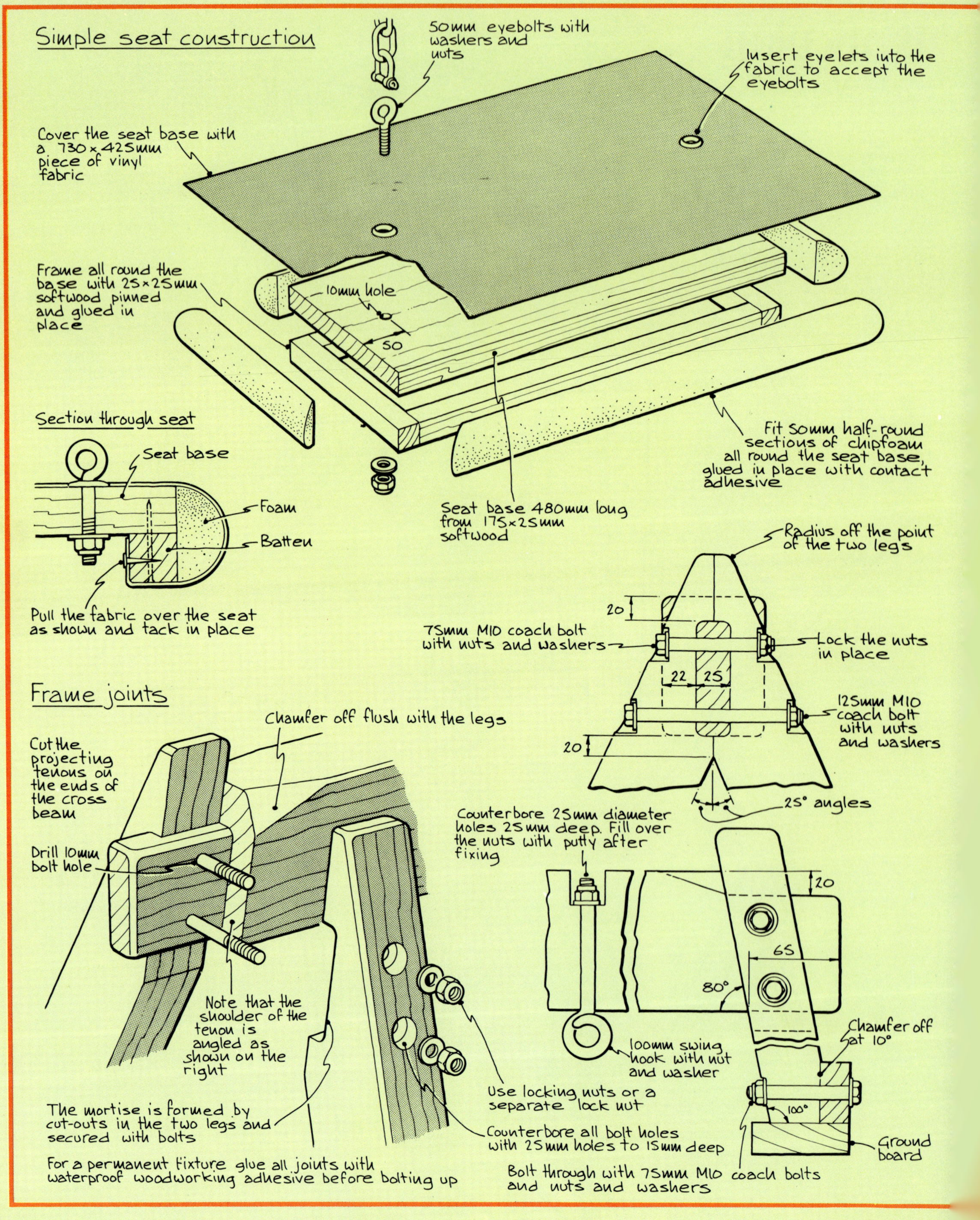

Simple seat construction
50mm eyebolts with washers and nuts
Insert eyelets into the fabric to accept the eyebolts
Cover the seat base with a 730 × 425mm piece of vinyl fabric
Frame all round the base with 25×25mm softwood pinned and glued in place
10mm hole
50
Section through seat
Seat base
Foam
Batten
Pull the fabric over the seat as shown and tack in place
Fit 50mm half-round sections of chipfoam all round the seat base, glued in place with contact adhesive
Seat base 480mm long from 175×25mm softwood
Radius off the point of the two legs
20
75mm M10 coach bolt with nuts and washers
Lock the nuts in place
22
25
125mm M10 coach bolt with nuts and washers
20
25° angles
Frame joints
Chamfer off flush with the legs
Cut the projecting tenons on the ends of the cross beam
Drill 10mm bolt hole
Note that the shoulder of the tenon is angled as shown on the right
The mortise is formed by cut-outs in the two legs and secured with bolts
For a permanent fixture glue all joints with waterproof woodworking adhesive before bolting up
Use locking nuts or a separate lock nut
Counterbore all bolt holes with 25mm holes to 15mm deep
Counterbore 25mm diameter holes 25mm deep. Fill over the nuts with putty after fixing
20
65
80°
100mm swing hook with nut and washer
Chamfer off at 10°
100°
Ground board
Bolt through with 75mm M10 coach bolts and nuts and washers

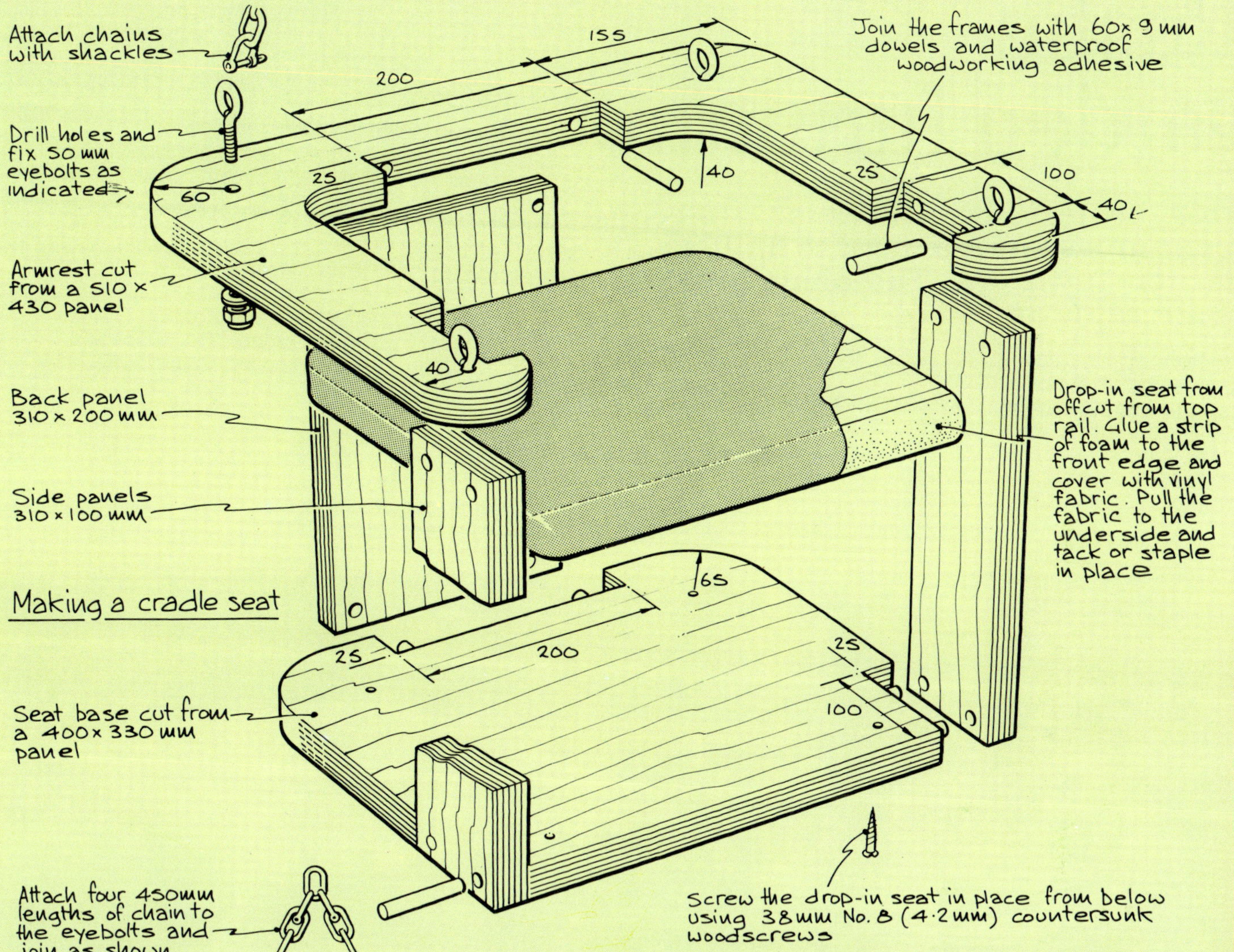

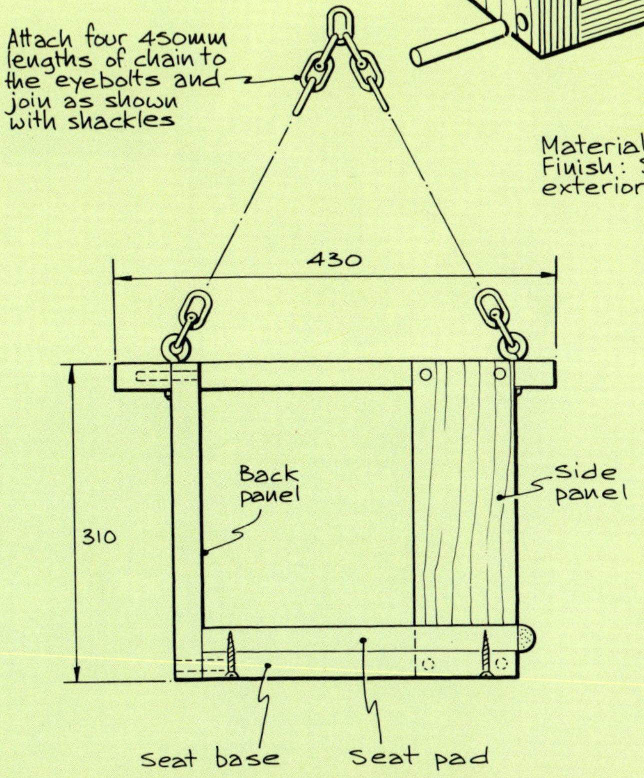

Materials: Cut all parts from 25mm plywood.
Finish: Seal all timber parts with at least two coats of exterior polyurethane lacquer

Cutting list
All sizes are in millimetres. Timber is planed all round, PAR (dressed four sides, D4S)

Part	Material	No.	Size
legs	75 × 50mm softwood (PAR)	4	2700mm
crossbeam	100 × 75mm softwood (PAR)	1	1825mm
ground boards	75 × 25mm softwood (PAR)	2	3100mm
side plates	50 × 25mm softwood (PAR)	2	2900mm
seat base	175 × 25mm softwood (PAR)	1	480mm
Cradle seat			
arms	25mm plywood	1	510 × 430mm
seat	25mm plywood	1	400 × 330mm
back	25mm plywood	1	310 × 200mm
sides	25mm plywood	2	310 × 100mm

Additional materials: Coach bolts, eyebolts, swing hooks, plastic foam (high density), chain, shackles, vinyl fabric, tacks
Finish: Timber preservative

Rustic garden furniture

This project introduces all the constructional techniques you will need to build traditional-style garden furniture. The plans give details of this chair, table and stool

Rustic furniture is ideal for any garden. It is simple and cheap to build, and the natural timbers harmonize perfectly with their surroundings.

The material used throughout is rustic larch poles, with the small side branches removed, but the bark left on. You can buy these from some timber yards, particularly in country districts, or from gardening centres. If you have some trees you want to prune or cut down, you can even use your own materials.

Because it is an untrimmed natural material, the poles have an irregular section, and vary in diameter. All sizes given in the working drawings are therefore approximate, and some dimensions will have to be judged by eye during construction. A little roughness, however, will add to the rustic charm.

Start by selecting timbers of approximately the right dimensions and length for all the parts needed. Cut the main structural members–such as legs and top rails to length.

The main tools you will need are a coarse cross-cut saw, a hammer and drill with a large diameter wood bit. An axe is also useful for trimming and making notched or halving joints.

All the joints are very simple, being variations on simple butts, housings and half-laps, and are held by nails. Galvanized nails will last better.

Start by making up main frames and tops, then join them and add the smaller braces, making all joints as shown in the plans. You can flatten the top boards with an axe and a coarse planer-file.

Cutting list (stool)
All sizes are in millimetres. All parts are cut from rustic larch poles. Dimensions are approximate due to the variation in the material.

Part	Pole diameter	No.	Size
legs	50mm	4	400mm
cross rails	35mm	2	400mm
braces	35mm	2	500mm
top rails	55mm	approx. 7	400mm

Additional materials: Round wire common nails in various sizes 75–150mm

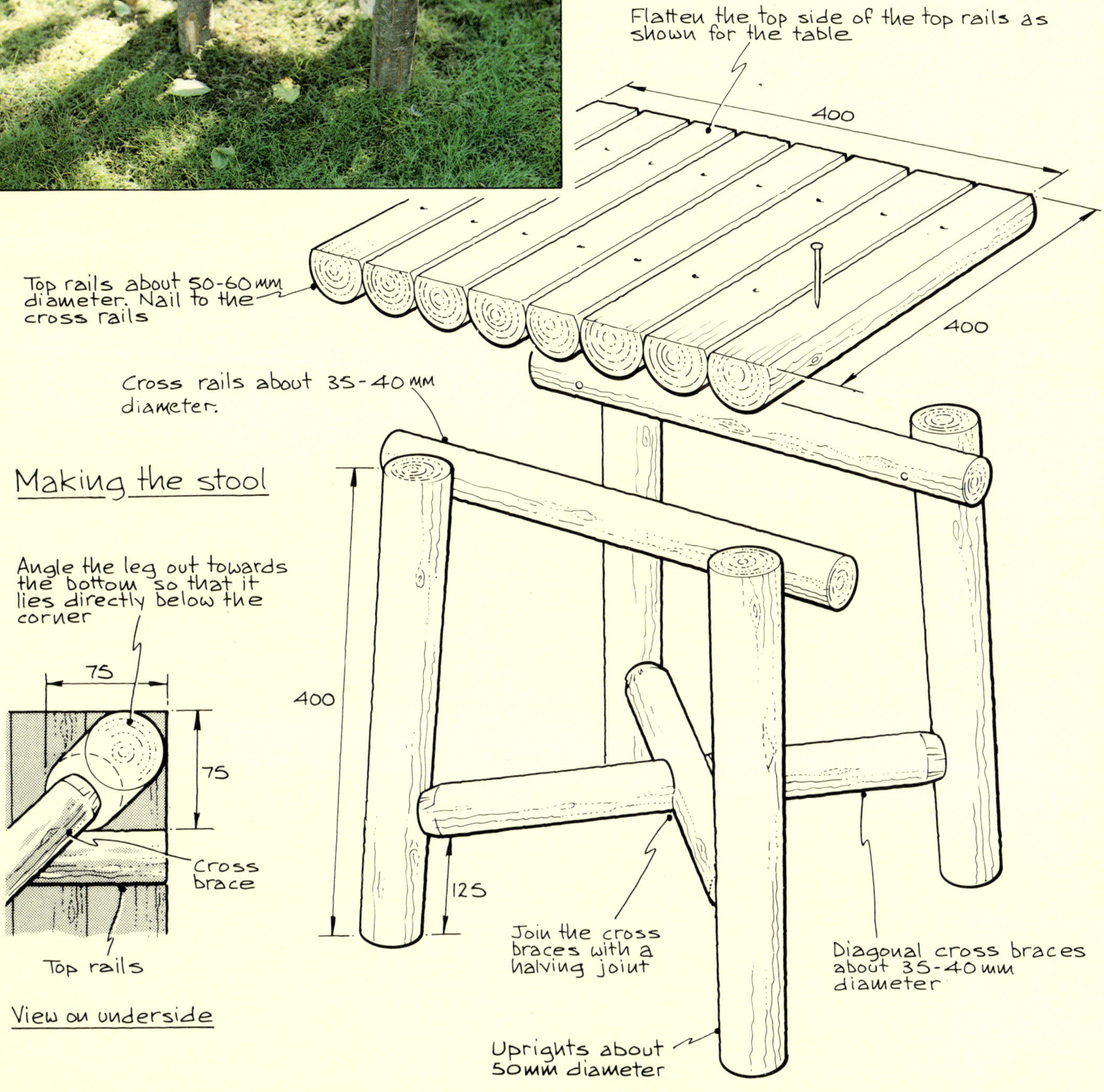

Workplan

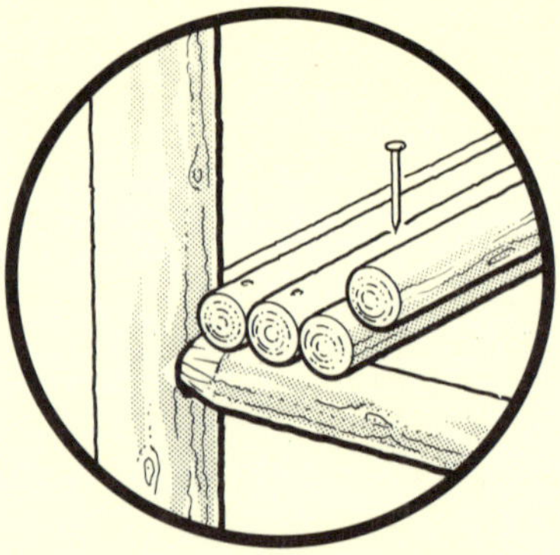
Join the seat rails as shown with simple butt joints. Use nails which will project through the rail by at least 25mm. If any nails project right through the side rail, the ends must be clenched over
N.B. The construction will be more durable if all nails used are galvanized, as these will not rust so quickly

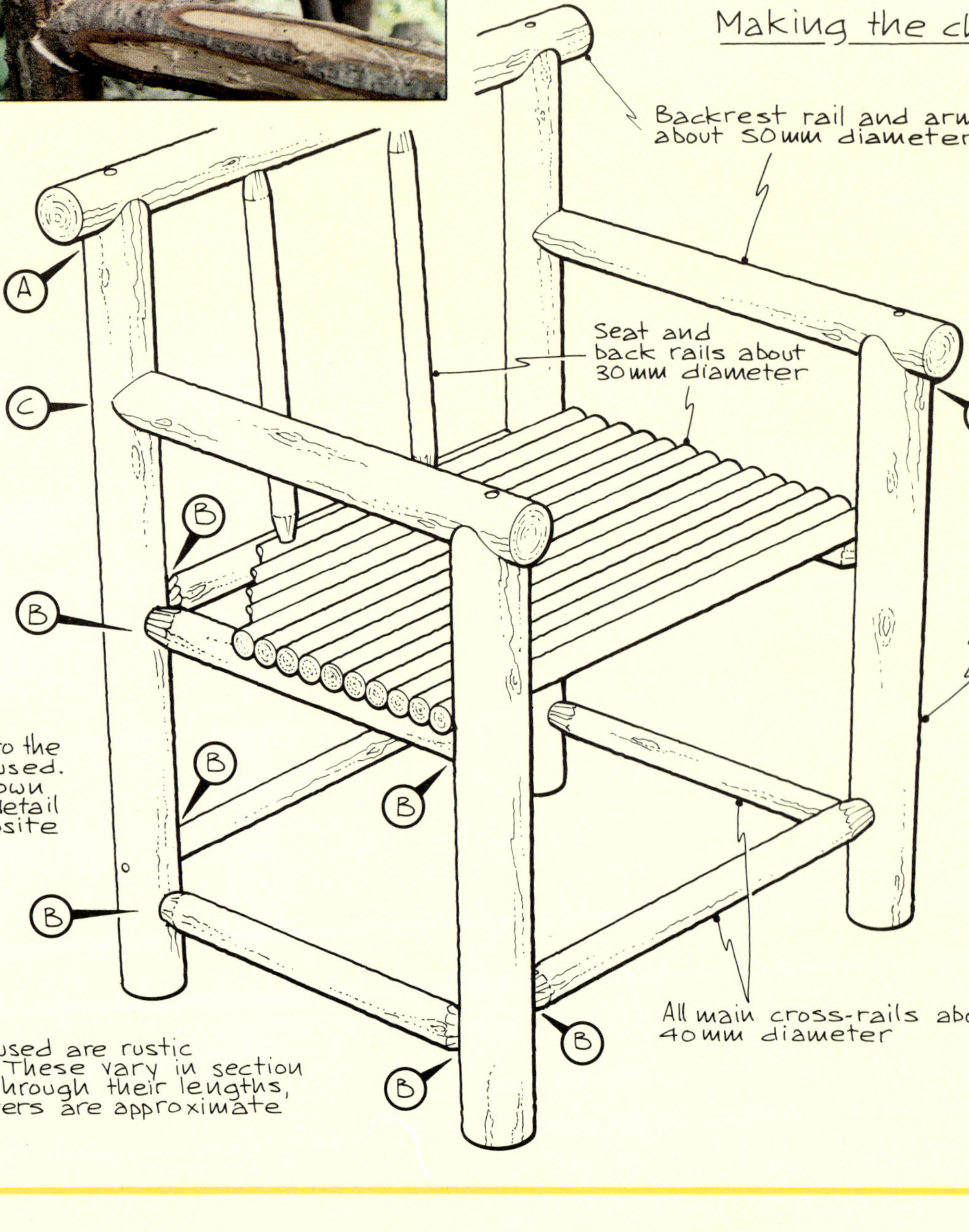
Making the chair
Backrest rail and arm rail about 50mm diameter
Seat and back rails about 30mm diameter
Uprights about 65-75mm diameter
A
A
C
B
B
B
B
B
B
B
The letters in circles refer to the type of joint used. These are shown in the small detail drawings opposite
All main cross-rails about 40mm diameter
All materials used are rustic larch poles. These vary in section and taper through their lengths, so all diameters are approximate

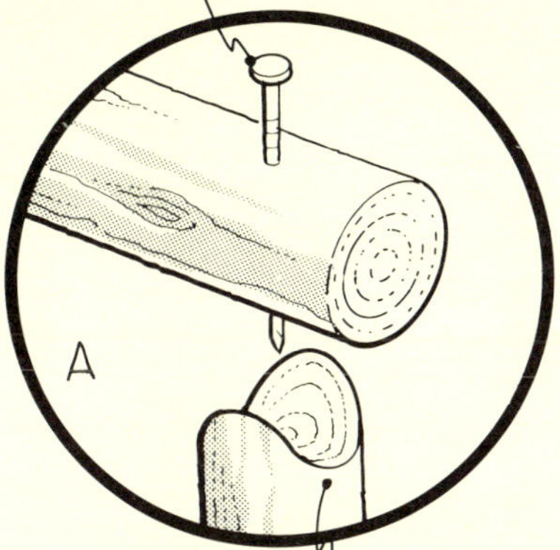

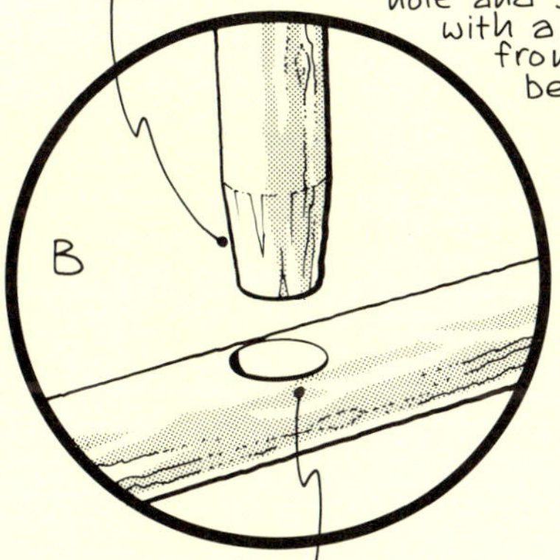

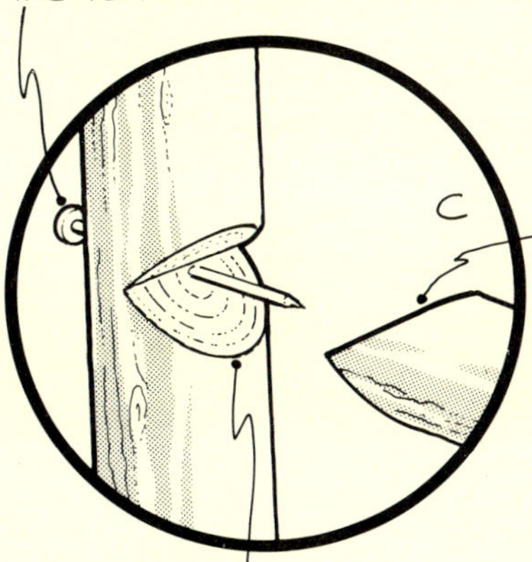

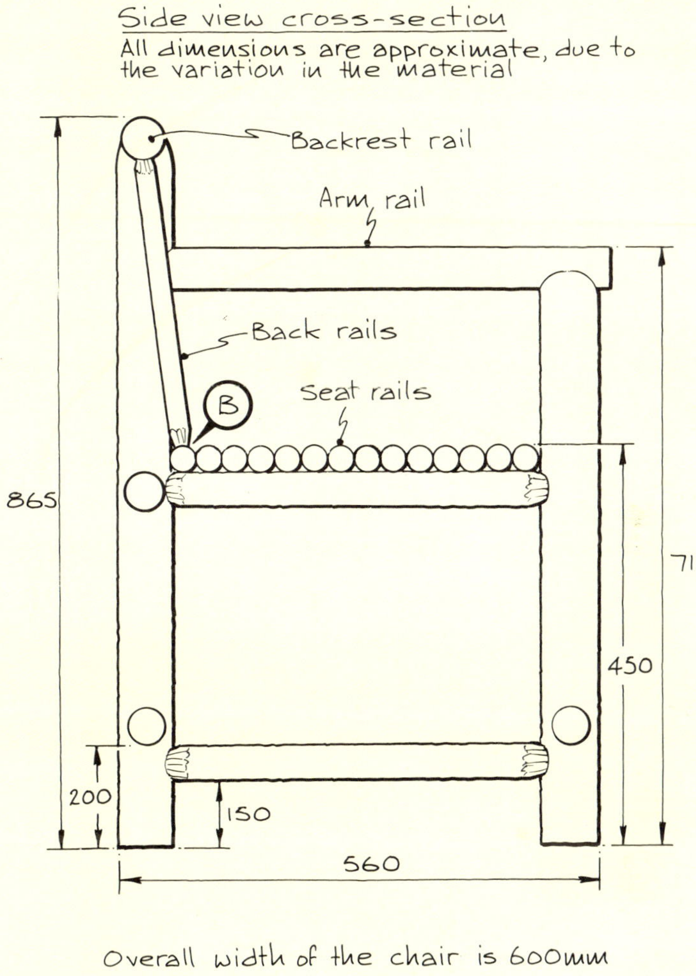

Cutting list (chair)
All sizes are in millimetres. All parts are cut from rustic larch poles. Dimensions are approximate due to the variation in the material.

Part	Pole diameter	No.	Size
back legs	70mm	2	850mm
front legs	70mm	2	700mm
backrest rail	50mm	1	600mm
arm rails	50mm	2	500mm
back rails	30mm	2	400mm
cross rails	40mm	3	500mm
side rails	40mm	4	450mm
seat rails	30mm	approx. 11	600mm

Additional materials: Round wire common nails in various sizes 75–150mm

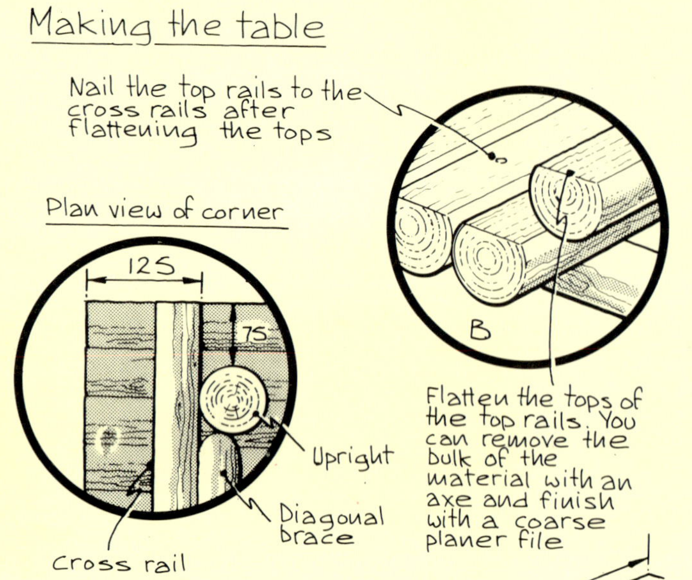

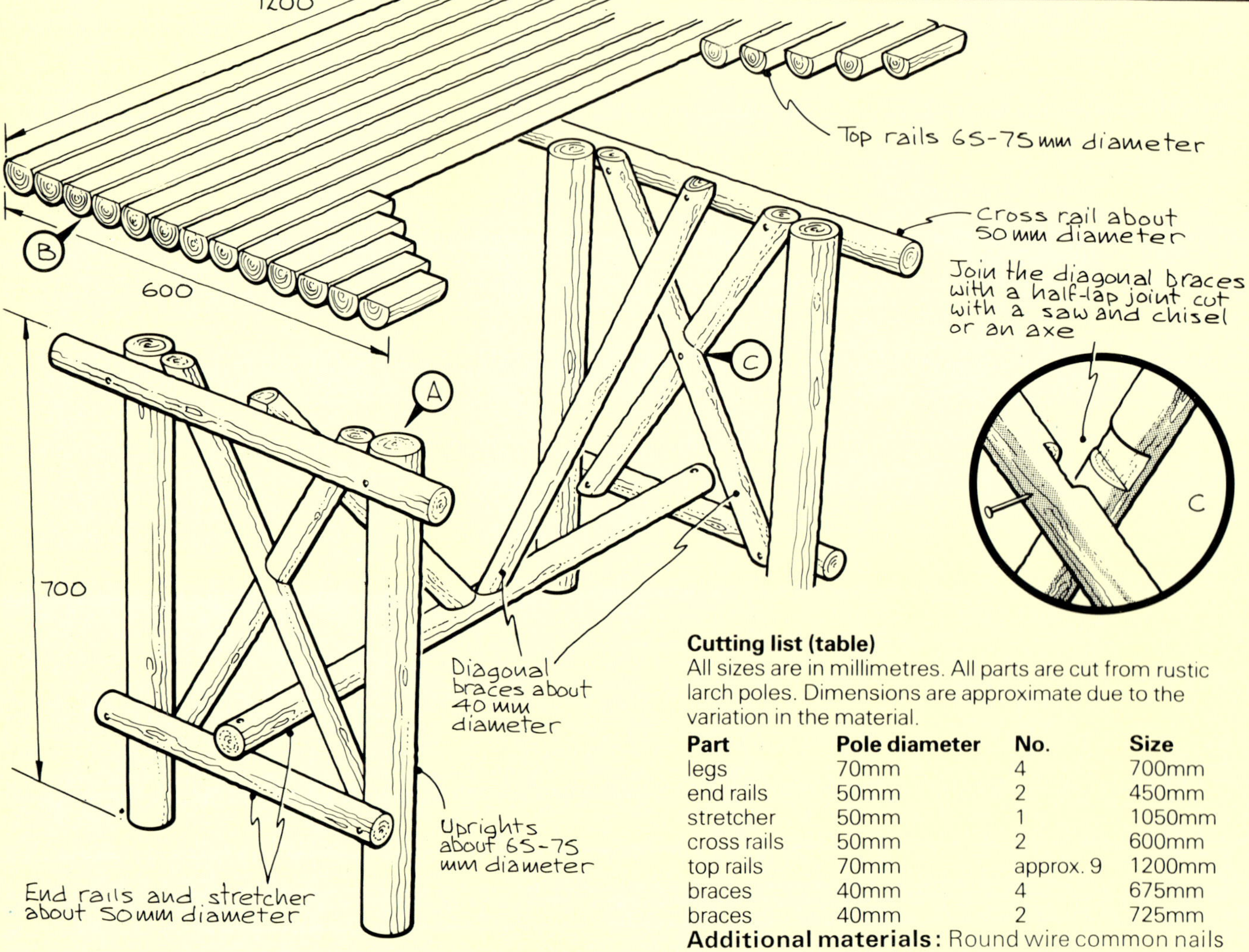

Cutting list (table)

All sizes are in millimetres. All parts are cut from rustic larch poles. Dimensions are approximate due to the variation in the material.

Part	Pole diameter	No.	Size
legs	70mm	4	700mm
end rails	50mm	2	450mm
stretcher	50mm	1	1050mm
cross rails	50mm	2	600mm
top rails	70mm	approx. 9	1200mm
braces	40mm	4	675mm
braces	40mm	2	725mm

Additional materials: Round wire common nails in various sizes 75–150mm

Garden furniture

Gardens are pleasant places to be, whether they are large and rambling or small and elegant. But add some garden furniture and your garden becomes an outdoor living area, adding an extra dimension to your home

Below: *A built-in brick bench seat and barbecue grill uses the minimum of space and provides the ideal barbecue area for a small town garden*
Bottom: *Simple, yet practical garden furniture can be created quite easily using natural bricks and stone slabs*

One of the joys of having your own garden is the simple pleasure of sitting out and relaxing in it in the evenings or at weekends. It does not have to be a huge garden – indeed, a tiny courtyard in the city can be just as pleasant a haven as a large estate in the country. The vital ingredient in either case is somewhere comfortable to sit – whether you just want to perch for a few minutes or relax for an hour or more – with a table on which to stand a glass, a plate of food, or a book.

General considerations

There is a wide choice of garden furniture available nowadays, ranging from simple deckchairs to elegant cushioned sun loungers with matching tables and sunshades. But perhaps the first thing you need to consider is whether you want your garden furniture to be permanent outdoor fixtures or units which are light and portable, to be stored away and brought out only when needed.

Of course, many people prefer to take their favourite chair from the house into the garden and this is fine if it simply means carrying the chair through the garden door. However, if your seating area is any distance from the house, then the portering element becomes less desirable and a permanent outdoor seat might be a more practical choice.

The style of your garden will to some extent dictate your choice of furniture. For example, a pleasantly informal, if not overgrown, garden is quite the wrong setting for elegant sun loungers. Similarly, a formal patio behind a contemporary-style house will look equally wrong with rustic benches.

Although most homes have a paved or other solid surface somewhere in the garden where tables and chairs can be placed, many people prefer to have their seating arrangements on the lawn. And here, the softness of the ground must be borne in mind when it comes to choosing styles and materials.

All wooden garden furniture is suitable for use on lawns as well as on paved surfaces, although it may be worth bridging adjacent pairs of legs with a batten nailed to the feet to help spread the load on soft lawns, so that the legs do not sink in and damage the turf. Metal furniture is generally heavier, with smaller section legs that tend to dig in even more in soft ground. It is therefore best confined to paved areas.

In any event, all furniture that stands on a lawn should be moved around at regular intervals to avoid marking or even killing the grass beneath it.

Another point to consider is the use to which your furniture will be put. You may want something simple like an upright seat or bench for occasional use, or something more elaborate where you can lie and sunbathe for hours in complete comfort. On the other hand, you may like to extend your office outdoors, and work in the fresh air, in which case you may feel it is worth providing some sort of shade and wind shelter as well.

Above: *Sections cut from a variety of tree trunks can provide unusual seating arrangements which are impervious to all types of weather*

Materials

If you decide on the type of garden furniture which may be kept in the house until it is needed, then your choice of materials is almost unlimited. A wide range of materials may also be stored safely in an unheated shed, summer house or garage, although any upholstery should at least be damp-proof.

Garden furniture which is to remain out of doors all year round must, naturally, be completely weatherproof. This means it should be able to stand up to wind, rain, frost and snow as well as the heat of the sun, without deteriorating in performance or appearance.

Natural timber, whether used rough or finished, is perhaps the finest material for outdoor furniture of all types. It is strong, durable, weathers well and blends with any type of garden according to the way it is fashioned and finished.

When choosing timber furniture it is worth bearing in mind that some woods are more durable than others. In general terms, hardwoods such as oak, elm, beech and teak are better than softwoods such as pine. However, cedar is a notable hard-wearing exception among the softwoods, which normally need preservative treatment if left permanently outside.

Rough, unfinished rustic timber may be good to look at, but it can also be uncomfortable to sit on for any length of time, and can snag clothes and cause

Below: *A permanently-placed wrought iron garden seat teams well with lightweight tubular tables and chairs brought out for summer picnics*

Above: *A sundeck with a touch of luxury, yet a relatively simple do-it-yourself project. Old floorboards treated with preservative will help cut costs* !

splinters. It also has a tendency to grow discolouring surface moulds in time, although rustic wood needs little or no maintenance providing it is well jointed and does not contain metal fixings that can rust or break.

Planed wood, on the other hand, must be jointed with care otherwise water may accumulate in the joints and permit rot to set in. For the same reason flat surfaces which allow water puddles to form should also be avoided.

The surface finishing of wood furniture also raises one or two points. Oil-based finishes should be avoided as they can stain clothes, while paint and varnish will not last long on furniture left permanently out of doors unless it receives regular attention. A natural or stained finish needs the least maintenance and carefully-selected hardwood such as teak, or a softwood like cedar, will weather to a pleasant grey colour when left unfinished.

The problem with using many metals for garden furniture is rust, which soon ruins the appearance of the framework and eventually destroys it. Even galvanizing, painting or the provision of plastic coatings will not provide permanent protection on mild steel furniture, since the first chip or scratch allows rust to gain a foothold and this quickly spreads underneath the coating. However, wrought iron – which rusts only superficially – is a popular choice for garden use.

Rust is not a problem with modern aluminium furniture, whether of tubular construction or of the more substantial cast type. And because aluminium is very light, units made from it are far easier to lift and move around.

Natural or man-made paving slabs set on a brick or stone base can make very attractive permanently-sited seats and tables which will, quite literally, last a lifetime. These can either be free-standing or built into a wall.

Styles and designs

The most popular form of permanent garden furniture is probably the two- or three-seater wooden bench, complete with arms and a back. Its slotted construction and sturdy frame minimize the effects of the weather, and if well designed, such furniture can be extremely relaxing and comfortable.

A lightweight alternative is the simple 'school bench' which is ideal for children and very useful when used in conjunction with a simple table for serving meals.

For sun worshippers, a simple and versatile lounger can be created using a slatted bench, with one end hinged so that it can be raised slightly.

For real luxury there are various types of Continental style loungers with padded cushions which can be removed and stored away while the framework remains permanently outside. And as well as sun loungers, you can get matching tables, upright chairs and sunshades to create a very attractive, if expensive outdoor dining arrangement.

Apart from the traditional designs, you

Left: *A basement garden with plenty of greenery provides a pleasant and secluded seating area with simple deckchairs and cane furniture*

might also consider some of the more unusual ideas for garden furniture. For instance, you can create a very simple bucket seat by cutting down a wooden barrel and setting a circle of wood into the middle of it. This forms the seat while half the upper part of the barrel forms the back. Simply add a colourful round cushion for comfort. Several of these could form an inexpensive garden set. Similarly, large logs, cut from trees 300mm or so in diameter make useful occasional seating, and these can be left out in all weathers.

If you have substantial trees in your garden, then swing seats can be great fun and most relaxing. There are simple one-seater types or more elaborate multi-seater versions. And if you have the patience to master the knack of getting into it, a hammock can be supremely comfortable. On the other hand, if you have room, you can also buy free-standing swing seats complete with sun shades.

Below: *Bucket chairs with padded seats can be brought into the garden to provide comfort while the dining set can be left permanently outside*

Barbecues

Once you have decided on your garden furniture, an obvious extension of the garden as 'living' room is the provision of a barbecue for parties and for evening or weekend meals.

Of course in countries where the climate is unreliable it may be difficult to justify the expense of building a permanent, tailor-made barbecue installation. But there are many relatively inexpensive portable types available and the sheer joy of barbecue entertaining more than justifies the expense and personal effort.

A very simple barbecue can be assembled in minutes from concrete blocks, a paving slab and a sheet of rigid metal mesh. The paving slab forms the hearth, while the other blocks shield it from the breeze and provide support for the grill, which is placed above the charcoal bed.

This type of barbecue can be set up almost anywhere on the patio or lawn and may be stored away in the garage or garden shed when not in use. This concept can be as flexible as you wish, to cater for a handful of people or a large gathering – you simply build a larger hearth. If you have more blocks, the barbecue can be raised to waist level for easier access, or the hearths can be placed at the edge of raised flowerbeds to bring them up to something approaching waist height.

When setting up your barbecue, do take care to pick a spot out of the breeze where the ground is level and where there are no overhanging trees. If you stay fairly close to the house, there will be less fetching and carrying of food and supplies – but check the direction of the wind to avoid smoke billowing towards the house.

Deckchair covers

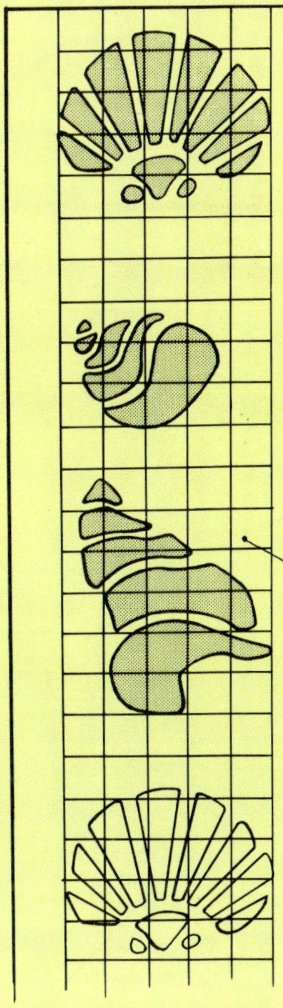

Overall size of the canvas after hemming is 1350 x 420 mm.

For the applique design, draw up 30 mm squares on a piece of pattern paper. Transfer the strawberry design to the paper. Cut out the two pieces of the design from red and green fabric. Pin in position as shown on the canvas. To stitch in position, use a sewing machine set to a wide, close stitch to overstitch the edges of the fabric all round. Use matching threads for each fabric.

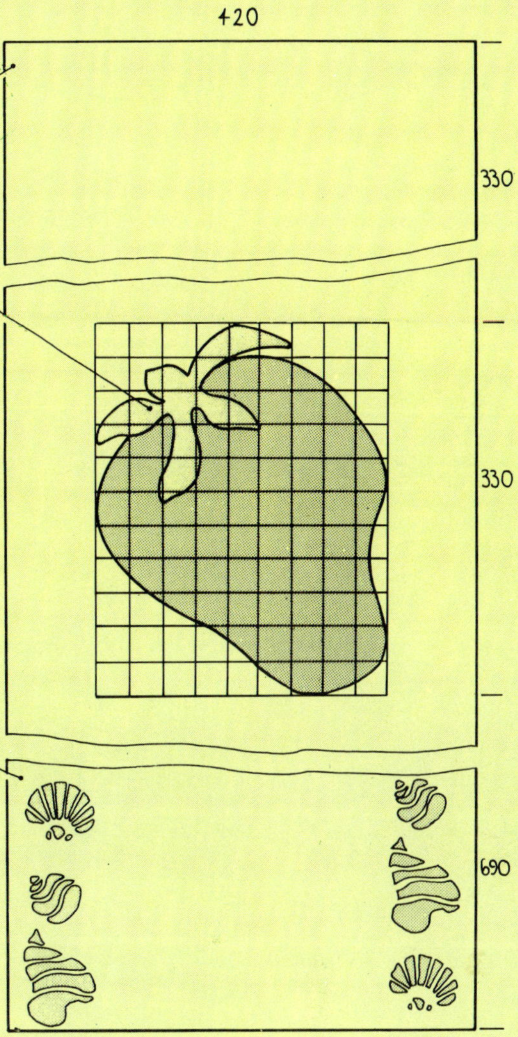

For stencilled designs, copy this pattern on to a piece of paper measuring around 300 x 75 mm. Draw up with 13 mm squares, then transfer the pattern. Cut out the shaded areas with a sharp knife to create the stencil. Stretch your canvas over a flat surface and pin or tape the stencil to it inset by 20 mm from the edge. Paint through the design using fabric paint and a stencil brush. Move the stencil along the fabric to create a repeated pattern.

Hem each side of the deckchair canvas to 15 mm.

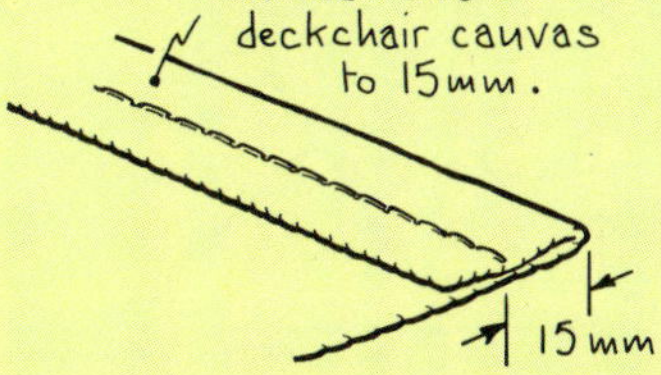

Fit the canvas to a ready-made deckchair frame as shown. Loop it over the top and bottom rails of the frame and secure with tacks, decorative upholstery nails or staples.

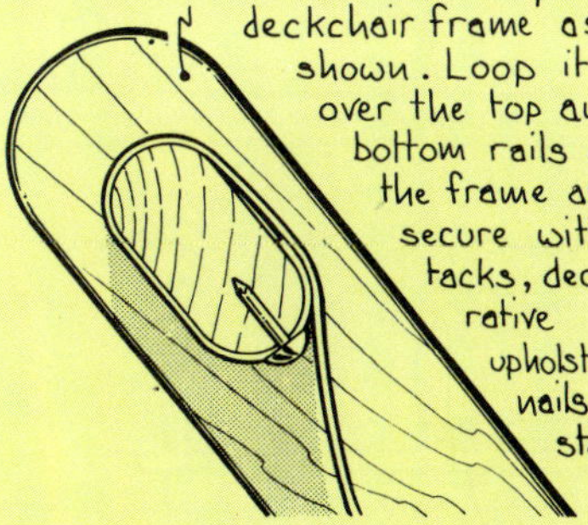

Although deckchair canvas is available in a wide range of colours and patterns, these two ideas will allow you to create something really different.

Start with a plain wooden deckchair frame. You can buy these new, or strip an old frame for recovering. You will also need a length of plain coloured deckchair canvas.

Follow the working drawings to trace up patterns and add either an appliqué or a stencilled design to the canvas before you fix it to the frame.

Make a sun lounger

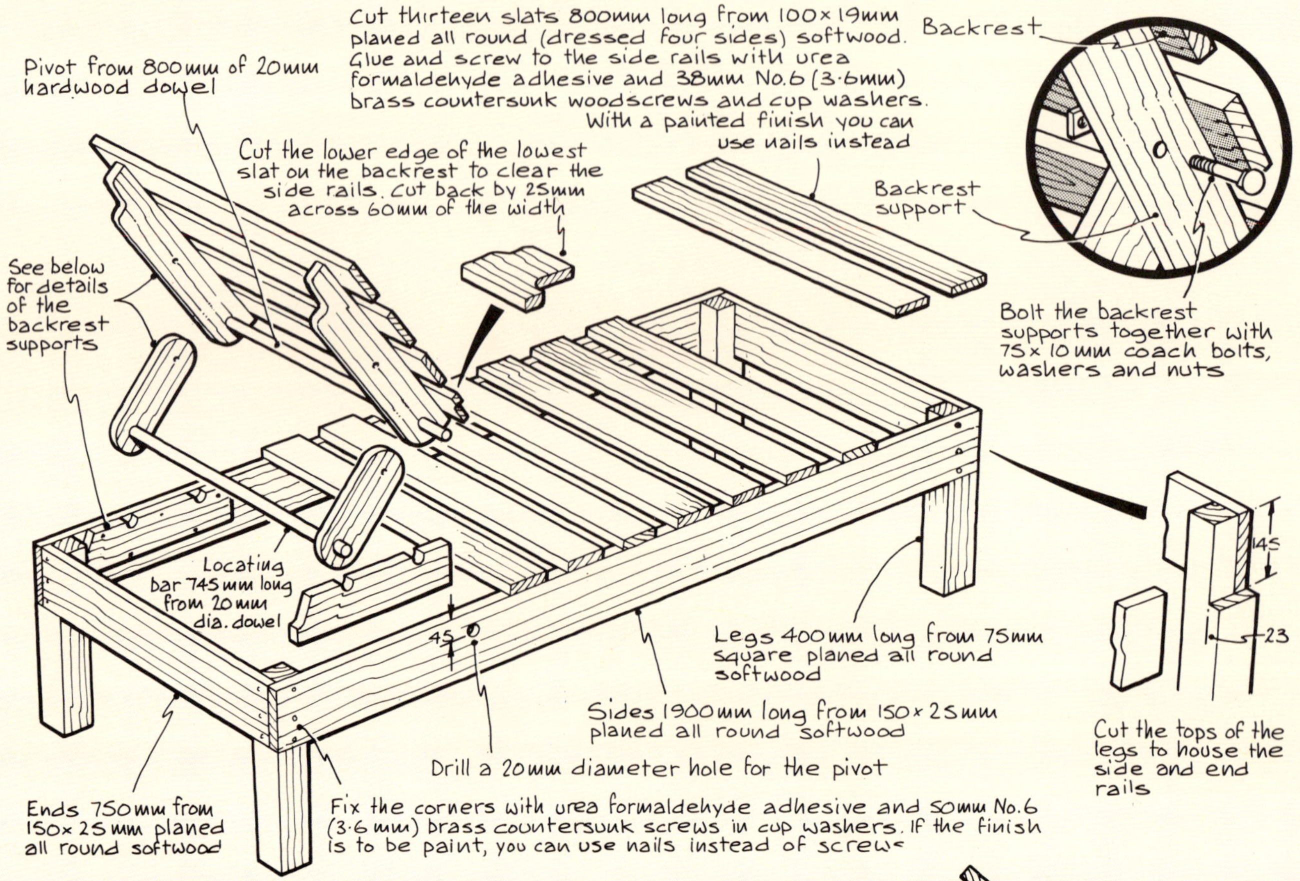

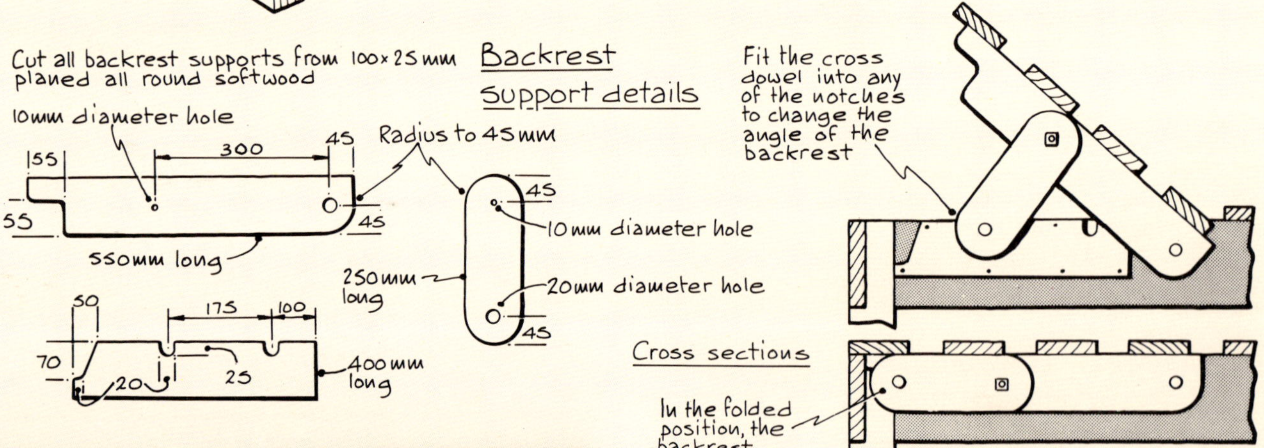

Finish: Use either an exterior quality lacquer for a natural finish, or primer, undercoat and gloss paint for a painted one

Chapter 4
BUILDING IN THE GARDEN

Which concrete?

Although concrete and mortar are two of the most basic building materials, they often give rise to a great deal of confusion. Deciding on which mix to use and what materials you need is frequently the hardest part.

Concrete

Concrete is a mixture of water and two dry ingredients: a matrix or binder, usually Portland cement, and aggregate. Portland cement comes in bags (usually 50kg in the UK) and is grey or white. The white type is more expensive but gives a better looking finish to the concrete, especially when colour additives are used (see below).

Aggregate is a term about which there is often confusion. Generally, it describes anything from fine sand, through shingle and river gravel, to small pebbles. But when builders speak of concrete 'mixes', they sometimes take the sand separately and call the gravel component 'large aggregate'. Hence a typical concrete mix would be 1 : 2 : 3, meaning one part cement to two parts sand to three parts gravel.

The size of the particles of gravel goes a long way towards determining the exact nature of a particular concrete mix. For example, one commonly used type of aggregate contains particles up to about 18mm or so in size, and this may be described as '18mm aggregate', or simply 'coarse aggregate'. This sort of aggregate, when mixed with cement and sharp sand, should give a concrete which is suitable for most DIY jobs.

Above: *The 'squeeze test' is a simple method for testing the consistency of your concrete. The water content is correct when the mix moulds to the shape of your palm without oozing or crumbling.*

Table 1 – general purpose concrete mixes

	Portland cement	Sharp sand	Coarse aggregate	Combined aggregate	Applications
MIX A	1 :	2½ :	4		Foundations, drives and floor slabs, fence post setting, any small job which requires a 75mm thickness of concrete or over
	1 :			5–6	
MIX B	1 :	2 :	3		Stronger than Mix A. For paths, pools, steps and jobs calling for a concrete thickness of less than 75mm
	1 :			3.75	

But it is far more convenient for the DIY enthusiast to buy the sand and gravel ready mixed as '18mm all-in ballast' or 'combined aggregate'.

All-in ballast may be available in

bags but if more than $0.25m^3$ is required, it is much cheaper to buy it in loose bulk form. When mixed in the proportions of 1 (cement) to 6 (ballast), it gives the ideal general purpose concrete mix for the DIY enthusiast (see table 1).

In the finer mixes of concrete used for some rendering and screeding jobs the large aggregate is replaced by 9–10mm gravel mixed with sand, or by sharp sand used on its own. At this stage, they are better referred to as mortar mixes.

Water content

The water content of concrete is a critical factor, but one for which there are unfortunately no hard and fast rules for the DIY person. Aggregate is usually damp when you buy it, so it is impossible to generalize.

The most useful rule of thumb is to add only as much water as you need to bind the dry ingredients together. Do this a little at a time, mixing as you go and taking great care not to leave any puddles in the mix.

Of the many tests you can do to find out whether the water content is right, the 'squeeze test' is perhaps the most convenient. Take two handfuls of the mixture and squeeze them tightly into a ball in your hands. If the ball stays together when you open your hands, the mix is about right. If it crumbles, add fractionally more water and try again. If the concrete is slimy and slips through your fingers, you have no choice but to add more dry ingredients.

Concrete additives

Although most concrete mixtures contain only cement, water and aggregates, it is sometimes necessary to include additives or admixtures to give the mix special qualities. For example, ready-mixed cement may contain an air-entrained admixture: particularly useful in Canada to protect the concrete from frost damage. Admixtures must be used properly, or they may ruin the mix completely. Obtain, and follow, manufacturers' or suppliers' advice carefully: do not add anything unless you are sure you need to.

Try, wherever possible, to avoid concreting in cold weather. If you must, get advice on what, if anything, you should add to the mix.

Concrete can be coloured by using a special type of aggregate or cement—only your supplier can advise on this—by adding pigment, or by painting the finished concrete with special colouring dyes which soak the surface.

Table 2–mortar mixes

Applications	Portland cement	Non-hydraulic lime	Builders' sand	Sharp sand	Plasticizer	Remarks
External walls and outer	1	1	5–6		×	
leaves of cavity walls	1		5–6		√	
above DPC	1	2	8–9		×	for calcium/silicate
	1		7–8		√	bricks—summer use only
External walls below DPC	1	½	4–4.5		×	
External free-standing walls	1		3–4		√	
Internal walls, inner	1	1	5–6		×	winter or summer
leaf of cavity walls	1		5–6		√	use
	1	2	8–9		×	summer use only
	1		7–8		√	
Copings & sills, also	1	0.25		3	×	
retaining wall and	1	0.5		3–4	√	calcium/silicate bricks
engineering bricks	1	0.5		4–4.5	×	
Parapets and domestic	1	1	5–6		×	
chimneys (rendered)	1		5–6		√	
	1	2	8–9		×	calcium/silicate bricks
	1		7–8		√	summer use only
Parapets and domestic	1	0.25	3		×	winter use only,
chimneys (not rendered)	1	1	5–6		×	not calcium bricks
	1		5–6		√	
Joints for paving	1		3–4		√	use fine sand
Bedding for paving	1			3	×	large and small slabs
	1			3–4	×	to take light traffic
		1		8	×	large slabs pedestrian
	1			10	×	traffic only

Above: *Typical mortar mixes for various applications. The figures refer to the proportions of each ingredient used. A tick in the plasticizer column indicates that the use of this additive is permissible*

Calculating quantities

When you are concreting, it is vital to have an adequate supply of materials with you: there is nothing more annoying than having to stop half way through a job in order to buy more.

Begin by finding out the volume of mixed concrete you need. This is simply done by multiplying the area to be concreted by the depth of concrete required and adding on about 10 percent for wastage. For example, on a drive 6m x 3m, the area is $18m^2$. If it is to be covered to a depth of 100mm you get $1.8m^3$ ($18m^2$ x 0.1m). Adding on 10 percent for wastage gives you a final requirement of about $2m^3$.

If the area is irregularly shaped, draw a scale plan of it on graph paper. Find out the area of one square, multiply this by the number of whole squares then make an estimate on the area covered by the part-squares. Be generous in your estimates: remember that it is better to have too much

1 *Start the hand-mixing sequence by adding cement to the coarse and fine aggregate. Try and keep the ingredients together*

Applications	Portland cement	Non-hydraulic lime	Builders' sand	Sharp sand	Plasticizer	Remarks
Pointing for brickwork	1		2		×	engineering bricks
	1	2	8		×	other bricks
	1		4		√	
Floor screeds	1			3	×	waterproofer/hardener may be added
Insulating floor screed	1				×	6 parts vermiculite (50kg cement + 2 × 110 litre bags vermiculite) lay 36–50mm thick
Topping screed for vermiculite substrate	1			4	×	
Repairing flaunchings round chimney pots	1	1		6	×	
	1			3	×	
Rendering, internal first coat	2		3	3	√	change plasticizer for waterproofer/hardener to prevent damp
subsequent coats	2		6	6	√	
Internal walls all coats	2		6	6	√	
	1	2	4.5	4.5	×	
Rendering, external first coat	2		3	3	×	plus waterproofer/hardener
subsequent coats	2		4.5	4.5	√	
Hard brick	1	2	4.5	4.5	×	

NB If colouring is added, a different mix may be required; follow colour manufacturer's instructions exactly.
Where alternative proportions of sand are given they refer to the grade of sand used. Use lower limit if sand is either coarse or fine, higher if sand is evenly graded.

2 Mix the dry ingredients thoroughly using a suitable spade. Fold the mix over as you add from the edge to the middle

3 Form a crater in the dry pile and add most of the water. Until you have some experience of mixing, add this in stages

4 Mix the material to an even consistency and colour, again folding edge mix into the centre so all the dry mix is used

5 Use a sprinkling water can to add water—very gradually—until the consistency and workability seems right

concrete than too little. Use any residue for odd repairs.

Having decided on your volume requirement, refer to table 2. This shows what quantities of dry ingredients you need to make up a specific volume of mixed concrete.

Buying concrete

Mixing concrete by hand is an extremely laborious business and for all but small quantities, is not worth the effort. This may leave you with three options: to hire a small concrete mixer, to order the concrete ready-mixed or to employ a specialist company to mix the concrete for you.

Ordering concrete ready-mixed saves you a lot of effort on really large jobs but most firms charge proportionately more for small amounts. Bear in mind that you will need access on-site for the lorry—and plenty of assistance to help lay the concrete quickly once it has been delivered. When you make your order, specify what you want the concrete for: the firm will then supply you with their most suitable mix.

For amounts between say $1m^3$ and $7m^3$ the choice is between hiring a mixer and getting a firm to mix the concrete for you on-site. The latter is preferable if there is a firm offering this service in your area and if you have enough room for their lorry. As with ready-mixed concrete, materials and advice on which mix to use both come as part of the service.

Though mixers can be hired quite cheaply from plant hire shops, using

6 *If a boot leaves a lasting impression in the mix—without oozing or crumbling—the mix is at the correct consistency*

7 *Test the workability of mortar for blockwork by seeing if it sticks to a metal float when this is held upside down*

8 *The 'squeeze test' for checking the consistency of concrete—the mix on the left is too wet, that on the right is too dry*

this method involves you in buying and arranging transport for your own supply of materials.

In the end, your choice must be based not only on how much concrete you need but also on the logistical difficulties of buying, transporting and storing it. And this is something you need to think about carefully in advance of making a decision.

Whether you are buying your own materials or ordering ready-mix, be sure to tell the supplier what you want them for. All forms of aggregate—both sand and ballast—vary widely from area to area, so your supplier will advise on the most suitable materials he has in stock. Also, remember that the larger the supplier the more likely you are to get what you want.

Storing cement

Cement deteriorates if it is stored for any length of time, so buy it in batches as required. Whether you store it indoors or outdoors, it is important to keep the cement dry and off the ground. If possible, make a timber platform and store the bags flat on this. If it is stored outdoors, keep the cement well covered with plastic sheeting to avoid any possibility of rainwater getting to it.

Keep batches separately so that old stock can be used first. Once opened, a bag of cement should be used as soon as possible. If you do have to store an opened bag, keep it in a large, dry, heavy-duty plastic bag. Never store cement next to lime or gypsum plaster.

Additions to concrete such as plasticizer are long-lasting but should be stored safely.

Mortar

Mortar differs from concrete in that it contains none of the heavier forms of aggregate such as ballast. It is simply a mixture of cement and sand.

Older forms of mortar used lime, instead of cement, to bind the sand together. This produced a flexible mortar which could take up quite large settling movements without cracking, but which had little resistance to the weather.

Cement-based mortar is much more robust. The addition of a small amount of lime or plasticizer to some mixes (see table 2) improves their flexibility and makes them easier to work with.

The cement used in mortar is Portland cement. For bricklaying and related jobs, this is mixed with a soft sand such as builders' sand. For rendering and screeding mortars, washed sharp sand is used instead.

Where lime is specified in the mix (see table 2), you may have a choice between hydraulic and non-hydraulic lime. The majority of bricklaying jobs call for the latter, which is dry or slaked and needs plenty of air around it if it is to set properly. Hydraulic lime sets under water and is therefore used in thick walls or structures which retain some moisture.

An alternative to adding plasticizer or lime is to use masonry cement, which has the correct amount of plasticizer already added. For small jobs, various dry-mixed mortar 'recipes' are also available.

As with concrete, pigments are available which colour the mortar. These are particularly useful for jobs such as repointing, where they can be used to match the mortar to the colour of the surrounding brickwork.

Mixing mortar

Mix mortar in the same way you would concrete: the dry ingredients first, then the water. Like concrete, the water content of mortar is always the most critical factor.

For bricklaying and rendering, add enough water to bring the mortar up to the consistency of thick cream. Pick a little up on your trowel, give a sharp upward shake, then turn the trowel over. If the mortar sticks to the trowel, it is of about the right consistency for ordinary bricks. For heavy block work and engineering bricks, the mix should be slightly thicker. Always bear in mind that if you are adding plasticizer to the mortar, slightly less water will be needed to reach the right consistency.

Flooring screed mixes require considerably less water. In this case, use the 'squeeze test' described above for concrete.

9 *Concrete (top) and mortar (below) differ greatly in appearance—reflecting the differences in the jobs that they do*

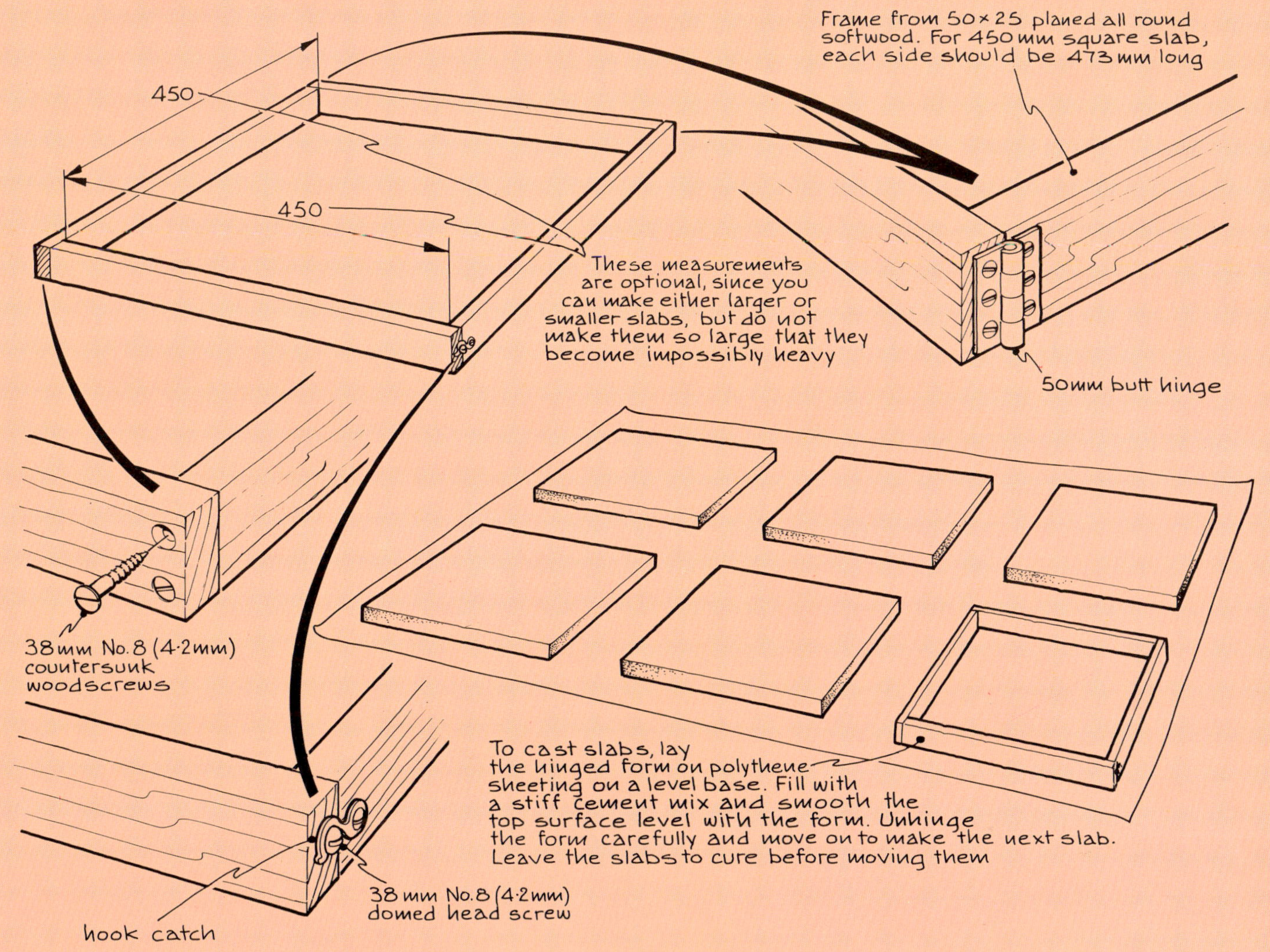

Making paving stones

Casting your own paving slabs is quite easy, and allows you to choose whatever texture or colour you want.

Make a simple hinge-apart frame like that shown. Use a stiff concrete mix that will stand up on its own without slumping. Make up enough mix for all your slabs, and cast them one after the other on a polythene sheet on a level smooth surface.

To cast coloured slabs, add concrete pigment to the mix—you will get a better colour if you use white cement.

Allow the slabs to cure fully before moving them. You can then lay the slabs on compacted sand or mortar to form a colourful path.

Concreting tools

● Machines and tools to make concreting easy ● How to break up old concrete rafts and screeds ● Compacting machines ● Types of concrete mixer ● Choosing a mixer ● Using and maintaining a mixer ● General safety precautions

As well as the smaller power tools–drills, saws, routers–which get regular use and are therefore worth buying, a wide range of larger tools is now becoming available for hire at specialist shops. These take the hard slog out of many heavier jobs and the hire charges are often very cheap when compared to the amount of time and effort saved in the process.

This part of the course deals specifically with machines to help mix and lay concrete–often the most backbreaking of tasks. Although small amounts of concrete can be mixed and laid by hand, where large quantities are concerned, it is best to enlist the aid of power equipment.

Concrete breaking

Quite often you need to break up and remove a poorly laid concrete screed in order to re-lay it properly or clear the ground ready for some other use. One way of doing this is by hand, using a sharp cold chisel and a heavy club hammer, but this would take a long time and might even be impossible in some instances.

One alternative is to use an ordinary power drill fitted with a large masonry bit to make a series of random holes at roughly 50mm intervals in the screed: on thin screeds this should weaken the structure enough to make it a lot easier to break up by hand. For tougher screeds (20-100mm thick) you could buy or hire a heavy-duty industrial drill fitted with a large diameter bit.

A. *There are plenty of tools available for hire to take the hard slog out of larger concreting jobs. A barrow type mixer like this is particularly useful*

1 *Heavy duty industrial jack hammers like this are supplied with a range of interchangeable heads, enabling you to use them for breaking or drilling*

2 *One of the most obvious uses for the jack hammer is in breaking up an old or badly laid screed. Keep the broken pieces for use as hardcore*

3 *Levelling off the site and picking out old roots and boulders is one concreting job that must still be done by hand–at least initially*

4 *Fortunately, plate tamping machines like this are available to help with the final levelling. They also compact the ground to form a solid base*

5 *Having pegged up the site and constructed suitable formwork, you can prepare the base as necessary. Here hardcore from the old screed is laid*

6 *The larger chunks of hardcore can be broken up with the jack hammer but you will probably find it just as easy to smash them with a sledge hammer*

But for really rapid concrete breaking there is no tool to compete with a jack hammer and small electrically-powered models suitable for do-it-yourself use can be hired (fig. 1). At first sight, jack hammers look rather like large industrial drills; but instead of being fitted with a bit they have a number of interchangeable 'heads', some of which are pointed, others spade-shaped rather like a cold chisel. The breaker has a vibrating up-and-down action and can force its way through practically any depth of concrete in a relatively short time.

When using a jack hammer, be sure to wear a pair of stout shoes with protective toecaps. Work systematically from one side of the screed to the other, breaking off sizeable chunks which can easily be disposed of. Push the whole machine down so that the head is forced into the concrete then, once you have broken through, pull back on the handles to loosen each chunk (fig. 2).

When the whole area has been broken up in this way the lumps can be loaded on to a wheelbarrow for disposal. You can then prepare the site as you wish. If you plan to lay a new screed, the sub-base should be thoroughly flattened first and all large rocks and vegetation removed.

Compacting machines

A compactor is a machine which flattens and consolidates hardcore and rubble bases prior to concrete pouring (fig. 7). By hand this usually takes a great deal of time and effort, so buying or hiring a compactor is well worthwhile–especially if you have a large area to cover.

The ideal compactor for home use is the type with a vibrating plate. This can be rolled across the site rather like a wheelbarrow while the plate vibrates and imparts a series of blows to the area directly underneath. It is usually unnecessary to go over the site more than two or three times to flatten it completely. Once this has been done you can prepare the area for concreting by erecting formwork (see pages 130 to 135).

Concrete mixers

For jobs requiring only a small amount of mortar or concrete it obviously makes sense to mix by hand. But larger projects where a great deal of concrete is needed can be greatly speeded up by the use of a concrete mixer.

The most suitable mixer for domestic use is the *barrow* type. This consists of a cylindrical drum (where the mixing takes place) mounted on two pneumatic or solid rubber wheels. At the rear of the mixing drum are two handles enabling the whole machine to be trundled around and tipped rather like a wheelbarrow (fig. C).

The main advantage of the barrow mixer is that it is relatively small and light, meaning that it is easy to transport in the back of a van or estate car to wherever it is needed. And once on site, you simply push it to the most convenient spot for mixing. If you are filling a footing, for example, you can move the mixer right up to the edge of the trench and deposit the mix without having to transfer it using a wheelbarrow (fig. 18).

The second type of mixer is much larger and cannot be moved around as easily as the lightweight barrow type. It consists of a fixed H-frame mounted on four wheels which carries the mixing drum (fig. C). The whole body of such a machine obviously cannot be tipped up on end when loading and unloading the drum. Instead, a large wheel mounted on the body of the mixer enables the drum to be turned to either side and a separate locking device allows you to lock it to any position (fig. C).

For many DIY jobs larger mixers can be too cumbersome: they are very difficult to move around without the assistance of at least two other people and can only be transported to the site by being towed behind a vehicle. However, on really large buildings jobs–such as building an extension–their greater capacity makes them practically the only type worth hiring.

7 *With the hardcore in more or less regularly sized pieces, you can use the plate tamper again to level and compact them into the ground*

Choosing a mixer

One of the first things to look for in a concrete mixer is load size. This tells you how much material (sand, cement, ballast and water) it can accommodate at one time.

The capacities of concrete mixers are described in various ways–sometimes as the volume of *dry* ingredients and sometimes the volume of *mixed* concrete that can be handled in one go. Usually both figures are given, so a mixer described as having a capacity of 140/100 is able to hold 140 litres of dry ingredients and 100 litres of concrete. When choosing a mixer do not be fooled by the size of the rest of its component parts; concentrate

B. *The ideal concreting site should have everything set out neatly, within easy reach. Where the formwork is above the surrounding ground, provide ramps for your wheelbarrow or mixer and take extra care when dumping a load*

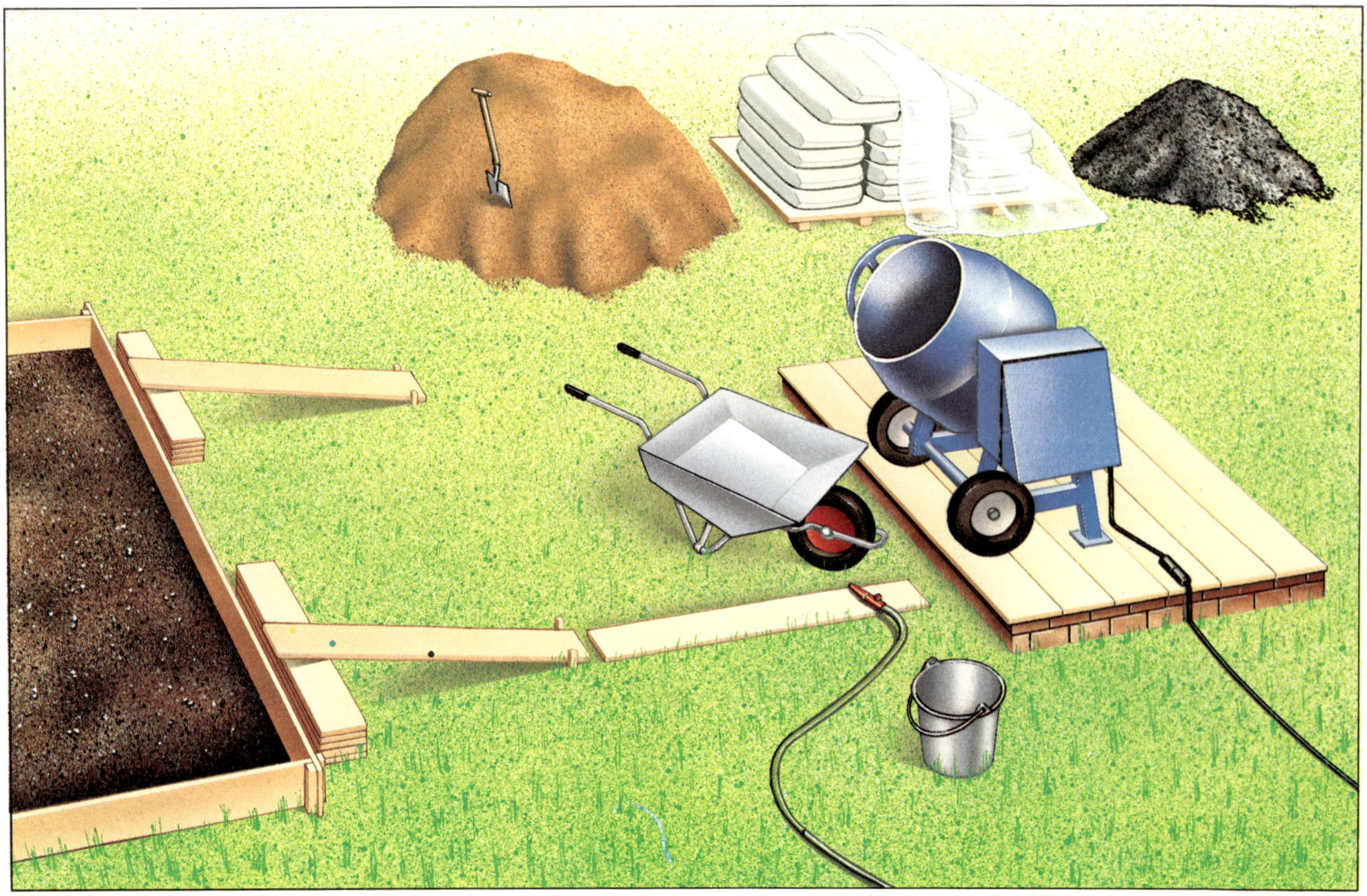

8 *Wheelbarrow type concrete mixers may be electric or petrol driven and are useful for transporting cement or ballast as well as for mixing*

9 *If the mixer is to stay in one place, use the stand provided or a platform of timber and bricks to bring it up to a convenient working height*

10 *If you have never used a concrete mixer before, use a bucket to help measure out the cement and ballast in their correct ratios*

11 *Later, as you get more experienced, you can shovel the ingredients straight into the mixing drum, taking care not to spill any on site*

12 *Lay bags of cement on a sheet of hardboard or polyethylene—this will protect them from moisture and make cleaning up easier*

13 *On your first load, shovel in half the aggregate and then add half the mixing water. Let them combine for a few seconds before adding all the cement*

instead on the capacity. A mixer with a capacity of 140/100 should be suitable for most do-it-yourself work.

Treat capacities as nominal only. The exact volume of materials you can safely load into a drum will vary considerably depending on the type of cement, sand and other materials you are using—and you can only really discover this for yourself by using the machine.

Next, have a look at the type of motor installed. The smaller wheelbarrow type usually have either petrol or electric motors while the larger four wheeled models are invariably petrol driven. Electric motors are quiet and give few starting problems compared to the petrol variety. But because they have a long lead stretching from a nearby electrical socket outlet to the machine you must be constantly on guard against accidents (see below).

If you want to consider getting a barrow type mixer, try to choose one that is easy to handle and tip—remembering that it will be full of concrete when you do so. The best mixers have a safety bar at the front end to stop the machine getting out of control while it is tipped.

Some manufacturers and hire shops make a small stand which raises the machine off the ground so that is it high enough to be tipped into a wheelbarrow. And on some models this stand allows the mixer to be swivelled through 360°, which can be very useful if you are working in a confined space or want to load the drum from one side and discharge from the other. If you cannot find a stand which is suitable, stand the mixer on a patch of ground slightly higher than the rest of the site or build a small platform of bricks and boards so that you can tip it more easily (fig. B).

Using a mixer

Mixing dry ingredients and moving load after load of wet concrete is not easy, even with a machine. Your first consideration should be to plan the layout of your site with this in mind, so reducing the amount of shovel work and travelling you need to do at any one time.

If you have sand and aggregate delivered in bulk, shovel these into neat piles on one side of the mixer so they can be loaded easily. You can keep the materials from getting soiled by placing a number of large clean boards on the ground and then loading the sand and aggregate on to them when it arrives at the site (fig. B).

Have another flat and clean area nearby where you can split open bags of cement and transfer them to the mixer. Remember that the cement should be covered overnight with tarpaulin or sheets of polyethylene in case of rain.

Lay on a supply of water by fixing a garden hose to the nearest tap. This might mean a lot of water splashing around while you are mixing but it avoids having to constantly refill buckets from the tap. If you can fix a device to the end of the hose enabling you to turn it off on site so much the better. In the absence of a convenient tap aim to use a large clean drum from which you can scoop buckets of water. If you intend transporting the mix in a wheelbarrow, make sure that you can get the barrow under the mouth of the tilted mixing drum. Build a platform if necessary (see above).

If you decide to tip the mixed concrete straight on to the ground prior to shovelling it into a wheelbarrow or directly into the formwork you have prepared, lay sheets of plywood beneath and around the mixer. This ensures that the concrete does not get mixed up with earth and stones, and also makes the site easier to clean up afterwards.

It is surprisingly easy to lose control of a wheelbarrow laden with heavy concrete, but the chances of you doing so can be reduced by providing a smooth pathway between the mixing site and the formwork. If the ground is particularly well-compacted and free from bumps you should have few problems; if not, lay a number of stout planks or scaffold boards across the site and drive pegs against the sides at regular intervals to stop them from moving (fig B).

You may need to construct a number of small ramps or bridges to smooth out any steps along the way: try to support these at least every 2m, either with bricks or trestles. You will need a similar run for a wheelbarrow type mixer if you intend to tip it directly into the formwork. In this case rig up a fairly gradual ramp consisting of two planks, parallel with one another and in line with the mixer

14 *Having shovelled in the rest of the aggregate, add more water gradually until the ingredients are well mixed and fall off the drum blades cleanly*

15 *If you are leaving the mixer in one place, empty the mixed concrete into a wheelbarrow. Be sure to keep the mixer turning as you do so*

16 *Use scaffold boards and bricks to smooth out any steps or bumps on the route to the site. Make sure the ramps are secure—concrete is heavy*

17 *Have a heavy timber baulk ready at the site and use it as a step against which to tip the wheelbarrow. Take care not to strain your back*

18 *With a barrow type mixer, you can often transfer the mixed concrete directly to the site. Again, use a step and keep the drum turning*

19 *Once you have poured the concrete, a heavy duty vibrator is very useful for settling it and removing airlocks which cause structural faults*

wheels. When using such a ramp make absolutely sure that the mixer wheels stay centred on the boards and that the mixer is under complete control at all times—especially when you are tipping.

Before you start mixing, decide on the quantity of concrete you want in each load. If you are a little uncertain, start with small loads and work up to larger ones: full barrows are very heavy and there is no sense in straining yourself or the walkway you have built.

Start off using a bucket as a standard measure; then, as you get more proficient, shovel the ingredients directly into the mixer (see pages 119 to 123). There is no need to hurl materials into the drum: it is far better to let them fall over the lip. Any waste which drops to the ground can be cleared away and re-used.

Start the mixing by putting half the aggregate into the drum. Follow this with half the water and then let the two mix for a few seconds before adding the whole of the cement. Then pour in the rest of aggregate and add more water gradually until you achieve the correct consistency. The mix should fall off the drum blades cleanly, but must not be too wet. If in doubt, turn off the motor and apply the 'squeeze test' (see page 119).

The time you allow the machine to mix will vary according to the amount of material and the exact ratio of cement and aggregate, but on average it should take no longer than three minutes. Once this time has elapsed, you can tip the concrete into a waiting wheelbarrow or directly into the formwork. However, do not switch off: instead keep the motor running then slowly but steadily tip up the machine or turn the control wheel until the whole drum has emptied of its concrete load (fig. 15).

20 *Afterwards, all that remains is to skim the concrete level with the top of the formwork and tamp it down using a timber tamping bar*

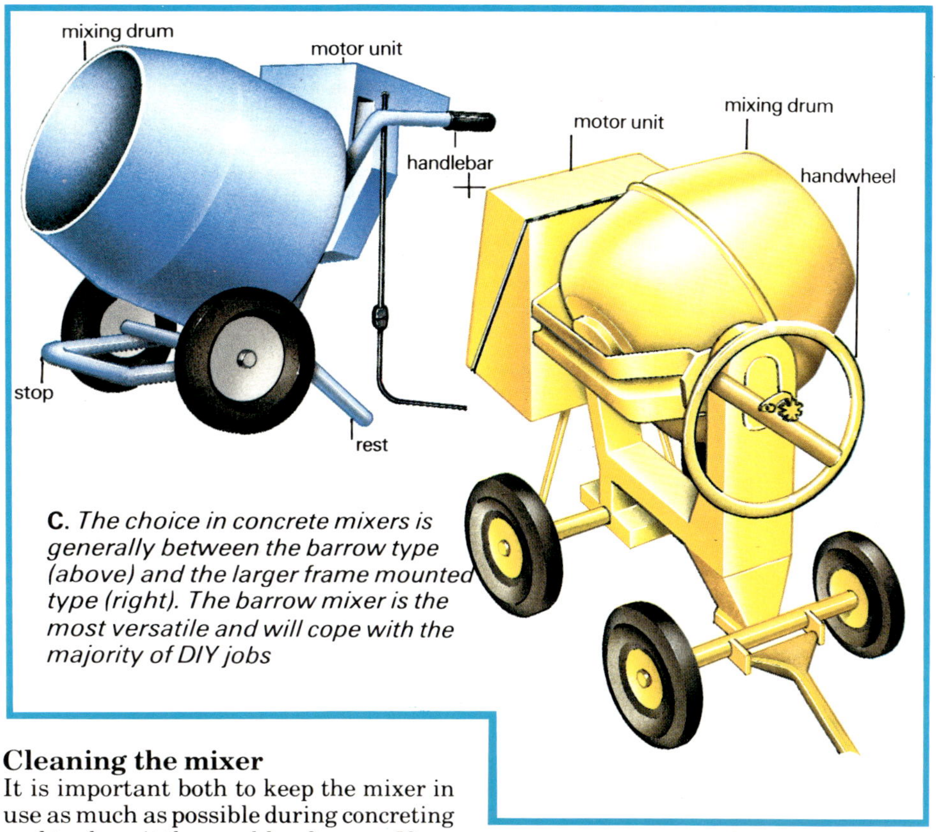

C. *The choice in concrete mixers is generally between the barrow type (above) and the larger frame mounted type (right). The barrow mixer is the most versatile and will cope with the majority of DIY jobs*

Cleaning the mixer

It is important both to keep the mixer in use as much as possible during concreting and to clean it thoroughly after use. If you do not, cement will soon harden on all the surfaces—especially the inside of the drum—and the mixer will become steadily less efficient to the point where it is almost unusable.

As soon as you have tipped one load, fill up the drum with half the aggregate and half the water and leave it running. Even in you do not intend to mix up another load immediately—because you are tamping the concrete, for instance—this will clear the blades ready for action.

At the end of the day clean the mixer thoroughly. Wipe the outside of the machine with a wet rag and leave the motor running for about 15 minutes with a mixture of aggregate and water inside the drum. Then switch off, dump the load and clean off any remaining deposits with a wire brush or the end of a piece of batten. Finally, hose down the entire machine (disconnect an electric mixer first) and leave it to dry off before moving it under cover for the night.

General safety precautions

- Stand to one side when loading the mixer; sometimes a machine will spit material out of the drum mouth.
- Make sure you are standing on a firm footing when loading or tipping the mixer.
- Keep well clear of moving parts. Never reach into the drum with hands or tools while it is rotating.
- Follow the manufacturers' instructions on maintaining motors, gearboxes, drive belts and so on. Lubricate all moving parts regularly and check bolts and mountings before starting work.

Electric motors

If you use a mixer powered by mains electricity you must of course run a power lead from a nearby power socket. In this case check the following:

- Keep the lead out of wet ground and make sure it cannot get damaged in any way. Use waterproof plugs and sockets as well as heavy duty cable. Never unplug intermediate connections unless the machine has first been unplugged at the power source.
- Try to choose a mixer which is double insulated, if possible. An earthed mixer should be fitted with a leakage circuit breaker to prevent accidents.
- Keep water clear of the motor. Never wash down the outside of the machine unless it is unplugged, and wait until it has dried before using it again.
- It is important to be able to switch the motor on and off at the mixer rather than at some remote power socket.
- If you notice a slight voltage drop, it may be that either the cable is kinked or the run between the mains and the machine is too long. If the voltage drop still persists once you have straightened the lead, fit a thicker cable.

Laying raft foundations

• Planning and setting out the project • Preparing the site • Constructing the formwork • Laying mesh for loadbearing foundations • Tamping the sections of concrete

Raft foundations are the large slabs of concrete on which rest garden sheds, greenhouses and outhouses. Their function is to spread the load of the structure above, together with its contents, over a wide area.

Laying a stretch of concrete—for a patio, path or driveway—is a good introduction to the concreting techniques used in making rafts. It also leaves some margin for error if you have never worked with concrete.

Above: *The final section of a large raft foundation is filled and tamped after the concrete in the adjacent bays has been laid and set*

Planning the project

Make a scale drawing of your proposed project before you start work. If you are planning a patio, path or driveway it will be much easier to run this right up to one wall of the house. Multiplying the final area of the project by the required thickness of concrete gives you a guide to how much concrete you need. For a drive, aim for a minimum thickness of about 100mm concrete over 100mm well-tamped hardcore. This can be reduced to 75mm concrete for paths and small patios or a minimum 50mm concrete over 75mm well-tamped hardcore. But if your soil is particularly soft, consult the local building inspector.

Ordering the concrete

For work of this kind use a mix of one part cement to $2\frac{1}{2}$ parts sand to four parts aggregate or gravel, plus enough water to bind the ingredients together. If your estimates call for more than $1m^3$ of concrete. Consider having it delivered ready-mixed by a local concrete firm. The extra cost may be more than offset by the savings in time and effort.

Remember that if you are concreting in large 'bays', you need two loads of concrete delivered on separate occasions. Allow for the cost of this in your estimates.

When ordering ready-mixed concrete, bear in mind that the company's truck will need access to the site. Be sure both of the mix and quantity of concrete you want and if there is more than one firm in your area, shop around for a competitive quotation.

If you are mixing the concrete yourself, the volume of concrete you will get will be roughly equal to the volume of the aggregate (only). Do your mixing on level ground as near as possible to where the drive or path is to be laid.

Setting out

You will find it helpful to choose a site which is more or less level: ground which is heavily sloping calls for more involved concreting techniques, and you should probably turn the job over to a professional.

If you are working from an existing house wall, take this as your base setting-out line and take other measurements from it. If not, drive in two wooden pegs and stretch a length of masons' line or twine between them. Ensure that the pegs are well outside either side of the work area.

Your second setting-out line will run at right-angles to the baseline and mark one side of the project (fig. C). Having measured and marked where the line will cross the baseline

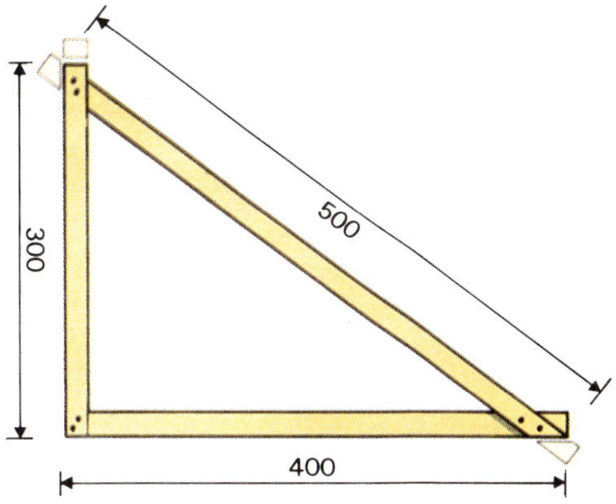

A. *Make a builder's square by nailing together offcuts of wood—vertical 300mm, horizontal 400mm and the diagonal 500mm*

B. *A length of 100 x 50mm timber and offcut handles makes a good tamping beam for compressing wet concrete*

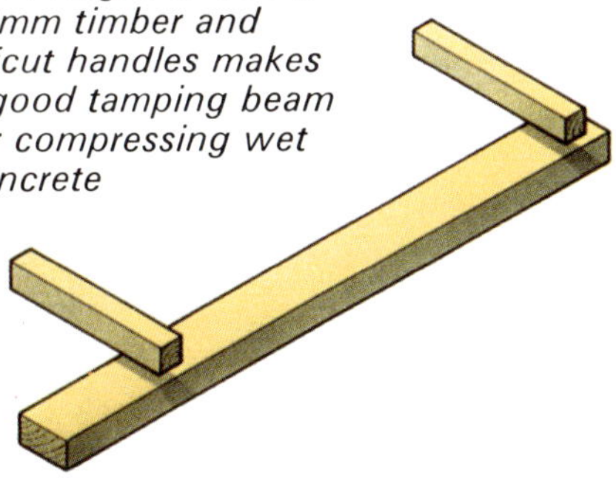

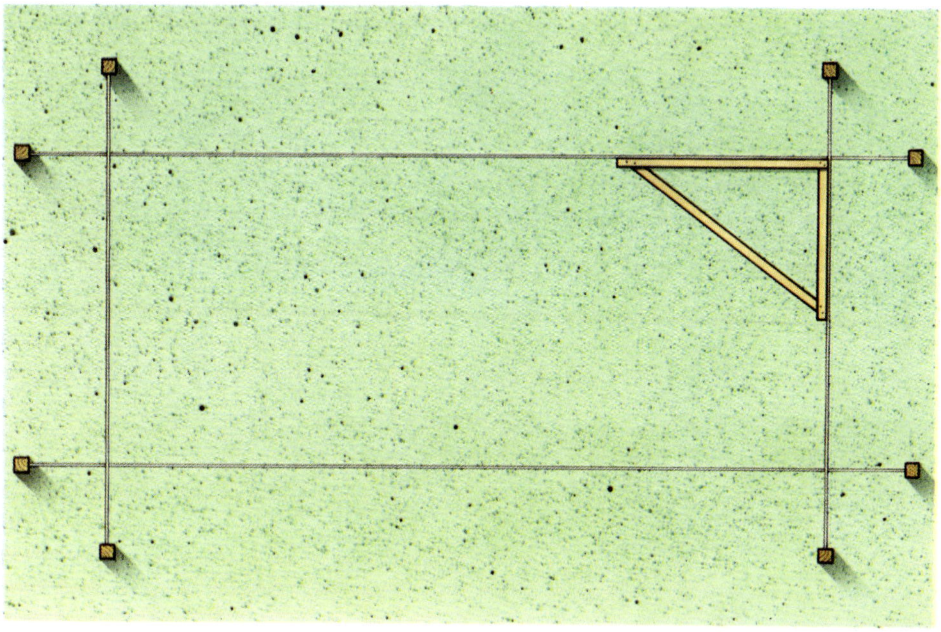

C. *Use the builder's square to ensure that the setting out lines are perfectly square*

(or wall), set it up with pegs and line. Use a builder's square (see above) to ensure that the angle between the two lines is exactly 90 degrees.

The third line—marking another side of the project—should run parallel to the baseline. Measure out from both sides to the baseline to ensure that this is so then set up the pegs and line. Again, use the builder's square to check that the corner with the second line is 90 degrees.

The fourth line—marking the final side of the project—runs parallel with the second. Measure and set it out in the same way as the others so that you have an arrangement similar to that shown in fig. C.

As a final check to ensure that the corners of the project will be square, measure across the diagonals. If the measurements are not exactly the same, adjust the positions of the pegs accordingly.

Preparing the site

Start by removing all obstructions and traces of vegetation—such as weeds and roots—from within the boundaries of the site. If there are some areas of existing concrete on-site, these must be broken up into rubble with a pick.

To get the site level, you need a straight piece of timber 2-3m long and a supply of wooden pegs, about half as long again as your proposed depth of concrete.

Decide where you want the final level of the concrete to be—normally against a lawn or base of the house—then drive one of the pegs into the ground on the edge of the site. The top of the peg will mark the final level of the concrete and is known as the datum. Ensure that the finished level of the concrete is a minimum of 150mm below any adjacent damp proof course—also that the concrete slopes away from the house in about a 1:60 fall to deal with surface water.

Use the straight piece of timber and a spirit level to check the height of the peg against the point you are taking your level from.

The site can now be excavated to the required depth, working away from the datum peg. As you progress, more pegs must be driven in to help you keep an eye on both the level and depth of the site. The pegs should be no further than the length of your straight edge away from each other—or from the datum peg.

You can then check each peg for level with a straight edge and spirit level.

Once the whole site is pegged out in this way, you can measure down the pegs to the required depth of concrete and level off the ground at this point. Keep the edges of the site sharp and in line with the setting out lines.

Foundations such as driveways which are going to bear the weight of

D. *Check that the excavation pegs are all equal with a spirit level*

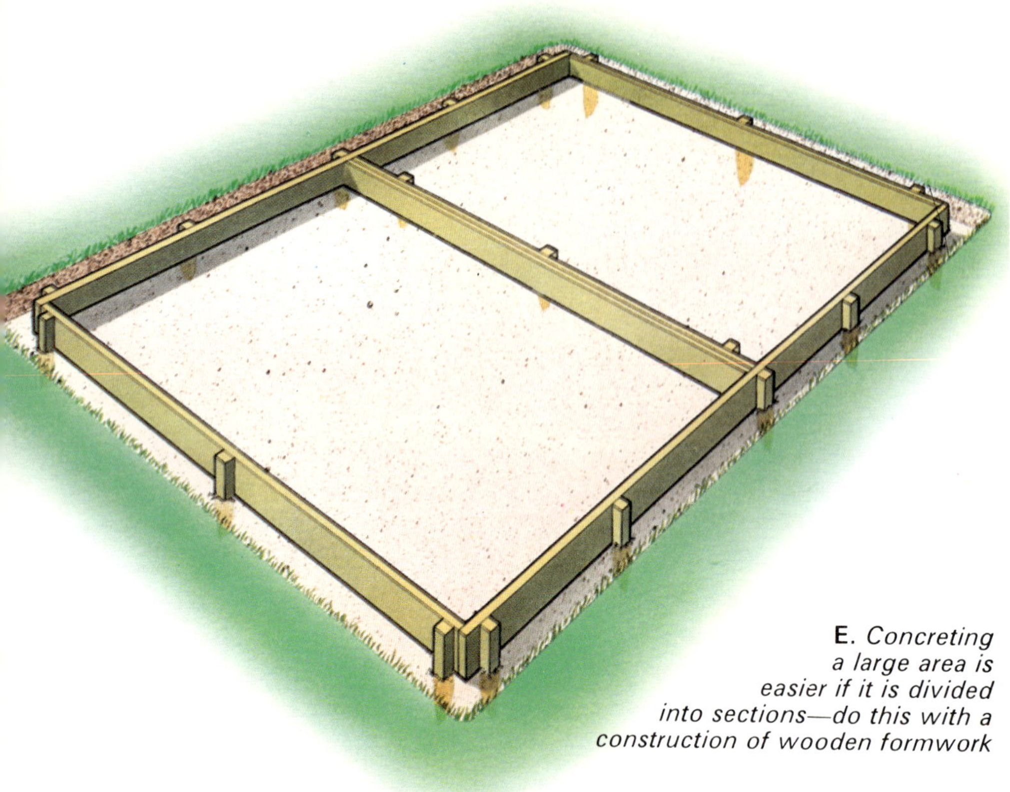

E. *Concreting a large area is easier if it is divided into sections—do this with a construction of wooden formwork*

1 *If necessary, the wire mesh for loadbearing foundations can be cut to size. Before concreting, box in obstructions such as drains*

2 *Lay the wire mesh on lengths of timber which have been checked for level and then another length on top to hold the mesh in place*

3 *Drive in wooden pegs against either side of the formwork and then nail all the pieces together to make a secure construction*

a car need to be strengthened. This is done with wire mesh of about 3mm diameter which can be cut to size with bolt cutters (fig. 1).

At this stage, any obstructions on the site, such as drains, should be boxed off to prevent them being concreted over (fig. 1). Remove the box and concrete round the edges when all the foundations are down.

Lay the mesh down on lengths of timber—which are level with your setting-out lines—prior to concreting. Nail another length of timber on top of the first to hold the mesh in place while concreting the various sections (fig. 2). These lengths of timber act as the sectioning formwork necessary for concreting large areas. They should be removed after the adjacent section has been concreted.

Constructing the formwork

The purpose of formwork (fig. E) is to stop the wet concrete from spilling haphazardly over the boundaries of the site. It can also be used to split large sites into smaller areas, which can then be concreted in stages.

Make the formwork from lengths of timber, as wide as the depth of your concrete and about 25mm thick. Place them around the boundaries of the site, butted end to end so that there are no gaps.

To hold the timber in place, drive in more wooden pegs against the outside faces (fig. 3) then nail all the pieces together.

If a large area is to be concreted or if the concrete is to run up to an existing wall, more formwork must be used to divide the site into sections of about $2m^2$. This will enable you to lay and level one section before starting on the next.

Where a path is being laid along a wall, the site should be divided into 'bays' (fig. E). Alternate bays can be filled, levelled and left to harden: you can then stand on them to fill and level the intervening bays.

Construct the sectioning formwork in the same way as that for the boundaries of the site. Remember to drive in the support pegs on the opposite side of the sectioning formwork to that being filled.

When all the formwork is in place (fig. 4), use the straight edge and spirit level to check that the top edges of the boards are level with the tops of your marker pegs (fig. 5).

Concreting

The actual job of concreting will be much easier if you have an assistant to help you. If the concrete is being delivered ready-mixed, make sure that the formwork is ready and the ground fully levelled off.

Shovel in the concrete by hand and level it off roughly 15mm above the height of the formwork (fig. 6).

4 *All the formwork is in place—including the sectioning timber—ready for the first bay to be filled with the prepared concrete*

5 *Use a straight edge and spirit level to check that the top edges of the boards are level with the top of the marker pegs*

6 *Shovel the concrete into the first bay and level it off to about 15mm above the formwork. It can then be tamped down level*

7 *Use a heavy length of timber as a tamping beam. To be effective, the beam must be at least 150mm longer than the width of the bay*

8 *With the help of an assistant, run the beam over the freshly concreted section in a chopping motion to give a rippled effect*

When you have filled a section, the concrete must be compressed, or tamped.

The tool for doing this is called a tamping beam. You can make one from a length of 100mm x 50mm timber with wood offcut handles at either end. The tamping beam should be at least 150mm longer than the width of the section (fig. 7).

With the aid of an assistant, run the beam over the freshly concreted section in a sawing, chopping motion. The weight of the beam should be enough to tamp the concrete down to the height of the formwork, while the 'chops' will give the surface a rippled effect (fig. 8).

The distance you leave between 'chops' depends on how rippled a surface you want: the normal allowance is half the thickness of the beam.

If the tamping shows up any low spots, fill them immediately and re-tamp. When you are happy with the surface, two passes of the beam should be sufficient to complete the tamping process.

The final surface

This can be left as it is—rippled—roughened, or smoothed. For a rough surface, brush over the concrete with a stiff broom. To smooth the surface

F. *A site alongside a wall should be divided into bays and alternate sections filled, levelled and left to dry*

9 *When one section is finished, remove the sectioning formwork between the first and the next. Then concrete this section as before*

10 *After the concrete of these alternate sections has set, remove all the formwork and fill in the last intervening bay*

11 *A steel edging trowel should be used to smooth off the edges of the concrete to give the foundation a good, smooth finish*

12 *Freshly-laid concrete needs at least a week to dry out—longer in damp weather—and heavy loads should be kept off it for ten days*

skim it over with a piece of timber or (better) a plasterer's wooden float.

Concreting subsequent sections

If you must complete the concreting in one go, you will need to provide expansion joints so that the concrete does not crack as it dries out. To do this, make up your sectioning formwork in the usual way. With the first section poured, place a thin (say, 9mm) board against the next length of sectioning formwork and check it for level. When you have poured the second section, carefully remove the formwork, but leave the thinner board permanently in place. Repeat this procedure for subsequent sections.

If you are concreting in 'bays' fill in alternate sections with the sectioning formwork left in place. After the concrete has hardened (see below), remove the formwork and fill in the intervening sections (fig. 10).

Use a steel edging trowel to flatten down the edges of the concrete for a really neat finish (fig. 11).

Drying

The freshly-laid concrete (fig. 12) should be given at least a week to 'cure'—longer if the weather is especially cold or damp. Heavy loads should be kept off it for seven to ten days.

In warm weather, the concrete must be prevented from drying too quickly. Do this by covering the whole site with dampened sacking or a similar material. Every day, sprinkle the covering with water to keep it moist.

In cold, wet weather, the concrete will be more in danger of frost than of drying too quickly. To guard against this, cover it with sheets of heavy-duty polythene or waterproof building paper.

Laying crazy paving

Laying crazy paving provides an ideal opportunity to demonstrate your artistic abilities, to use up oddments of paving slabs and form an attractive design with random shapes.

It is a most economical way of laying a path as even the smallest oddments of paving slab can be used up. These should, however, be kept towards the centre of the path with the larger pieces around the edges, so that maximum support is given to the structure.

The foundations are laid in the same way as for all raft foundations and since these provide a good, firm base, almost any type of paving slab can be used to form the crazy, jigsaw pattern.

If the site of the path is on very firm ground and it is not likely to take any great load, the 100mm of concrete need not be laid. The paving slabs can be put straight down on the bed of lime and damp sand.

The most important part of all such foundation work is to constantly check that the site is level. Check it as you excavate the site, as you lay the hardcore and the mortar bed, and finally as you lay down the paving slabs. Careless work at this stage will ruin the finished look of the path.

To make doubly sure that the path is level across its length as well as its width, use the spirit level and board across pegs A-B as well as A-A, B-B, C-C and so on.

It is even more important that the path is allowed to set for a few days before any weight is put on it, otherwise the foundations may be disturbed and all your good levelling work gone to waste.

Crazy paving looks good in any garden—front or back—and can be made even more attractive by giving it curves. A curved crazy path is no more difficult to lay than a straight one. It just takes a little more patience to find the right pieces to fit the jigsaw puzzle.

Crazy paving is also one of the few external constructions which look better as it gets older. Moss and lichen may grow between the pointing but this only makes the path look more attractive.

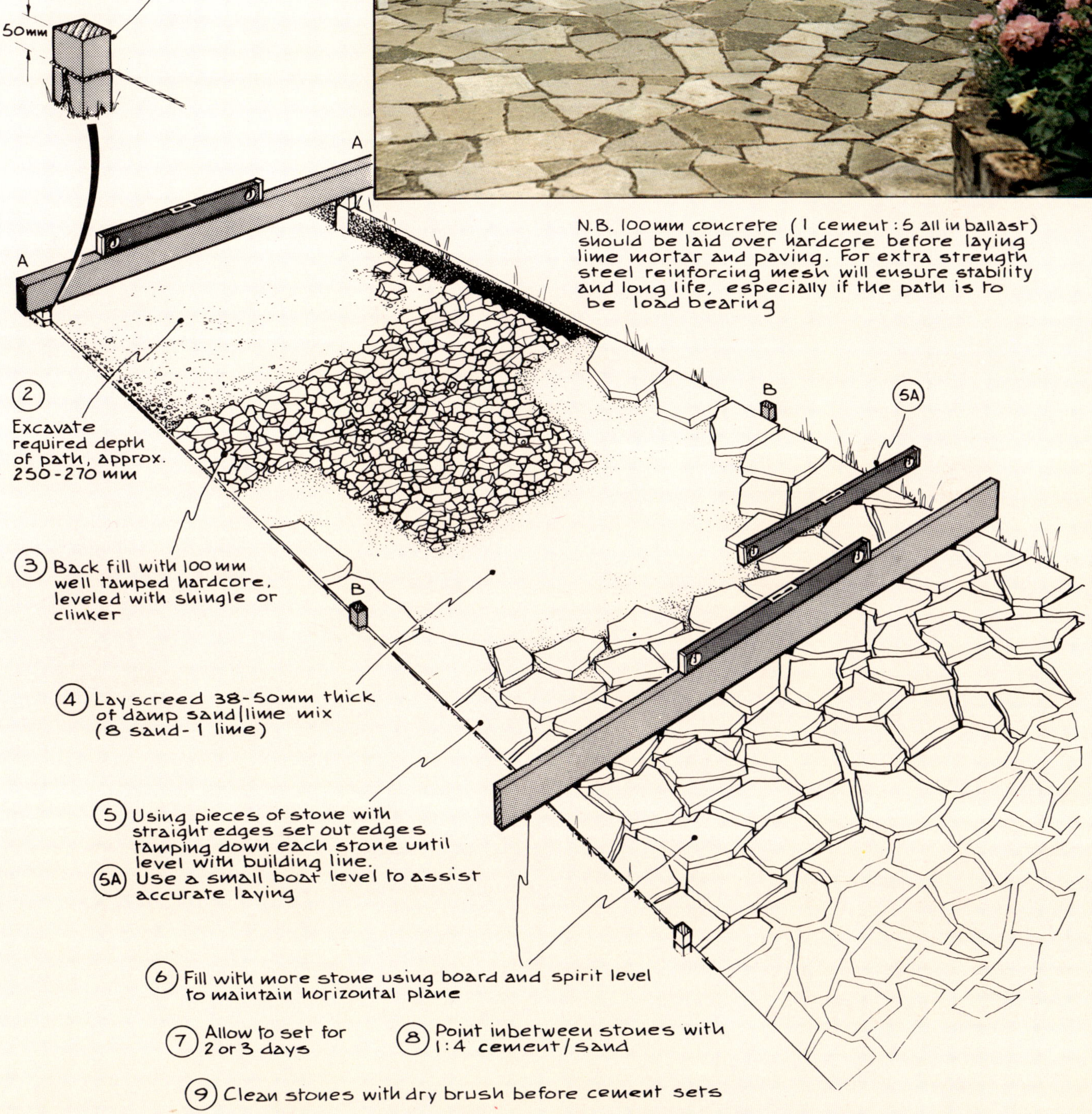

1 Use wooden pegs 50×50×450mm and building line to set out path. Line is fixed at identical distances from top of all pegs. The line indicates top outer finished edges of path
50mm
A
A
N.B. 100mm concrete (1 cement: 5 all in ballast) should be laid over hardcore before laying lime mortar and paving. For extra strength steel reinforcing mesh will ensure stability and long life, especially if the path is to be load bearing
B
5A
2 Excavate required depth of path, approx. 250-270 mm
3 Back fill with 100mm well tamped hardcore, leveled with shingle or clinker
B
4 Lay screed 38-50mm thick of damp sand/lime mix (8 sand-1 lime)
5 Using pieces of stone with straight edges set out edges tamping down each stone until level with building line.
5A Use a small boat level to assist accurate laying
6 Fill with more stone using board and spirit level to maintain horizontal plane
7 Allow to set for 2 or 3 days
8 Point inbetween stones with 1:4 cement/sand
9 Clean stones with dry brush before cement sets

Turning a corner

Bricklaying terms explained • Different types of bond • Types of bricklaying mortar • Setting out a quoin • Building quoins • Building the intervening walls

Above: *A completed quoin must be straight on all its edges—the quality and accuracy of the quoins determines that of the entire structure*

Once you have learned the correct way to lay bricks quickly and accurately, the next stage of bricklaying is to become familiar with the various patterns—or bonds—in which bricks are laid. At the same time, you will come across quite a few bricklaying terms: it is important to learn these, as they crop up time and time again.

Brick terminology

In bricklaying, bricks cut to different sizes are all given different names. Cut in half across its width, a brick becomes a *half-bat*. Cut to three-quarters of its length, it becomes a *three-quarter bat* and to a quarter of its length, a *quarter-bat*. A brick cut in half along its length is known as a *queen closer*. This is used for building strengthened corners, or *quoins*.

The way in which bricks are laid also has its own terminology. A brick laid so that one of its longest sides is visible in the finished wall is known as a *stretcher*. If it is laid so that one of the ends shows, it becomes a *header*.

Bonding

All bricks conform to a specified arrangement to ensure maximum strength, load-bearing property and a uniform appearance. This arrangement is called a *bond*.

As a general rule, no brick should be laid directly on top of another: instead, it should overlap the joints between the bricks above and below it so that there are no straight joints running up the wall. The various bonding patterns in use all follow this rule and ensure that the vertical joints between bricks are staggered over the whole wall.

Stretcher bond (running bond): This is the simplest of all bonds. It is used in walls which are half a brick (102mm) thick—the minimum thickness of any brick wall (fig. A). Each brick overlaps the one above and the one below it by half a brick's length to provide a simple, strong bond which involves cutting half-bricks only at the ends of courses. About 50 bricks (75 in the US and Canada) are needed for each 1m² of brickwork.

English bond: This bond (fig. B) makes a wall one whole brick (215mm) thick. The strongest of all bonds, it is used wherever high load-bearing qualities are called for—such as foundations and man-holes. About 100 bricks (150 in the US and Canada) are needed for each 1m² of brickwork. It consists of alternate rows, or courses, of headers and stretchers.

As the bricks overlap by only a quarter of a brick's length (56mm), care must be taken to keep the perpendicular joints aligned and staggered on each alternate course. Otherwise the bond tends to 'creep' as the courses progress and form straight joints where a crack may appear when stress is applied.

To keep the bond aligned at its corners, a queen closer is laid end-on next to the corner brick (fig. B).

Flemish bond: This bond (fig. C) also makes a wall one whole brick (215mm) thick. But because it has numerous internal straight joints, it is not as strong as English bond and is used more in decorative work, such as garden walls. When British houses had solid 9 inch brick walls instead of cavity walls, it was the bond most used to build them.

Flemish bond consists of alternate headers and stretchers along a single course. Each stretcher has a header above and below it forming what is called the 'Flemish star' and the decorative properties of the bond are accentuated if this is laid in different coloured bricks.

This bond takes a long time to build and also has a tendency to creep if sufficient care is not taken in aligning the vertical joints of alternate courses. To start each course correctly, it too requires a queen closer next to each corner brick.

English garden wall bond: More complex and not as strong as standard English bond, this incorporates two overlaps—one of half a brick's length (102mm), the other of a quarter brick's length (56mm). It is an arrangement of

A. *Stretcher (running) bond*

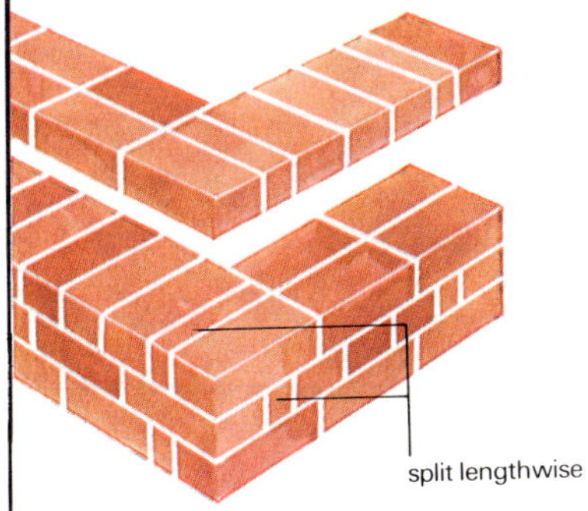

B. *English bond*

C. *Flemish bond*

D. *English garden wall bond*

E. *Flemish garden wall bond*

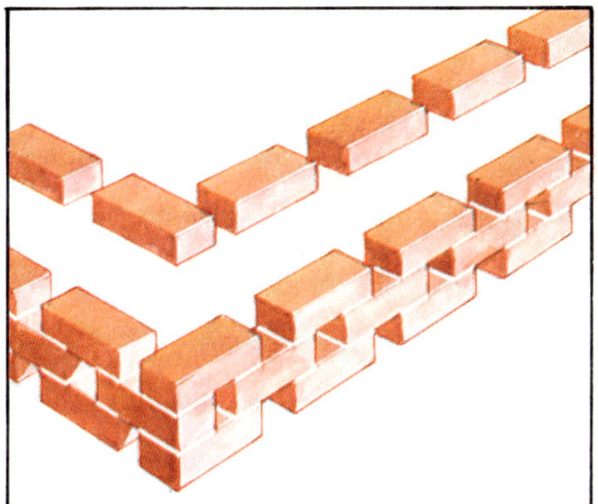

F. *Open bond*

three or five courses of stretchers for every course of headers. Care must be taken to ensure that the joints on the header courses align vertically.

The English garden wall bond is economical because it incorporates a lot of stretchers, so there is less wastage from cutting bricks.

American bond: This is similar to English garden wall bond, except that it has one course of headers to every five or six courses of stretchers, and—because of the deep perpendicular joints between the bricks on the face of the wall and those at the back—is correspondingly less strong. Like English garden wall bond, it is used only for decorative outdoor brickwork, not for building construction.

Flemish garden wall bond: This is a complex arrangement used in decorative brickwork and consists of three or five stretchers followed by a header repeated along the same course (fig. E). The headers are arranged so that they are centred in the block of stretchers in the course above.

Open bond: This bond is purely decorative. Consisting of stretcher courses with a quarter-bat spacing (fig. F), the spacing is decreased at the corners to maintain the bond. The top of the bond can be finished with either a solid course of stretchers or with a course of coping slabs.

Mortar composition

Mortar, the material which binds bricks, is composed of a binding material—such as cement or lime—and a fine aggregate—such as sand—and water. Bricklaying sand for general use should be graded either 'soft' or 'fine' for best results.

For all mortars, the specified quantities must be mixed to correct and constant ratios over the whole of the project. Where this rule is not observed, cracking caused by uneven expansion and contraction occurs and the difference in the mortar mix shows through as colour changes in the finished work.

For general and normal house construction four parts of sand to one of cement is the correct ratio—but variations on this mix can be used according to the needs of the bond. Take advice from the brick supplier to ensure that the mortar is neither stronger nor weaker than the bricks it is being used with.

To test the water content of a mortar mix, press a trowel into it. If the impression made remains for a minute or more, the mix is of the correct consistency. If the edges around the impression crumble, the mix is too dry. If the impression fills up with water, the mixture is too wet and more cement and sand in the correct ratio should be added.

Water gives mortar its bonding power. When making up the mix, it is most important to use only fresh, clean water. Dirty water or water from a rain barrel will cause the mix to quickly break up.

Gauged mortar

Many companies now are producing a form of ready-mixed mortar—gauged mortar—which is sand and lime mixed to a ratio of approximately six of sand to one of lime. As this mixture does not contain any cement, it does not set hard and will retain its water content for extended periods. The cement is added according to the manufacturer's recommendations.

1 *Bang two pegs firmly into the ground at each corner of the foundations. The twine stretched between the pegs must be taut*

2 *When the twine is in place, check that the angle between the two lines is square with a builder's square*

3 *Another way to check the angle is by 3-4-5. If two sides of the triangle measure 3 units and 4 units, the diagonal must measure 5 units*

4 *Directly under the twine, at each corner, lay down a thin screed of wet mortar extending about 600mm along the foundations*

5 *Carefully hold a spirit level against the twine, check that it is plumb, then score a line where its base touches the screed*

6 *Join up the scored lines at both the front and side edges. Once the pegs and twine are out of the way, these provide the building line*

Plasticizer

To make the mortar easier to use during bricklaying, additives called plasticizers are added. These aerate the mortar and spread the water content evenly throughout the mix, making it more malleable and easier to use for longer periods.

For non-structural brickwork, washing-up liquid makes a suitable plasticizer. For structural brickwork, a proprietary plasticizer — available cheaply from builders' merchants—should be used. The correct quantities to use for different jobs are printed on the back of the container. Gauged mortars contain lime and do not need a plasticizer. Similarly, the *masonry cement* sold in the US and Canada already has a plasticizer added.

Foundations

Strip foundations are suitable for garden walls, as they only support light loads. Foundations for house or garage walls are much more elaborate, and vary from area to area. In countries subjected to hard frost in winter such as the UK and Canada, for example, they must extend at least 1200mm below ground level (below grade) to avoid 'frost heave'. Building such foundations is unnecessary for most garden walls.

Setting out a quoin

With the foundations laid, the following simple setting out procedure must be carried out before construction of the quoin begins.

- Set up two upright pegs at each corner of the foundations. Stretch twine between them along both the front and side of the proposed structure (fig. 1 and fig. G).
- Check that the corner angle is square using either the 3-4-5 method or a builder's square (figs. 2 and 3).
- In the corner of the foundation, lay down a screed (thin layer) of wet mortar—extending about 600mm along the foundation (fig. 4).
- Hold the spirit level vertically against the string—without bending it—and score a line with the trowel where the bottom of the spirit level touches the screed (fig. 5). The mark must be directly under the string. Repeat this about 500mm along the screed and using a straight edge join up the two marks (fig. 6). Do the same along the side of the foundation so that both the building lines have been transferred down from the twine to the concrete.
- The upright pegs and twine can now be removed so that they do not interfere with the bricklaying.
- Lay the bricks 'dry' outside the line of the main wall, following your chosen bonding arrangement.

The idea is to adjust the width of the vertical joints, or *perpends*, between the bricks until the wall 'works brick'—that is, until there are just a

7 Carefully lay down a mortar joint, in preparation for laying the first bricks. Take care not to cover the building line

8 Promptly, but carefully, lay the first three bricks. Align the face of each with the scored line on the foundations

9 Only when these bricks have been checked for level should the remaining bricks of the quoin's first course be laid down

10 The side bricks of the quoin can now be laid, using the spirit level on end to check that all the bricks are in line and level

11 Each course after the first should be shortened by one brick and the quoin built up so that it ends in a single brick on top

12 At this stage, the 'racking back' of the quoin should be checked along its diagonal edge to ensure that the structure is level

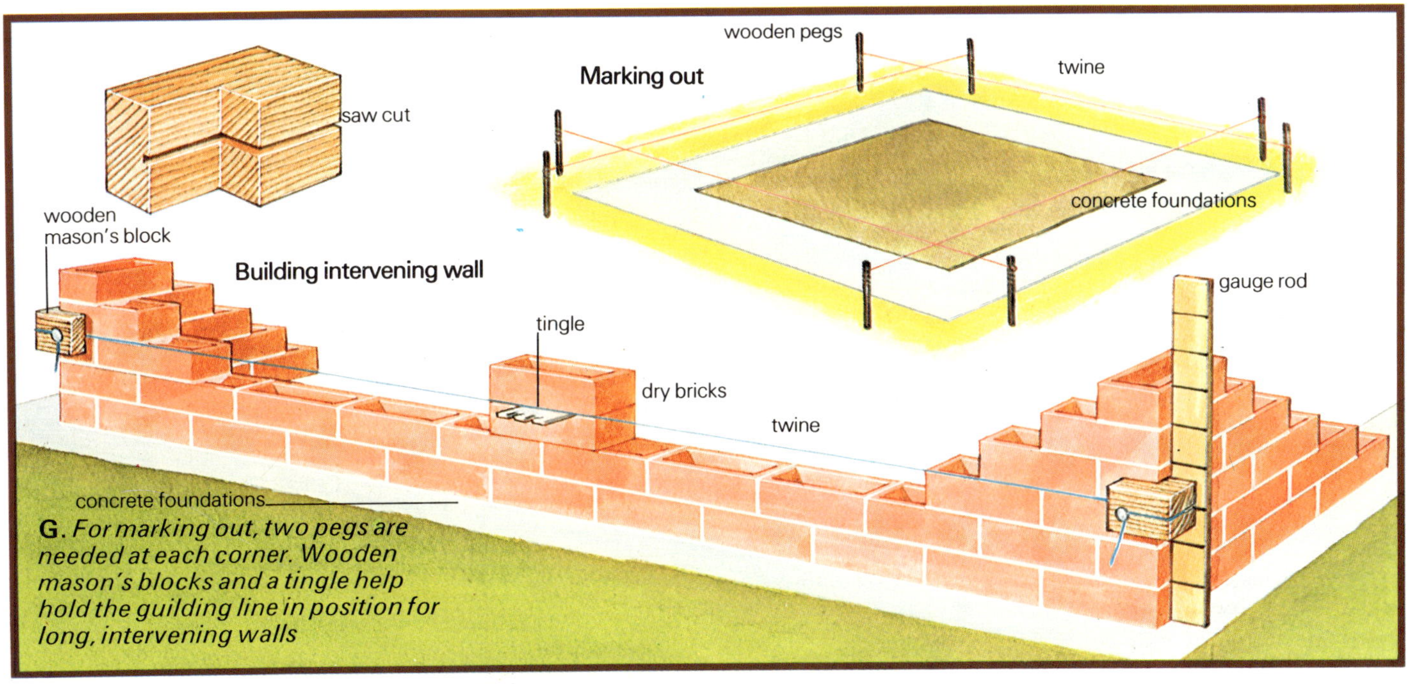

G. For marking out, two pegs are needed at each corner. Wooden mason's blocks and a tingle help hold the guilding line in position for long, intervening walls

small number of cut bricks or, better still, none at all. A cut brick in the wall is a weak point and too many will destroy the bond altogether.

This complete setting out procedure must be carried out for each corner of your proposed project. You are then ready to start building your quoin.

Building a quoin

- Lay down a mortar joint inside the scored line, taking care not to cover it (fig. 7).
- Carefully lay the first three bricks from your dry run along the mortar joint, keeping the face of the bricks aligned with the scored line of the foundation (fig. 8).
- Using the spirit level, check these bricks for horizontal (fig. 9) and then lay the remaining bricks forming the first course of the quoin.
- Repeat this procedure down the side of the corner to form a right angle. The corner is then described as being 'set out' (fig. 10).

Racking back

You can now continue building up the quoin following your chosen bond. Shorten each course after the first one so that you 'rack back' the quoin to eventually end in a single brick (fig. 11).

As you build, constantly check the quoin for plumb, line and level using your spirit level (fig. 10). You must also check the width of the horizontal, or cross, mortar joints. (fig. 11) Do this with a gauging rod—a straight piece of wood marked off at intervals of 75mm. The 75mm corresponds to the height of a brick and one mortar joint.

A final check across the diagonal racking back with a spirit level (fig. 12) should confirm that the quoin is properly aligned. When all the quoins of your proposed structure have been completed, you can fill in the intervening walls.

Building intervening walls

To build the intervening wall between two quoins, you need a set of mason's lines and blocks (fig. G). The tension on the line between the blocks holds them in position (see previous page). The line should be in the same place as the proposed mortar joint and act as a guideline between the quoins. With this in place you can build up the wall following your chosen bond.

On very long walls, the line may tend to sag in the middle, In this case. you need a tingle—a piece of metal supported on 'dry' bricks (fig. G)—to support it in the middle.

Brick types

Most general building bricks are made of clay or calcium silicate. Others are made of concrete, pottery waste, clinker and even crushed and moulded cinders. This variation in brick-making methods gives rise to an enormous variety of different types of bricks, few of which will all be available in the same area.

A more convenient way to classify bricks is by use. Here, four different types can be distinguished.

Common bricks: These are general-purpose bricks, used for such jobs as internal house walls and external walls which are to be rendered. Common bricks are usually roughly and unattractively finished and are also subject to frost damage. They should not be used for large areas of bare brickwork.

Face bricks: More expensive than a stock brick, these are used wherever bare brickwork is to be left showing. Face bricks are available in various colours and textures, are well finished and have a fairly good resistance to water and frost. The mortar joints on face brickwork should always be finished off neatly with a pointing tool.

Loadbearing bricks: These may be either face bricks or commons in appearance, but will conform to specified compression strengths and stress loadings. They are used, for example, where a load-bearing internal wall has been knocked down and brick pillars are to be erected to support the steel joist put in its place to take the load.

Engineering bricks: These are the hardest bricks of all and are made of clay, burnt at high temperatures in large kilns. They are designed to carry heavy loads and can also be used where exposure to the elements is likely to be a problem. The term does not apply to calcium silicate bricks, which are hard, but may not quite reach the specified strength and compression requirements of engineering bricks.

A point to remember when stacking bricks is that they should all be stacked on edge, in opposing directions, on each alternate row. Otherwise, bricks could topple off the stack and damage their edges—expensive if the whole pile collapses.

An open bond wall

The decorative open bond has been used to build this sturdy but attractive garden screen wall. It is made up of seven stretcher courses with a quarter-bat spacing. The spacing is reduced slightly at the corner and middle plinths to give the bond its strength.

Here, the top of the bond has been finished off with coping slabs and corner copings. But a solid course of stretchers could also be used to good effect.

If you decide to use the coping slabs—and they do help to protect the wall—treat them as carefully as possible. The uniform appearance of the copings is instantly lost if they are cracked. Go gently with the hamme and bolster chisel when cutting them to size—several gentle blows are better than one massive hit which could easily crack the coping in entirely the wrong place.

Although a generous, but even amount of mortar is needed to secur the coping slabs in position, take car not to get any mortar on their to sides. The mark left by the wet morta is almost impossible to remove.

Also, take time to remove an excess mortar from the bond's ope spaces—untidy lumps of mortar wi detract from the finished look.

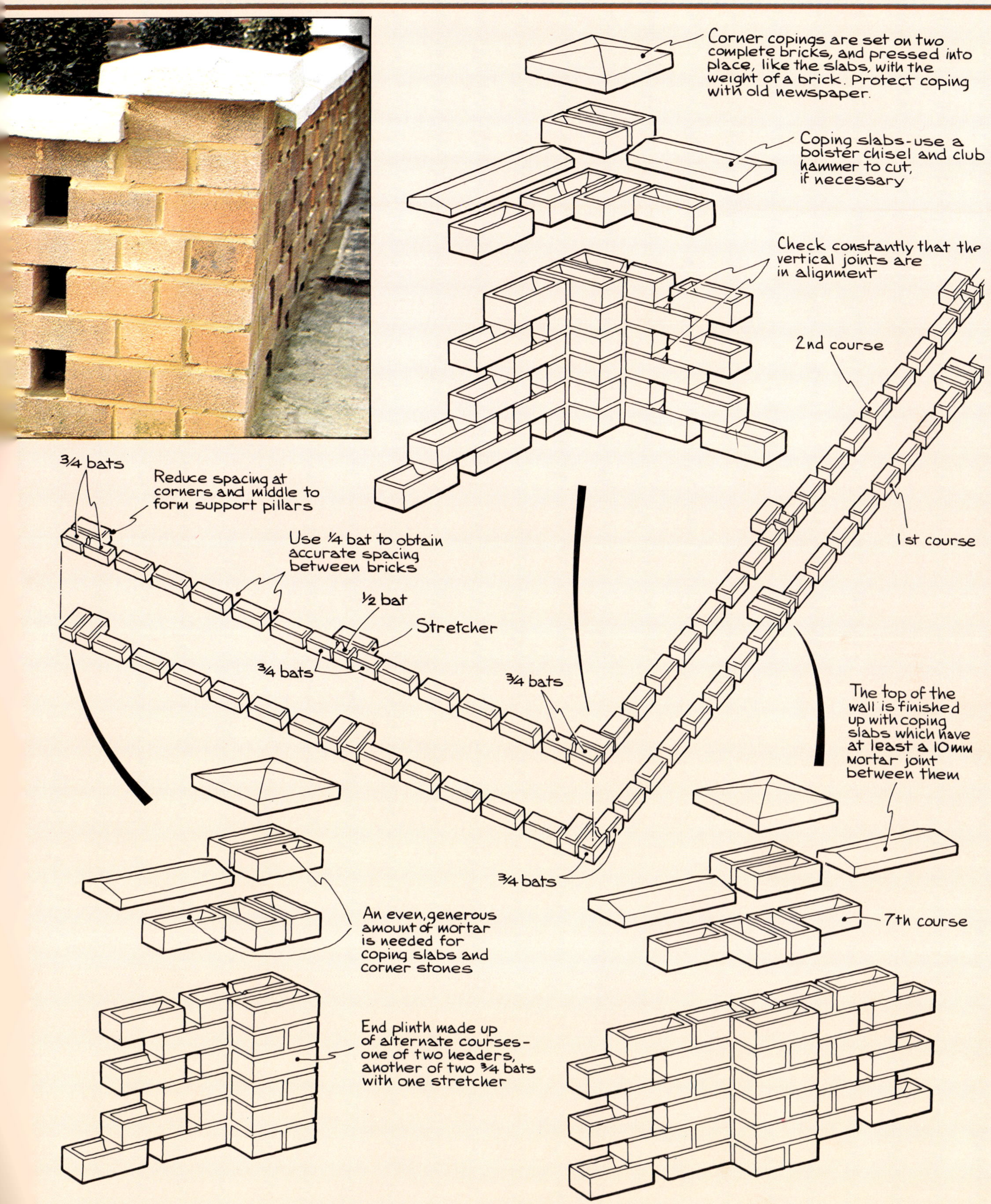

Corner copings are set on two complete bricks, and pressed into place, like the slabs, with the weight of a brick. Protect coping with old newspaper.
Coping slabs - use a bolster chisel and club hammer to cut, if necessary
Check constantly that the vertical joints are in alignment
2nd course
1st course
3/4 bats
Reduce spacing at corners and middle to form support pillars
Use 1/4 bat to obtain accurate spacing between bricks
1/2 bat
Stretcher
3/4 bats
3/4 bats
3/4 bats
The top of the wall is finished up with coping slabs which have at least a 10mm mortar joint between them
7th course
An even, generous amount of mortar is needed for coping slabs and corner stones
End plinth made up of alternate courses - one of two headers, another of two 3/4 bats with one stretcher

A brick terraced planter

This masonry project will help you to make the most of an awkward sloping garden. It uses brick walls to divide the site into a series of stepped planters, forming an attractive display on several levels

A sloping site can make it difficult to organize your garden effectively. Rainwater running down the slope can also cause problems with drainage and soil erosion.

The classic answer to both of these problems is to build terraces, dividing the slope into a series of flat steps with solid retaining walls. This makes it easy to control the drainage, as all the earth is held in position, and the flat surfaces make gardening very much simpler.

This design uses terracing to provide a series of stepped planters. These are incorporated into a scheme which spans the whole garden, with paving on two levels, steps connecting the levels, and a tall planter to provide an additional display on the upper level. You can easily modify this basic scheme to suit any particular site, incorporating some or all of the ideas as you wish.

The basis of the whole construction is a series of concrete formwork steps. These are exposed at one point to become steps on the finished structure. On each side, the same steps form the foundation for the brickwork of the planters. Level your site and cast the steps behind shuttering boards as shown.

Build up the brick walls on the formwork, installing weepholes for drainage as you go. Add paving, and surface the steps with bricks or paving slabs laid on the concrete.

Fill the planters with earth over rubble, and your terrace is complete.

Workplan

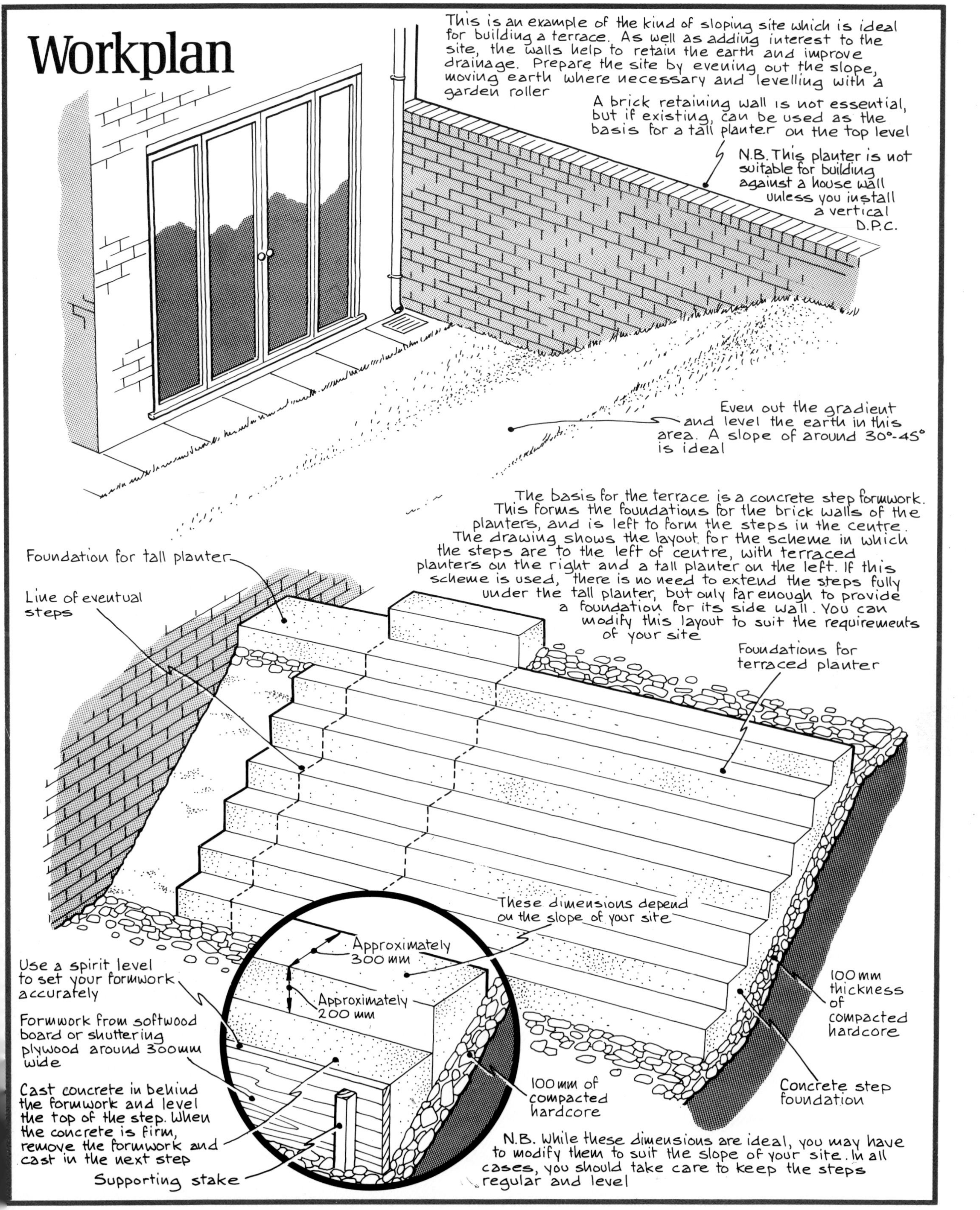
This is an example of the kind of sloping site which is ideal for building a terrace. As well as adding interest to the site, the walls help to retain the earth and improve drainage. Prepare the site by evening out the slope, moving earth where necessary and levelling with a garden roller
A brick retaining wall is not essential, but if existing, can be used as the basis for a tall planter on the top level
N.B. This planter is not suitable for building against a house wall unless you install a vertical D.P.C.
Even out the gradient and level the earth in this area. A slope of around 30°-45° is ideal
The basis for the terrace is a concrete step formwork. This forms the foundations for the brick walls of the planters, and is left to form the steps in the centre. The drawing shows the layout for the scheme in which the steps are to the left of centre, with terraced planters on the right and a tall planter on the left. If this scheme is used, there is no need to extend the steps fully under the tall planter, but only far enough to provide a foundation for its side wall. You can modify this layout to suit the requirements of your site
Foundation for tall planter
Line of eventual steps
Foundations for terraced planter
These dimensions depend on the slope of your site
Approximately 300 mm
Approximately 200 mm
Use a spirit level to set your formwork accurately
Formwork from softwood board or shuttering plywood around 300mm wide
Cast concrete in behind the formwork and level the top of the step. When the concrete is firm, remove the formwork and cast in the next step
Supporting stake
100 mm of compacted hardcore
100 mm thickness of compacted hardcore
Concrete step foundation
N.B. While these dimensions are ideal, you may have to modify them to suit the slope of your site. In all cases, you should take care to keep the steps regular and level

A brick terraced planter

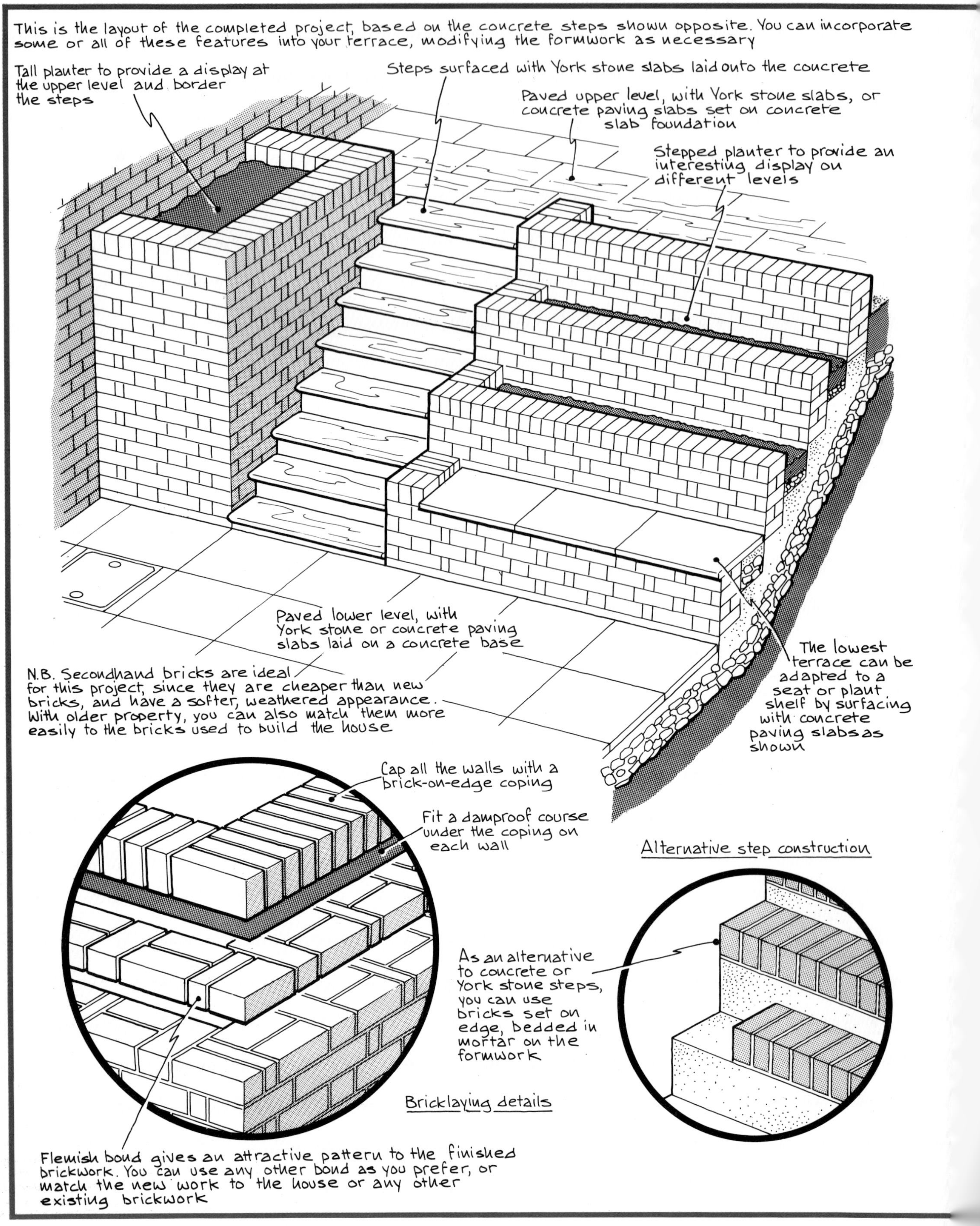

Section showing steps and tall planter

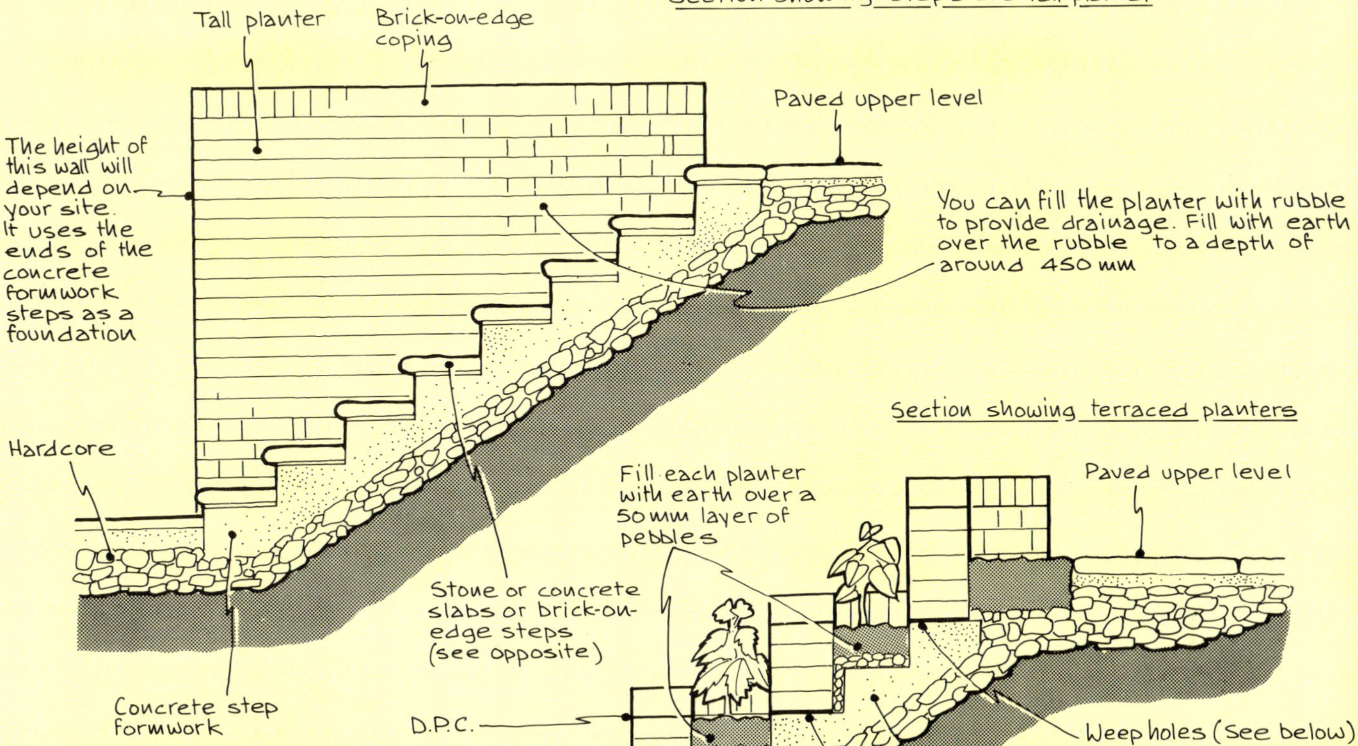

Section showing terraced planters

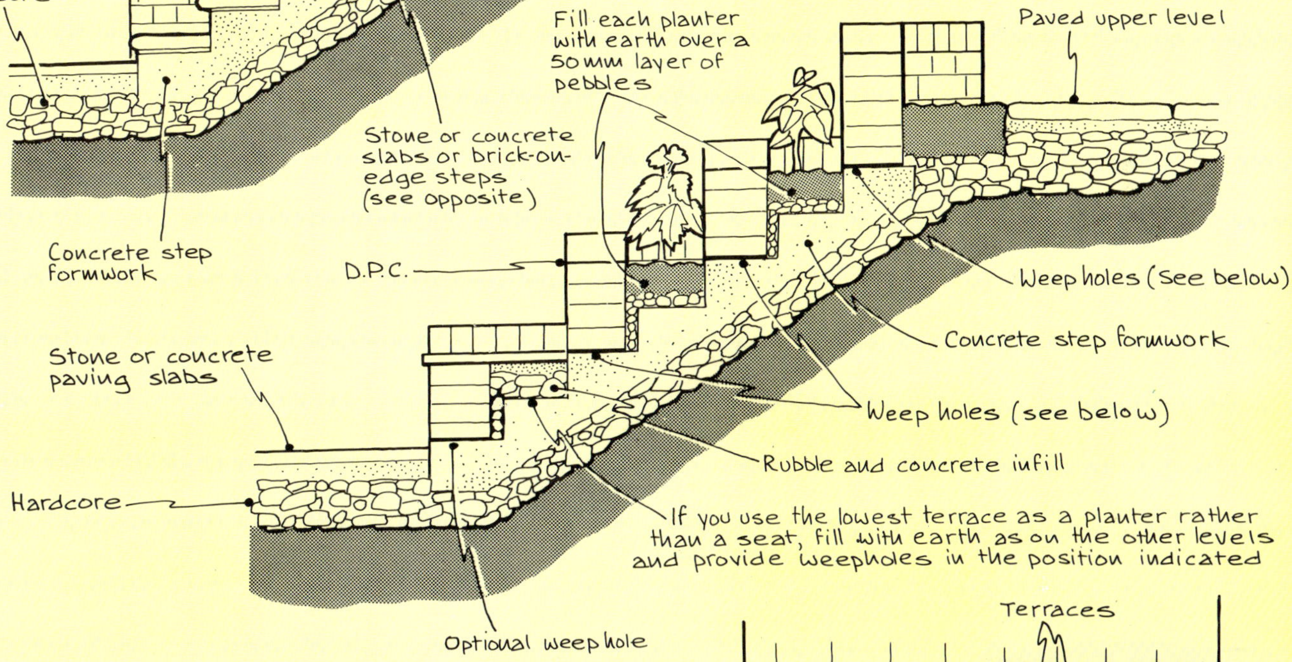

To provide weepholes for drainage, instal lengths of plastic tubing, such as 12 mm plastic overflow pipe squashed flat, in the perpendicular mortar joints at 450 mm intervals

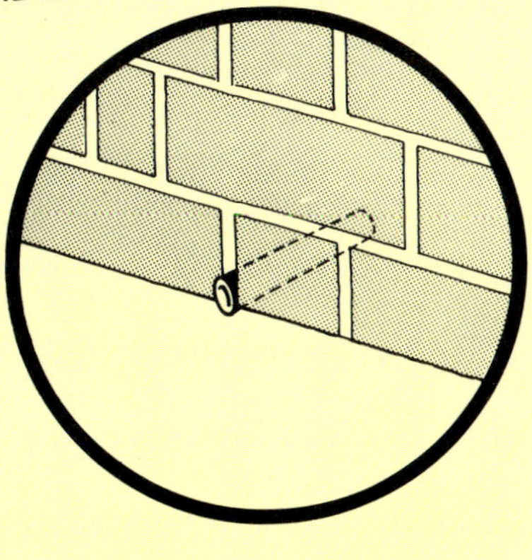

Installing weep holes

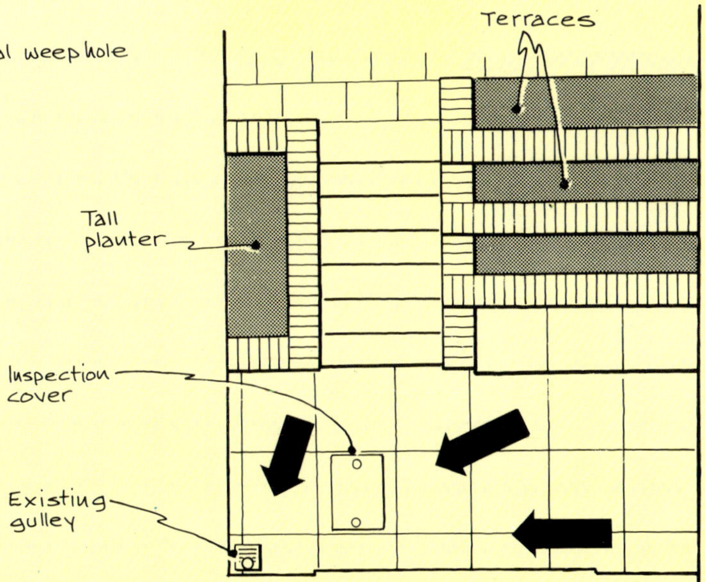

To ensure that the entire structure drains properly, provide a slight slope on the lower paved area to allow it to drain towards an existing gulley. In the drawing above, the gulley is at bottom left, so the paving is sloped in the direction of the arrows

Planning a swimming pool

Choosing the right type and size of pool for your garden and family ● Selecting the best site ● Site survey ● Designing the pool surrounds ● Planning the work schedule ● Services ● Marking out ● Excavating the hole

Private swimming pools are no longer the impossible luxury they once were. With over 10 million private pools in the world (a figure that grows by some five to ten percent every year), relative costs have been reduced to the point where you can buy and instal a swimming pool yourself for as little as two percent of the price of your home.

Unlike public pools which are more likely to be used exclusively for swimming, private pools tend to become an extension of the living room: people spend their time sitting around the pool socializing, eating, sunbathing, and generally relaxing. As this is the key to a successful installation, this series of four parts is concerned not only with the siting and installation of the pool, but also with the layout of the surrounds. Read all four parts—and make careful drawings to help you plan the landscaping—before starting work.

Installing a swimming pool is not an undertaking to be approached lightly: a typical pool about 9m × 4.5m and 1.5m deep has a volume of $60m^3$—all of which may have to be excavated, and the spoil disposed of. Careful planning and the correct choice of pool type for your garden and soil conditions is vitally important, but if you get these right the 30 or 40 man-days spent actually installing the pool and its plumbing is time well spent.

A. Below: *When designing your swimming pool, remember that it will become the natural focal point of your garden even when not in use. The surrounds may have to accommodate many adults and children so a nearby patio and tables and chairs is ideal*

Types of pool

Various types of pool are available to suit different ground conditions and levels of skill on the part of the installer. The simplest pool system is a lightweight above-ground unit which is made up from prefabricated steel panels; these can be assembled in two or three days. The panels are engineered to withstand the outward thrust of water, so they must not be sunk into the ground. A heavier duty version can be partially set into the ground or into a shallow slope, providing no external pressure from the soil is brought to bear on it.

A similar system for in-ground installation uses heavy gauge interlocking

steel panels, the unit being designed to equalize the outward pressure of the water and the inward pressure of the surrounding soil. This type can be built partially out of the ground if required and a landscaped bank built up alongside to conceal the panels.

The last pool type is made from reinforced concrete, and is usually an in-ground installation. Construction is by concrete blocks or hollow bricks with steel reinforcing rods which are then filled with concrete. Both this and the in-ground panel systems use a concrete screed as a floor, and they can be lined with PVC. One advantage of concrete pools, however, is that they can be lined with a more permanent material such as mosaic or a waterproof render coat made from white cement and marble dust.

This series concentrates on the last two pool types, partly because they are likely to create the greatest problems to installers but also because the potential they offer for landscaping and decoration around them is far greater.

B. Below: *The cunning use of synthetic grass in this pool enclosure preserves an aura of greenery close to the water while providing a practical, though expensive, surface for wet feet*

C. Right: *The choice of pool depends on budget, ground conditions and swimming requirements as well as the effect you want to create. The most permanent forms of lining are only possible on concrete blockwork pools*

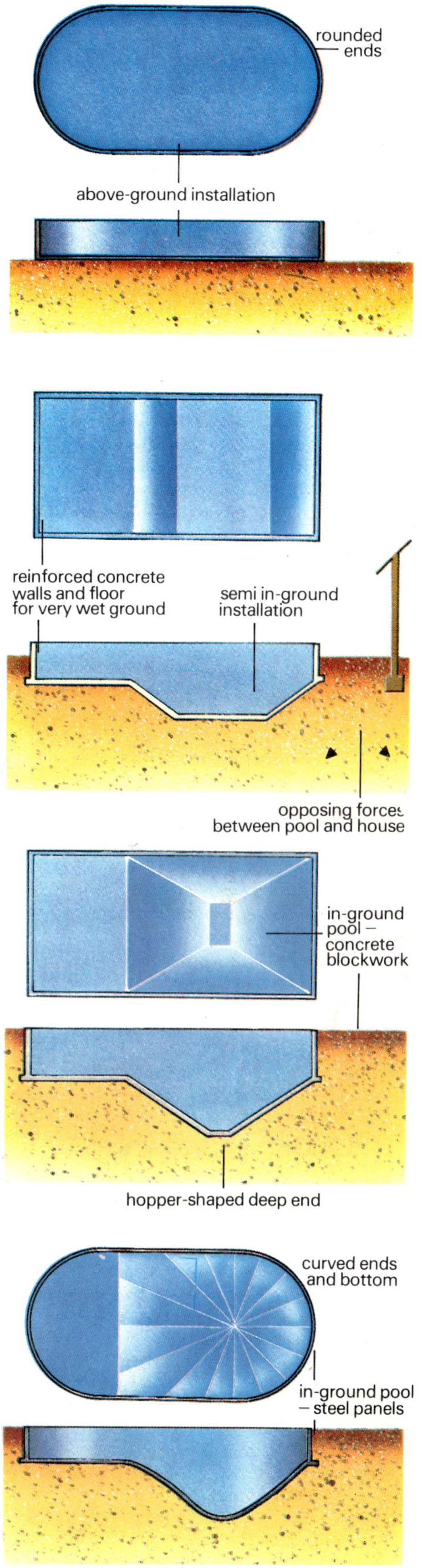

Choosing your pool

Your choice of pool type will be dictated by such diverse factors as ground conditions, local authority regulations, and the amount of money you have available but there are a number of considerations to be taken into account whatever type of pool you are buying. Many shapes and sizes are available to suit imaginative owners or awkwardly-shaped gardens, but a good practical choice is one of the oval or rectangular models offered by most manufacturers. These normally include a shallow area for children to play in, a reasonable length for swimming, and a section about 2m deep for diving. If you want to instal a springboard as well, the deep end should be at least 3m deep for safety.

When sizing up the pool allow about 4-5m^2 of water for each swimmer, and double the number of your family to arrive at a reasonable minimum size. Around the side of the pool allow the same space in hard decking for sunbathing and

POOL SURROUNDINGS

1. Topsoil for vegetable garden
2. Compost
3. Slope up
4. Bank
5. Trellis and hedge
6. Decking
7. Underwater light
8. Skimmer
9. Inlet
10. Rail barrier
11. Spoil beneath raised pool area
12. Wet seat
13. Gates
14. Planters
15. Filter
16. Heater
17. Plant room
18. Loggia
19. Patio
20. Drains
21. Mains water
22. Mains electricity
23. Telephone
24. Carport
25. House

D. Left: *Planning your pool location is a complex matter of balancing the factors of sun and shelter, privacy for swimmers and a view from the house for watching children. Site the shallow end close to the house for safety*

playing so that children do not get their feet dirty playing on grass and then transfer the dirt to the water.

Consider the pool services such as heating and filtration as well: proper filtration is essential for hygiene, while heating allows you to use the pool in chilly weather during the spring and autumn. There are many systems on sale, most of which can be adapted to suit different pool types, so choose the services at the same time as the pool so that they can be properly matched. Choosing and installing filters and heating units is covered later on in the series.

Planning

Your first concern before choosing and ordering a particular pool type should be the regulations governing its installation and operation. In certain areas there are no regulations at all as long as you do not build any kind of permanent weather-proof structure over it. Some local authorities rigidly define the minimum distance a pool should be sited from roads, boundaries, sewers and buildings while others specify standards for safety fences, energy conservation and water usage.

Check all these points with your local planning and engineering authority, and at the same time find out about any drains, gas and water mains, and underground cables that cross your property. Get information about their depth and direction so that you can plan your pool around them.

Site inspection: Before making your choice of structure investigate the condition of your planned site. Most installations require no special techniques, but you should get a surveyor or engineer to check the subsoil conditions.

If the ground is very rocky below the topsoil you may have to build a pool above ground, or else sink it only as far as the topsoil. If there is a high water table (that is, if a lot of water appears when you dig a hole, or if the ground is very wet and marshy) you must either build above ground, or drain the site by pump while you are installing the pool. This can be very expensive, and the pool could even be lifted out of the ground by flotation when the shell is empty.

The best answer to a high water table is to build elsewhere, if possible. The same applies to steep slopes or at the top of a steep bank or cliff where the soil may move suddenly under the weight of water in the pool or after heavy rain.

If your site has a corrosive or expansive soil (your surveyor or pool contractor can tell you if it has) you will have to replace it when you come to backfill around a submerged pool to prevent damage to the structure and fittings.

Layout: Armed with all the relevant information supplied by your local authority, take an architect's scale rule and draw an accurate scale plan of your property, including in it the boundaries, the position of your house, the depth and direction of underground services, the direction and fall of any slopes, and the access routes of any heavy plant such as trucks and excavators. Mark on it also the direction of the prevailing winds during the summer months and the arc the sun follows during the hours of daylight.

Make a scale cut-out of approximately the same size and shape as the pool you want and start moving this about on the plan until you find the best possible position for the pool.

A pool should be placed in the sun within easy reach of changing facilities and – for both comfort and economy – out of the wind. Try to keep the pool fairly close to the house: not only does it become easier to keep an eye on children, but the water and electricity supplies to the pool machinery can be more easily installed.

Consider the access to the site of excavators and trucks bearing sand and earth: they will require adequate space to manoeuvre and some sort of hardstanding on which to park. Consult a contractor on this point before making any final plans.

Ensure that there is sufficient working area for the excavator, and that there is enough space to store the excavated soil, which expands by about 50 percent. If you intend to dispose of it you could get it removed as soon as it is dug, but if you want to re-use it for garden landscaping you should allow at least the same area for storage as the pool occupies.

Planning the work

This is vitally important: a job that drags on for weeks and months because of an oversight at the planning stage can be disruptive and infuriating as well as expensive. Divide the pool installation into distinct phases that can be completed one at a time over a few weeks or during your holidays. The main parts of any job of this kind can be divided into: site clearance; marking and excavation; pool construction; services installation; and landscaping (this aspect is covered in detail later on in the series and also in the Home designer course).

Many of the tasks can be completed more quickly and for only a little more expense by using sub-contracted labour. For example, by hiring an excavator you can dig the hole in a day or by getting the pool supplier to recommend a contractor you can reduce the base concreting to a one-day job, along with the installation of the surrounding deck and the perimeter coping of flagstones on concrete.

Your schedule should be fairly flexible and must take into account the type of pool you are building. You could finish a prefabricated or modular pool within two weeks if you were to work during your holidays, while a concrete block system of

1 *Mark the outline of the pool on the ground with string and pegs. Allow an extra 600mm all round and mark this digging line with sand or lime*

2 *Before digging, place the datum peg in the highest piece of surrounding ground at least 2m from the pool area and mark it with a rubber ball*

3 *An excavator will dig the hole in less than a day. Brief the operator beforehand so he knows exactly what to do and does not go too deep*

4 *Set up a Dumpy or Cowley level on a piece of firm ground near the pool. Adjust its position according to the height of the datum peg*

5 *Now you can use a home-made surveyor's pole to check the depth of the hole at various points in conjunction with the level*

6 *When the excavator has finished digging the main part of the hole you can trim it by hand using the level to check the exact depths*

construction is more adaptable to casual weekend working over a period of months. You should in any case allow at least 30 man-days for a modular system, and as many as 50 for a concrete block swimming pool.

Services

You do not have to have a heated pool, but you must have a filtering system that recirculates the water and purifies it. The rate of flow obviously varies with the size of pool, but a system that completely changes the water every 12 hours or so while it is in use is the minimum requirement. There are a number of filtration systems available, as well as a wide choice of heating systems. All are discussed further on in this series, but it is worth considering at this stage where they will be located.

If necessary you can house them all in a corner of your garage, but a separate enclosed space at least 1m × 2m is preferable. If you do include heating in your plans for the pool, then a plant room at least 2.5m × 1.5m in area with provision for storage of chemicals and cleaning equipment will be useful.

Marking out

Consulting the layout that you have already drawn up lay a datum peg in the ground at least 2m outside the pool area and out of the way of construction traffic and stored earth (fig. 2). The top of the peg should be about 30-40mm above the surrounding land and marks the finished level of the pool and its surrounds. This is the point from which all levels and heights will be measured, so on no account must it be moved.

It also helps if you align the pool with a fixed object – such as a fence or the side of the house: this creates another useful reference point during installation.

Using this second point, measure and mark out one side of the pool in its correct position. Drive a peg into each end of the line. Taking your 15m steel tape measure, mark the approximate position of one adjacent side of the pool by drawing an arc with sand or lime of the correct radius from one of the pegs. Moving to the other peg, draw a second arc of the same radius as the pool's diagonal measurement, and where these two arcs coincide place a third peg (fig. F).

Repeat this procedure at the opposite end of the line you drew first to get the third side so that you end up with four pegs placed in the ground forming a perfect rectangle. The exact dimensions of the pool and its diagonals will be

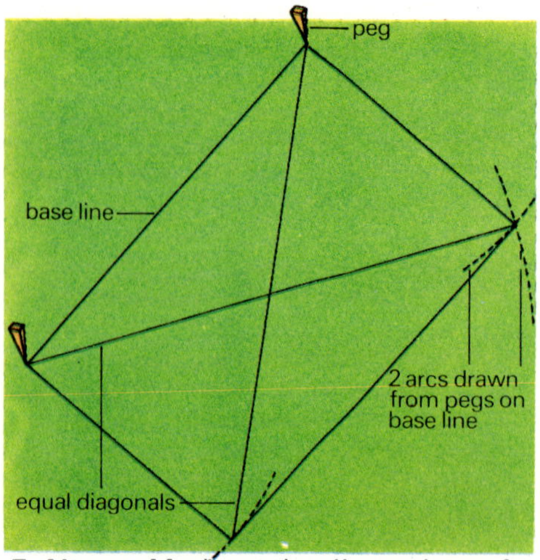

F. Above: *Mark out the dimensions of the pool using pegs. You can work out a perfect rectangle by drawing arcs from the first two pegs with a steel tape*

G. Above right: *If your garden has a tree-lined corner, this could provide privacy and shelter from the wind. Complement a woodland setting with natural materials for the surround*

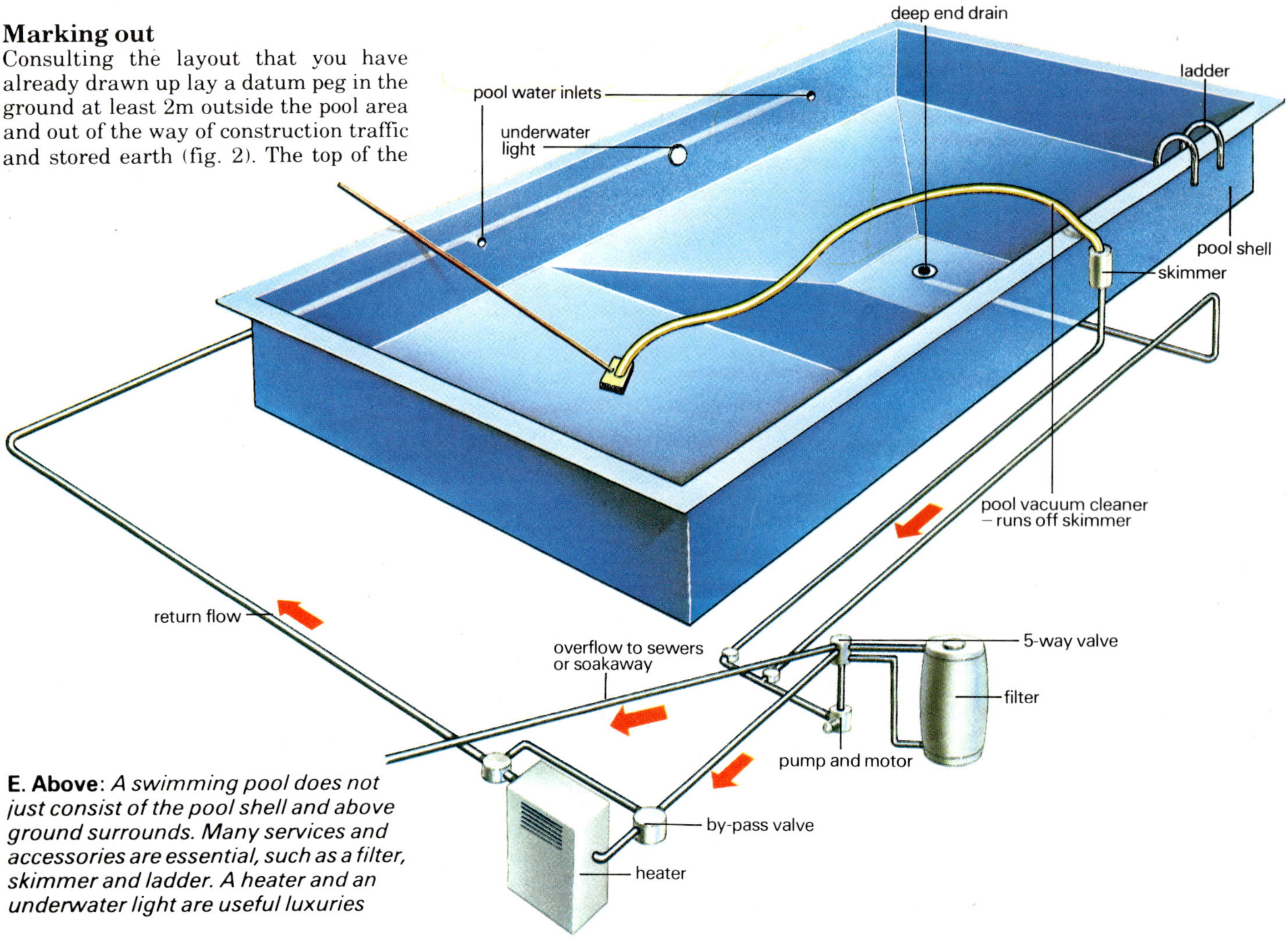

E. Above: *A swimming pool does not just consist of the pool shell and above ground surrounds. Many services and accessories are essential, such as a filter, skimmer and ladder. A heater and an underwater light are useful luxuries*

supplied by the manufacturer but to ensure a perfect rectangle, make certain the two diagonals are exactly the same length and cross in the middle.

Where the pool has rounded ends, find and mark the centres from which the radii of their arcs will be measured and then mark the rounded ends themselves.

To allow for the thickness of the pool walls and to create a certain amount of working room, allow an extra 600mm all round and mark this larger perimeter on the site. This new line marks the digging area for the excavator.

The third part of the series describes how to position and instal the filtration and heating units. Referring to this and the manufacturer's instructions, mark the position of any piping around the pool and follow the runs right up to where the heating and filtration equipment will be located.

A sloping site must be levelled before you mark it up. Dig down to the correct level–do not build up soil as this will remain unstable during excavation.

Excavation

The manufacturer's instructions will include the various pool depths and the shape of the pool floor, so you will be able to brief the driver of your hired excavator. Do not start work until the operator knows exactly what he must do, and until you have impressed upon him the importance of not over-digging.

Check the levels constantly during excavation: the importance of certain dimensions varies from one type of pool to another, but try to get them all right. Use the Dumpy or Cowley level to check the depth of the hole at the corners, at changes of gradient, and all the way across the pool.

If you are storing the spoil for subsequent landscaping, make sure it is well away from the sides of the hole and that it cannot collapse under its weight. If you are getting rid of it, however, keep about $18m^3$ for backfilling later (providing of course it is suitable material).

When the hole is roughly the right depth all round–but not too deep–the excavator can be sent away. Trim the hole by hand using a spade.

Wet sites: There are three methods of drying these out–assuming you cannot dig elsewhere. The first is to dig a bore hole deeper than the pool and just outside the pool area. Water will drain into it and you can pump this away.

The second, in pools where there is a drain at the deep end, is to instal the drain with a hydrostatic relief valve. The valve allows water into the drain from where it is pumped away by the pipe normally attached to the filtration unit (see part three of the series).

The third method is to instal a series of land drains below the pool floor which channel the water down to the hydrostatic relief valve, but this should only be used in extremely wet sites, and the concrete pool floor laid above it must be reinforced with steel rods. Your supplier or surveyor will tell you which method is most suitable for your site.

Pool checklist

	Planning	Tank	Surroundings
Determine:	type of pool	type of tank	type of decking
Consider:	budget and contingency; reserve pool uses and users; feasibility	gradient; ramps; steps and datum level; soil disposal; water table	site clearance; pool enclosure or fencing; new and existing landscaping
Check:	local planning codes; water, gas, electricity supplies nearby	water table; soil conditions; subsoil drainage; special reinforcement	nuisance value to neighbours
Select or locate:	pool orientation; size; shape; sunshine; wind; services; access for machinery	method of excavation; working and storage areas; drains; gulleys and sumps; pool lining; water level; energy conservation	levels and contouring; features and walling; trees and planting; terraces and wet seating; decking surfaces and finishes; deck accessories

Pool construction

● Constructing the pool shell from steel or glass fibre panels ● Concrete blockwork ● Installing the pool floor ● Waterproof render and PVC linings ● Fitting steps, drains and skimmers ● Backfilling ● Decking

The hardest part of any swimming pool installation is the construction of the tank itself and this, the second part of the series, is devoted to this crucial phase.

Having made your choice of pool type and drawn up your workplan according to the information in part one of the series, order the pool kit from the manufacturer. Because each kit is tailored to a slightly different layout and set of ground conditions, find out in advance what extra equipment and tools you will need for the job so that you can have them all ready when the kit is delivered. Then check the contents of the kit against the parts list that should be supplied with it and read and understand the instructions before you go any further.

Installing the pool shell

The pool shell is basically a large watertight tank engineered to withstand the weight of up to 100m^3 of water and the inward pressure of the surrounding soil. The walls are usually erected first and the floor rendered afterwards.

A. Left: *In a relatively small city garden an irregular pool sited off-centre leaves plenty of space for relaxing and also for plenty of greenery*

B. Below: *Cross section showing two forms of pool construction – panel (left) and blockwork (right) – plus the deep end drain and soakaway*

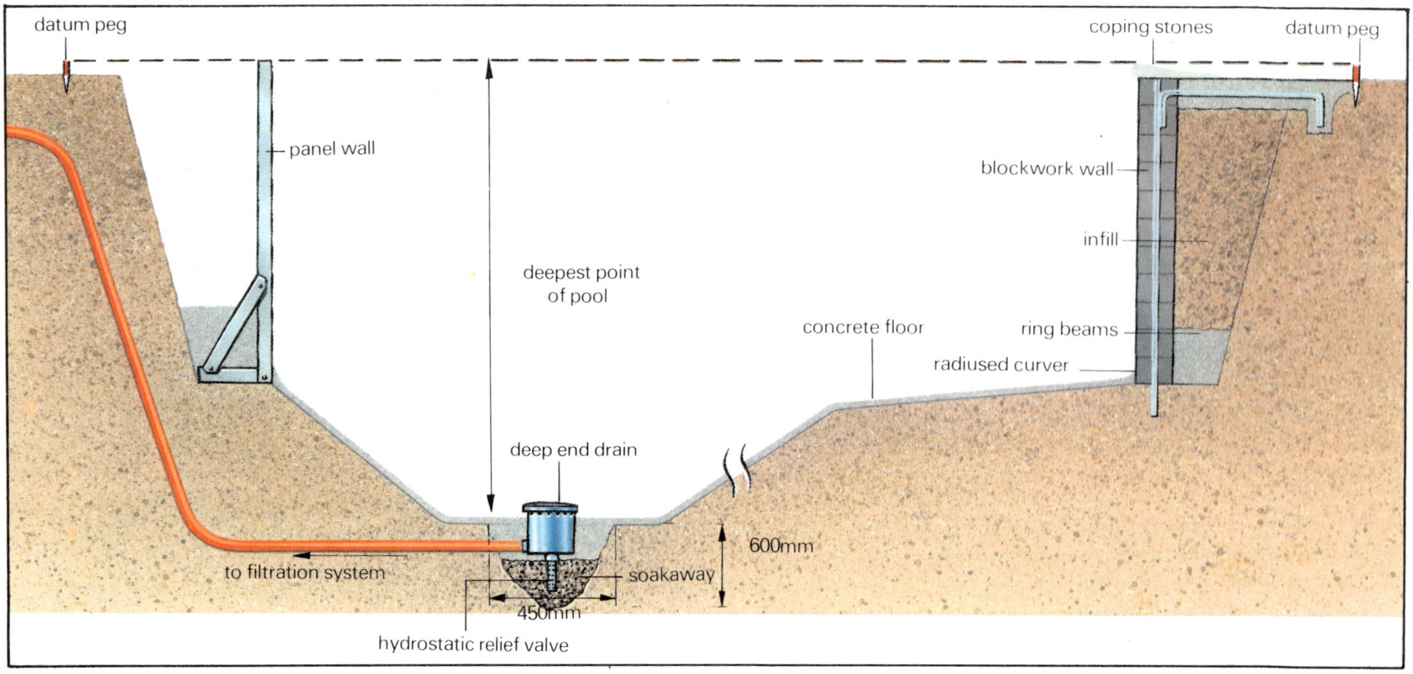

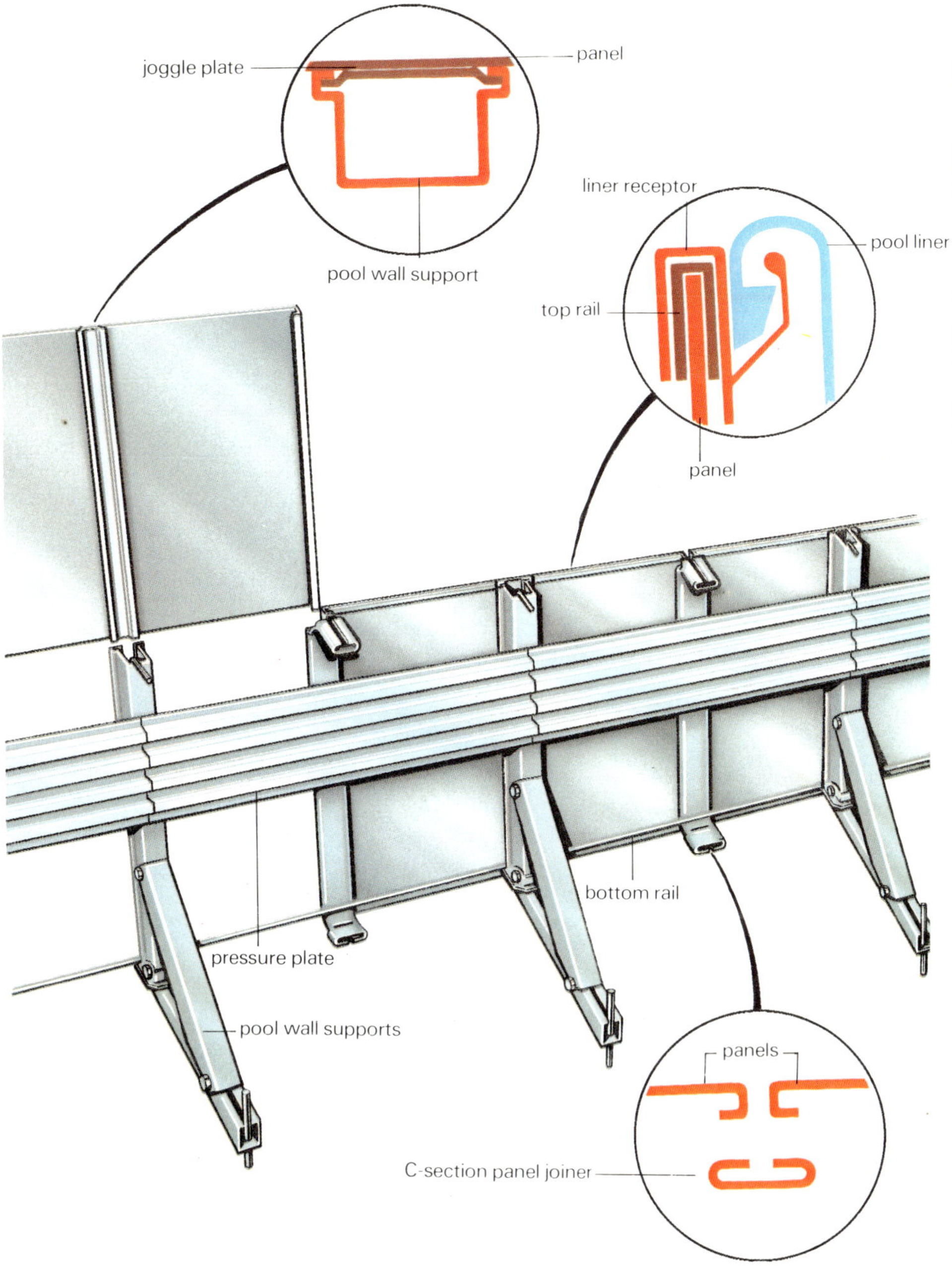

C. Above: *Panels are joined by C-sections slotted into wall supports. The rails and pressure plates strengthen the walls and the liner is secured to the top rail*

1 *When installing a panel pool start by assembling the angled pool wall supports. These simply bolt together—use a spanner and self-locking wrench*

First check all the excavation depths and re-trim the hole if necessary, then choose the positions of the lights, drains, and skimmers (this will be covered in detail in part three of the series).

Panel pools: In a panel pool system your first job is then to assemble the panel supports. These are typically angled brackets made from galvanized steel which bolt together (fig. 1). Lower these into the hole in approximately their correct positions and locate them with the tie bars and panels which connect them all together. The steel wall panels can then be fitted in place; like the supports they are simply bolted or slotted together, according to the pool type. In most kits certain panels are cut to accommodate such things as lights and drains so make sure that these are in their correct places.

One type of panel pool consists of glass fibre panels which simply slot together and which are reinforced with a concrete ring beam at top and bottom: these are even more quickly assembled.

Blockwork pools: These are more versatile and durable than panel pools, but also considerably more time-consuming to assemble. Most systems use hollow plastic 'bricks' which are filled with concrete after erection, and the simplest of these consists of walls erected on a levelled pool floor (fig. D).

In this case simply build the four (or more) pool walls, assembling the hollow bricks according to the manufacturer's instructions. The bricks are divided into certain types so make sure the *footing* bricks form the first two courses and that bricks intended to accommodate fittings such as skimmers and lights are in their correct positions.

When the walls are assembled and you are certain they are level, instal the wall fittings and make sure they are protected from the infill concrete by masking them with tape or polyethylene. If the instructions state that the walls need steel reinforcement, drive reinforcing rods of the correct length through the walls and into the ground at this stage. Infilling with concrete is normally done using a funnel-like hopper to feed the concrete mix into the first three or four courses of bricks only. After this concrete has set, you can repeat the procedure for the remaining courses.

The strongest pool shell, and the one which allows the most flexibility in terms of work schedules, uses a similar blockwork construction laid on top of a mortar bed. The blocks used are hollow core units laid core-upwards so that they can be reinforced with steel rods every 300mm or so and then filled with concrete.

With this type of pool the entire floor must be rendered first and the concrete ring beam around the base laid before the walls are erected. With every other type, however, the ring beam is laid around the outside of the wall before the floor is screeded.

Ring beams: First ensure (where applicable) that the gap between the base of the wall and the edge of the hole is constant

2 *Now assemble the side pressure plates which strengthen the panels as they connect the wall supports. They are secured with self-tapping screws*

3 *Where the pool wall supports meet the edges of the hole you may have to dig additional small channels for the supports to fit into*

4 *When the supports along the side of the pool are erected, check that they are all at the same height and also that this height is correct*

all round, then seal any joints in the wall with tape or paper. Use steel pegs set into the ground to mark the correct concrete level, then pour a 1:2:4 concrete mix into the void so that it just covers the pegs (see checklist on concrete and mortar mixes overleaf). Allow it to set before going any further with the pool.

Flooring

The instructions should tell you how thick the pool floor must be and what concrete mix to use but if they do not, use a 1:6 screed mix of cement and sharp washed sand. Check that the mix is not too wet (it should remain in a ball after being squeezed in the hand) and aim for a screed depth of about 25mm. The huge weight of the pool water will hold the liner and flooring in position.

Mark the screed depth with pegs set into the tamped earth of the pool floor at regular intervals and, if you are fitting a drain at the deep end, instal this now. Make sure that the drain is set out of the

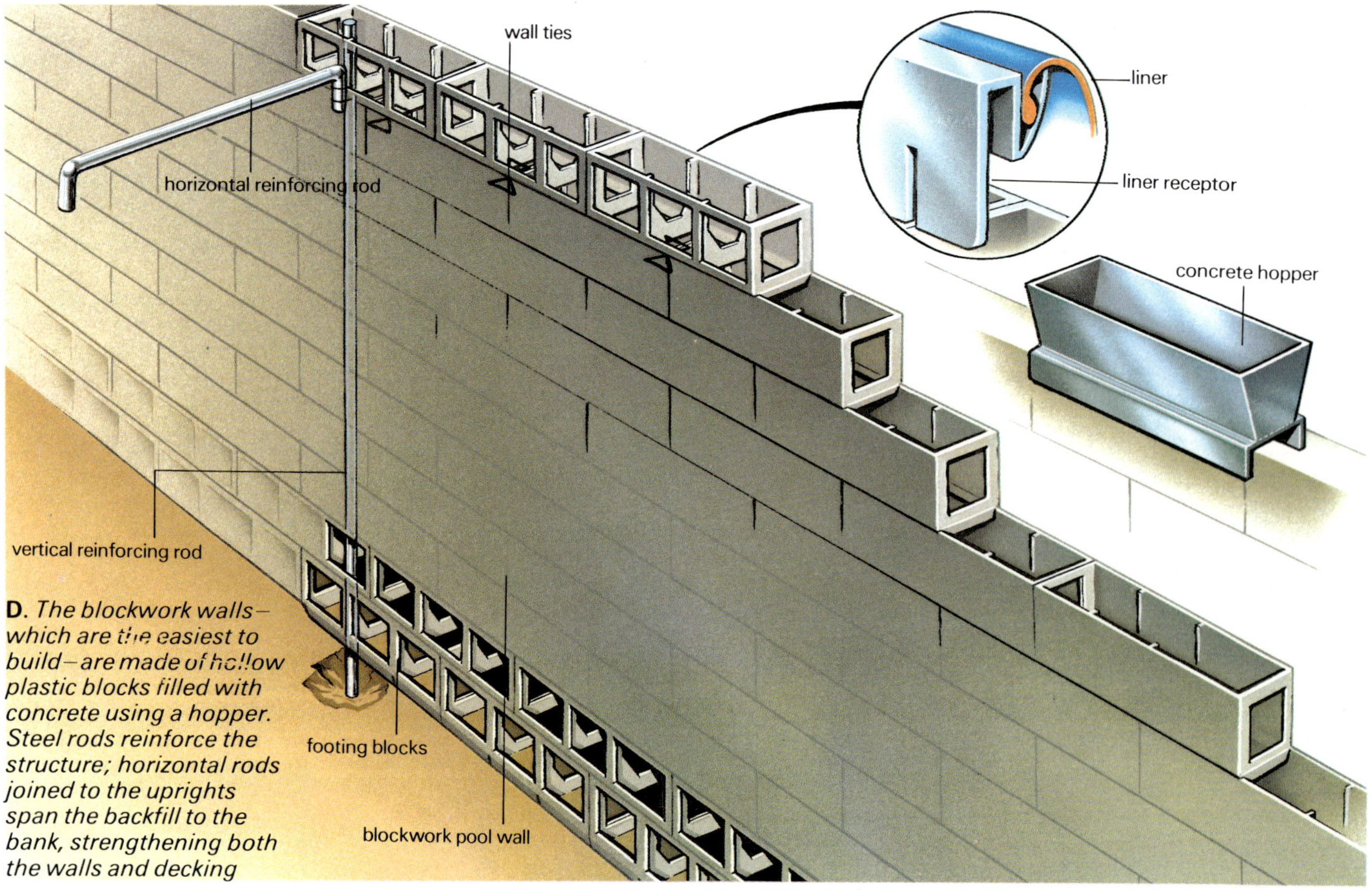

D. *The blockwork walls—which are the easiest to build—are made of hollow plastic blocks filled with concrete using a hopper. Steel rods reinforce the structure; horizontal rods joined to the uprights span the backfill to the bank, strengthening both the walls and decking*

5 *If any of the supports are not high enough, pack them out with compacted earth. If they are too tall, make their holes slightly deeper*

6 *Before going any further make absolutely sure that the pool is regular in shape by checking that the diagonals are the same length*

7 *Now secure the supports by driving 450mm steel pins through them and into the ground. Leave about 150mm of the pins exposed*

8 *Where the pool has rounded ends mark the radius of the curves from a centre point by drawing a steel pin through the earth*

9 *Fit the wall panels into place with the joggle plates attached. These then slot into the grooves provided in the pool wall supports*

10 *Fit the intermediate wall panels into place. These should be secured to the adjacent panels with the correct C-section panel joiners*

soil as high as the finished screed.

Mix the concrete, load it into your wheelbarrow, and move it down to the deep end on a path made from planks or scaffold boards. Starting at the junction of floor and wall around the deep end, get an assistant to shovel the concrete on to the earth. Then, working towards the bottom, tamp it down with a wooden beam and smooth it off with a steel float. Remove each depth-marking peg as you reach it and take care not to over-trowel the screed or you will cause laitence to form on the surface.

Continue screeding back up the pool, leaving a suitable path so that you screed all except one corner at the shallow end. Afterwards climb out of the pool and lean over the wall to finish the job. At the edges of the screed, run the concrete up the walls for 50-75mm so that there is a gentle curve between the floor and the wall surfaces. Make sure you clean any splashes of concrete off the walls well before it sets.

The pool liner

There are two types of liner. The traditional one consists of several coats of waterproof render with a painted or tiled finish. More common nowadays (and cheaper) is a PVC liner which can either be supplied ready-cut or else cut and solvent-welded to the exact required shape on site.

PVC liner: This is secured around the top edge of the pool wall by a retaining strip which engages a bead in the liner's edge (fig. C). To protect the liner from abrasions you can instal an underlay. This usually comes in sections which must be glued separately on to a perfectly clean and dry pool floor or wall, and the joints must be taped together. Make sure it is perfectly flat and then cut around all the lights and fittings in the pool wall with a sharp knife. Fit gaskets to all the fittings before installing the liner itself.

Choose a warm day to instal the liner and unroll it on the lawn—not on tarmac or concrete—before getting several assistants to help you carry it carefully to the pool without letting it drag on the ground. Depending on the type of pool, you must locate at least one corner of the liner with a reference point in the pool itself. When you have done this locate the edge bead in the retaining strip around the top of the pool wall and let the liner settle in the pool shell. Smooth out any wrinkles in the liner with a soft broom and then tape over the joint between the edge of the liner and the wall (fig. 20).

Now, using an industrial type vacuum cleaner with the hose either slipped in between the liner and the wall or through

11 *At the appropriate point, assemble the skimmer, join it to its panel and fit this into the previously selected position*

12 *When all the panels are in place, check very carefully that they are all level and all at the correct height using a sight stick and a theodolite*

13 *Extras such as steps should be installed at this stage. Secure steps with self-tapping screws and fit a gasket between them and the walls*

14 *Lay a concrete ring beam at least 75mm deep around the base of the pool walls after checking that these are all level and upright*

15 *Tape over the panel joints and screed the floor in sections. Smooth the concrete with a float and run it up the pool walls about 50mm*

16 *As the concrete dries, fit the top rail and liner receptor and wire-lock the necessary reinforcement rods around the pool perimeter*

Concrete and mortar mixes

Concretes	Cement	Sharp sand	Soft sand	Aggregate (10mm)
Oversite blinding	1	4		4
Footing and foundations	1	2		4
Floor slab – block pool ring beams	1	2		4
– liner pool	1		6	
Screeding	1	4		
Wall infill/backfill/decking	1	2		3
Decking	1			6
Mortars				
Walls — below ground	1		3	
– above ground	1		6	
Coping	1		4	
Jointing	1		5	
Render	1		6	

17 *With the aid of assistants, lay the liner in the pool. Make quite certain that it is correctly aligned with the sides of the pool*

18 *Clip the bead in the edge of the liner into the liner receptor, pulling the liner around to distribute it evenly across the pool*

19 *Tape the liner around the edges of the pool steps so that you can fit a gasket around the opening before cutting the liner away later*

E. *When building concrete blockwork pool walls fit banking plates into blocks protruding at corners to stop the concrete infill leaking out*

F. *Fit the skimmer, wall-mounted drains and inlets as you erect the walls. Mask these with polyethylene or tape to protect them from the concrete infill*

G. *Use string stretched between pegs to check the levels in the pool walls. When the walls are erected instal the drain in the bottom of the pool*

H. *Fill completed walls with the correct concrete infill. Compact the concrete in the first four courses and let it dry before filling the rest*

one of the skimmer outlets, draw the air out from under the liner so that it moulds itself to the pool floor (fig. 21). Smooth out any further wrinkles by shifting the liner bead around in its retaining strip or by physically getting into the pool—in stockinged feet—and pulling them out with moistened fingers.

Now you can start filling the pool (see part three of the series). Switch off the vacuum cleaner when the water level in the shallow end is about 100-150mm.

Render coating: In this case start off by brushing a slurry mixture of cement and water on to the walls and floor to act as a key for the render coats. Afterwards render the floor and walls with a 1:6 mix of cement and sharp sand incorporating a

Installation programmes

	Substructure	Plumbing	Services	Surroundings
1.	tank excavation	trenching	allocation	clearance
2.	subsoil drainage	hydrostatic relief valve	drains and sewers	surface drainage
3.	subfloor	pool gravity outlet	conduits and infilling	subsoil disposal
4.	base	main drain or	plant room base	contouring
5.	walling	inlets and skimmers	underwater lighting	backfilling
6.	lining	pipeline layout	storage facilities	decking foundations
7.	coping	plant room layout	electrics	paving/decking
8.	poolside accessories	water treatment plant	controls and valves	walling and features
9.	safety equipment	water heating plant	bather changing	landscape structures
10.	finishes	commissioning	maintenance	planting and turfing

proprietary waterproofing agent in the mixing water. Use a scratcher to key this as it goes off and then, when it is fully dry, apply a final 10mm render coat of the same mix. Finish this with a wooden float as a final surface to which you can apply an appropriate paint or mosaic finish.

A wide variety of specialized paint finishes are available, most of them requiring several coats. The most durable (and expensive) finish of all remains mosaic or ceramic tiling, and either can make an attractive pool outstanding.

Backfilling

Your initial survey will have told you whether your garden soil is suitable for backfilling and if it is not you should by this stage have imported some suitable material (about 18m³ for an in-ground installation). Shovel the material into the void between the pool wall and the edges of the hole, tamping it down in layers 150-200mm thick.

Test the plumbing system before burying the pipework (see Filtration and Circulation) and then backfill to the level specified in the manufacturer's fitting instructions.

Most installations require you to run tie bars from the top of the wall to the edge of the hole at about 1m intervals. As the normal backfill level is about 200mm below the top of the pool wall, this allows you plenty of room to pour concrete into what remains of the gap around the pool. The tie bars and concrete then reinforce the decking which will be laid above.

Smooth off the concrete and allow it to set. Then lay a decking of coping stones on top, arranged to protrude slightly over the edge of the pool. The stones should slope away from the pool towards a gulley at a gradient of not less then 1:50 so that water splashes can be channelled back into the water system after filtration (see parts three and four of this series).

20 *Remove all the creases in the liner by tugging them gently with your hands. Alternatively you can smooth them out with a soft broom*

21 *When you start filling the pool, remove any air between the liner and pool shell by fitting the nozzle of an industrial vacuum cleaner between them to draw the air out*

Pool fittings

Suction

Main drain
- situated at deepest point
- 200mm pot with anti-vortex cover
- provision for hydrostatic relief valve stem

Skimmer weir
- situated to face prevailing wind at water level
- floating weir overflow taking 80 percent of pool water to filter
- includes leaf basket, equalization line and provision for underwater suction sweeper

Return

Flow inlet
- situated in wall 500mm below water level multi-directional control

Extras as required

Underwater light	wall niche fitted within pool shell
Underwater sound	500mm below water level
Cup anchors	bolted and plugged
Handrailing brackets	50mm above water level

Tools and plant

Garden tools:	Spade; shovel; rake; pick-axe; yardbroom; soft broom; dustpan and brush; two garden hoses
Hand tools:	Screwdriver set; pliers; hammers (light, heavy, and claw); hand saw; tenon saw; hacksaw; razor knife; electric drill with masonry bits and hammer attachment; extension lead
Masonry tools:	Spirit level; 15m steel tape measure; 3m steel tape measure; bucket; trowel; steel finishing trowel; wooden float; string; plumb-bob; concrete tamper
Plumbing tools:	Pipe wrench or adjustable spanner; emery paper; paintbrush; pipe pliers
Plant hire:	Wheelbarrow; concrete mixer; dumper; excavator; bolt croppers; Dumpy or Cowley level and surveyor's pole

Filtration and circulation

● The importance of filtration ● The circulation system ● How to lay it out ● Sizing the filters ● Installing the pipework and filter equipment ● Finishing off ● Electrics ● Disinfection

A. Below: *A swimming pool is more than an enormous bath full of water: it must be kept clean and free of algae and bacteria. Installing a proper circulation system to cope with this is a necessity, but it can be done comparatively easily*

A swimming pool is more than a tank that you can simply set into the ground and fill with water—if it is not cleaned regularly and if the water is not properly filtered and disinfected it will very soon become a stagnant pond full of bacteria and algae.

Proper filtration is vital to a successful pool installation and this, the third part of the series, is mainly concerned with the problems of choosing and installing filtration equipment.

A basic system comprising a pump and motor, control valves and a filter unit, combined with chemical disinfectants of one kind or another that are added by hand, allows you to keep the same water in your pool for years with only occasional topping-up. This keeps your water rates lower than if you refilled it every year.

Circulation

The pool and filtration plant form a completely self-contained system. The dirtiest water—the top 50mm or so on the surface—is drawn through a skimmer mounted in the pool wall at water level. The water passes through two strainer baskets which filter out leaves and hairs before it is pumped through a filter bed.

Filtration and circulation

It is also possible to instal a filtration system that incorporates a drain at the bottom of the deep end of the pool. This will only filter at most 20 percent of the pool water, but this does include the dirt which invariably settles on the bottom, so this system can be a good investment if your pool is designed to take such a unit.

Cleaned water is pumped from the filter and can then be heated before being fed back into the pool at the opposite end or side from the skimmers.

Laying the system out: Before laying out the system choose your filter type and size (see below)—as a basic rule always oversize the filter slightly to accommodate any temporary increase in the number of swimmers.

The filter, the size of the pipes, and the capacity of the pump must be correctly matched. Generally speaking the further the filtration plant is from the pool, the greater the pipe diameter and the stronger the pump must be. The pump is weakest on the suction side, however, so you should try to position it as close to the skimmer as possible.

The majority of pool installations place the pump within about 10m of the pool and 0.5m above or below the surface water level. This allows the use of 40mm low pressure ABS or uPVC pipework with a 500-1000 watt electric pump, but if

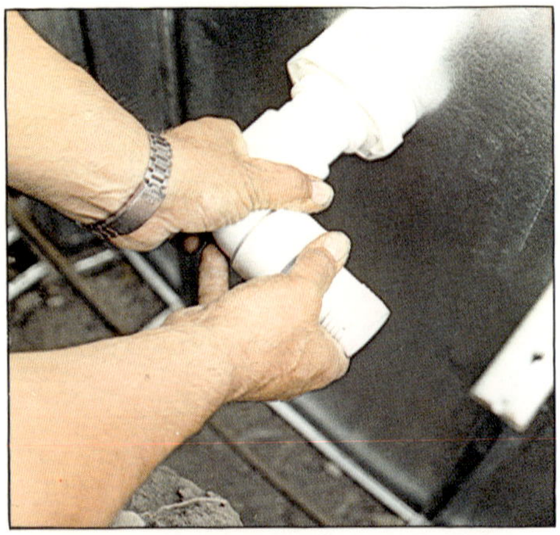

1 *Secure the pool water inlet to the pool wall panel through the pre-drilled hole and secure it with the plastic backnut supplied*

2 *Fit the skimmer unit to its panel before this is assembled to the pool, and secure it through the panel with the brass nuts and screws supplied*

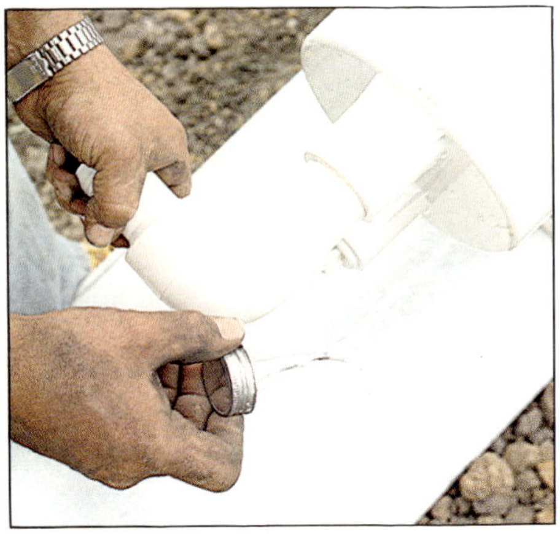

3 *Cement the water pipe connections and fittings in place using the correct ABS solvent, and wrap PTFE tape around any threads*

4 *Tape a gasket to the edges of the skimmer unit, water inlet, and underwater light holes before you fit the PVC pool liner and fill it with water*

B. Below: *A typical pool circulation system: the wind blows dirty water into the skimmers and from there it is pumped through the filter and heater back to the below-surface water inlet*

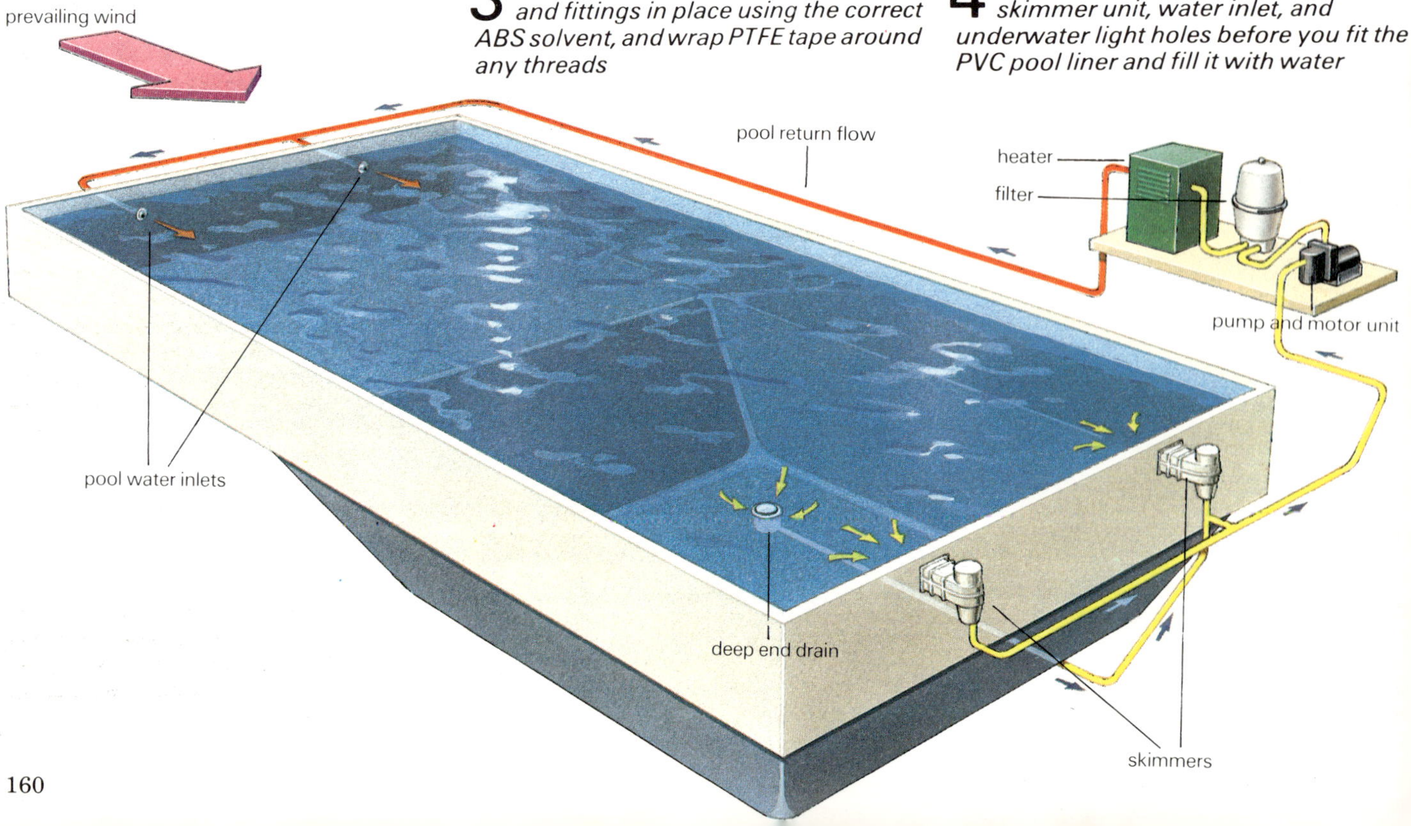

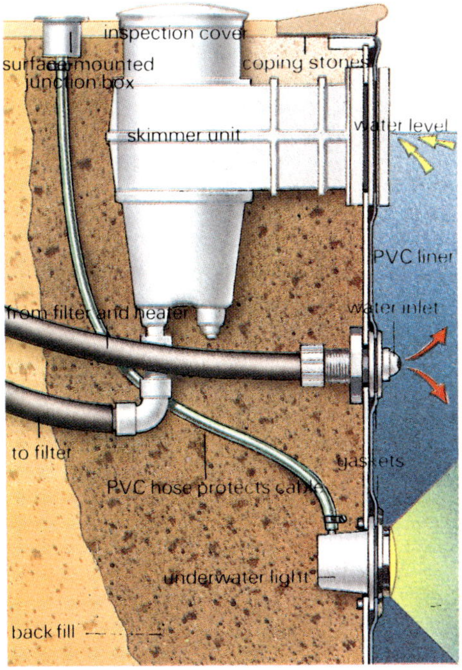

C. *The skimmer, water inlet, and underwater light installed in a panel pool wall. Note the gaskets between the panel and liner, and the buried pipework*

5 *Rather than dig trenches for the water pipes to and from the plant room, you can lay them in the pool excavation for some of the way*

6 *When the skimmer is installed make sure its weight is supported by a concrete block until you backfill round the outside of the pool walls*

7 *In a blockwork pool system the skimmer unit, pool water inlet, and the underwater lights must be installed in their final positions as the walls are erected*

8 *Run the cables to the underwater lights through length of watertight PVC hose. These should be secured at each end to the fittings with worm-drive hose clips*

you are in doubt consult your supplier.

Inside the plant room mark the function and flow direction of all pipes and valves, and include gate valves within each line so that you can completely isolate any part of the system without having to drain the pool.

Filters

There are two main filter types, both available in a variety of sizes and capacities. The cartridge type consists of a porous membrane mounted on a frame through which the water flows. When it becomes clogged up and impedes the circulation – which you will notice either because the pressure gauge on the filter unit shows a higher reading, or because the water in the pool starts looking dirty – the membrane should be removed and it can either be hosed down or replaced. This type of filter needs regular servicing but it is economical to use as it does not require much power from the pump to force the water through it.

The sand bed filter has a greater capacity and is very simple to maintain. The water flows through a bed of finely graded sand which traps the dirt. When the sand is totally clogged up the pressure in the system rises due to the restricted flow of water.

At the point of maximum pressure you merely reverse the direction of flow through the filter (a process called *backwashing*) and clean water purifies the sand before being channelled into a drain or soakaway. This process takes only a couple of hours once a week.

Installation

As stated on page 153, choose the positions of the skimmers and inlets before erecting the pool walls. In an ideal installation the prevailing winds would blow surface water towards the skimmers where it would be sucked a short distance to the filters. From here the clean water would be pumped round to the other side or end of the pool and fed into the tank below water level through the inlet fitting (fig. B).

After erecting the pool walls, and before you fit the liner and backfill around the pool, fit the skimmer and inlet fittings. Offer them up to their respective holes in the panels and blockwork: the skimmer is fitted from outside the shell, the inlet fittings from inside the pool shell. Secure the inlet fittings through the pool wall with the backnut supplied.

Using the bolt holes on the skimmer's mounting flange as a guide, mark and drill the required number of bolt holes through the panel. Bolt the skimmer loosely in place and position bricks or a concrete block underneath it to support its weight. In the case of a blockwork pool do this before you start infilling the blocks with concrete, and protect any working parts from the concrete with masking tape or polyethylene.

Before fitting the pool liner tape a gasket around the skimmer and inlet fittings. Instal the liner as described on page 154 and start the filling. When the water is about 25mm below the level of the fittings fit another gasket over them and bolt the face plates through the liner, gaskets and pool wall to the fittings

9 *Instal the heating and filtration units on a concrete base in the plant room and start connecting the ABS or uPVC pipework and fittings*

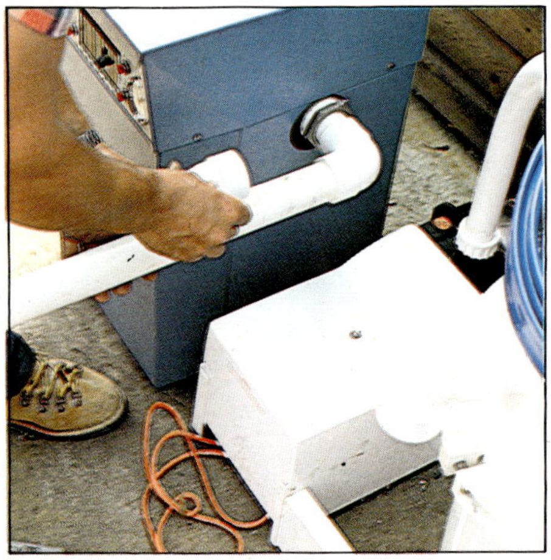

10 *Before cementing pipes and connections together assemble the plant room pipework 'dry' to ensure that it all fits without undue strain*

themselves. Only then should you cut the hole in the liners to allow water into and out of the skimmer and inlets.

If you wish to fit underwater lights, these are installed in much the same way, except that they must be installed from inside the pool before the liner is fitted. Leave enough extra flex in the light fitting for the light to be dismounted and held above the surface when you change the bulbs.

Pipework

In most swimming pool kits, the pipework and connections are made from ABS or uPVC with a flexible plastic pipe running from the skimmer and pool drain to the filter, and from the pump back to the inlet. The rigid fittings and pipes are connected in the normal way using the correct solvent. After you have warmed the end with a gas torch the flexible pipe is connected with worm-drive hose clips to the various fittings.

Connect the pipework and equipment in a dry run to make sure they all fit together properly before installing the pipes in their trenches. When digging the trenches make sure that the pipes run horizontally from the pool to the plant room and then rise vertically to the filter and pump. The actual rise should be less than 1m. Compact the earth in the bottom of the trenches, lay a foundation of soft sand in the base of the trench, then lay and connect the pipework.

Allow the welded or glued joints to harden for 24 hours before testing the plumbing for leaks and malfunctions. Once you are certain the circulation system is working properly you can switch it on and start getting the water clean while you backfill around the pool and fill in the pipe trenches. Both jobs will take quite a time.

The plant room

Whether you are installing the pump and filter in the garden shed, the garage, or in a specially built plant room, they must be placed on a stout concrete base. Make sure they are as close to the pool surface level as possible so that the pump is not overstressed, and ensure that the equipment area is well ventilated.

D. *When installing the ladder, use a wedge anchor to secure it in the concrete and fit rubber buffers over the bottoms of the ladder strings*

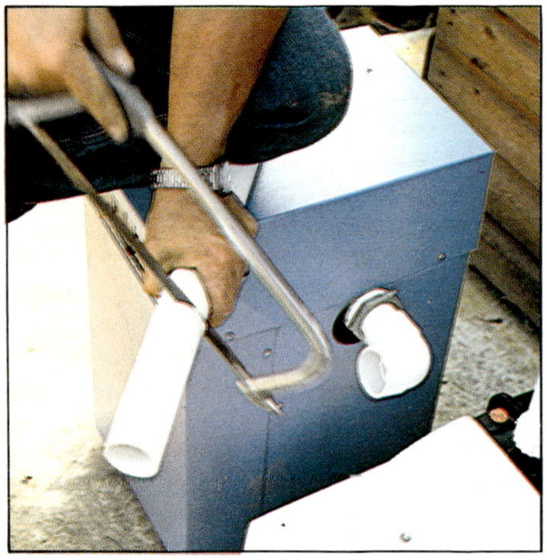

11 *Plastic piping can be cut easily using a hacksaw, but you must remember to deburr the cut edges with abrasive paper before assembly*

12 *It is important that the pipework fits properly. Any strain on the joints could be aggravated by vibration, leading to breakages and leaks*

13 *Before you start up the circulation system instal the filter medium. In this case a pre-weighed amount of filter sand is added to the filter body*

Finishing off the pool

As stated in Pool Construction (p.152), the top of the pool wall must be reinforced with a concrete ring beam. This runs right round the pool and serves not only to anchor any tie bars between the pool wall and the edge of the excavation, but also as a support for coping stones or concrete decking around the pool side. Before laying the concrete, however, you must instal the skimmer access hatch and the inspection cover for any underwater light connections (see above). These lie flush with the top of the finished deck and, in the case of the skimmer, simply bolt on to the top of the skimmer unit.

Before laying the ring beam select the position of the pool ladder so that you can pour the concrete in a circle starting from one side of the ladder and finishing on the other. Ladders usually consist of two hand rails and three or four rungs which must all be assembled before the concrete is poured. Fit a rubber buffer at the bottom of each rail where it will rest against the pool wall.

The other end of the hand rail is curved and must be set into the concrete using wedge anchors, so assemble these as well before laying the concrete (fig. D).

Now, using the datum peg (see page 153) to mark the level of the ring beam, start pouring the concrete. When you have gone all the way around the pool sink the ladder into the wet concrete. The instructions will state how deep the wedge anchors should be set, and you must use a builder's spirit level to ensure the ladder is upright. Go around the ring beam now and smooth it with a wooden and then a steel float, and when it is nearly dry key it with a scratcher so that you can mortar coping stones on top.

Some pool kits supply a set of coping stones matched to the shape and size of the pool: once the concrete ring beam has hardened lay them in their correct positions around the pool to adjust the pointing gaps. When you are satisfied with their layout mortar them in place. Make sure that they slope away from the pool at a gradient of about 1:50, with their inside edges either flush with, or slightly overhanging, the pool walls. Allow the mortar to set and then grout between them using the correct mortar mix.

Some pools are intended for use with concrete decking rather than coping stones, and these come with a metal or plastic retaining strip for the top of the pool wall. Clip this into place before you pour the ring beam, and lay the decking concrete after the ring beam has hardened. The retaining strip prevents the new concrete from falling into the pool and you can grade it by hand so that

14 *Replace the lid of the filter unit, reconnect all the pipework, and then fit a locking ring around the joint between the body and the lid*

15 *The pump should be mounted as close to the pool water surface level as possible so that it does not have to draw water more than 1m upwards*

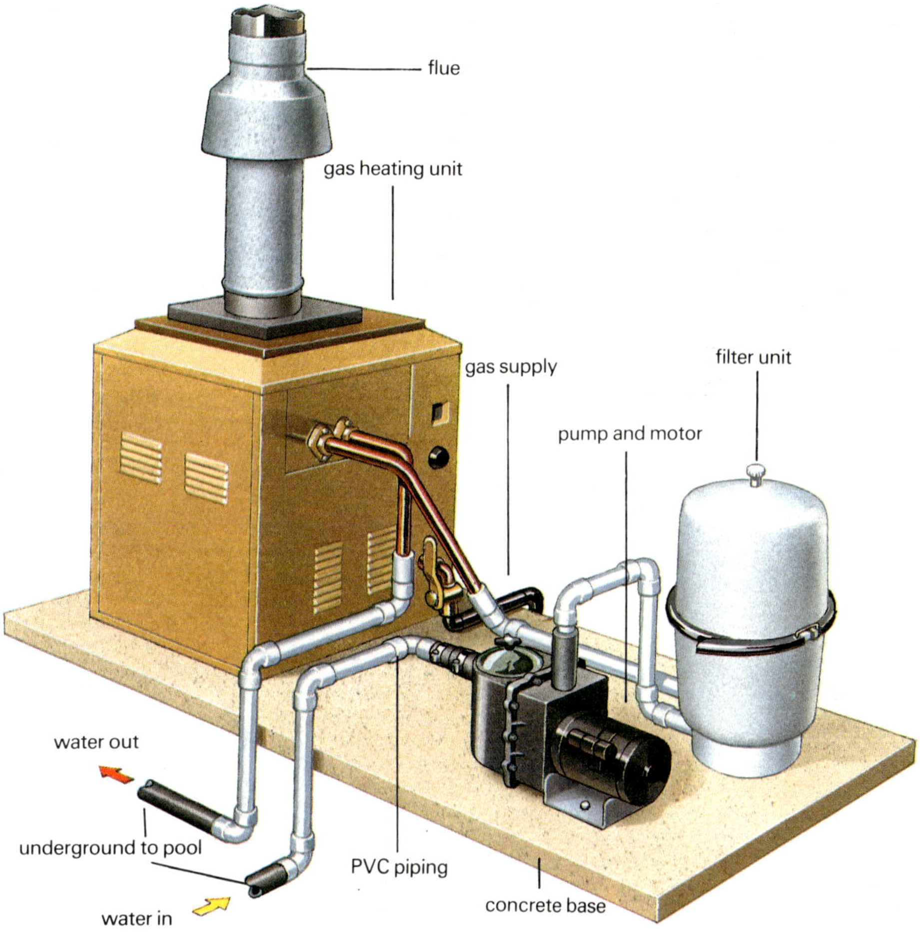

E. *A typical plant room layout: the pump and motor are mounted as low as possible so that they do not have to raise the water from the pool higher than is necessary. The water is carried in a PVC piping to the filter (a membrane filter in this case) and from there to the gas heater. For neatness as much of the pipework as possible is buried underground, and a flue disperses the gas fumes safely*

16 *A completed installation showing how the filter, pump, and heater are mounted on concrete bases, with the gas and water pipes buried in the ground*

17 *Another typical installation with the water pipes passing through the plant room walls to avoid the concrete foundations before being buried*

18 *Where you are using flexible pipe between the plant room and inlet, warm the ends using a gas burner so that it fits over the connections easily*

19 *Make all electrical connections for the underwater lights and enclose the cables in PVC hose before burying them and the junction box*

the deck slopes away from the pool edge.

It is sensible to lay the same area of hard decking as the pool itself occupies (see part 1 of this series) and you can do this with concrete, crazy paving, or stone flags. The layout and method used are purely a matter of personal choice and some ideas along these lines are discussed in a Home designer article which follows this series.

Electrics

The three main consumers of electricity in a pool installation are likely to be the pump, underwater lights, and an electric heater or heat pump. Heating is a subject that is covered in depth in the fourth part of this series, so this part is concerned mainly with the pump and lights.

A large pool with a lot of water to be filtered needs a pump developing about 1500 watts although a 500 watt pump may be sufficient for a smaller pool. This is easily catered for by running a power supply out to the plant room from the house's consumer unit. The advantage of installing the pool and plant room near the house is that the power supply can be run to the electrical equipment with the minimum of fuss. If there is a wall running between the house and plant room fix the cable to this, otherwise bury it or run it overhead.

In the UK, use PVC-sheathed wire armoured cable or mineral insulated copper sheathed cable except for overhead installations. Inside the plant room use waterproof fittings, and instal a fused master switch so that you can isolate the entire pool circuit. From here run a separately-fused supply—with all the appropriate precautions—undergound to the underwater light fitting (fig. 19).

20 *Enclose the skimmer unit in cardboard to protect it from the concrete ring beam, and so that you can backfill around it later*

21 *Instal the pool ladder before the ring beam dries by sinking it into the concrete. Make sure that it is upright and level before the concrete sets*

22 *A typical pool finish: coping stones which overlap the pool edge are mortared to the ring beam, with a brickwork decking mortared around it*

23 *The finished pool edge. The skimmer inspection cover is flush with the decking while the ladder strings are finished off with decorative mouldings*

24 *A measured amount of chlorine should be added to the pool water while the liner is being filled to prevent the growth of algae and bacteria*

25 *An alternative to hand-mixing and pouring chemicals is an automatic dispenser containing chemical tablets which floats on the surface*

Disinfection

The air is full of bacteria and fungus spores, while each swimmer carries millions of viruses and bacteria. Proper disinfection is therefore vital for safety and hygiene. The most common chemical disinfectant is chlorine which is available in tablet, powder, or dilute liquid form. This is usually added by hand after the state of the pool water has been tested, but you can get automatic dispensers that feed properly metered amounts of disinfectant into the circulation system.

Other chemicals used include bromine which smells less than chlorine but costs more, cyanurate compounds which are slower acting but more persistent, and liquid biocides.

Correct concentrations of chlorine are vital if swimmers are not to suffer from sore eyes: most pool kits supply a colour coded chemical test set with which you can check the concentration and vary the dosage accordingly.

The same test set will also tell you the pH – or acidity level – of the water. This ranges from 0 (highly acidic) through 7 (neutral) to 14 (highly alkaline). Adjust the level by adding sodium bisulphate (acid) or sodium bicarbonate (alkali) until the pH is 7.5 – the same level as the fluid in human eyes. This takes only a few minutes on each occasion.

Leading pool manufacturers and pool care companies offer specialized guides to pool care and disinfection, as well as chemicals and test sets. The problems are complex as each chemical and type of bacteria has a different effect on the water. The simplest way to alleviate some of these problems is to instal a shower and insist that swimmers use it before entering the water. This can clean off up to 50 percent of body dirt and bacteria.

Pool water turnover

The turnover of pool water by the filtration plant is an indication of its performance. Turnover is affected by: filter rating; number of swimmers; and the condition of the water. When sizing your filter use this formula:

$$\text{filter rating } (m^3/\text{hour}) = \frac{\text{pool capacity } (m^3)}{\text{pool water turnover (hours)}}$$

when paddling pools require a 1 hour turnover
teaching pools require a 2 hour turnover
school pools require a 4 hour turnover
club pools require a 6 hour turnover
private pools require an 8-12 hour turnover

Pool equipment

Circulation: ABS or uPVC pipework and fittings
solvent and thinners
valves and manifolds
main drain and pipe with hydrostatic relief valve
skimmer weir and pipetail with vacuum cleaner connection
pool water inlet and pipetail

Filtration: facing pipework and multiport control valve
filter tank with filter material
self-priming pump and motor with strainer basket

Disinfection: dispenser unit
water test set
chemicals – chlorine, acid, alkali, algicide

Accessories: pool ladder
underwater light – 300 watt
diving board
hand rails

Heating your pool

● The importance of heating ● Conservation of heat ● Types of heater ● Heat pumps ● Solar heating ● Tube-in-mat solar collectors ● Pool covers ● Insulation ● Pool enclosures

There are very few places in the world where an open air pool remains warm enough for swimming throughout the year. Comfortable water temperatures may come about naturally for three months or so during high summer in temperate zones—but even in summer there will be times when the water is too cold to enjoy a swim.

For this reason it is well worth installing some kind of pool heater—not only for comfort's sake, but also so that you can get a return on the money you paid for the pool. This, the fourth part of the Home improvements series on installing a pool, is about pool heating and the conservation of heat.

Heating and conservation

With the cost of heating rising all the time, conservation has become just as important to the pool owner as an efficient heater. Conventional heaters usually warm pool water by about 1°C every hour, but if four or five degrees are lost while the heater is switched off overnight, you may have to pay for four or five hours extra heating in the morning before the temperature becomes comfortable again.

Conservation mainly involves preventing heat loss from the water surface to the surrounding air though in rare cases a high water table may cause heat loss through the pool walls. Specific conservation methods are discussed in detail below.

Pool heating

If you poured a kettle full of boiling water into a pool full of cold water, a swimmer would not notice the difference. If you raised the pool temperature by 1°C, however, he would. This is the whole basis of pool heating: large quantities of water heated only a few degrees rather than small quantites heated to the temperature of bathwater.

Heaters are usually set to raise the pool temperature by about 1°C an hour up to the desired level, when they can be shut off and either manually or thermostatically controlled. As a rough guide, the heater rating should be about 0.5 kW/m^3 of water. So for a 60m^3 pool, you would need a 30kW heater. This rating will vary, of course, with such factors as pool surface area, air temperature and exposure to wind. Your supplier will be able to advise you on the correct heater size for your installation.

Pool heater units are fitted into the circulation system downstream from the filter so that they do not get clogged up with dirt which would make them less efficient. There are several types available to suit your pocket and pool installation.

Oil-fired heating: There are two ways of heating a pool with oil. The first is to instal a boiler, heat exchanger, and oil tank specifically for the pool. This is expensive, however, and the boiler will need regular maintenance if it is to operate efficiently.

The second method—where the pool and plant room are near the house—is to run a circuit from the house's domestic boiler to a heat exchanger in the circulation system. This is only really effective if the boiler is a large one and if the house and pool heating seasons do not coincide.

A. Left: *A solar heating system is the cheapest way to heat your pool in the long run and is not prohibitively expensive to instal. Here a flat garage roof provides space for the collector–the plant room is in a greenhouse*

1 *A popular make of gas water heater in a plant room. The gas supply runs underground from the house gas main and rises next to the heater*

2 *Ventilation is vital where gas is being used; here a flue carries the fumes outside the plant room where they can be harmlessly dispersed*

3 *Heat pumps are another extremely efficient method of heating pool water. This unit for a large pool draws heat from the surrounding air*

4 *This is the 'traditional' type of aluminium flat plate solar collector. It is quite efficient but can be rather ugly and wasteful of space*

5 *Flat plate collectors should be used like this–angled towards the sun for maximum efficiency–but the shade this creates is not always welcome*

Gas-fired boilers: These may be cheaper than oil to instal and run but in some parts of the world gas heating of swimming pools and other installations is banned. They can be plumbed directly into the circulation system or operate through a heat exchanger. The gas can be supplied from the mains or you can use bottled gas although this is often inconvenient. As with an oil-fired domestic boiler, however, you can run a hot water circuit from the house to a heat exchanger in the plant room.

If you do instal a mains or bottled gas unit in the plant room, make sure it is well ventilated and that fumes cannot drift across the pool or into the house.

Electric heaters: These are the cheapest to instal but often the most expensive to use. You can instal a heater in the circulation system or lay heater elements in the concrete pool floor. Units over 20kW in power require their own 3-phase supply, however, and this can be expensive to lay on privately. Perhaps the most economical use of electricity is where an electric heater is used to supplement solar panels (see below).

The chief advantage of electricity is that it is clean, odourless, and easily controlled. In addition you may be able to take advantage of cheap off-peak rates during the night.

Heat pumps: These are a comparatively new development and are basically refrigeration units working in reverse. Whereas a fridge draws heat from the air inside it and expels this as waste, a heat pump draws heat from the surrounding air or earth and uses this to warm the pool water.

The pump's efficiency is described as a coefficient of performance (COP). In average summer conditions a pump might use 1 kilowatt-hour (kWh) of electricity to extract the equivalent of 5 kWh of heat from the air. This gives it a COP of 5:1. In winter when the air and ground temperatures are lower this figure may fall as low as 3:1, and the pump will heat the water more slowly as a result.

Solar heating

Every garden pool which absorbs direct sunlight is a passive collector of solar energy. When some additional method of circulating the warmth is added it becomes an active system.

One way to increase the heat-retaining ability of the pool is to paint the pool sides white and the bottom a dark colour—energy passing through the water warms it before being reflected off the white sides and on to the bottom. Here it is absorbed where it automatically warms the water at the bottom of the pool.

The simplest form of active solar collector is a length of large-bore hosepipe coiled on the decking or strung along the garden fence. Filtered pool water is pumped through this on the way to the pool and the sun warms it as it passes through the pipe. Extra heat can be gained by surrounding the pipe with metal foil reflectors or by encasing the pipe in glass bottles with tops and bottoms removed.

The most effective solar heating method—and most familiar to many people—is the purpose-built solar panel. These used to be made from expensive copper and aluminium but most have been replaced by lightweight plastic panels or flexible tube-in-the-mat systems. In fact many systems use heat-

Solar heating and conservation

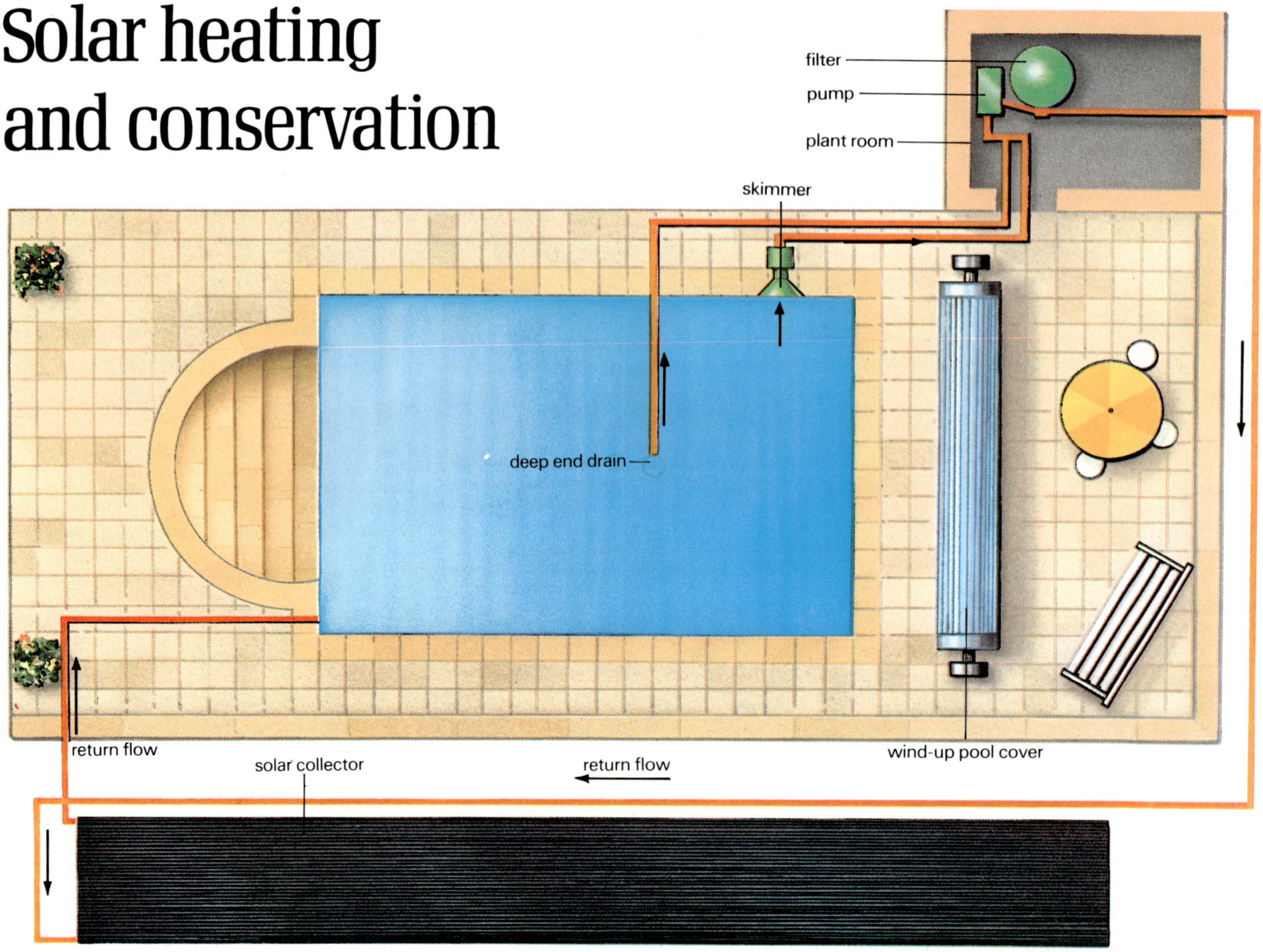

B. Above: *Before installing solar heating, consider the space needed for the collector and also the cost of an efficient and convenient pool cover*

C. Right: *By installing a tube-in-mat collector under poolside decking you can take advantage of solar energy without wasting valuable space*

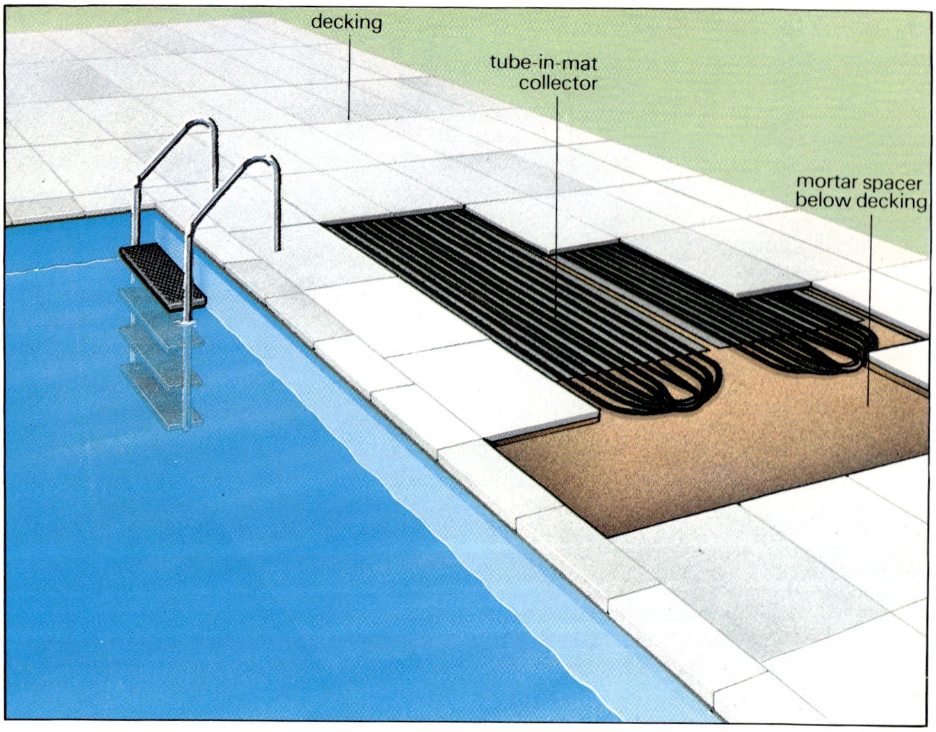

absorbing concrete paving stones laid over a bed of water pipes.

One disadvantage of solar energy outside the tropics is that the amount of energy falling on a square metre of ground becomes less the farther from the equator you go. Therefore a solar collector must occupy a proportionately greater surface area in temperate climates: as much as 75 per cent of the pool's surface area, in some cases.

The operating principle of a solar panel is fairly simple: sunlight falls on a dark panel and warms it up. Water is then pumped through this panel and absorbs the heat before passing on to the pool. Lagging behind the panel prevents heat loss by conduction while one or two layers of glass, separated from the black panel by an air space, prevent heat loss by convection and radiation.

In the case of a swimming pool the emphasis is on raising the temperature of a lot of water by a small amount, so a great deal of insulation around the panel is not necessary. The water can be pumped through continuously by the pool filter pump, but more expensive systems use a thermostat or solar sensor to isolate the system when no heating is required.

Narrow bore tubing in the heat exchanger constricts the flow of water and creates back pressure in the filter, which can reduce its efficiency. In this case a separate solar heater circuit with its own pump and pool inlet and outlet grilles will be necessary.

Conservation

To reduce heat loss to the atmosphere a pool should be installed in a sheltered spot protected from the wind, and exposed to as much sunlight as possible. In some cases heat may be lost through the pool shell to wet ground but only in the worst cases will foam insulation be required.

Insulation of the pool shell may be quite effective in the case of an installation above ground, but this should be removed during daylight to allow the sun to warm the water through the pool walls.

The majority of heat lost from the pool is in the form of evaporation and radiation—especially on cooler nights. A cover over the pool can therefore save you a great deal of money.

Insulating covers: The simplest of these is a floating, quilted plastic cover which simply lies on the pool surface. It can cut heat loss at night by up to 60 per cent, but also prevents sunlight from warming the pool during the day. These can be laid manually or fixed to a roller at one end of the pool (fig. B).

A variation on this theme consists of a layer of ping-pong balls or expanded polystyrene balls floating on the surface. This performs much the same function as a mat, but can be difficult to remove.

Solar trap insulation: This consists of a floating translucent sandwich that insulates the water and prevents heat loss, but also allows sunlight to warm the pool. Lighter weight materials, while allowing plenty of sunlight to reach the water, provide comparatively poor overnight insulation. Heavier materials reduce the passage of sunlight.

Structural covers: Rigid covers can be excellent at both preventing heat loss and allowing sunshine to warm the water. Designs include hydraulically operated floating roller blinds, suspended PVC sheet, pneumatically lifted canopy decks, and hand assembled glass fibre modules which can be simply lifted on and off the pool surround. These tend to be expensive, however, and sometimes a nuisance if they have to be replaced every night.

Pool enclosures

Because an open-air pool in a temperate climate can only be used for a few months many owners look for a cover or enclosure which allows swimming all year round.

The cheapest permanent enclosures may cost as much as 25 per cent again as the pool, while custom-built structures will at least double the initial cost.

Russian shelter: This is the cheapest of enclosures and consists of nothing more than an all-round wind-break with an

6 Capitalize on available sunshine by painting the pool sides a lighter colour. Sunshine can then be reflected on to a darker, heat-retaining bottom, perhaps in a shade of blue

7 This brick-built diving platform incorporates a small fountain—ideal for aerating chlorinated water before it passes into the pool. This type of structure also creates a feature

8 Here the plant room is built very close to the pool, helping to cut down the stress on the pump and also any heat loss between heater and pool inlet

9 Access to the skimmer inspection cover and to gate valves in the circulation system is through this flush-mounted paving stone

10 A garden fence near the pool gives both privacy and shelter and can also provide useful storage for some bulkier pool care accessories

Pool heating

Heater sizing

Heater rating depends on variables such as pool surface area, depth and volume; air temperature, insulation, and exposure to wind; average temperatures during the coldest months in which it will be used.

Typical rating for the UK: 0.5 kW/m³ of water.

Example: A pool containing 60m³ of water requires the following heater ratings to achieve extra pool water temperature above the mean air temperature:

Pool water temperature above mean air temperature:	+5°C	+10°C	+15°C	+20°C
Fast heater rating:	15kW	30kW	45kW	60kW
Slow heater rating:	10kW	20kW	30kW	40kW

Solar energy

Solar supplies

	Annual sunshine (hours)	**Annual solar radiation (kWh/m²)**
UK/Northern Europe	1000–1500	900
New Zealand/Mid Europe	1500–2000	1100
Canada/US Border	2000–2500	1300
S. Australia/N. America	2500	1500
S. Africa/Southern USA	3000	1700
W. Australia/Arizona	4000	2200
Sahara Desert	4500	2600

Solar collector sizing

Proportion of collector area to pool water area	Pool use	Fuel saving
0.5:1	summer	75%
0.75:1	spring to autumn	50%

Solar collectors

Glazed: Trickle flow flat collectors require backing insulation and rely upon the 'greenhouse' effect to prevent heat being radiated back through the glass.

Unglazed: Flood flow, honeycomb sandwich plastic panels do not need insulation or framework stands. Best installed facing the sun and angled to catch its rays flat-on—a sloping roof is an ideal site. Tube-in-strip flexible matting is designed to be laid flat.

Structural: Solar collectors are space consumers. Pool surrounds offer an ideal site for heat-collecting paving stones which incorporate an invisible network of water circulation pipes. A combination of this and either gas or oil-fired heating is a most cost-effective system.

overhanging canopy. This reduces heat loss to the wind, but can also cut down heat gains from sunlight when the sun is low in the sky.

Airdome: This is a pressurized airtight dome inflated over the pool. It prevents most types of heat loss while allowing a certain amount of solar heat to warm the air and water inside. Airdomes are usually ugly, but they are comparatively cheap and efficient. They do require an air pump to keep them pressurized, however, and an airlock door to prevent the air escaping when the door is opened.

Modular structures: These are often the most cost-effective pool enclosures. There are many different types of design available—ranging from geodesic domes through elaborate aluminium-framed greenhouses to prefabricated sliding roof units. You must secure planning permission from your local authority before erecting a permanent structure of this kind, however.

One more development which is gaining in popularity is the pool room or natatorium. This can be anything from a house extension which covers a sunken pool to an underground pool built in the cellar. These tend to be very expensive indeed, and are usually beyond the scope of all except the most determined and skilled do-it-yourselfer.

Front garden facelift

Use brickwork and tiling to create this neat conversion for a small front garden. Only simple techniques are required, and the finished result is an ideal complement to the traditional brick-built cottage

It is often difficult to produce an attractive display within the confines of a small front garden. There is very little space for plants, and those that you can fit in are all too easily lost behind a front wall.

The planter wall which forms the basis of this project is an ideal solution. It brings the plants up to a level where they are easy to tend and shows them off at their best. You can then tile the remaining area between the house and the wall to keep it neat, tidy and easy to clean.

The basis of the construction is a raft-type foundation as described on page 130. This provides a solid footing for the walls and also forms a base on which to tile. The entire foundation is sloped or 'dished' to allow water to drain off the surface. You can fit proprietary recessed drain fittings into the concrete to hide any existing inspection covers.

The planter is formed by two leaves of brickwork and supported by solid piers at the corners of the enclosure. Try to use bricks which match the original house wall (if this is exposed brick) in colour and texture.

You can form a small enclosure for deliveries or a boot scraper by building a recess in the inner leaf. Finish the top of the wall with a small, cast lintel before adding the final soldier course of brickwork.

When the wall is complete, you can finish the piers with capstones. The drawings overleaf give details of casting your own using wooden formwork.

Tile the area behind the wall with quarry tiles, laid over the concrete raft on a sharp sand/cement mortar bed (see pages 130 to 135).

Fill the planter with topsoil over drainage stones. You can add a trellis to the top of the wall as a basis for climbing plants, or fit timber bars between the piers. Alternatively, use a wrought iron gridwork.

Above: *The planter wall will house border plants as well as climbers*

Workplan

Begin by clearing your site and setting out the foundations (see pages 130 to 135). When you cast the concrete, be sure to arrange a slope for drainage, and to allow for the thickness of the tiles. If you have an inspection cover or gulley, set its frame into the foundations at the same time.

Set out and build up the planter walls and the brick piers, including the damp-proof courses in each leaf and the vertical damp-proofing where they touch the house wall. Tile the enclosed area with quarry tiles, using them to conceal drainage fittings.

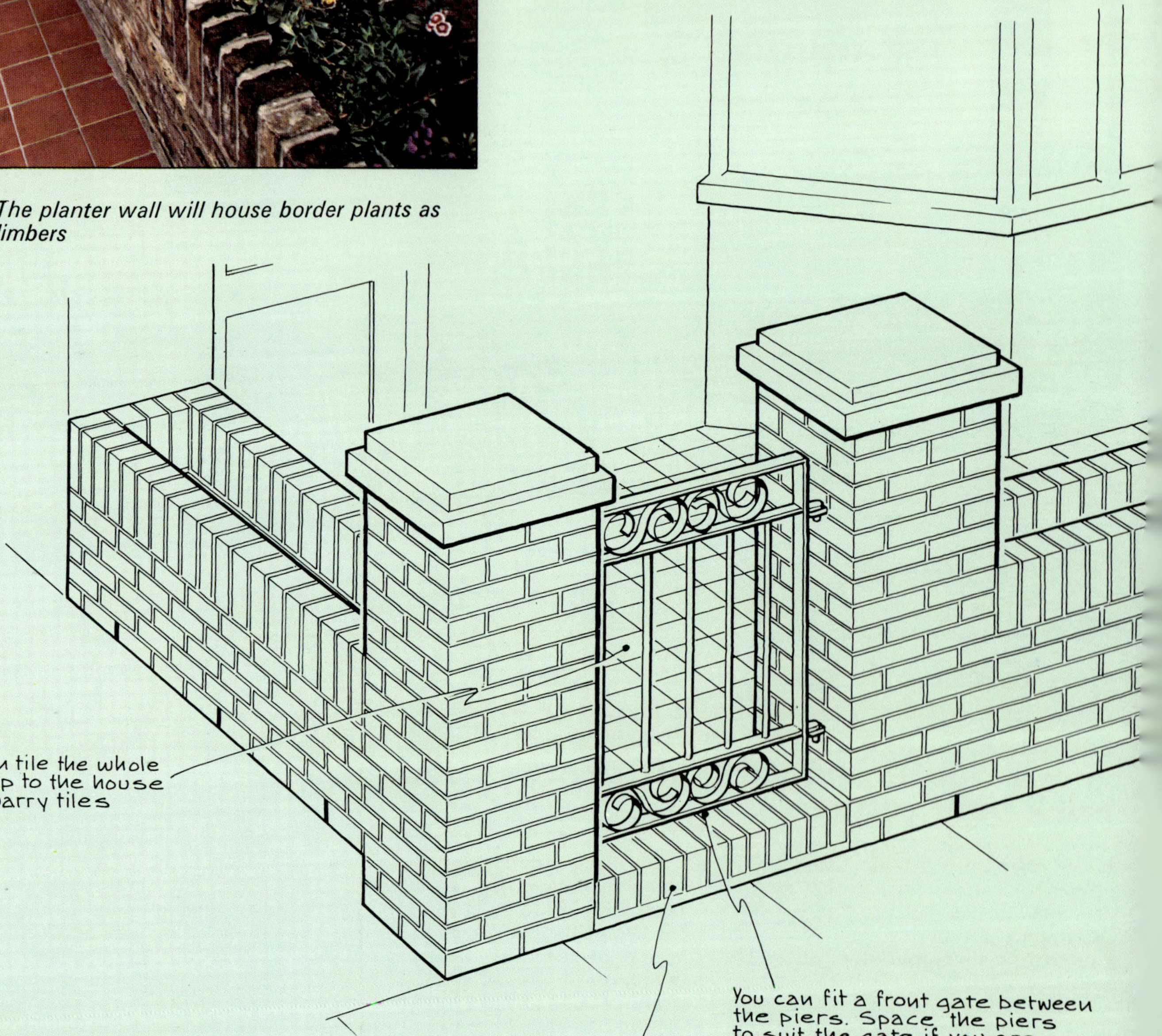

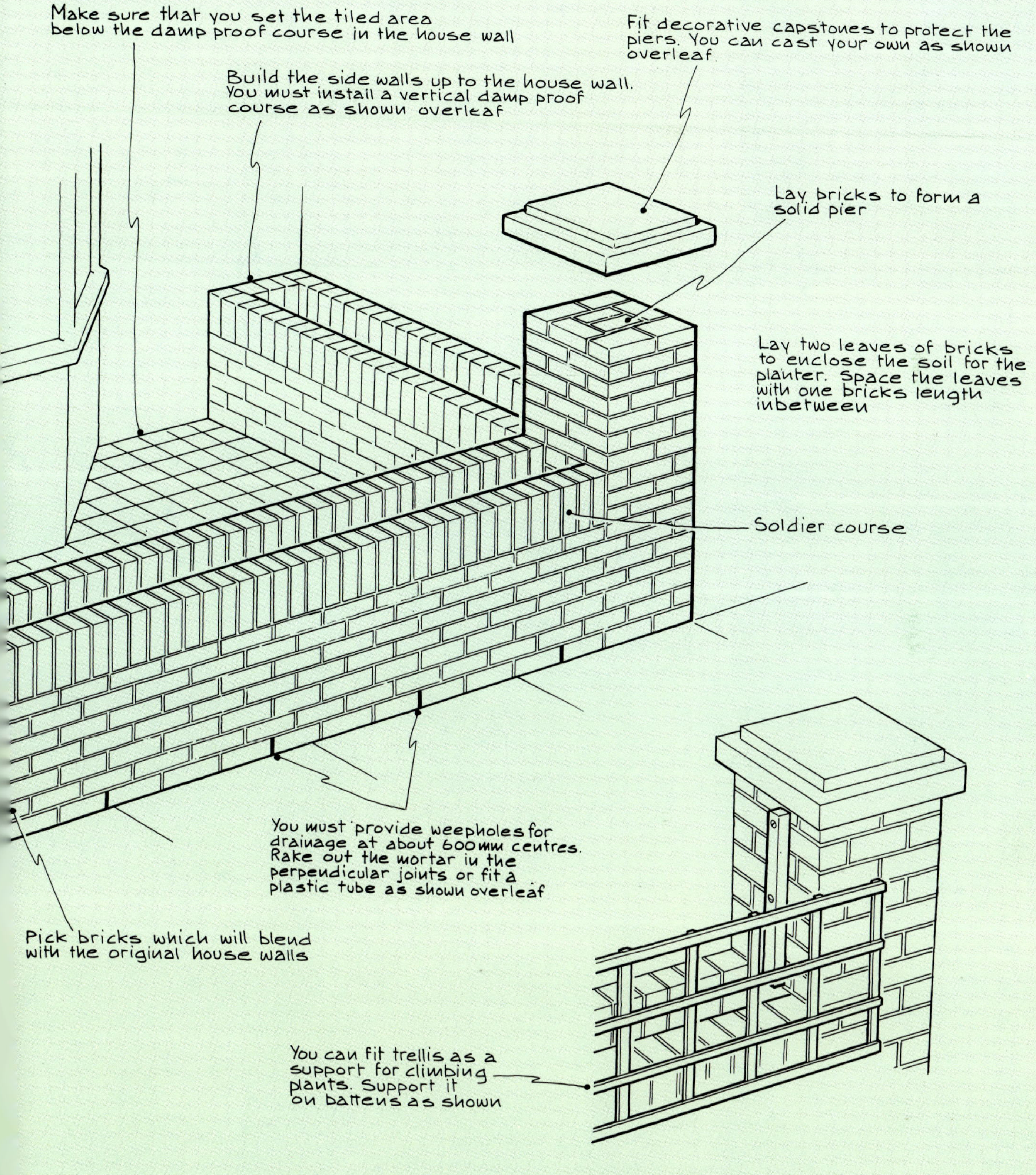
Make sure that you set the tiled area below the damp proof course in the house wall
Build the side walls up to the house wall. You must install a vertical damp proof course as shown overleaf
Fit decorative capstones to protect the piers. You can cast your own as shown overleaf
Lay bricks to form a solid pier
Lay two leaves of bricks to enclose the soil for the planter. Space the leaves with one bricks length inbetween
Soldier course
You must provide weepholes for drainage at about 600mm centres. Rake out the mortar in the perpendicular joints or fit a plastic tube as shown overleaf
Pick bricks which will blend with the original house walls
You can fit trellis as a support for climbing plants. Support it on battens as shown

Above: *You can cast your own cap stones to almost any pattern. All you need is a wooden mould*

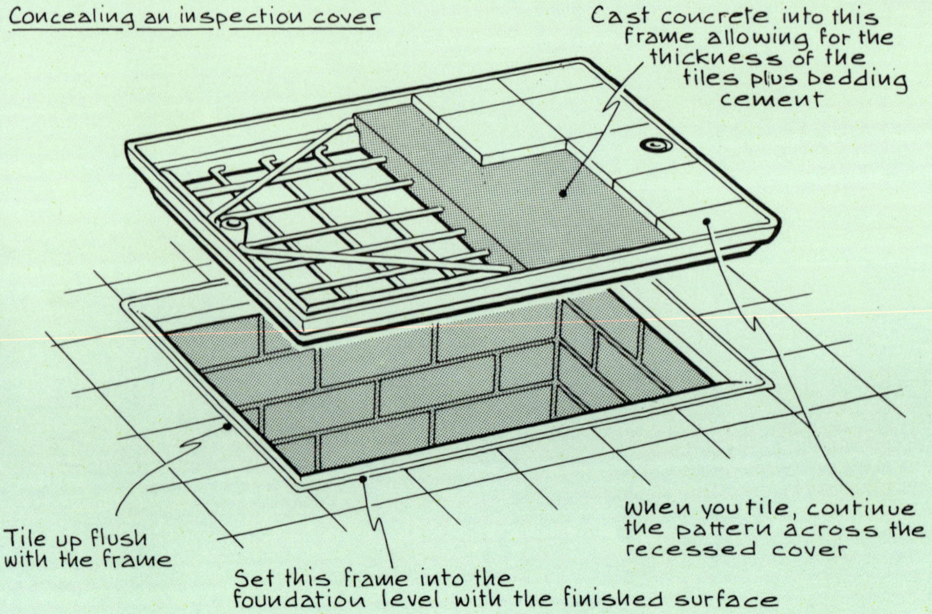

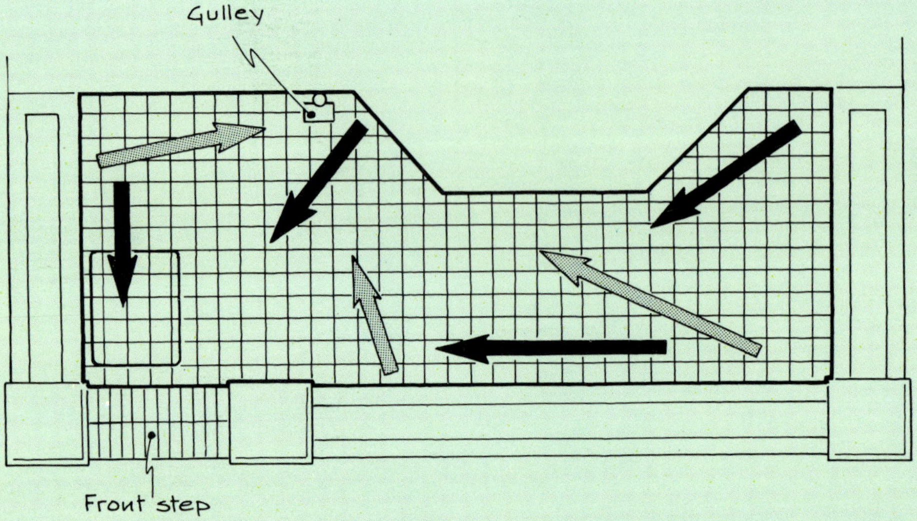

Drainage

It is important to arrange for a slight slope across the tiled area if it is to drain properly. Lay the slab foundations with a slope of about 1 in 60 along the arrows shown. Use the black arrows to arrange drainage over the step. If there is a gulley, you can drain towards it as shown by the grey arrows

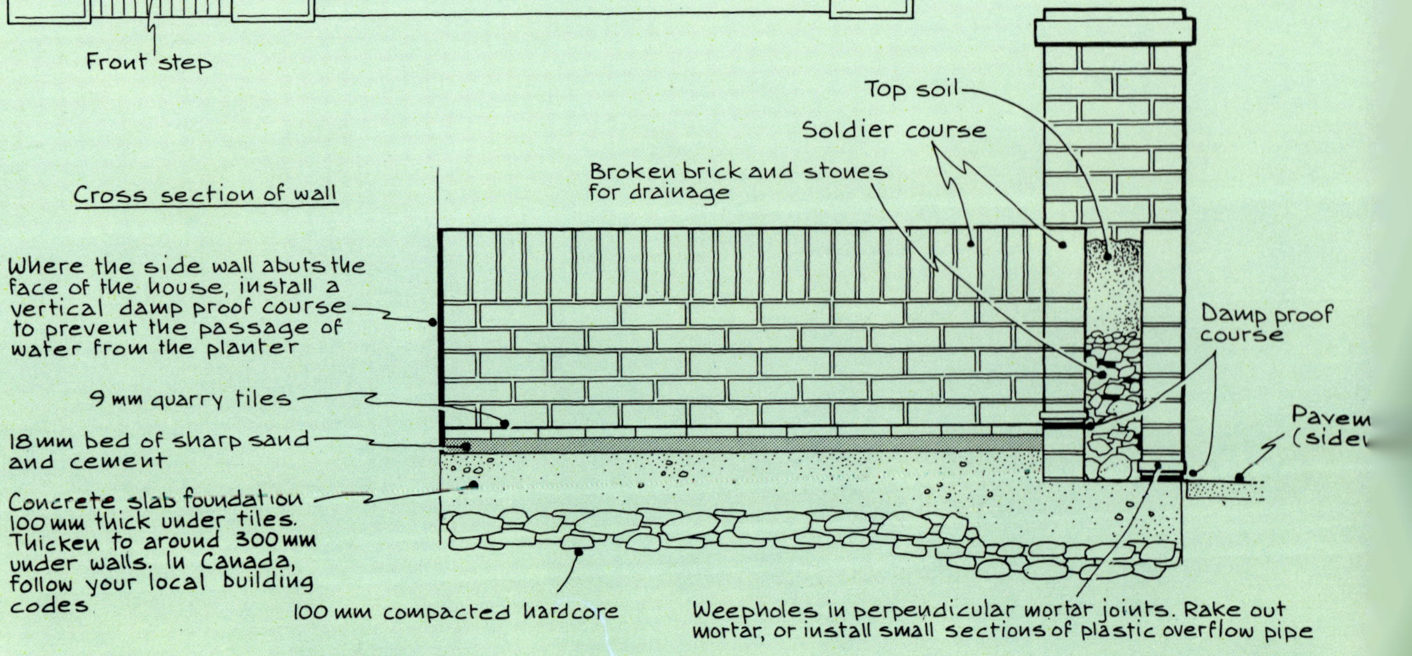

Casting your own capstones

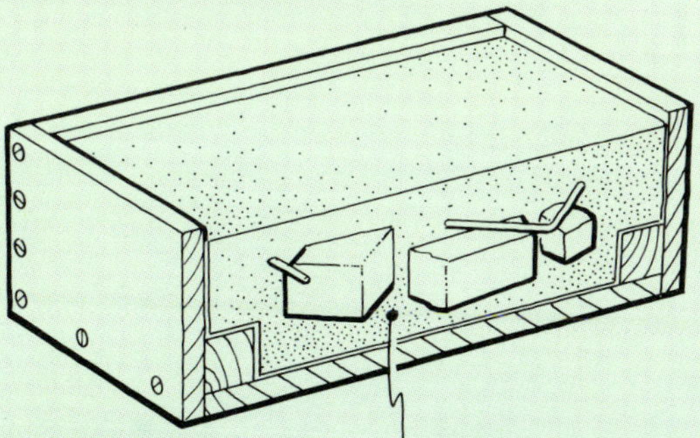

Fill the mould with a mix of sharp sand and cement. You can fill the central area with rubble, such as broken brick. Pieces of wire, such as old coat-hangers will add strength, but make sure that they do not protrude

Above: *Fit a trellis as a decorative background to the plants and as a basis for training climbers*

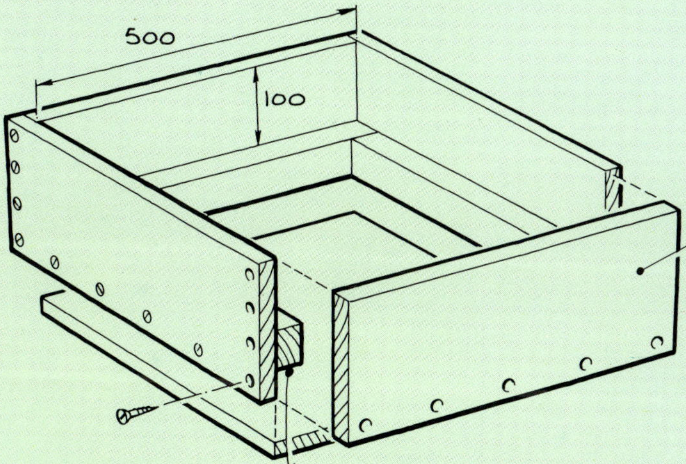

Make the mould from shuttering plywood, chipboard or softwood screwed or nailed together. Line the entire mould with polythene, or grease the surface to ensure that the cement will not stick. Adjust dimensions if necessary to suit the size of your piers

Fit pieces of 50×50 planed all round softwood inside the mould. This will form a step effect in the finished capstone

Below: *The recessed inspection cover lets you fit tiles on top for an unobtrusive flush finish to your tiling*

Small cast lintel

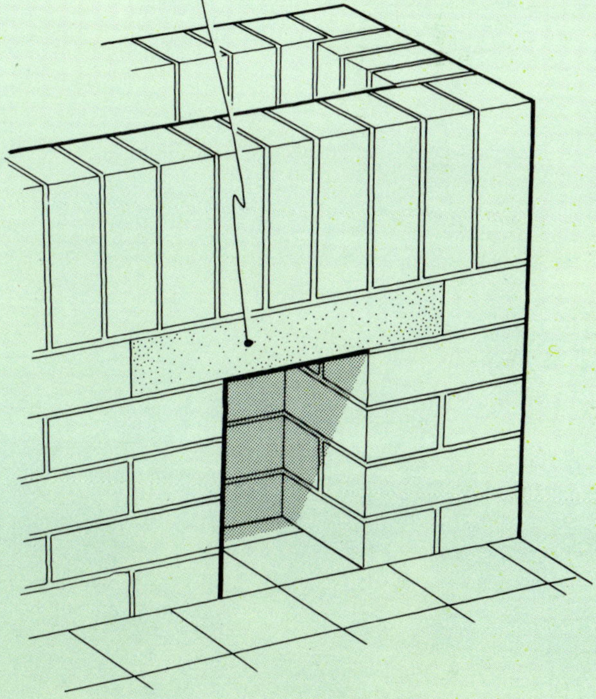

You can make a recess in the inner leaf of bricks to house a boot scraper or to collect deliveries. Construct it as shown

An attractive stepped planter

This stepped planter project adds an attractive focal point to any garden. The design is based on the simplest of all brickwork bonds—the stretcher or running bond—but uses half-bricks all the way along the top courses as a decorative feature.

Depending on where you want to site the planter, the ground in front can be covered with 915mm x 610mm concrete slabs, laid on a base of tamped hardcore topped with mortar. These keep the feet dry as well as giving the planter a 'finished' look. Alternatively, you can leave the area as bare soil or as grass.

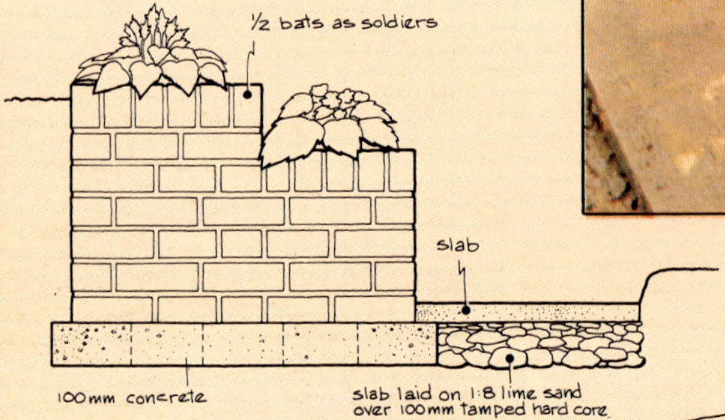

For the planter, you need 265 bricks plus an allowance for breakages. Forty-five of the bricks, cut in half, are used as 'soldiers' to finish off the top courses. For the mortar, allow one 50kg bag of cement and four 50kg bags of soft sand. The optional concrete slabs rest on a bed of mortar laid over 100mm of well-tamped hardcore.

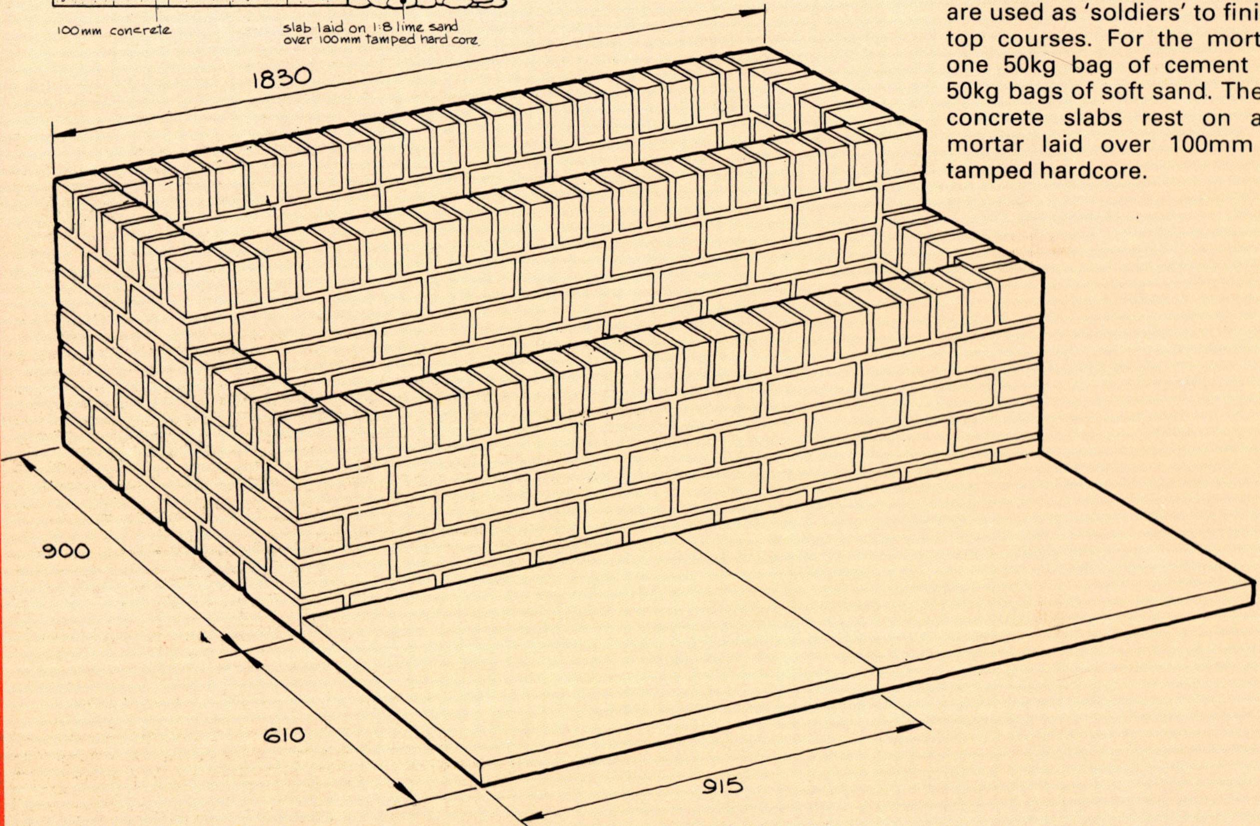

Chapter 5
FENCES AND WALLS
Walls and hedges

To many people, walls and hedges mean little more than a barrier to keep the outside world at bay. Yet a garden wall or hedge can serve many purposes beyond that of a boundary and make an attractive feature in any garden, as below, where rough flintstones have been used to make this unusual and decorative wall. This one is particularly interesting because of its circular opening which 'frames' a view from either side. The stock bricks used as a border provide an interesting contrast with the flintstones.

Walls and hedges are essentially dividing lines, whether you use them to mark where your property ends and another begins, or to sub-divide your own garden into separate areas. Which you choose is largely a matter of personal preference, but apart from some of the more obvious points which might influence your decision, there is one external factor that is often forgotten—the character of the locality.

For example, if you plant a hedge along the front of your property when every other house in the road has a wall of locally-quarried stone, it will look totally out of place. Just as a red-brick wall topped with screen blocks would look wrong in an otherwise leafy, tree-lined avenue. By following the character of the entire street you will contribute something to its overall appearance and also make your home part of a unified whole. Apart from the purely visual benefits, this could actually help to increase the value of your property.

That aside, there is a variety of other factors to consider. For instance, a hedge takes time to grow, so if you are impatient for results a wall would be a more obvious choice. A wall is solid and permanent and needs virtually no looking after, whereas a hedge, although softer-looking, needs just as much care as any other garden plant and will soon become an eyesore if neglected. A wall is harsh and unyielding to the eye compared with a hedge, and does not encourage birds and butterflies to your garden as a hedgerow will. And, perhaps most important, a wall can be expensive, even if you build it yourself, while a hedge, if set out with small cuttings or plants, need cost very little.

Above: *Clematis and valerian add a touch of colour and softness to this rough stone stepped wall. The lower 'step' provides a handy garden seat*
Right: *If privacy is not a priority, pierced screen walls provide the perfect boundary and also introduce a delicate form of pattern*

The garden wall

Boundary walls virtually site themselves. But if you are dividing your garden into sections, perhaps to mark changes of level of use, your decisions must be made carefully. Draw up scale plans of the area involved, trying out all the possibilities on paper before laying the first stone.

In particular, position openings or breaks in the wall run with care; steps, arches and gateways often turn out to be in quite the wrong place. Some driveway entrances make it almost impossible for a car to manoeuvre, because the opening is too narrow or the gateway is wrongly sited, yet a simple experiment with two bamboo canes for gate-posts would quickly indicate the right positions and width.

Height and thickness are the next considerations. In the UK boundary walls must not exceed 1m in height along road frontages, or 2m elsewhere, unless planning permission is granted by the local authority.

Although walls can be as thick as you like within the bounds of common sense, there are minimum thicknesses to observe if the walls are not to fall down. For a free-standing wall under about 760mm in height, a single skin of bricks or blocks is adequate but additional reinforcement in the form of a strengthening pier will be needed for every 3m or so of wall length.

Right: *Cut stone slabs in a variety of shapes and textures are set into ordinary mortar to make a most unusual and decorative wall*

Walls higher than this, or those acting as retaining walls, should be of double-thickness brick or blockwork.

Walls of pierced screen blocks over six courses high, or with a distance of over 3m between any piers, need expanded metal mesh reinforcement in the mortar bed to improve the bond strength, and if hollow pier blocks are used, these should always be built around metal reinforcing rods set in the wall's foundations.

Foundations are important too. Not only must they be strong enough to support the wall, they must not encroach on neighbouring property (you must build on your side of the boundary line, not astride it), nor must they interfere with drains or underground gas, water or electricity supplies.

Badly built foundations are an all too frequent cause of wall failure; get the site surveyed if you are in any doubt about its suitability.

Choosing materials

There is a wide range of building materials from which to choose—from the ordinary brick with all its local colour variations to manufactured walling blocks of various types and, of course, natural stone. Each can be used on its own, or materials can be intermixed—either using different colours of one material, or mixtures of quite different materials such as natural flint and brick. Pattern can easily be introduced and looks particularly effective with bricks laid in herringbone or other patterns.

Walls do not have to follow straight lines; often a curve, or the introduction of features such as raised and lowered sections and alcoves, can create a far more pleasing effect, especially where changes of ground level are involved. Again, it is best to experiment with your ideas on paper before committing yourself.

Remember, too, that a garden wall does not have to be just a wall. You could decorate it to match your house —perhaps with smooth or textured mortar rendering, pebbledashing or split stone. You could plant climbing vines in beds at the foot of the wall, or perhaps include a narrow flowerbed between a dwarf double wall. If you are particularly artistic, you might even consider painting your own mural on to the wall. Otherwise you could opt for the attractive combination of wall and hedge.

The garden hedge

A boundary hedge performs virtually the same functions as a boundary wall, giving privacy, acting as a windbreak, keeping trespassers out and the children and the family dog in. But hedges have important advantages over walls—they provide the perfect backdrop for display borders, flower beds and individual specimen shrubs, and because of their shape and colour, hedges can also provide attractive features in their own right.

Above: *Though it needs care and attention, topiary can be great fun to do and enables you to introduce exotic shapes into your garden*

When siting a hedge, be sure that it comes within your own property: since even a small hedge may be up to 600mm thick, the original planting line must be at least 300mm inside the boundary line.

The most appropriate height for a hedge can best be estimated by 'planting' a line of bamboo canes along the proposed hedge line, then viewing it from various parts of the property. The desired height will, to some extent, then determine the species of hedging plant most suitable.

Choosing hedging plants

The range of species for hedging plants is immense, but as a rough guideline it can be divided arbitrarily between formal and informal hedges. Formal hedges are the hedgetrimmer's and topiarist's delight, since they can be clipped into neat or even fantastic shapes. Informal hedges sprawl delightfully, needing only the lightest pruning to keep them broadly within the bounds of your property.

The other major classification factor is whether you want to plant an evergreen or a deciduous hedge. For formal evergreen hedges box, lonicera, privet, cypress, yew and holly are among the most popular and widely-grown, though honeysuckle and pyracantha could also be considered. Among deciduous plants, beech is probably the commonest, although hawthorn, hornbean and plum are also in widespread use. For an informal hedge the choice in evergreens is dominated by the conifers, but berberis, lavender, lilac and in warmer climates fuschia and tamarisk will all make a very attractive informal hedge.

The type of soil you have in your garden will also have a bearing on the best hedging plants to choose. Broadly speaking, plants such as honeysuckle, hornbeam and lilac thrive on heavy soils; holly, lavender and tamarisk on light soils, and beech, box and yew on chalky ones. Lonicera and privet seem to grow well almost anywhere.

One further point to consider before planning your hedge is the amount of clipping it will need, particularly if you are an occasional and not over-enthusiastic gardener. Some plants such as yew need clipping only once a year, whereas lonicera needs as many as four clippings a year to keep it looking neat and tidy. Most other hedges need around two to three clippings a year.

Growth rate and ease of propagation are also worth taking into account. For example, lonicera cuttings take very easily and grow quickly, as does

Right: *Cotoneaster lacteus makes a perfect evergreen hedge, even during wintery months. Its brilliant red berries are particularly eye-catching*

privet, and many fast-growing conifers will give you a substantial hedge in only a few years. Yew, on the other hand, is extremely slow-growing. So if you are in a hurry with your hedge, check this point with your local nursery before buying.

Colour can play an important part in the aesthetic appeal of your hedge but is mainly a question of personal taste. Most people seem to prefer a monochrome hedge, whether it is of golden privet or purple beech. But the mixed hedge, or one created from flowering shrubs, has a very distinct attraction. Perhaps the best way of reaching a decision is to go hedge-spotting around your neighbourhood or visit garden centres.

Getting expert advice on local conditions is also important at this stage; soil type, prevailing winds and whether or not your garden is sheltered could all be deciding factors.

Below: *A firm favourite, this attractive multicoloured prunus hedge is achieved by alternating plantings of two green, then four crimson. bushes*

Above: *Lavender makes an excellent dwarf border and its brilliant mauve flowers add refreshing fragrance to the garden during warm summer months*

Planting and pruning

The basic planting requirements are similar for all hedging plants: a deep-dug trench, damp, well-prepared soil and firm planting, with additional support in windy or exposed positions. Spacing is critical—if the plants are too close, they will choke and starve each other as they grow; too wide a spacing will create a gappy appearance. For most plants, 450mm is ideal, although plants such as privet, beech and hornbeam should be a little closer and bushy plants and shrubs further apart (depending on the species).

For a thick boundary hedge, plant double staggered rows 225 to 300mm apart, up to 1m inside the boundary line to allow for subsequent growth.

To encourage your hedge to grow thickly at the base, careful pruning is essential. Naturally leggy plants such as privet and lonicera should be cut back to 150mm or so at planting to encourage side-shoots, while other deciduous shrubs should be cut back after one year's growth. Evergreen should have the side shoots and leaders shortened after two year's growth. Prune evergreens (except conifers) in spring, conifers and deciduous plants in mid-summer, box and privet at any time during the growing season.

Getting more ideas

Unless you already have quite definite ideas on the kind of look that you want to achieve, try to find out how similar problems have been solved in the past.

Some of the very best garden walls and hedges are to be found in stately homes. And although these will obviously be on a much larger scale, you should nevertheless be able to adapt the ideas for your own garden.

Fences and gates

Fences and gates might serve to mark the boundary lines of your property, but with thought and planning, they can also add greatly to the exterior appearance of your home

Fences and gates do more than simply mark the border between your garden and the neighbouring ones or indeed the public street. They say something about you and your home even before your visitors get as far as the front door. In spite of this, however, very little thought is given to them as design features and they often end up as dreary, unwelcoming eyesores.

Fences

There are many different types of fences and you will almost certainly find one which is ideally suited to your style of house and your particular needs. But before choosing, it is worth considering exactly what functions you want your fence to fulfil beside marking the boundary.

For example, you might want to

protect fruit bushes from a cold wind, be concerned about the safety of children, require privacy for sunbathing, or simply need to mark the end of your garden without concealing decorative flower beds.

The simplest form of fence is solid or close boarded fence, consisting of upright or horizontal strips of wood, 150mm wide, nailed to two or more supporting rails. A slight variation of this is the feather board fence which is very similar but consists of wedge-shaped boards which overlap each other by about 20mm. This style of fence affords the greatest degree of privacy and protection against wind and can be tall or short according to your needs.

Both these types of fences are fairly economic to construct, easy to maintain and quite hardwearing. Individual parts can easily be replaced if they get damaged or worn, without the expense of replacing whole sections.

Left: *A traditional vertical close-boarded fence provides privacy and protection and acts as an attractive backdrop for plants and shrubs*

However, regular treatment with preservative is essential for timber fences, to help protect them from the elements.

One drawback to plain timber fences is that they are not very attractive and can look dull and boring unless decorated or combined with other types of fencing, such as trellis, to provide a contrast. An excellent way of disguising them, without losing the advantage of privacy, is to grow a screen of small shrubs and plants in front—although you should be careful not to allow soil to build up against the gravel boards at the bottom or it will rot the wood.

Another very good way of relieving the monotony is to shape the top of the fence—for example, along the sides of a garden. Use tall boards at one end and shorter boards at the other, with boards graduating in size between them, to give the effect of a sweeping curve. There are all kinds of possible variations here, as long as you take care in measuring and construction to produce a neat, clean-cut finish along the fence top.

Below: *These palings, painted white to match the house, appear even more attractive draped with greenery supported from a simple structure behind*

Another very popular form of fencing, particularly on modern housing estates, is interwoven or lapped fencing. The basket-weave effect achieved is quite attractive and the fence still offers considerable privacy. It is usually supplied in 1800mm panels, which are nailed to upright wooden posts or inserted into grooves on concrete posts.

Although cheaper to construct than feather board, interwoven fencing is not as tough. Tall panels are easily damaged by strong winds, though the posts may be reinforced with concrete spurs to help counteract this. Any damage usually requires complete replacement of the affected panel, which can often prove rather expensive.

Overlap fencing is similar in style to interwoven in that panels are fixed to wooden posts. Usually made of larch, it consists of strips of wood with uneven edges overlapped horizontally.

Another possibility where privacy is your main consideration is to have a

dwarf brick wall topped with timber fencing. Feather board, interwoven and overlapped fencing are all suitable for this treatment, and the wall helps to improve their durability.

Where privacy is not your main consideration, the scope is even greater. Many families regard their back gardens as a sort of outdoor extension to their home and, naturally, do not want to be overlooked all the time. Front gardens, on the other hand, often provide an opportunity to display your gardening prowess and present a welcoming façade to visitors.

If the garden is to provide a safe play area for children, however, the fencing must be sturdy and secure—it is no good choosing one which is easy to get over, through or under.

Post and rail ranch fencing is inexpensive, easy to maintain and suits almost every style of house. It is usually fairly low and this, combined with the fact that it is not solid, helps to create an impression of space, making it especially suitable for small gardens and crowded streets.

The broad, horizontal rails, spaced about 300mm apart, are fastened directly on to upright posts. Traditionally, they are painted white which, again, adds to the general feeling of spaciousness.

Palings are well suited to cottages and 19th century terrace houses and 'villas'. This style consists of an upper and lower rail—fastened horizontally to two end posts—with upright slats attached at regular intervals inbetween. The upper ends of the palings are usually rounded, although they may be shaped to a point and look most attractive when painted to match the house.

The palisade or picket fence looks rather like a tall version of palings. It can be bought in rolls and is very useful for fencing off awkwardly shaped areas. The stakes are more roughly shaped than palings and have one flat and one curved side. They are usually pointed and 1800mm high. The individual stakes are wired top and bottom to strong, horizontal wires and the rolls are attached to oak posts with wire.

Trellis fencing is cheap and ideal as a support to climbing or trailing plants. It consists of panels of 30mm thick laths of wood fastened across each other horizontally and vertically to form squares. It is not very sturdy and is best used in conjunction with other types of fencing or as a screen within the garden.

Rustic fencing is becoming increasingly popular, even in towns, and looks particularly appropriate with a country-style garden. It is usually made from larch or pine in a variety of different designs—the most popular being diamond shapes. You can buy it with or without the bark, but either blends in very well with the garden.

Gates

Gates can be divided into two basic categories—wooden and iron—but this does not mean that the choice of design is in any way limited. Most types are available in a considerable range of heights and widths, but it is essential to measure the aperture accurately—allowing for supporting gate posts—before ordering.

The type of fence you have should influence your choice of gate and it is often best to plan them both at the same time. For example, if you have decided on a tall, feather board fence for the sake of privacy, then a plain,

Left and below: *Wrought iron gates are available in a variety of styles and look decorative either on their own or—for a country look—below an arch of colourful climbing plants*

Below centre: *A strong, yet attractive fence—the rich golden colour of lapped, waney-edged timber panels is accentuated by the supporting concrete posts and gravel boards*

Above: *Bright, contrasting colours look perfect on these unusual double gates and are particularly effective between the white painted walls*

solid board gate would be more appropriate than a lacy patterned, wrought iron gate. Equally, a traditional wooden gate is best with palings and a picket fence. Height is an important consideration and the simplest rule is to choose a gate the same height as the fence. It is is possible to combine a low fence and a tall gate, but the result often looks strange.

Wooden gates are relatively cheap, easy to maintain and fairly durable. They should be painted or treated with protective sealing regularly.

There are three basic types. Solid board gates are severely practical and often used—singly or in pairs—for back and side entrances, where security rather than decoration is the main concern. They can be fitted with bolts which lock into the ground and are virtually 'peep proof'.

Other wooden gates are more decorative and consist either of a row of slats fastened to cross pieces and a diagonal, or of a solid base with a decorative open top.

There are all kinds of more unusual possibilities, but remember that ease of access is essential. If you decide on an unusual gate, make sure that it is easy to open from the outside as well as from the inside, not too heavy to move and, if it is covered, that there is plenty of headroom.

Wrought iron gates are more expensive than wooden types but are very durable. They are available in an immense variety of patterns, ranging from plain, vertical bars to barley sugar twists and swirling scrolls.

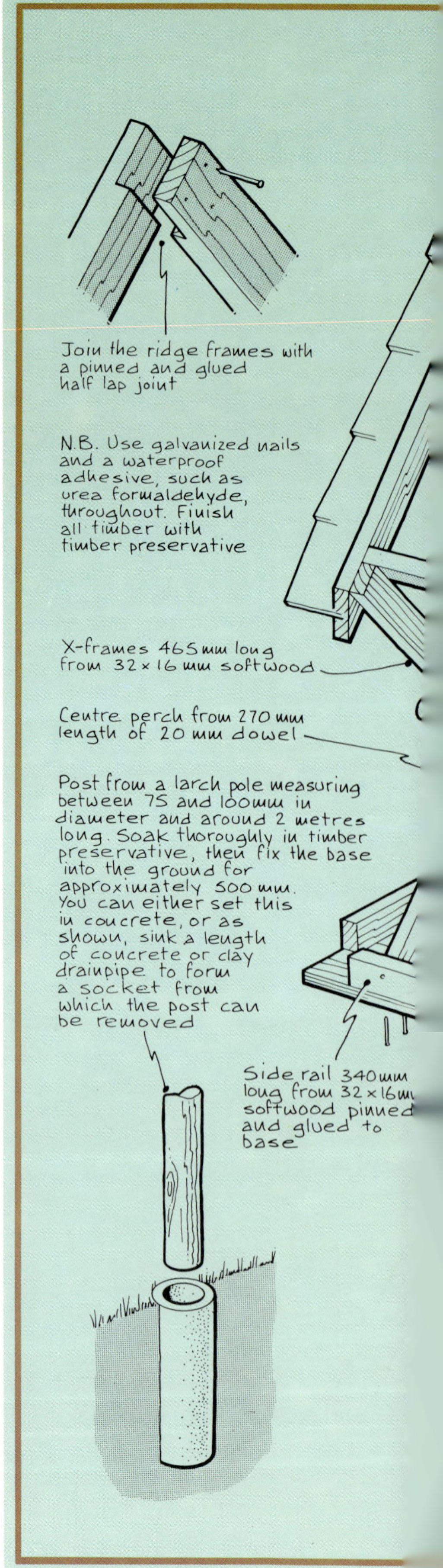

Build a bird table

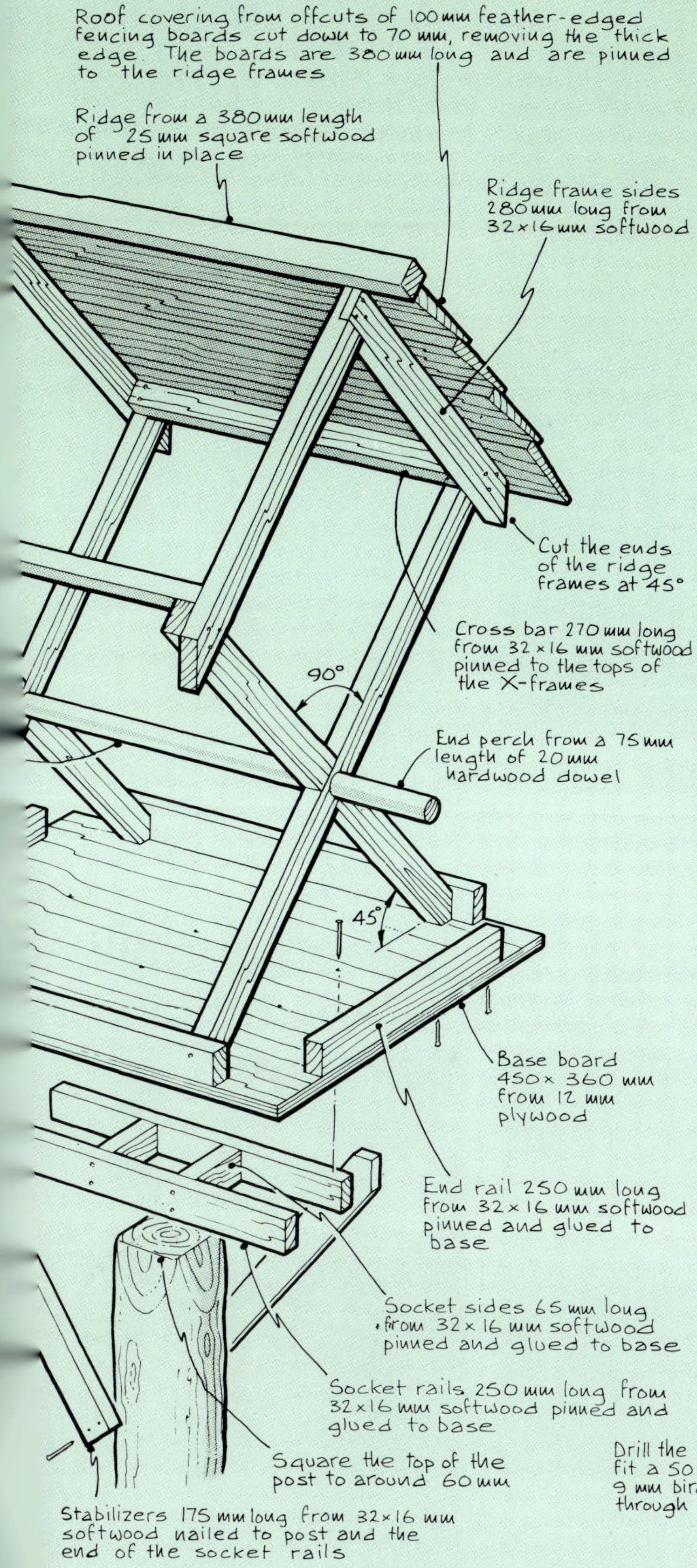

You can build this attractive, rustic bird table for very little cost by using offcuts of timber and fencing materials. You can use either sawn or planed wood for the frame, or even the thick edges of the feather edged boards used for the roof. Be sure to use exterior grade plywood for the table.

Give all the timber a thorough coating with timber preservative. Fit the table to a larch pole, either bedded in concrete or fitted into a pipe as shown. Bird seed or nuts can be put out on the table, and you can fit cuphooks for hanging containers of nuts or coconut halves.

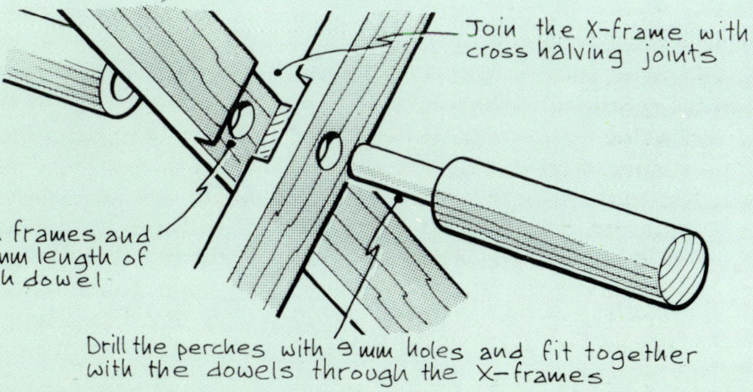

Repairing fences

Left: *The galvanized steel bracket is extremely useful for a number of fence repairs.*

Getting your fences in good order goes a long way to making the garden more attractive. You can replace them, repair them or even add new sections quite simply and cheaply

For wooden fences to be an asset in a garden, they must be regularly treated with preservative and repaired as soon as damage becomes apparent. Like any cut wood which is exposed to the elements, fences are susceptible to rot and infestation—so unless renovations are conscientiously carried out, they can quickly fall into a state of disrepair.

Preservatives

Most new posts have already been impregnated under pressure with a solvent to protect against wood-boring insects and fungus infections. But if there is any doubt as to whether this is the case, soak the post for at least two days in a preservative before putting it in the ground.

One external wood preservative that can be used is creosote. This has a tar and oil base, and in the UK a brand to BS 144 is recommended for fencing. In Canada, a preservative containing creosote and pentachlorophenol is often used.

The main drawback to creosote is that it stains the wood a dark, not very attractive colour. Also, once the wood has been coated with creosote it cannot normally be painted over.

Creosote must be applied to dry wood—either by soaking or applying with a brush. If you brush it on, bear in mind that it will penetrate only about 3mm into the wood and that the whole process will have to be repeated in a couple of years. Remember also that creosote and other solvents are poisonous to all life forms.

A more expensive form of preservative but one which can be painted over is the organic solvent—a preservative chemical which has been dissolved in white spirit or petroleum oil. Organic solvents can even be used

1 *Remove the concrete spur from the supporting post using the bolts as handles to lever and ease it out of the ground*

2 *Replace the rotten supporting post having cut new mortises for the arris rails. Angle-cut the top for water to run off*

3 *Set the concrete spur to overlap about 100-150mm below the bottom of the post and mark the new positions for the bolts*

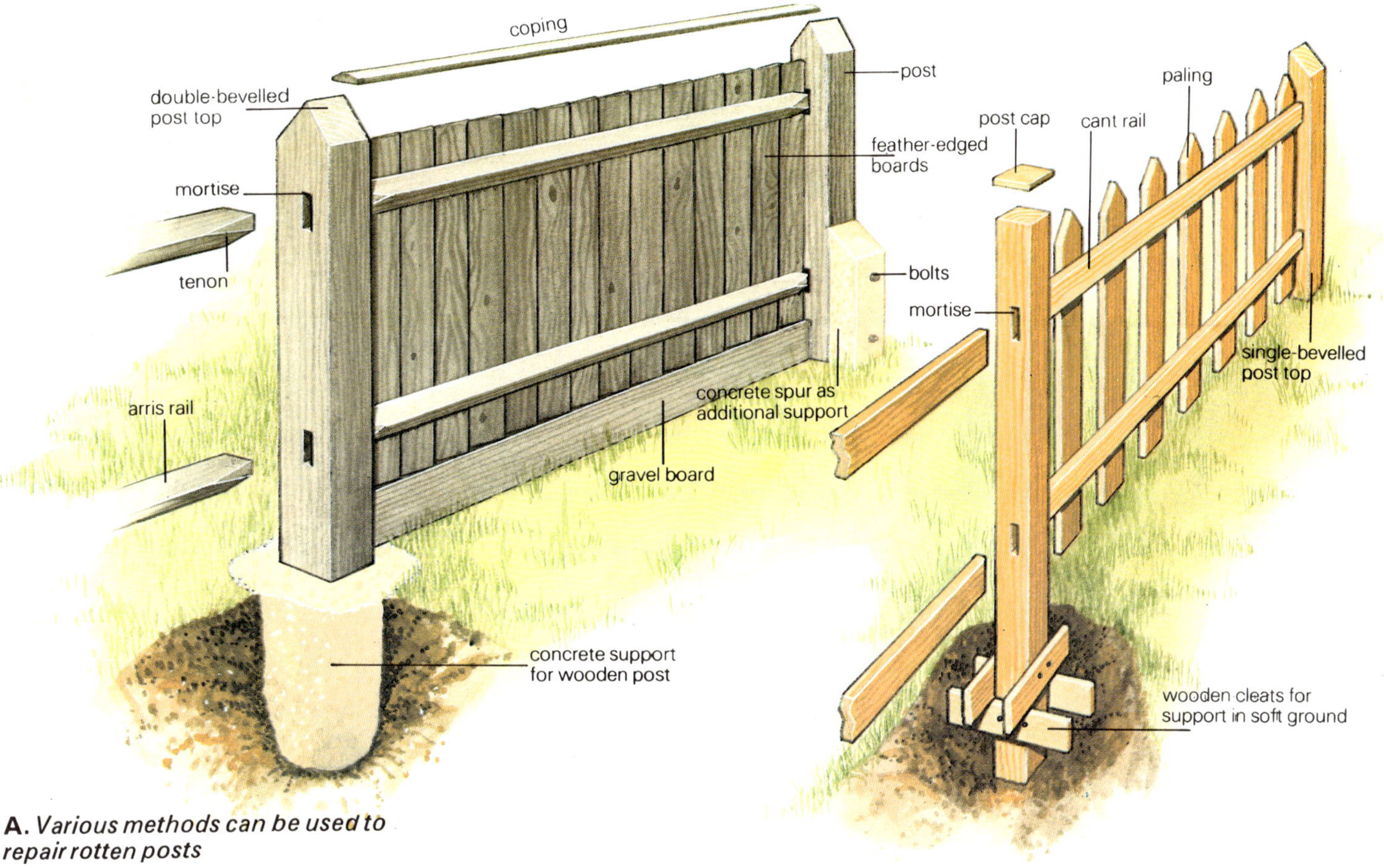

A. *Various methods can be used to repair rotten posts*

to treat wood which has already been attacked by fungus or insects.

Whenever a post or piece of fence is being replaced, the new section must be treated with a preservative, or it will quickly rot.

Paint acts as an effective barrier for wood only if a new coat is applied immediately the old one shows signs of flaking or blistering.

Remember when using wood preservatives to wear protective clothing and eye protection. Always apply the preservative in the open air or at least in a well ventilated room.

Repairing a post

The most likely place for a fence post to become damaged is at, or below, ground level. At this point, the wood is almost permanently damp, causing it to rot. Once a post is rotten, it can give no support and the section of fence butting up to it tends to lean out of alignment.

To repair the post you must cut off the affected part and attach a supporting spur (fig. A). This involves temporarily supporting the fence and then digging a hole around the post about 600mm square and 300mm deep. Saw off the rotten part of the post once it is completely exposed and bolt on the

4 *When the base hole is dug and the timber preserved, set the post and spur in position and find the vertical with a spirit level*

5 *If the arris rail tenon is also rotten make a mortice from timber blocks and screw them firmly to the post around the arris rail*

6 *Pack a mix of concrete firmly into the hole at the base to give a solid support for the spur and the fence post*

7 *Saw off a particularly weak arris rail tenon at the mortise joint, removing the end board of the fence to get access*

8 *Position a galvanized steel joining bracket to bridge the gap between the solid part of the arris rail and the supporting post*

9 *You can also temporarily repair an arris rail that has broken between two supporting posts by using a steel bracket*

10 *Make sure the fence is back in alignment then place the bracket centrally over the broken section and screw it in position*

concrete spur—150mm or 200mm coach bolts are suitable.

The straight face of the spur should be against the post (fig. A). When it is in position, use a spirit level to check it is upright. Hardcore should then be packed around the bottom of the spur and the hole filled with a 1:3 cement and coarse sand mix. In Canada, set the cement below the frost line.

This method of repairing a post will withstand fairly severe weather conditions. Another method for a fence post which is not exposed to strong winds is the use of a metal spike.

After the rotten part of the post has been cut off, the ground must be tightly packed back into place. The metal spike is then driven hard into the ground, while gently holding the fence out of the way. Then bolt the spike to the post.

Repairing an arris rail

An arris rail—the horizontal bar of a fence—can be repaired temporarily if broken at the tenon (pointed end) or in the shaft by using a metal bracket to bridge the broken part (fig. 8).

If the tenon is broken, first level it off and then soak it with a preservative. Using galvanized or sheradized screws, fix the arms of the bracket to the post in the same place as the rail was originally fixed. With the bracket in place, screw both sides of it to the shaft of the arris rail.

When using a metal bracket to repair the shaft of an arris rail, screw it to one side and then with the aid of an assistant push the other side inwards and screw the bracket to that.

It is most important to use galvanized or sheradized screws in external woodwork. Ordinary screws will simply rust away—causing unsightly stains—or fuse with, and split, the wood.

Fitting a new arris rail

When ordering a new arris rail, measure the distance between the two upright posts and add at least 75mm for the tenons. You may need to whittle away at the rail so that it fits into the mortise (rectangular slot) in the post (fig. A). Treat tenons and mortises with preservative.

If you cannot force the posts far enough out of line to enable you to spring the ends of the rail into the post, you will have to use metal brackets or wooden chocks.

For the latter you need four 25mm × 20mm offcuts of wood to fit around the mortise. They must all be coated with preservative and then all but the top piece screwed into position. With this done, the rail can be slotted into place and the fourth strip of wood screwed tightly down for a firm grip around the tenon. Do this at both ends of the rail.

New boards in feather fencing

A feather fence is one which is made up of slightly overlapping vertical strips of wood (fig. A). It is a simple matter to replace either one single board or to erect a whole series to form a complete new section.

When only one board needs replacing, remove the nails which are securing it and make sure that those securing the boards on either side of the damaged board are well banged in. Then slide the thin edge of the new board under the thick edge of the old one and nail through the overlapping edges with galvanized nails.

If a whole series of boards needs to be fitted, follow exactly the same procedure except for using a spirit level every fourth board to check that they are vertically level.

Gravel boards

As all wooden fences are at their most vulnerable where they touch the ground, a gravel board is usually fitted to minimize the risk of damp rising through the fence (fig. A).

Most gravel boards are made of 150mm × 50mm hardwood. Alternatively, the fence can either be set on a single course of bricks topped with a strip of roofing felt, or on a custom-designed concrete panel.

To fit a wooden gravel board, clear away any soil or debris from around the base of the fence to form a recess for the board. Treat the board with preservative and either fit it into pre-cut mortises in the wooden posts

B. *Follow this method and you can add any length to a woven panelled fence with little difficulty*

or nail it through wooden blocks attached to the inside of the post. The blocks can be of the same wood and need to be set back from the edge of the post so that the gravel board will be flush with it.

If the posts are concrete, drive pegs into the ground butted right up to the post. The pegs should be made from treated 50mm × 50mm hardwood and at least 600mm long. Leave about 150mm protruding from the ground and—after measuring and cutting the board so that it fits tightly between the posts—nail it to the pegs.

Concrete gravel boards are also available, designed for use with concrete posts. Such posts have a groove on the inside surfaces, into which the concrete gravel can be slotted. Fencing panels are ideal for use with this system because they too can then simply be slid into position.

Panelled fencing

Interwoven panelled fencing (fig. B) is the simplest type of fencing to erect but it has the drawback that even the slightest damage to a panel usually means that the whole section has to be replaced. Being very light and often tall, woven panels are especially susceptible to damage from strong winds. Since it is an expensive business to replace entire panels, such fencing should always be set on a gravel board.

The slats which make up woven fences are very difficult to obtain individually—unless a second-hand panel is available from which slats could be taken. It is usually always necessary to buy an entire panel. They are sold in standard sizes.

Panels can be cut to size, if necessary. To do this, hold the panel in the correct position and mark off the overlap. Carefully remove the end battens with a claw hammer. These will be longer than the middle battens because they extend up level with the top rail. They should be re-nailed inside the marked lines and underneath the top rail so that the excess protrudes from the bottom. It can be sawn off when the batten is in position. The surplus part of the panel can also then be sawn off, using the end batten as a guide (fig. B). With this done the panel is ready to be positioned alongside another and hammered into its correct place.

Do not forget that panel fences, like other wooden types, must be regularly treated with preservative if they are to stay in good condition.

11 *In order to replace a rotten picket fence first measure the height of the palings and the length of the arris rails*

12 *When the rails and palings are removed, mark the positions for the tenons at each end of the new arris rail*

13 *Mark out the shape of the tenon on the new rail and cut it out by sawing or whittling with an axe. Treat the cut end with preservative*

14 *Set the new rail tenon into the mortise in the supporting post and paint the post liberally at this stage with a wood preservative*

15 *Mark out the triangular shape at the top of the paling timber and saw the first one carefully to use as a template for the others*

16 *When the palings have been painted with preservative, set the first one in position and check it for spacing and plumb*

17 *Set the second paling at the exact height at the other end of the section then secure both palings with galvanized nails*

18 *Stretch a string attached to nails in the supporting posts to act as a guideline for the horizontal line of the palings*

Removing a wooden post

It is sometimes very difficult to remove an old wooden post which has been set into concrete. However, the job can be made easier by using a strong rope-leverage system.

First, temporarily support the fence by tacking a sturdy batten to the top arris rail on either side of the post. In the case of a slatted fence, remove one board from either side of the post. Afterwards, dig out as much soil as possible to completely expose the base of the post in its bed of mortar.

Hammer in a 100mm nail about 300mm from the ground on either side of the post then tie a strong rope round the post immediately below the nails, leaving enough of the rope to tie around a suitable levering post. The levering post must be of very sturdy wood. Two nails should be hammered into it about 30mm from the end to provide a grip for the rope.

Stack some bricks under the levering post about 100mm higher than the nails in the post. Push hard on the stick to ease out the post, adjusting the height of the bricks as necessary for maximum leverage.

The new post should already be pre-treated. Insert it in a hole at least 600mm deep and after packing in some hardcore, fill in the hole with a 1:3 cement and coarse sand mix. The top of the new post should either be cut slanted at an angle of 30° and painted with creosote or have a hardwood or metal cap screwed on to it. Either of these methods helps prevent penetrating damp by protecting the exposed end-grain of the wood.

C. *With an assistant holding the post, lever extraction is easy*

Repairing gates

● The various types of gate designs ● Replacing unsound gate posts ● Constructing new post foundations ● Dealing with faulty hinges ● Repairs to metal and timber gates

A. Below: *A timber gate can last a lifetime if it is well maintained. On a large five-bar gate like this wear is inevitable, but repairs are usually simple and cheap providing you spot the trouble in time*

Wherever there is a fence, wall or hedge you are likely to find a gate. Unfortunately, both gates and their associated hardware are often ignored until something goes wrong–usually when the gate itself becomes difficult to open or shut. Getting frustrated and forcing the gate shut only makes matters worse; it is a lot less trouble to make a few simple repairs as soon as the need arises.

There is a vast range of gate styles fashioned from timber, metal and even plastic, but all share the same major components: the gate itself, the hinges, the latch or bolt, the gate posts, and the foundations of the posts. The gate posts are identified as the latch and hinge post.

The first sign of trouble is likely to be a binding, either against the ground or the latch post, or a general insecurity of the structure because something has broken

1 *A worn bolted joint and a broken brace are typical causes of a sagging gate. But first, check that the gate posts and hinges are secure*

2 *A bolted brace is easy to remove. Often the bolts are rusted and can easily be sheared off, but otherwise you can saw through them*

or become loose. In all cases you should start your investigation with the gate posts, then move on to the hinges and finally to the gate itself.

Faulty gate posts

It goes without saying that gate posts must provide a firm anchorage and be strong enough to withstand the weight of the gate. In the UK the best timber posts are made of English oak or larch, but you may find softwood posts of fir, redwood or pine. Ready-made metal gates are usually supplied with hollow metal posts, but more substantial than any posts are brickwork, stone, or pre-cast concrete block piers.

For light single gates, 125mm × 125mm timber posts are adequate; 150mm × 150mm is the minimum size for light double gates, increasing to 230mm × 230mm for heavy double gates. In the case of free-standing piers, light gates need piers of 35mm × 35mm, medium gates 46mm × 46mm, and heavy double gates, piers of at least 56mm × 56mm. Remember these are minimums.

To start with check that the posts are firm in the ground, perfectly vertical and, in the case of timber posts, free from rot. Although it is possible to repair a gate post that is rotten at the base by fixing a ready-made concrete spur to it, this is actually a false economy because you must still disturb the ground to make solid foundations of concrete.

If the post has good foundations, the best remedy is to remove the post and substitute a new one of the same dimensions without disturbing the ground any more than is necessary. Do this by tying a length of levering timber to the post and levering it out of the foundations over a pile of stone or bricks.

Prepare the new post by sawing the end into a blunt point so that it will easily fit into the hole. Clean out the hole, then position the post in it with the help of a spirit level. Nail two supports to the post to keep it upright as shown in fig. B, then fill the hole with concrete and tamp down beside the post to exclude any air pockets.

3 *Where a bolt has rusted through, push it out of the joint using a hammer and punch—taking care not to damage the good timber*

When the concrete has set, remove the supports, wedge the gate in place, and mark the position of the hinges or latch. All that remains is to attach the hinges or latch to the new post, while supporting the gate in its correct position.

Unsound foundations: Your investigation may reveal that the actual post foundation is unsound in which case you must dismantle the gate and construct new foundations. When doing this, bear in mind that the posts should extend at least 900mm below ground level (1200mm in the case of double gates). Unless the ground is very hard, it is normal to construct a bridge between the gate posts to prevent differential settlement which might cause the gate to bind or fail to close properly.

To start with, dig out the old foundations and prepare a trough linking them. If, as may be the case, the old latch post was set directly into the ground, dig a hole around it as large as the hole for the hinge post foundation. Use a square ended piece of scrap timber around 250mm × 250mm and about a metre long to tamp down the earth within the excavation. Then set up both the gate

4 *Lay the broken brace over the replacement piece of timber—which must be the same type and size—and clamp them together*

6 *Next use a hammer and punch to transfer the position of the bolt holes to the new brace, then pre-drill the holes to accept the bolts*

C. Below left: *The Kent is a pressure impregnated softwood gate in the traditional Kentish five-bar style*
Below right: *The Yeoman features a distinctive curved hanging stile which provides additional strength*

5 *As long as the original profile has not been destroyed you can trace the correct angle directly on to the new piece of timber*

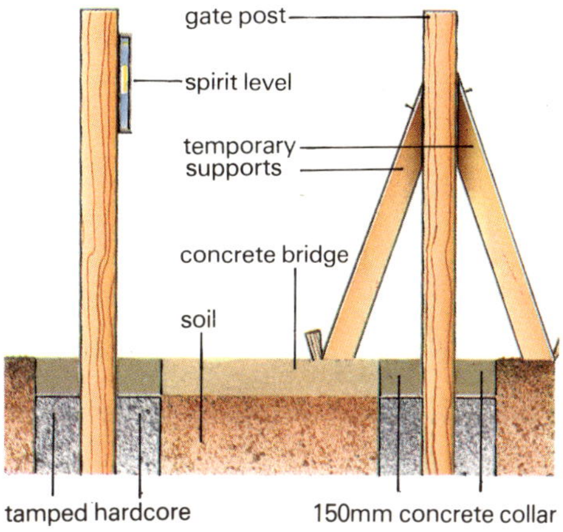

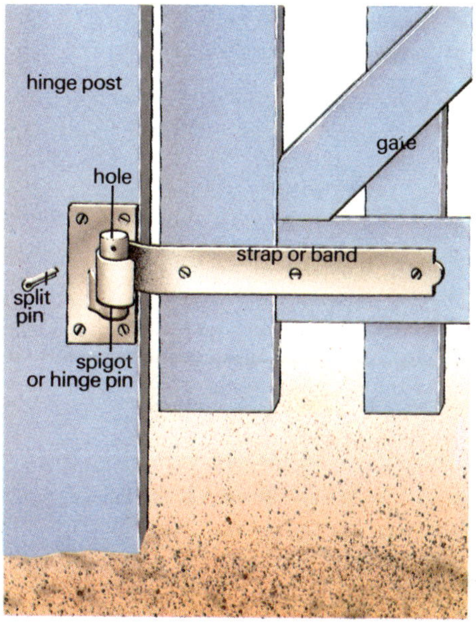

B. Above: *Gate posts must be anchored in hardcore and concrete foundations—add a concrete bridge in soft ground* **Right**: *To thief-proof a strap and spigot hinge, insert a split pin in the spigot*

7 *When you have marked out the new brace, pre-drill the holes then remove the original and saw off the waste areas*

posts with a spirit level and support them as described above with scrap wood battens temporarily nailed to the post.

Tamp in hardcore around the posts and the bottom of the bridge to within 150mm of ground level, fill the rest of the hole with concrete and allow this to set for at least 48 hours before removing the temporary supports and fixing the gate.

Timber gateposts: These will simply rot away unless treated against damp. New posts are best impregnated with preservative, preferably by pressure treatment at the timber merchant. If this is not possible, either char the lower end of the post over a bonfire or soak it in a drum of proprietary wood preservative.

In the case of older gate posts, you should test them for rot once a year by pushing a penknife blade into the timber near the ground. If it penetrates easily and deeply, you should replace the post with a new impregnated one. Once a year, paint all exposed gate timbers with creosote (when the timber is dry) or, if the appearance of the timber is important, with a proprietary organic solvent.

If older gate posts have not been impregnated, you can reduce the risk of soil-level rot by the following method. Drilling an angled hole near the ground halfway through the post, pour creosote into the hole then plug the hole with a rounded scrap of wood. Like the other processes, this should be repeated no less than once a year.

Hollow metal gate posts can also be given foundations as described above, but in this case you should treat all of the post below ground level with a thick coat of carefully applied bitumen.

If your initial investigations show that the gate posts are secure, free from rot and vertical, proceed to the hinges.

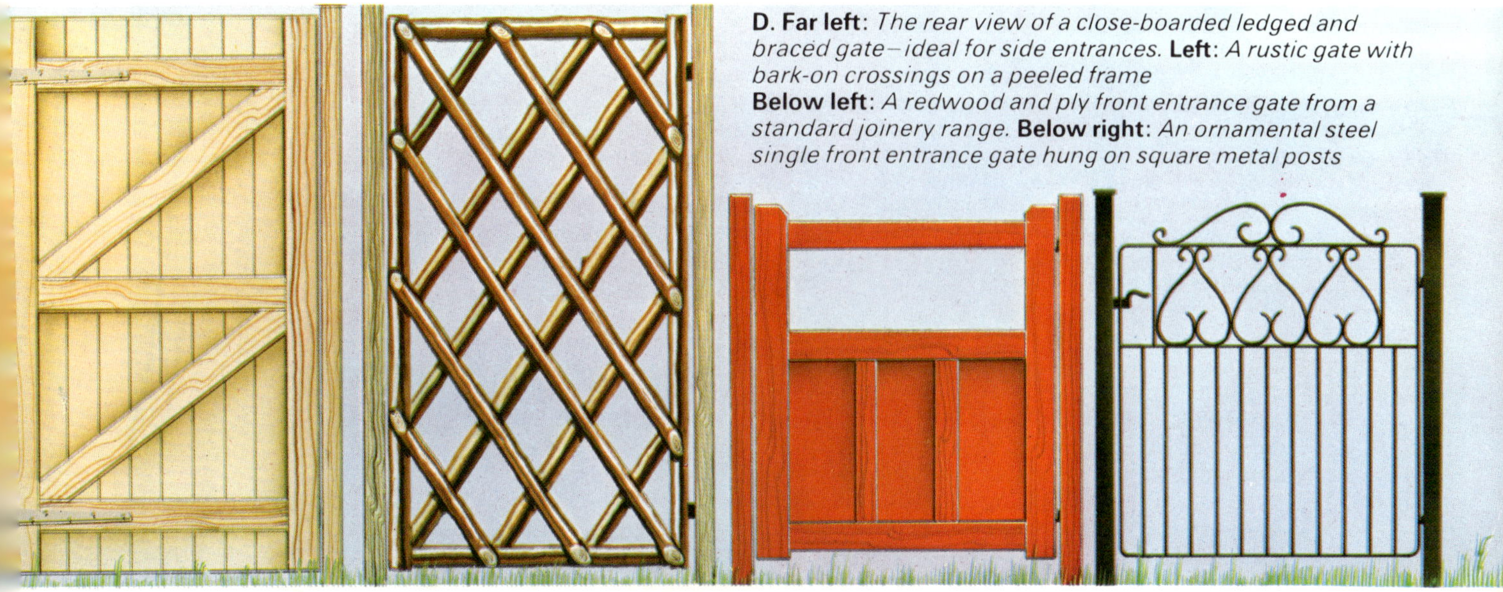

D. Far left: *The rear view of a close-boarded ledged and braced gate—ideal for side entrances.* **Left**: *A rustic gate with bark-on crossings on a peeled frame* **Below left**: *A redwood and ply front entrance gate from a standard joinery range.* **Below right**: *An ornamental steel single front entrance gate hung on square metal posts*

Repairing gates

Faulty gate hinges

In almost all cases steel hinges will show signs of corrosion: although heavily affected hinges must be replaced, you can clean, lubricate and reseat lightly corroded ones. Bent hinges must always be renewed. And if you are in any doubt about the basic strength of the existing hinges, you should replace them with a set of strap and spigot hinges.

The strap and spigot combination is particularly suitable for large gates because it rests the weight of the gate on one strong fixed point. Its only disadvantage is that you can bypass any locks on the gate by simply lifting it off the spigots. However, you can make the hinges more secure by drilling through the spigots and fixing split pins through them as shown in fig. B.

Before renewing a loose hinge, check that the fault is not simply loose fixing screws. If this is the case, wedge the gate shut, remove the old screws completely and pack the screw holes with a proprietary wood filler. To slow down the corroding process, roll the new screws up and down an ordinary candle to coat them with wax then, once the screws are in place, tip the heads with wood filler or metal primer. Do not try to solve the problem by driving in larger screws because you may split the wood.

Where the timber around the screw holes has split you can either fill the split with adhesive, using G-cramps (C-clamps) to close it up or, in very bad cases, patch in new timber using a scarf joint.

Fitting new hinges is exactly the same as refitting old hinges with new screws, but remember always to coat them with metal primer after first cleaning off their oil covering.

The major difficulty when renewing hinges is very often removing the old ones. It is not unusual to find the screws so badly corroded that there is no purchase for the screwdriver, or that the screw is fused to the hinge. To avoid damaging the gate or post, it is sometimes possible to prise the hinge carefully away from the surface then cut through the screws with a hacksaw. Use a self-gripping wrench to unscrew the stubs and fill the holes with a proprietary filler before fixing the new hinge.

Alternatively, you could drill off the screw heads, lever away the hinges, then unscrew the stubs as described above.

Rehanging a gate is not as critical as rehanging a door because there can be a space between the gate and the post, but you must watch the open arc of the gate, particularly where there is sloping ground. In any case it is good practice to support the gate on blocks just as when rehanging a door.

8 *It is essential to weatherproof timber used outdoors—be sure to apply preservative to the blind portion of the new brace before you fit it*

9 *Put the new brace in place on the gate, then bring the gate back into its correct position by levering it up and chocking it with waste wood*

10 *Holding the new brace in place with one or two G-cramps, bring the bolt holes into alignment by jacking the bars with a sash cramp*

11 *Insert new bolts into the holes in the new brace and hammer them through the joint with careful but deliberate blows*

Faulty gates

As mentioned above gates may be made of timber, metal or plastic, and whereas it is perfectly feasible to repair a faulty timber gate it is generally best to renew a metal or plastic gate that is badly damaged or corroded.

Plastic gates like the Ashford ranch style need no maintenance and indeed, this is their main attraction. Metal gates, however, have a major enemy in the form of corrosion. Wrought iron gates are relatively rare today, most metal gates being steel. Yet both rust if left untreated, and it is essential to remove the first signs of corrosion with a proprietary rust remover before priming and painting. Metal gates should be redecorated annually as a matter of course, and their hinges lubricated at the same time. The best lubricant to use is a lithium-based grease.

13 *The new bolts will almost certainly be too long: to avoid nasty accidents with the protruding bits, saw off the excess*

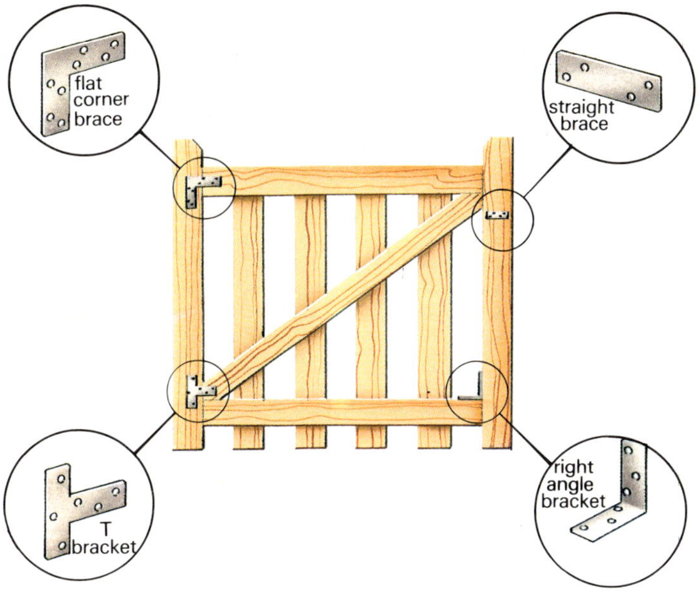

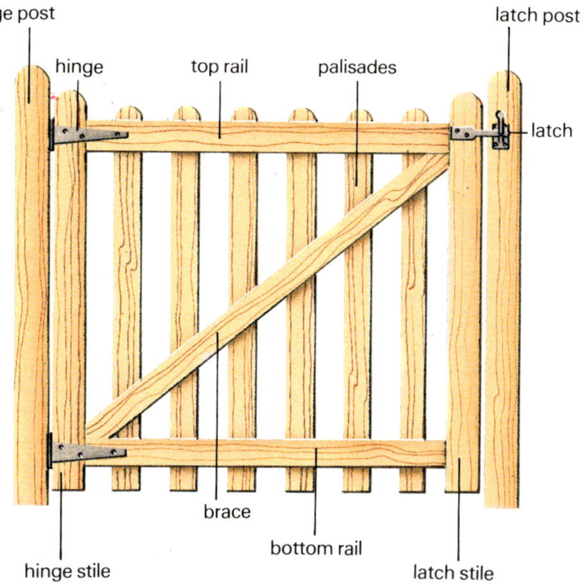

E. Above: *Galvanized steel reinforcing brackets are available in a variety of styles and are a good way to extend the life of a rickety single gate*

F. Above: *The basic elements of a timber gate. If it sags first check the security of the posts, then the hinges and finally the gate itself*

12 *Put a washer in front of the nut, then tighten the nut and bolt to pull the square shank of the bolt into the new brace to stop it turning*

14 *Finally, put on appropriate protective gloves and apply a liberal coat of creosote to all surfaces of the new brace, particularly the joints*

Repairs to timber gates

How you repair a timber gate depends on the type of unit in question. Gate construction can be divided into two basic types: ledged boarded and braced (fig. D); and the farm type, which can be based on a cantilever (such as the Kent) or suspension design (fig. C).

Horizontal rails are usually tenoned into the vertical stiles and secured with dowels rather than wedges (which tend to fall out). Braces are normally notched into the rails or the stile/rail joint. Boards and vertical palisades are always nailed to the ledges/frame and brace, but the cross bars on farm gates are tenoned or bolted into the stiles.

There are no hard and fast rules where gate repairs are concerned—each fault must be tackled according to its own specific characteristics.

Where strained joints cause the gate to sag and jam, it may be sufficient to trim the upper edge of the stile with a plane. If this fails and the gate is not braced, insert a brace diagonally from the hinge end of the lower rail to the latch end of the upper rail. Notch this into the rails or simply screw or bolt it on.

On a single span gate where the timber is sound but the joints are loose, you can strengthen the gate and restore its shape by using galvanized metal reinforcing brackets (fig. E). On a farm type of gate, the weight of the construction necessitates the use of a diagonal brace—either a metal bar or a tensioned wire across the 'long' diagonal.

Dealing with rotten timber: Perhaps the worst enemy of a timber gate is rot. In severe cases you must renew the gate, but if the rot is confined to small areas, you can patch in new pieces of timber in exactly the same way as you would on a door.

Rot is caused by moisture attacking the timber fibres, and to prevent further attacks you must treat the new timber with knot and weatherproof sealer before priming and painting.

Where the rot is more extensive but confined to—for example—just one stile, you can replace the stile and save the gate. First remove the gate and place it on a flat surface. Drill out any dowels or mortise wedges in the joints, using a wooden block to protect the edges of the timber. Then knock the stile outwards from the rails with a hammer so that the tenons on the rails separate from their mortises. Use a softwood block to prevent the hammer blows from damaging the stile itself or the surrounding timber.

Work your way slowly from joint to joint until the stile is released, then measure up the tenons on the rails and cut corresponding mortises in the new stile. Knot and prime the new part before applying the adhesive and sash cramps (bar cramps). Be sure to use a waterproof adhesive such as urea or resorcinol formaldehyde.

Alternatively, you can saw through the stile immediately adjacent to the joints and chisel away the rotten wood from around the joint area before replacing it.

Either method can also be used on any part of a gate which is affected by severe rot as long as the rest of the assembly is in reasonably good condition.

Erecting a close-boarded fence

Above: *Building a timber fence like this is surprisingly easy, providing you use the right materials and tackle the work in a logical order*

● Construction materials ● Preserving timber ● Preparation ● Installing the posts, gravel boards, arris rails and vertical boards ● Building a fence on a slope ● Masonry plinths

A garden fence built from overlapped vertical boarding is an attractive addition to any home. Close-boarded fencing—as it is called—is not difficult to build and uses pre-cut material, making it a realistic alternative to the cheaper but less durable 'woven panel' fencing now so popular for garden use. The tenon joints used in its construction do not have to be perfect, and the rail ends which slot in to them are simply rough-hewn to shape.

Three things make all the difference between a shoddy fence and an attractive, solid, long-lasting one. First and foremost the posts must be adequately supported. Many people try to save money by skimping on the length of the posts or the amount of concrete used to bed them, but this is false economy, as the first gale may quickly demonstrate.

Also, the timber must be adequately protected against rotting. Although fencing timber is sometimes sold pre-treated against rot, it pays to give it the extra protection of a good soaking in preservative before erection. Additionally, all cut ends and every joint must be well soaked in preservative before they become inaccessible.

Finally, the fence should be straight and its post tops level or, if on sloping ground, descending in steps of equal sizes. If your land slopes, you need to work out in advance whether to have a sloping or stepped fence, and whether you will use gravel boards or a plinth beneath it.

Construction materials

Though oak is the traditional fencing material, purpose-cut, low grade softwood is used in preference nowadays because of its lower cost. This can be perfectly acceptable provided the timber is properly treated with preservative. The posts are of 75mm × 75mm sawn timber—sometimes available as prepared 'fencing posts'—which are sunk at least 600mm into the ground and sleeved in concrete. Two or three arris rails—depending on the height of the fence—fit into mortises in the posts. These are triangular in section usually 100mm on one side, 75mm on the other two.

The vertical boards are feather-edged softwood, 100mm wide and tapering from 20mm at one edge to about 6mm at the other. When erected, they are overlapped by about 25mm.

To prevent the bases of the boards rotting, a horizontal gravel board is fixed between the posts just above ground level. Lengths of 100mm × 25mm timber are suitable, and should be fixed to 38mm × 38mm wooden cleats. As an alternative, you can use a masonry plinth—a dwarf wall—of either bricks or concrete walling stones set on a concrete pad.

You can make your fence even more durable by fixing capping pieces and a weathering strip (fig. C).

Preservation

Fencing timber is particularly susceptible to rotting, especially the softwood type. The most vulnerable area is the 100mm or so at, and immediately below, ground level; sometimes this will rot through, leaving the wood above and below it more or less intact. This is why it pays to carry your supporting concrete at least 50mm above ground level and give it a finishing 'crown' to run off the water.

Pressure or vacuum-impregnated timber (such as the Tanalised variety) is best for fencing but is expensive and sometimes difficult to obtain.

If you cannot get pre-treated timber, treat the wood yourself by soaking it in a bath of exterior timber preservative. To make the bath you need about two dozen old bricks and a 3m wide sheet of heavy-duty polythene (fig. A).

Find a suitable flat surface and arrange the bricks on edge to form a rectangle—slightly longer than the largest fencing post and wide enough to take all the timber. Lay the polythene over the bricks to form a bath then carefully pour in the preservative, taking care not to cut or otherwise puncture the sheeting. Steep the fencing materials for up to a week if possible. Cover the bath during this time if children and pets are around.

If you have to store timber out of doors for any length of time, lay it on a flat surface and cover to prevent warping. Leave plenty of ventilation space between individual boards.

As you erect the fence, paint preservative on all timber surfaces that you will not be able to reach later—for example, where the vertical boards overlap. Give all end grain an extra coat to protect it.

Initial preparation

Begin by using a line and pegs to set out a straight line for your fence. Nylon fishing line is best for this, and especially for some of the levelling you may need to do later, as it does not sag when damp.

Decide how far apart your posts are to be—but to save cutting, base this on the length of the arris rails. If your arris rails are 2440mm long, set the posts 2440mm apart, measuring from the centre (not the outside edge) of one post position to the centre of the next. If this means that one fencing panel must be narrower than the others, arrange for it to be at the least conspicuous end, or corner, of the run of fencing.

Next, prepare your posts. The mortises are cut to take 100mm × 75mm × 75mm arris rails. Cut slots 75mm high × 25mm wide, inset 20mm from the face of the post, for the gravel boards.

For a fence on level ground, begin the upper mortise 250mm from the fence top, and the lower one 300mm above ground level—that is, 900mm from the bottom of the post if this is bedded to a depth of 600mm.

If the fence is to be more than 1200mm high, add an extra mortise at the mid-point to accept the third arris rail which is necessary to strengthen the construction. Mark out the mortise positions with a try square and pencil, drill from both sides with a brace and 25mm bit, and use a 19mm or 25mm mortise chisel to square the holes neatly.

For a stepped fence on sloping ground (see below), the mortises on the 'uphill' and 'downhill' sides of the post will have to be offset, and drilled only halfway through the post.

If you do not intend to use post caps (page 200), cut the top of each post so that it slopes away at 45° on the side to which you will be fixing the boards. This ensures that rainwater runs off the vulnerable end grain.

Next, using a small hand axe, taper the ends of the arris rails enough for them to jam into their respective mortises. For a level fitting, try to leave the face of the longest side intact and cut instead into the top edge, bottom edge and back. An exact fit is not necessary, but the neater you are the easier the assembly becomes. Remember to dab preservative around the insides of the mortises and the cut ends of the rail. Also, try to make all the cut ends of the arris rails of equal length—this greatly enhances the overall appearance of the fence (fig. 14).

A. *If you are building an entire fence, it is well worth constructing a bath for timber preservative. Leave timbers to soak as long as possible*

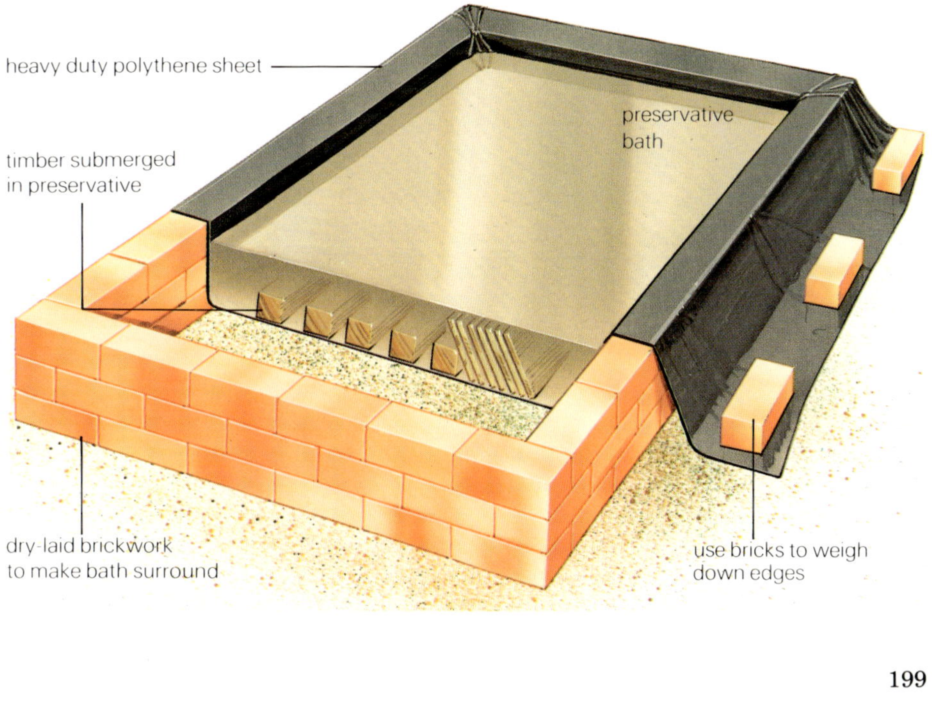

Erecting a close-boarded fence

Making the post holes

Once you have checked that your rails go halfway through the posts—and that your proposed post spacing is therefore accurate—you can mark the positions of the post holes.

Post holes need to be wide enough to allow for a decent sheath of concrete around the posts, but not so wide that they waste material. A narrow hole 600mm deep is hard to dig with a spade; a better tool is a post hole borer—sometimes called a *ground auger*—available from a tool hire shop. To use it, you just drive it in like a corkscrew.

Use the spade to trim the hole to about 200mm square. If you have the strength and the ground is soft enough, you may be able to 'pile drive' the post into its final bedding depth. Remove any loose material from the bottom of the holes.

If you are planning to build a masonry plinth (see below), dig the footings at this stage.

Next prepare shuttering from scraps of timber or plywood so that you extend the concrete sleeve above ground level and so protect the post at its most vulnerable point. Quite how far you extend it depends on whether the fence is beside loose soil, gravel, or concrete, and whether you are using a plinth. Do not go too far or it will be difficult to fix the cleats for the gravel boards.

Erecting the fence

When installing posts, ramming material around the base of a post loses much of its effect unless the bottom of the hole itself is really hard. So use a half brick or lump of concrete as a sole pad in each hole.

Erecting fence posts is much easier if there are two people, because one can hold the post plumb while the other rams in the concrete.

But if you are alone, stand the first post upright, fit a timber brace on each side, then use a plumbline or spirit level to check that it is vertical. When it is, fix the other ends of the braces to pegs driven into the ground.

Use a concrete mix of one part cement to six of all-in ballast. Pour it into the hole a little at a time and ram it well down with the end of a length of timber (fig. 8), checking as you go that you are not knocking the post out of plumb. Slightly over-fill the shuttering with concrete, then use a trowel to slope it to a smooth finish like the flaunching around a chimney.

Leave the concrete to set enough to hold the first post firmly and stand the second post on its sole pad. Fit the first set of two (or three) arris rails between the two posts. Check that the top rail is level. If it is not, scrape out more dirt from the second post hole or pour a little concrete under the sole pad. Then pour just enough concrete to steady the second post while you check that it is properly vertical. When it is, pour, ram and trim off the rest of the concrete.

Continue in the same way until you come to the final panel. Then measure off the last arris rails to the required length and erect your last post.

B. Below: *Gravel boards are secured to fence posts with hardwood cleats.*
Bottom: *Protect the tops of fence posts using one of these methods*

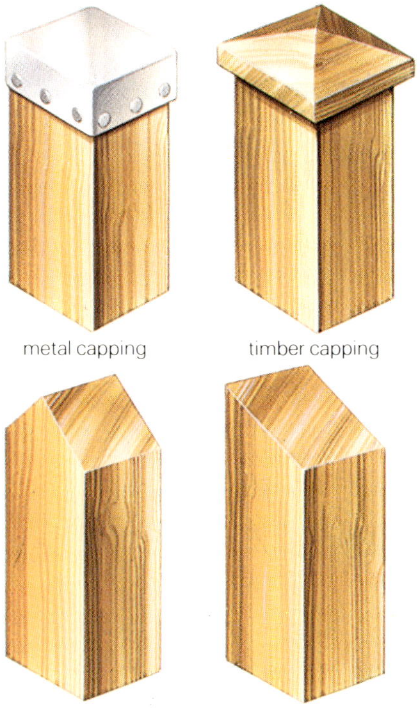

C. Right: *Constructional details of a close-boarded fence. Note that where a slope is involved, you can either slope the panels to match or step them and use masonry plinths to provide a firm base*

1 *Start cutting the mortises for the arris rails by drilling two or three large holes. Afterwards, finish off with a mortise chisel*

2 *Even if the fencing timber is already coated with preservative, you should apply more of the compound to all cut areas*

3 *Use a small axe to trim the ends of the arris rails roughly to shape. You can use a saw instead, but this does take longer*

Installing gravel boards

The next stage is to install the gravel boards or build a plinth (see below). Unless you are deliberately sloping the gravel boards, keep the top edges a constant distance from the tops of the posts. Doing so means you need only measure once—not several dozen times—when you come to cut the vertical boarding to length. Mark the height you want on a rod or an offcut of timber, measuring from the top downwards, and use this to gauge the height required on all posts.

Make the cleats to hold the gravel boards from 38mm × 38mm timber, the same length as the boards are wide. Inset them 25mm on the posts so that the faces of the gravel boards lie flush with the posts, and secure them with 65mm galvanized nails. Cut the gravel boards to length and nail them to the cleats. Ensure, in the future, that soil does not build up against them.

Close boardings

To keep the vertical boards level at the top of the fence, stretch a nylon line between the posts 25mm below their tops. Then cut a quantity of the feathered-edged boards to length.

Nail the first board in place, using 50mm galvanized nails, so that its thick end is against a post and the top is just brushing against the nylon guideline above.

Successive boards look neater if

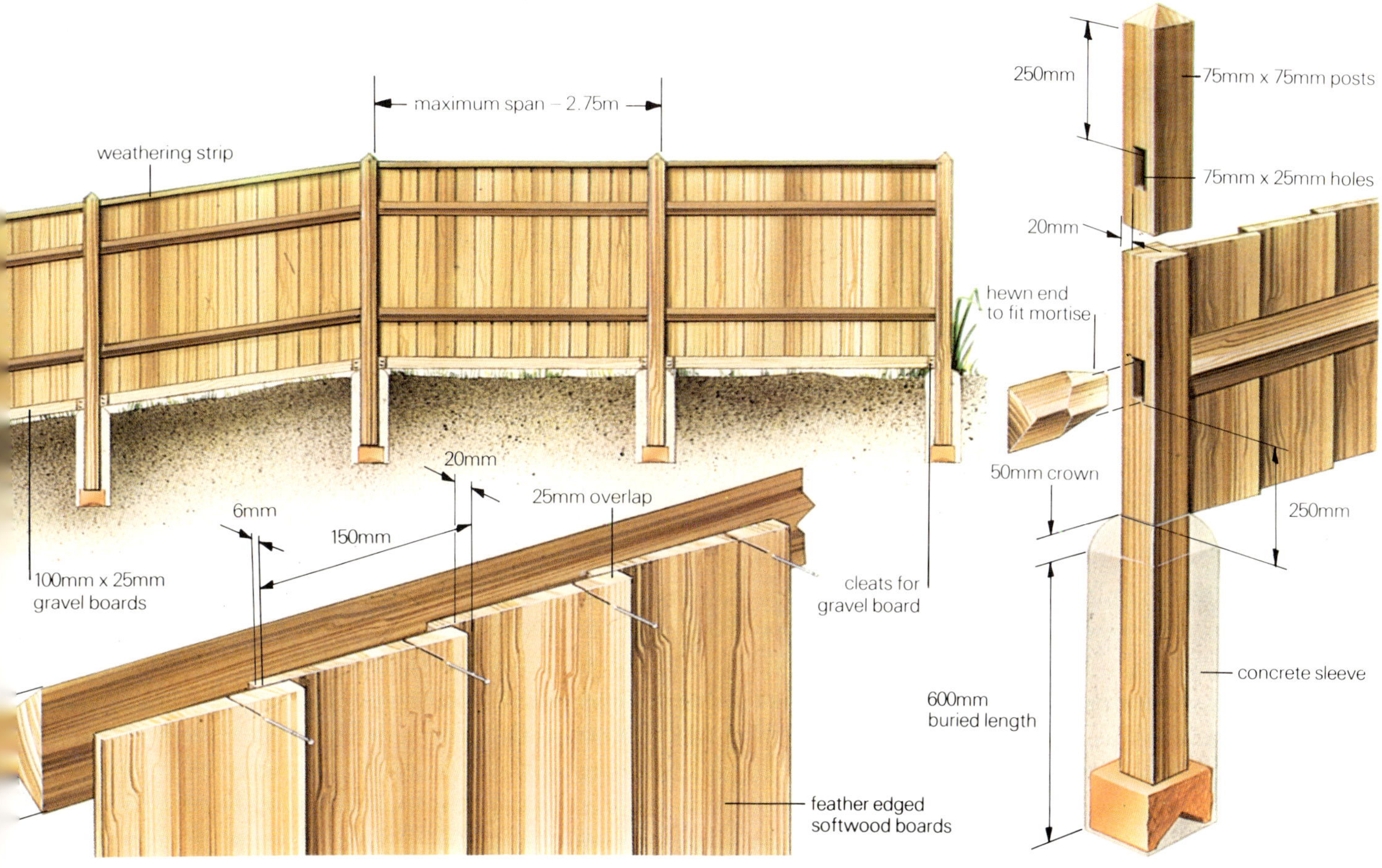

4 *Be sure to try each arris rail for fit in its mortise, otherwise you will run into difficulties during assembly of the fence*

5 *Make certain that the cut ends of the arris rails get an extra coat of preservative, or they may become a focus for rot in the future*

6 *A line is used to mark the positions of the post holes. After you have dug them, set up a post and rail to form a first panel*

overlapped by a consistent amount, and although there is nothing to stop you gauging progress by eye, it is wiser to measure and mark on the arris rails the positions of the individual board edges. Alternatively you can use a measuring gauge for this. To make one, take a spare board and rule lines across it at intervals the width of your boards, less 25mm to allow for the overlap.

Tack-nail the board in place between the two posts, or lean it against the gravel board. Then line up each vertical board with the appropriate pencil mark as it is nailed firmly in place. Nail each board through its thicker end only, so that the nail just misses the overlapped board below it (fig. 13).

Try varying the overlap slightly in the later panels if it looks as though you must trim the final board. A variation of 3mm in the overlaps will not be noticed from one panel to the next but, over the width of 2.5m panel, this can give you over 100mm of margin for adjustment—that is, plus or minus 50mm.

Caps and weathering strip

Wooden capping pieces are useful for protecting the end grain on the tops of the posts, and are sometimes supplied with them. If not, you can make your own from 100mm × 25mm timber (as used for the gravel board), sawing it into 100mm squares. These are secured with galvanized nails.

Also useful is a weathering strip along the tops of the boards. You can make this by cutting 38mm × 25mm battens to length. Nail them on at the thick end of the board edges, carefully, to avoid splitting (fig. C).

Dealing with slopes

Whereas most other types of fence and, indeed, constructions of all kinds must be stepped on sloping ground, a vertically-boarded fence can have a sloped top if the ground below it slopes only slightly. To maintain a consistent slope at the top of the fence, the procedure is to erect and plumb the highest post first, then temporarily erect the lowest post, plumb it, and hold it in position with cross braces. Stretch a nylon line between the two posts and use this as a height guide for the intermediate posts.

Otherwise proceed as for a level fence. Posts and boards must both be vertical. The arris rails are sloped, but the slight step between successive boards which this creates is barely perceptible.

On steeply sloping ground it is still possible to slope the top of the fence, but a stepped top looks much better. Slightly longer posts are needed, however, and the first thing you need to know is by how much the ground falls away. It is no use trying to estimate this by eye, because ground falls are highly deceptive and usually greater than they look.

Start by temporarily erecting the highest and lowest posts. Sink them in the ground by only the usual 600mm and when plumb, use temporary braces to steady them.

Next, take a nylon line and fix it between the top of the lower post to an approximately level position, partway down the higher post. Measure the exact centre of the line and mark it with a dab of paint or tape. Then carefully level the line at the centre spot using a spirit level. Finally,

9 *Secure the arris rails as shown, by nailing through the mortises in the fence posts. Use a club hammer to stop the post from jarring*

measure the height from the line to the top of the higher post: this is the amount by which the ground falls between the two posts.

Now divide the total fall by the number of panels—not posts—your fence will contain between the highest and lowest posts. If, for example, your fence is to have eight panels, and the ground slopes by 1850mm, you will want eight steps of about 230mm.

To achieve this, make the mortises on the 'uphill' side of each post at the normal level, as described above, and those on the 'downhill' side 230mm lower. (The first post, of course, has mortises only on its 'downhill' side, and the last post only on its 'uphill' side.) This means that, in this example, all the posts will need to be 230mm longer than standard.

7 *Use a spirit level to check that the post is plumb as the first panel comes together. Hold the base of the post with pieces of hardcore*

8 *Once you have fixed shuttering around the post hole, ram in more hardcore then pour in the concrete and allow it to set hard*

10 *The gravel boards can be fixed as soon as the framework of the fence is complete. Nail them to cleats secured to the fence posts*

11 *Before you fix the vertical boarding, calculate the spacings needed to fill the panel then mark these on the arris rail*

12 *Use a line, stretched taut between the first and last boards of a panel, to gauge the heights of the intervening boards*

13 *Once you have got started, use a wooden former to judge the overlap between boards, adjust this to save having to cut the last board*

At the bottom of a stepped fence like this, you must make some provision for following the slope of the ground, and you have a choice between sloping gravel boards or a masonry plinth.

Sloping gravel boards

On sloping ground, gravel board ends must be angled so that the boards follow the ground contour (fig. C). This calls for slightly longer gravel boards than would otherwise be necessary and you will need vertical boards of varying length, which rules out the use of a standard fence kit. The only alternatives are to use two or more gravel boards one above the other—which looks ugly—or build a masonry plinth.

To mark the gravel boards correctly, start by running a nylon line along the length of the fence and about 150mm above the ground. Lay each board against a pair of posts, aligning its top edge with the nylon line. Then use the posts themselves as marking guides while you scribe each board end to the correct length and angle. Number each board to ensure that it goes in the right place.

Fix the gravel boards to their cleats, as described, and then stretch a line across the post tops in the normal way. Stand each vertical board against the gravel board with the top just brushing the nylon line, then mark the correct length and angle. Use the spirit level to check the plumb of every other board.

Masonry plinths

A masonry plinth is almost as easy to construct as gravel boards, and certainly more durable. On sloping ground, it has the advantage that the top of each section can be level, so you do not need to scribe a lot of boards to varying lengths.

A plinth can be constructed of brick or walling stone. It is laid only between the fence posts (not continuously), and because it carries no weight, it needs only the lightest of foundations—concrete 75mm thick if the ground is reasonably firm.

To build a plinth on anything but dead level ground, you need to step the foot between post positions (fig. C). Make the height of each step equal to one course of the building materials you choose to use, and the length a straight multiple of the brick or block length.

When you do this, do not forget to allow for a mortar bed between the foundation and the bottom course of masonry—and a double thickness of

14 *A panel of close-boarded fencing. The overall appearance is improved by regular spacings between boards and neatly cut rails*

15 *To weatherproof the tops of the fence posts, you can either cut them at a 45° angle or fit hardwood capping pieces as shown*

concrete where one step joins the next—or you will have nothing to bind the two steps together.

To avoid wasting material, cut the trench with a garden trowel or bricklayer's trowel—the average spade is too wide—and use the soil itself as shuttering. A couple of pegs driven into the bottom of each trench length and levelled with the spirit level will help to keep the foundation concrete level. And an offcut of timber hammered into the ground can be used to retain the end of each step.

If the soil is of a badly uneven consistency—topsoil patches, clay patches, rocky patches—and settlement seems likely, you can stabilize the wall by incorporating a length of galvanized expanded-metal wall reinforcement into the mortar joint between concrete and masonry.

While the concrete is hardening, stretch a nylon line across the fence posts above. Then, as you lay the masonry, use a gauge rod to keep each course at a constant height.

A dustbin screen

This practical dustbin screen will help to keep your garden neat and tidy. Simply build it as an extension to your close-boarded fence, using the techniques outlined in the preceding pages. You can easily adapt the basic design to the layout of your garden and the access to it.

The first thing to decide is the most suitable location, taking into account where you need access to the dustbins and on which sides you want them screened. The drawings on the right show four typical alternatives.

The screen is supported on one side by joining into one of the main fence posts, or in some cases, into two of them. When you are setting out the fence, you should take this into account, and site the posts accordingly. Cut extra mortises in these posts to take the arris rails for the screen. Stagger these to avoid weakening the timber unduly.

Set in the additional posts and fit the arris rails. Add the boarding, gravel boards and caps, treating all the timber with preservative. For a neat finish, you can pave over the enclosed area.

This simple dustbin screen is a useful addition to your fence. You can build it using the techniques and materials outlined on the previous pages. You may even be able to build it using left-over materials from the fence such as offcuts from the arris rails. You can build it to the same height as the fence as shown here, or economise on materials by building it lower, around 150mm taller than the bins

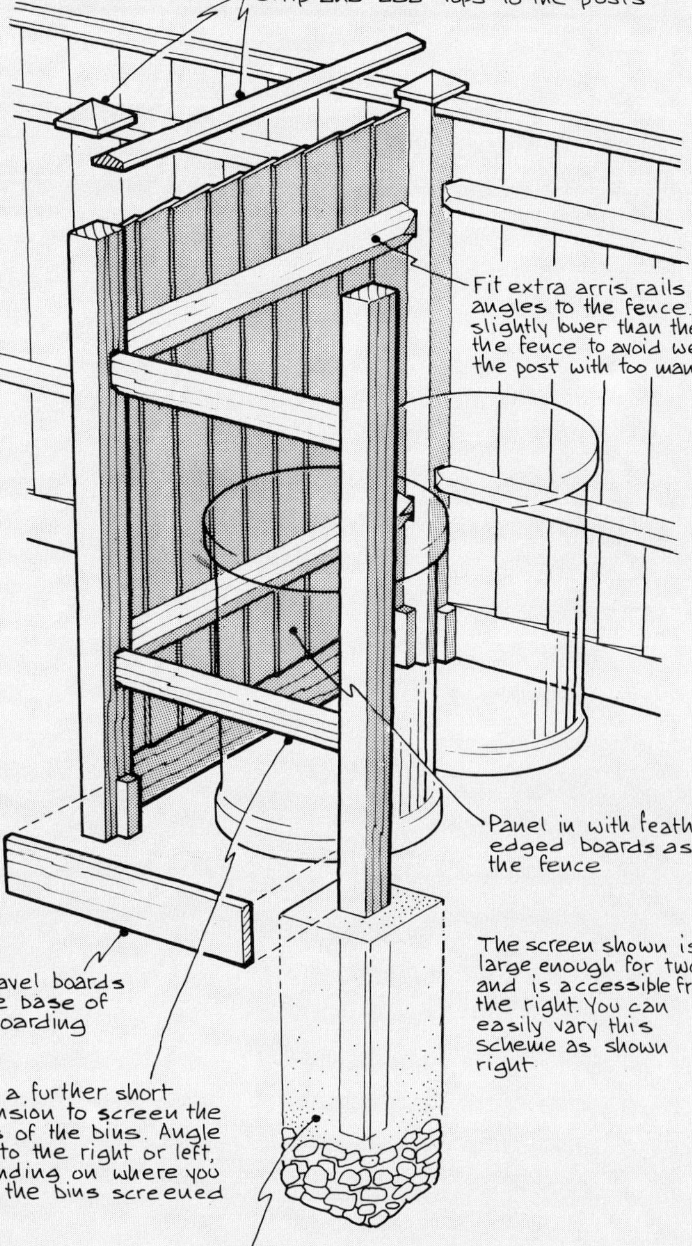

The screen shown is large enough for two bins and is accessible from the right. You can easily vary this scheme as shown right

<u>Alternative layouts</u>

Depending on the number of bins you have and where you want them concealed, choose one of the options shown on the right

To screen a single bin from both sides build two short extensions as shown

To screen a single bin, build a small enclosure in an 'L' shape. This could be angled to the right as shown, or to the left

This arrangement will screen two bins from each side, leaving them accessible from the end

Chain link fencing

● The advantages of chain link fencing ● Types of fencing mesh ● Planning and preparation ● Digging post-holes ● Erecting fence posts and bracing struts ● Fixing the support wires and mesh ● Steel and concrete fence posts

1 *Dig holes for the fence posts, fit the posts, and pack them out with stones so that they are all sunk to the same depth along the run*

Chain link fencing may not be the most attractive of fencing methods, but it is robust, practical, and secure—good reasons why it has become widely used all around the world.

The practical uses of chain link fencing are almost limitless: fences of various heights can be used to keep dogs and children safely in (or out of) your garden; as a burglar deterrent; and even as a climbing frame for some popular garden plants. Whatever use you intend to put it to, chain link fencing is easy to erect, although you may need the help of an assistant for certain parts of the job.

Materials

There is a wide choice of chain link mesh types, most of which can be used with either concrete, timber, or steel fence posts. When buying your fencing materials find out from your supplier exactly what is available and what most suits your needs. All the different types of fence are erected in much the same way.

A series of fence posts are erected first and support wires slung between them at various heights to support the mesh. When the mesh is erected this is secured to the first post in a run, and then stretched between each subsequent post where it is attached to them and wire-locked to the support wires.

Chain link netting: This is often sold as a package complete with the necessary fence posts and support wires for a given length of run. The netting is available in lengths of between 10m and 50m, and in widths varying from 300mm to 3.6m. The gauge of wire used in the mesh is variable, as is the fineness of the mesh itself. For general purposes 45mm or 50mm mesh made from 11 gauge wire should suffice.

You can buy the mesh with a galvanized or aluminium-coated finish, but the most durable and attractive finish is plastic coating which is available in a variety of colours of which dark green is the most popular.

Welded mesh: This is similar to chain link mesh. Because each intersection in the mesh is welded the material is stiffer and stronger, but also more difficult to work with and more expensive. Although not so widely available as chain link mesh, welded mesh can be bought with a variety of finishes and mesh sizes.

Chicken wire: Also known as wire netting, this is much lighter than chain link or welded mesh, and is only suitable for lightweight fencing. Because it is weaker it requires more horizontal wires to support it, although you can also staple it to a post-and-frame fence.

Decorative mesh: This is limited in range and function. The most widely available is woven picket which is a hoop-topped interlocking design of plastic-coated light gauge wire. It comes in 10-25m lengths and ranges from 250mm to 900mm in width, but however it is erected (and some types are self-supporting) it is really only suitable for decoration.

Planning and preparation

Before you start work check any pertinent building regulations with your local authority: in some circumstances you may need planning permission to erect a fence. And if the fence is to form a

A. *Five different types of mesh. From the left they are: decorative mesh; welded mesh; a decorative welded mesh; chicken wire; and chain link. Decorative mesh is usually self-supporting*

2 When you have dug holes for all the posts and any angled bracing struts, fill the post-holes with a dry concrete mix and tamp this down

3 With very light fence posts like these chestnut stakes you can chamfer the end of the bracing strut rather than cut notches in the straining post

4 Fit temporary struts to keep the posts upright while the concrete is setting, and use a plumbline to ensure that the posts are vertical

5 Permanent angled struts can be bolted to the posts, but in the case of this decorative fence they were set in concrete then nailed to the posts

6 Use a string line stretched between the end posts to check that all the intermediate posts are properly aligned and at the correct height

7 When the concrete has set drill a 10mm hole through the top and bottom of each straining post to take the eyebolts which secure the support wires

B. *Instead of cutting chain link mesh you can break it—or knit two lengths together—by unravelling or refitting a single loosened strand*

shared boundary between yourself and your neighbours, it wise of course to seek their co-operation first. Although the deeds to your house will define the limits of your property it may still be necessary to check with the local authority surveyor's department. At the same time check the depth and direction of underground services such as water and gas pipes and drains around your property.

Having gained the approval of your neighbours and the local authority, start marking the line of the fence with string and pegs. Drive the pegs into the ground to a uniform depth so you can check easily where the ground is high or low, and use stakes 450mm high to mark the corners and changes of gradient.

If the boundary is an odd shape, or if there are frequent changes of gradient, you must decide now whether the fence would not look better and be easier to erect if the boundary followed a slightly different line.

When you have settled on the line of the fence mark the position of any gates or breaks in the perimeter. Establish the widths of the gates you intend to use and clearly mark the positions of the gate posts. Do the same at any other breaks in the fence where there are to be no gates.

You can now calculate how much wire mesh and supporting wire to buy; when ordering ask for the nearest number of full rolls so that you have a little left over. At the same time calculate how many fence posts you will need. Your first consideration must be the gate posts and the straining posts at the corners. If you are using steel or concrete fence posts,

8 *If you intend using a stretcher bar to support the mesh, fix its mounting with the eyebolt and leave this loose so that you can tighten the wire*

9 *Secure the wire to the eyebolts and stretch it tight simply by tightening up the backnuts on the straining posts with a spanner*

10 *Thread the stretcher bar through the mesh at one end of the roll and bolt this to the mounting brackets on the two eyebolts*

11 *Unroll the mesh along the fence and, at the far end, unpick a knot between two strands so that you can break the mesh without cutting it*

12 *Feed a second stretcher bar through the end of the mesh and bolt this securely to the mounting brackets on the straining post*

13 *Before securing the mesh to the support wire, nail it to the intermediate fence posts using wire staples at top and bottom*

you can buy specially-designed straining posts; otherwise you may have to make up your own timber straining posts with angled bracing struts. Work out how many of these you will need and mark their positions with chalk or paint on the string lines.

Between these you must place ordinary fence posts no more than 2.8m apart, though on longer runs you may need intermediate straining posts. Mark the position of the fencing posts on the line.

The amount of support wire you need depends on the height of the fence as well as its length. Fences under 1.2m high require a wire at the top and bottom, while fences up to 2.25m high require a third support wire in the middle. Remember that you will need an eyebolt and a turnbuckle or bottlescrew for each straight line of wire to tighten it. And do not forget to order all the appropriate fittings for the straining posts and for securing the netting–these are detailed below but most suppliers will provide a complete kit with the mesh and posts.

C. *Concrete and steel fence posts are erected in the same way as timber ones, but the methods of fixing the support wires and chain link mesh are slightly different from those for timber*

Digging post holes

Aim to instal gate posts and straining posts first and dig holes both for the posts and their angled bracing struts. You can use a pick and shovel to do this, but it is easier to hire or buy a post hole digger. There are different designs available to suit most types of ground but auger or clam-shelled diggers will be perfectly adequate for most jobs.

The holes must be 600-750mm deep and about 450mm square at the top expanding to 500mm square at the bottom. For fences over 1.2m high increase the depth to about 1m. As a general rule of thumb at least one-third of the fence post should be underground.

Where the ground is rocky, remove stones and rocks by prising them out of the hole. Alternatively you can reposition the post slightly. If you cannot remove a large rock, use a star drill to make a small hole in it then mortar a steel pin in this. Drill a corresponding hole in the bottom of a timber fence post and slip it over the pin, than backfill the post hole.

Erecting fence posts

Wooden fence posts should be of pressure impregnated timber at least 100mm × 100mm in thickness, and all fence posts should be the same length. Mark the posts with a knife cut or dab of paint at the proposed ground level so that when installed they are all the same height.

Cut angled notches in the straining and gate posts, about 300-400mm from the top, to accommodate the angled struts. Bolt the struts to the posts with coach-bolts after you have installed them.

Soak all those parts of the timber which will be below ground in creosote or a similar preservative for 24 hours before installing them. If you wish to paint them, use a preservative such as penta-chlorophenol instead.

When the posts are ready slip them into their holes, packing them out with stones and gravel until they are at the correct height. Fill the hole with a relatively dry concrete mix of one part cement to six of all-in ballast and check that the posts are vertical with a plumbline or spirit level before tamping the concrete down. Leave the finished level a few millimetres above the ground to protect the posts from rot.

Keep the post level while the concrete is setting by nailing temporary braces against two adjacent faces. When all the corner posts, straining posts, and gate posts are in position and the concrete has set, instal their angled braces. Concrete them into the ground in the same way as the posts themselves, allowing two braces

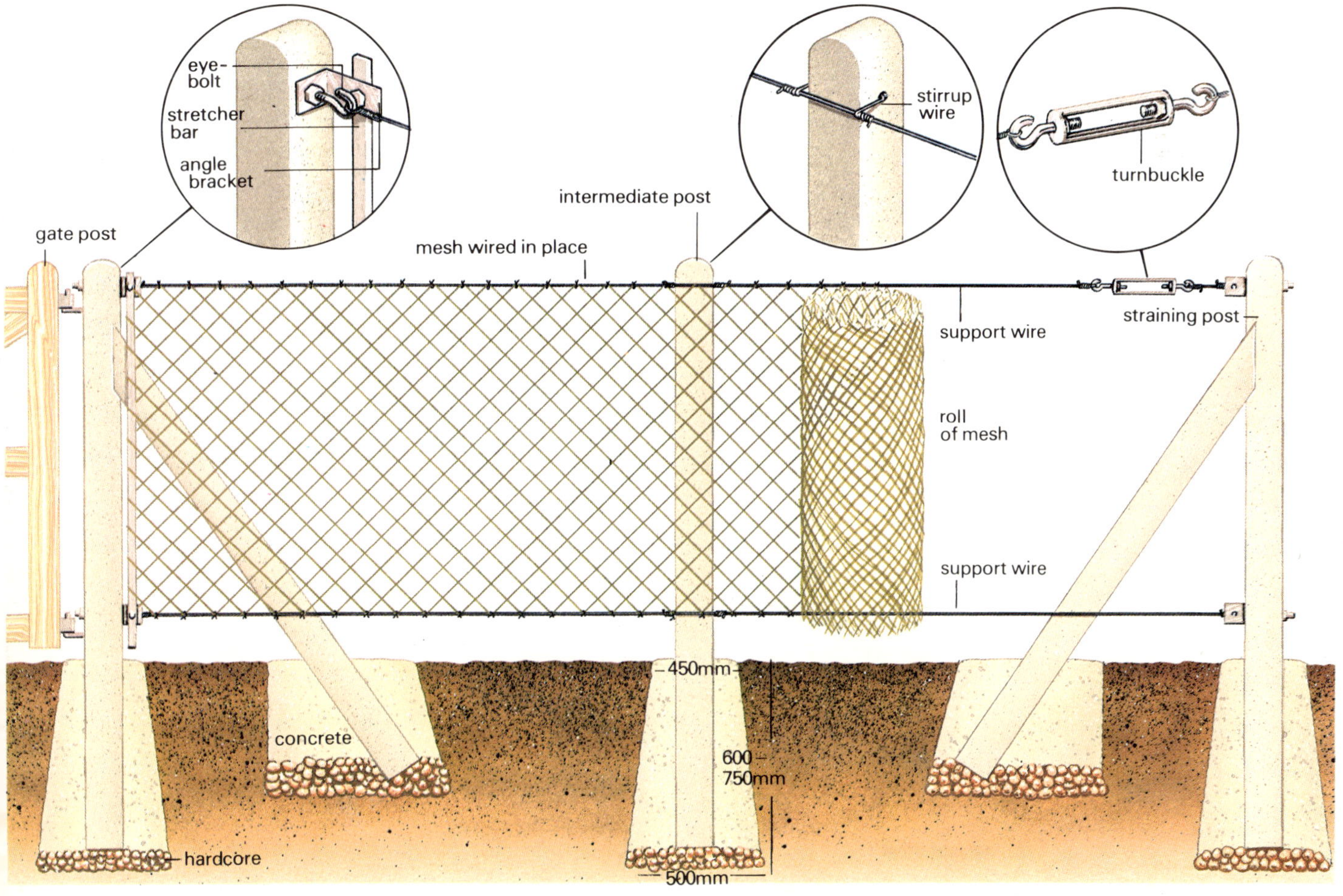

14 *Now attach the mesh to the support wires by knotting short lengths of wire around each at about 150mm intervals*

15 *To take the strain off the support wires, nail the mesh to the intermediate posts along their lengths with more wire staples*

16 *The finished fence: this one is intended only to support plants and hide a compost heap, so fence posts and braces are very light*

for corner posts and straining posts and one each for gate posts and end posts. Bolt the bracing struts to the posts first leaving the other end dangling in their holes; pack these ends out with stones and gravel, and then backfill with concrete.

Another way of fixing fence posts securely is to screw two timber battens about 600mm long to the bottom of each post before it is installed: these form a cross which cannot easily be torn out of the ground.

Fixing the mesh

You can now fit the support wire and the mesh itself. Start by drilling 10mm holes through each straining and gate post at the top and bottom, and secure two eyebolts to the post at each end of a run. Thread the end of a roll of 3mm galvanized steel wire through the eye of the upper bolt at one end of the run and twist it around itself three or four times with a pair of pliers to secure it. Run the other end of the wire to the top eyebolt at the other end of the run and either attach it to this or, if the run is a long one, attach it to a turnbuckle which has been wirelocked to the eyebolt. Tighten the wire up as much as you can and repeat this procedure at the bottom of the two end posts (fig. 9).

When the lines are tight use 15mm 16 gauge wire staples to secure them to the intervening timber fence posts. The procedure for securing the lines to metal or concrete posts is explained below.

When you fix the netting start by standing the roll upright next to the first post. Release about 600mm of the roll and align the top edge with the upper run of support wire. Staple this top corner to the post and staple the rest of the exposed end of the mesh in a vertical line down the post to the ground.

When the end is secure unroll the mesh along the line of the fence, pulling it taut as you go. Fix the mesh to the supporting wires every 150mm with a short twist of thin galvanized wire, and then staple the mesh to each post. Make sure that the mesh pattern remains regular and is not distorted by too much tension.

Do not bend the mesh around corners. Instead cut the roll by unravelling two spirals of the mesh and staple the loose end to the post concerned. Because of the structure of chainlink mesh unravelling it is very easy: use a pair of pliers to loosen the 'knots' at top and bottom of one strand of wire and untwist the wire from the mesh by turning it anti-clockwise. You can repair a fence or join two rolls together by reversing this procedure.

Steel and concrete posts: Although you can staple mesh to timber fence posts you cannot do this with steel and concrete units. Nor can you easily drill them to accommodate eyebolts and supporting struts. The majority of steel and concrete posts are pre-drilled for this purpose. But securing the mesh remains a problem.

Instal the fence posts as described above, aligning the pre-drilled holes along the line of the run. Insert the eyebolts in the end posts as normal, but use them to secure an angled steel bracket to the posts at the same level as the support wires. Instal and secure the support wires as normal, but fix them to the intermediate posts by running a stirrup wire through the holes in the post to hold the support wire on each side of them (fig. C).

Unroll the first 600mm of mesh and align the top edge with the top support wire. Thread a length of 20mm × 5mm steel bar the same height as the straining post through the mesh at this end and bolt it to the angled brackets.

Run the mesh to the other straining post on the run and secure it there with a similar steel bar. Secure the mesh to the support wires in the normal manner, and wirelock the mesh to the posts.

Some fencing kits with steel fence posts are supplied with different fixtures to replace the eyebolts and turnbuckles, but instructions should be supplied with the equipment, and in any case the principles of erecting a fence are identical whichever equipment you use.

Special considerations

Where you are building a pen for animals such as dogs and rabbits which may burrow their way out under the fence it is a good idea to purchase fence posts and mesh that are about 300mm higher than you require. Dig a trench 250mm deep and 100mm wide along the line of the proposed fence and dig the post holes in the bottom of this. Erect the fence as normal, but turn the mesh in slightly at the bottom of the trench and replace the soil you have dug up.

You can prevent the onset of damp and rot in timber fence posts by capping them as described on pages 198 to 205, but it will occasionally become necessary to replace one. In this case loosen the eyebolts at the end of the affected run and remove the staples securing the support wires and mesh to the damaged post. Dig out the post and fit a new one at the same height as the others, staple the wires and mesh back in place, and tighten up the support wires again.

If the netting sags due to vandalism or people attempting to climb over the fence you must rehang it. Remove all the tie wires holding the mesh to the support wires and also the staples securing it to the intermediate posts. Afterwards, working from one end to the other, pull the mesh tight and refix it.

Basic blockbuilding

● Types of concrete blocks ● Calculating quantities ● Mortar mixes ● Building a screen block wall ● Constructing a supporting pier ● Conventional blockbuilding

Concrete building blocks are a particularly versatile type of building material. Lighter, cheaper and often easier to work with than bricks, they have become popular for all kinds of indoor and outdoor projects.

Blocks are laid using all the usual bricklaying tools and many of the same techniques. But the key to successful blocklaying is ensuring that your project is structurally sound.

In the case of a garden wall or partition, the guidelines on structural strength are not hard to follow. Loadbearing walls in blockwork require building or planning permission.

Types of concrete block

Pre-cast concrete blocks come in all shapes and sizes. The term building block properly refers to the rectangular units used for building solid walls. These in turn are classified as either common or facing blocks.

Pierced blocks are the open, decorative kind used for garden screen walls like the project on page 216. As they are non-loadbearing and always laid unbonded (not overlapping), pierced block walls must be supported by piers or pilasters.

Special, hollow blocks are available for building piers, though bricks can be used instead. Thin, dense blocks known as copings or cappings are used to line the top of such walls and help protect the pierced blocks from adverse weather conditions.

A. Common types of building block: (1) Aerated building blocks, used in Britain in cavity walls and sometimes for solid exterior walls (2) Two types of screen wall patterned blocks (3) Dense aggregate blocks (4) Pilaster block for the end of a garden wall (5) Hollow lightweight block (6) Decorative facing block

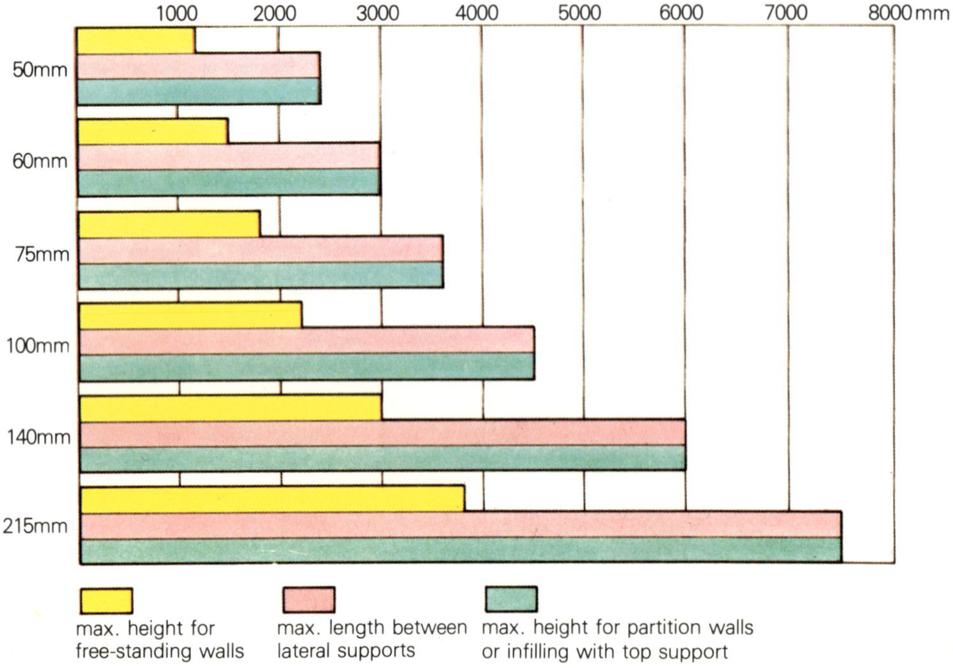

B. *When building with blocks it is important not to exceed the maximum dimensions specified for each size*

Calculating quantities

Try to plan your wall so that it is an even number of blocks, in both length and height.

Remember that blocks are always sold in nominal sizes, to take into account the 10mm mortar joint around each block and make calculating quantities easier. Thus, a block of nominal size 450mm × 225mm × 150mm in fact measures 440mm × 215mm × 140mm — an important difference.

In Britain, common sizes of building block are 450mm × 225mm, 400mm × 200mm, and 450mm × 150mm. Common thicknesses are 60mm, 70mm, 85mm, 100mm, 150mm, 200mm, 250mm.

Pierced screen blocks are normally sold in a nominal size of 300mm × 300mm × 100mm.

Before calculating quantities, the safest course is to visit your builders' merchant and actually measure the sizes of the blocks available. Work out how many blocks you will need for the length of the wall (do not forget the 10mm for the mortar joint). Then work out how many you will need for the height, and multiply the two figures together.

Building blocks

Concrete building blocks come in a variety of materials, depending upon what material is available locally from which to make them, and what structural and/or insulating properties are desired.

Dense aggregate blocks: Made from heavy aggregates such as granite, limestone and gravel, these heavyweight blocks can be used both below damp-proof course level and for wall structures. They are difficult to handle, hard to cut or chisel and can be laid only two or three courses at a time, since the mortar must be allowed to dry out at this stage. Thus they are rarely used in do-it-yourself work.

Lightweight aggregate blocks: Made from a huge variety of materials, including clinker aggregate, pumice aggregate, pottery dust, clinker or fuel ash. They come in both solid and hollow forms and in both loadbearing and non-loadbearing grades. Some are unsuitable for garden walls, and (in Britain) all must be rendered externally if they are used in house construction, to comply with the Building Regulations.

Aerated blocks (for example, Celcon, Thermalite, Lignacite): Formed of similar materials to lightweight aggregate blocks but by a different process, these are much lighter blocks and have better insulating qualities. These are the blocks that are much used in Britain for the internal skins of cavity walls, since two skins of brickwork no longer comply with the insulation requirements of the Building Regulations. Thicker blocks can also be used to build solid house walls, provided that they are rendered on the outside and plastered inside.

Mortar mixes

As with brickwork, the mortar used to bond blocks should never be stronger than the blocks themselves. Because the strengths of blocks vary so widely, manufacturers normally give very specific instructions on the correct mortar mix to use for any one block.

As a rough guide, loadbearing blocks

C. *To build a conventional block wall, gauge the width of the mortar joints with a 10mm wide offcut from a scrap of wood*

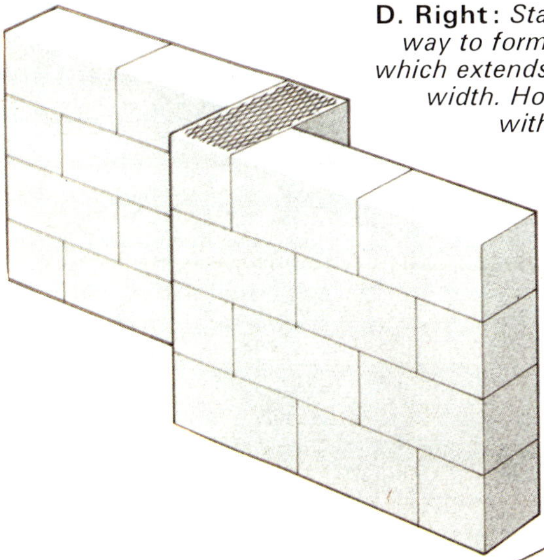

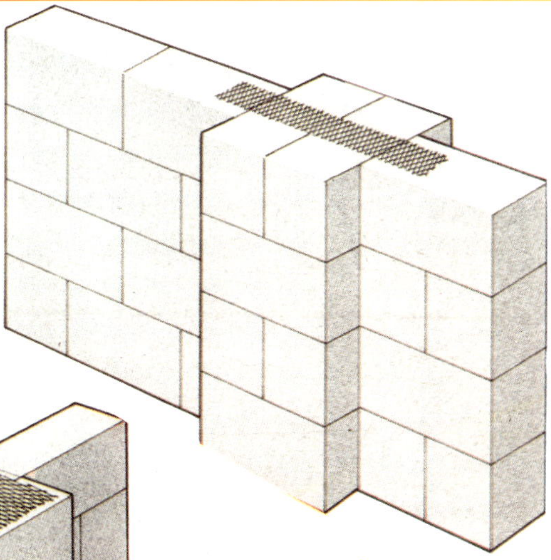

D. Right: *Stack-bonding is a good way to form a pier in a block wall which extends beyond its maximum width. Hold the blocks together with expandable wall ties*

E. Above: *A parallel wall will act as a brace to support a long run of a conventional block wall. Use an expanded metal tie to hold the blocks together*

F. Left: *An alternative method of building a stack-bonded pier is to have one side of it flush with the block wall. Use a wider piece of expanded wall tie to secure the pier*

take a mix of around one part Portland cement to six of sand while the lighter, non-loadbearing type require a one to eight mix.

G. *Having built up four courses to form the quoins, stretch a length of twine between them to act as a guide for the intervening wall*

Foundations

Where the foundations for lightweight, loadbearing and non-loadbearing blocks are concerned, there are no special factors to consider. Simple footings or rafts can be constructed in the same way as for brickwork. The only constructional difference occurs in the foundation for a screen wall. Here, steel reinforcing bars for the piers must be set in the wet concrete.

The foundations for heavyweight blocks may need to be 1.2m below ground level—your local building inspector can advise you on this point. The building inspector should, in any case, be consulted if you are planning a loadbearing block wall.

Piers

If it is necessary for a block wall to continue beyond the maximum permissible free-standing height and length (fig. B), some form of support must be used. This can either be a parallel wall which forms a lateral bracing (fig. E) or a pier.

Piers can be made in brick or from more blocks (fig. F) and should be twice the thickness of the wall. In both cases, the pier must be incorporated into the structure of the wall with wall ties.

Use either standard, galvanized wall ties or strips of expandable wall tie, set into the mortar joints on each course (fig. F).

Pilasters made from hollow con-

1 *When you have pressed the reinforcing bars into the wet concrete—making sure that they fall in the middle of the pilaster block—check that the foundations are level before proceeding further*

2 *Once the concrete in the foundations has set, a bed of mortar can be laid down around the base of the reinforcing bar. Lay down enough mortar to form a good base for the first block of the proposed pier*

3 *Slide the first pilaster block over the reinforcing bar, making sure that the slot for the pierced block is facing the right way. When it is in position, tamp it down with a piece of wood and check for level*

4 *When you have established that the pilaster block is level, its hollow can be filled with concrete. Make sure that the concrete is tightly packed in around the bar so that sufficient support is given to it*

crete blocks are a special kind of pier, particularly suited to supporting screen walls. Their sturdy construction also makes them ideal for gate posts.

Constructing a pilaster

The strength of a pilaster is derived from a hook-ended steel reinforcing bar which runs through the hollow blocks into the foundations below.

Having dug your footing and filled it with wet concrete, decide on how many pilasters are needed. Then, mark at the side of the footing exactly where the first block of each pilaster will go—bearing in mind that an exact number of pierced blocks must run between them.

Use the marks as guides to positioning the reinforcing bars—which must fall roughly in the middle of the pilaster blocks—and press the bars into the concrete (fig. 1).

When the concrete in the footing has gone 'off', lay down a bed of mortar around the first reinforcing bar and slide on the first pilaster block (fig. 2). Make sure that the slot for the pierced blocks is facing the right way for the construction.

Next, fill the hollow in the block with concrete, tamp it down with a piece of wood and check the block for line and level (figs 3 to 5).

The pilaster can now be built up to the desired height as follows:

- Lay down a 10mm mortar joint around the block already in position
- Slide a further block on top
- Fill the hollow with concrete and tamp firmly
- Check for line and level
- Repeat for the next block

When you have built up the pilasters to the desired height, leave them to set. When hard, any protruding reinforcement can be sawn off and the pilasters finished with coping blocks for neatness.

Building screens

Pierced blocks for screen walls are always laid unbonded, to preserve their pattern. The slots in the pilaster blocks are sufficient to bond the screen to the pilasters but intervening vertical joints must be strengthened with

5 *Check that the first block is still level, and then lay down a 10mm mortar joint on the top. Slide the second block into position and press it down on to its mortar bed. Check it is level and fill as before*

6 *Having built up the pilasters to the desired height, they should be left to set and the top of the bar cut off as appropriate. Set the first screen block in position on a 10mm mortar bed and check it for level*

7 *When this block is level, stretch a piece of twine between the two ends of the wall and use this as your guideline to position the intervening screen blocks. Check that each block is level as you lay it.*

8 *Always build up at least four courses of a pier before you build the intervening wall. When the wall is completed it can be topped with coping blocks, both as protection from damp and for a neater finish*

strips of expandable metal wall tie. The strips are laid across the vertical joints between blocks on every course and must be well bedded in to the mortar. To make sure of this, lay down a thin bed of mortar, position the tie and then cover it over with more mortar, up to a 10mm thickness.

When filling in a screen of blocks between pilasters, start laying according to the arrangement shown in fig. 6. With a length of twine stretched between ends, you will then have a guide to positioning the intervening blocks. Check each block, as you lay it, for line and level (fig. 7).

Like the pilaster blocks, screen blocks can be topped with coping blocks for a neater finish.

Conventional blockbuilding

Building a wall with blocks calls for much the same techniques as building with bricks.

Normally, only the half-lap (running) bond—where one block overlaps those above and below by half its length—is used. This involves some cutting.

For lightweight aggregate blocks, the cutting technique is to mark off the block then chip around it with a club hammer and bolster until it splits of its own accord. This is much easier on solid—rather than hollow—blocks, though pre-cut half blocks are sometimes available.

Heavyweight blocks can be cut in the same way, though more force is required. Aerated blocks can be sawn, using either a masonry saw or general-purpose saw.

When planning the first course of a blockwork structure, you can keep cutting to a minimum by laying out the blocks in a 'dry run' and then adjusting the width of the vertical joints between them.

Unlike brick walls, long concrete walls need expansion joints (control joints) every 6m or so along their length. These must run the full height of the wall. The usual method is to build a strip of bituminized building paper into the vertical joint, then fill in the rest of the joint with mortar. Pilasters fulfil the same function, if they are not mortared to the blocks on either side.

Build a garden screen wall

A screen wall constructed in pierced blocks is a useful way to divide up a large garden or to break up an uninteresting view. You can construct quite large walls with no special reinforcement, or you can make them as small or low as you like. The blocks are not intended for load-bearing structures, but you can use them to support a lightweight roof, such as a softwood frame covered in translucent acrylic sheeting, which makes them suitable for covered patios or carports. This project is for a simple free-standing garden divider, but it could easily be adapted to use in this way by adding a simple light roof framework.

The table on page 212 gives the maximum sizes for free-standing walls without special reinforcement, and this wall is constructed to these limits for ease of building. It uses standard pierced screen wall blocks with matching pilaster blocks and coping stones. Use whatever sizes are commonly available in your area. In the design shown, exactly 48 blocks are used between the piers, the edges of which are recessed to take the screen blocks. Special blocks are available for corners and ends of the wall to give a neat finish.

The building methods are those shown in the photographs on pages 214 and 215. You start by laying and levelling the foundations. This is most important, as it governs the stability and evenness of the finished wall. Do not omit the steel reinforcing rod which provides a starter for the pilaster blocks.

Lower pilaster blocks on to the rods, bedding them on mortar between 7 and 9mm deep and filling the central hole with liquid mortar. Check alignment as each block is laid until three pilasters are built up in each pier. Lay a bed of mortar on the foundation and in the groove of the pilaster block and position the first screen block, checking it is level. Work from both ends to the centre until the first course is complete. Continue in this way until you reach the finished height, then add the capping. Be careful not to get mortar on the decorative surface of the capping as it stains easily and is difficult to remove.

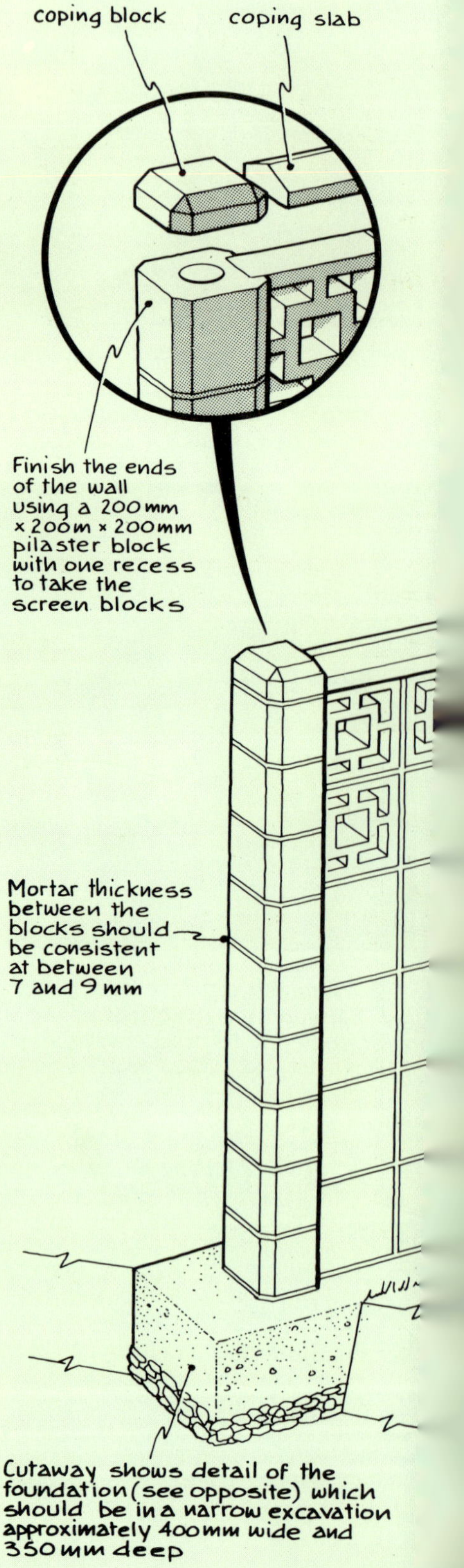

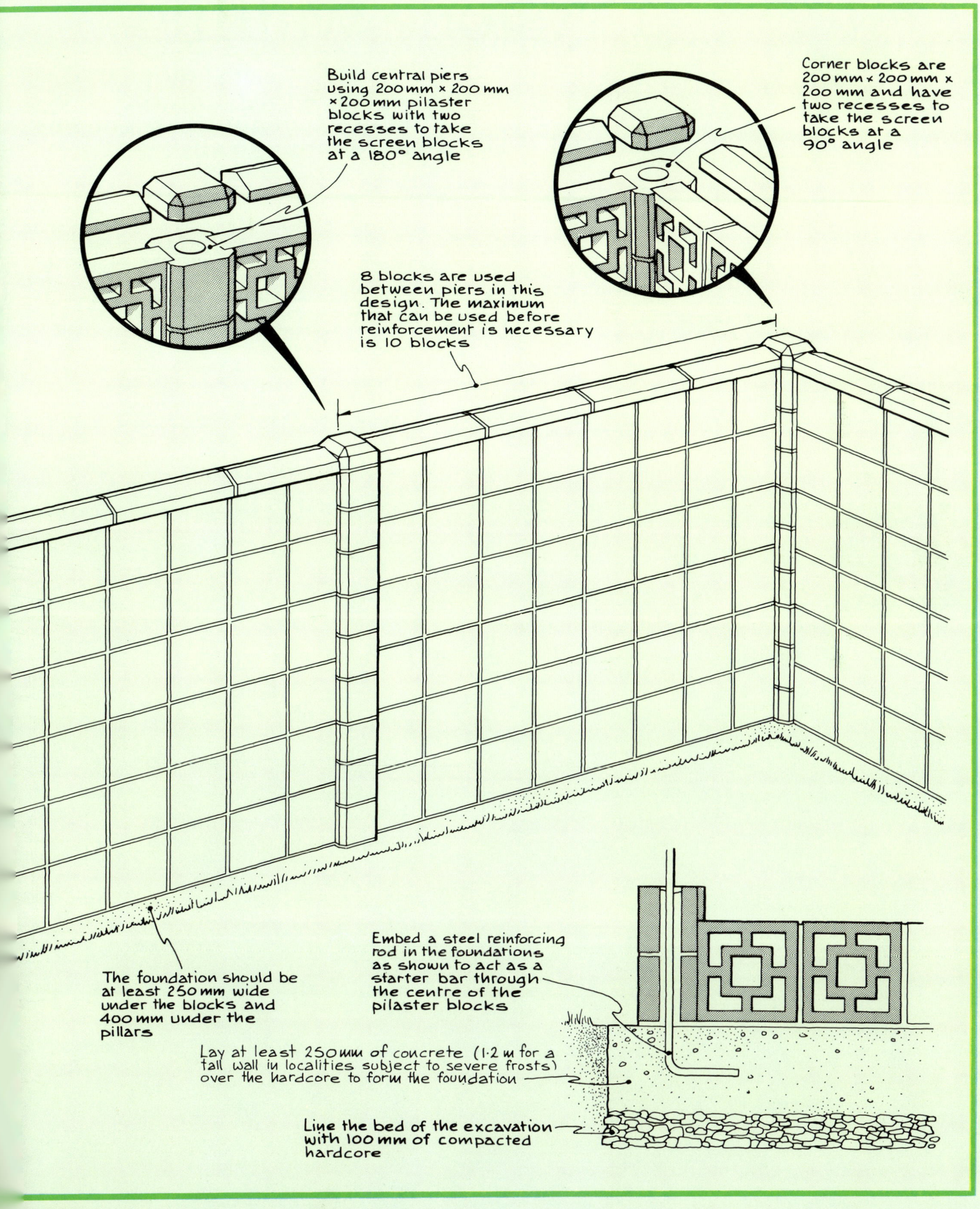
Build central piers using 200 mm × 200 mm × 200 mm pilaster blocks with two recesses to take the screen blocks at a 180° angle
Corner blocks are 200 mm × 200 mm × 200 mm and have two recesses to take the screen blocks at a 90° angle
8 blocks are used between piers in this design. The maximum that can be used before reinforcement is necessary is 10 blocks
The foundation should be at least 250 mm wide under the blocks and 400 mm under the pillars
Embed a steel reinforcing rod in the foundations as shown to act as a starter bar through the centre of the pilaster blocks
Lay at least 250 mm of concrete (1·2 m for a tall wall in localities subject to severe frosts) over the hardcore to form the foundation
Line the bed of the excavation with 100 mm of compacted hardcore

Drystone walling

● Component parts of a drystone wall ● Ordering materials and preparing the site ● Foundations ● Building techniques ● Topping the wall ● Drystone retaining walls

It is not difficult to see why drystone walls are so widely used in many country areas and why they also have an instant appeal to the home improver. Although sometimes difficult to erect, they last for literally hundreds of years and still retain their natural attractiveness when other types of walls and fences need to be replaced or repaired.

A drystone wall uses no mortar in its construction and depends instead for its strength and durability on the correct choice and placement of uncut stones of various sizes. The skill needed to do this is difficult to master and professional drystone wallers often take years to perfect their craft. Yet there is no reason why the average home handyman, with care and attention to detail, cannot erect a small drystone wall and use the techniques learned in doing this to construct other features such as a planter wall or a banked terrace for flowers.

Component parts

Most free-standing drystone walls are made up of five basic stones which vary in size and shape. Once in place, each stone binds on others to strengthen the whole structure and help waterproof the wall.

Below: *Appealing and attractive, yet extremely functional, a drystone wall forms an impressive and durable boundary around a garden*

To give the wall a solid base on which to sit, a shallow trench is dug just below the proposed site. This is then filled with two or three layers of flat stones which are carefully levelled off with the surrounding ground (fig. A).

Above this the wall is built using a combination of medium-sized edging stones, and larger stones—*throughs*—which span the whole width of the wall at random intervals to help strengthen it. Between the edging stones, the centre of the wall is packed with smaller stones—the *infill*—to stop the whole structure collapsing inwards (fig. A).

After a final course consisting entirely of throughs the wall is given a topping of rounded *coping* stones set on edge. As well as being decorative these help to stop driving rain finding its way into the heart of the wall where it can erode the inner stones and lead to collapse (fig. A).

Drystone walls are constructed so that both their external faces lean inwards towards each other. This gentle slope—the *batter*—stops the wall becoming top heavy (fig. A).

1 *Once the load of stones arrives on site, divide them into a number of neat piles according to size and shape*

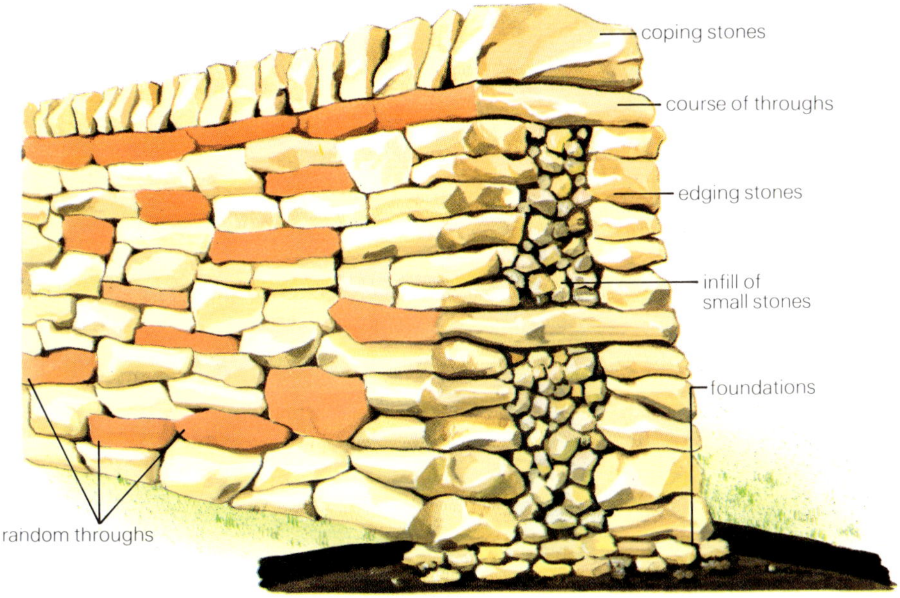

A. Above: *The component parts of a drystone wall, using five basic stones which vary in size and shape. These are positioned carefully so as to waterproof the wall, and give it strength and rigidity*

2 *Make the foundations 100mm wider than the base of the wall. Mark these dimensions by driving stakes into the four outside corners*

B. Above: *Insert large throughs at random intervals. Try to position each stone so that it overlaps the two stones directly beneath it*

3 *Extend a string around the outside of the plot. Lay it along the ground and tie it firmly to each of the stakes in turn*

Planning the work

Before you order any materials, go to the site of the proposed wall and carefully plan its exact length, height and width. Bear in mind that only very rarely should you need to exceed the dimensions of an average farm wall—1.3m high with a 650mm wide base. Nor should any absolute beginner attempt to build a wall more than 6m long—except in sections so that a small gap can be left for a gate.

From these dimensions you can calculate the amount of stones needed. Reckon on a ton of stone for each 1.3m^3 of wall above ground level; this will allow enough material for the foundations as well.

Getting enough stones of a suitable size and type is difficult unless you have already collected a large amount from your own garden or are lucky enough to live in an area where they can be found lying around. If neither of the above sources is available, a quarry or large builders' merchant should be able to help you.

Almost any type of stone can be used but the best are hard rocks such as granite, basalt or sandstone. Try to choose stratified rock with regular flat edges, rather than using irregular-shaped or rounded stones.

Remember also that the rocks you use should be of a suitable size and colour to blend with each other and with their surroundings. Check carefully for colour match and avoid very large stones which are difficult to lift and may look out of place built into a short section of wall.

So that you have a variety of stones from which to choose, order a range of different sizes—from small stones 50–100mm square for the infill, to the large throughs long enough to span the width of the wall.

Before the load of stones arrives, clear the site so that you can work from both sides. Try to ensure that the stones can be unloaded as near to the working area as possible so that you save yourself a great deal of unnecessary effort.

Once the stones arrive, divide them into at least three or four neat piles, according to size and shape. This makes it easier to quickly select the ones you need later (fig. 1).

Building the foundations

A rigid structure like a drystone wall has very little 'give' in it. To avoid collapse it must have solid foundations, even on well-compacted or stony ground. Marshy ground and land which is liable to subside are both

4 *Using the lines as a guide, dig a 150mm deep plot for the foundations. Make sure that it is squared off around the outside*

unsuitable for drystone walls.

Make the foundations the same length as the proposed wall and about 100mm wider than its base. Mark these dimensions by driving four wooden stakes into the ground at each of the outside corners. Tie marking strings between the stakes and lay them along the ground to mark the outside of the plot (fig. 3).

Using the inside of the lines as a guide, dig a shallow trench 150mm deep all around the outside of the area. Then shovel out the earth in the middle to the same depth. Finally, compact the earth in the bottom of the plot by trampling all over the area (figs 4 and 5).

Select a number of large, regular-shaped stones to line the outside of the plot. Lay them side by side, face downwards, so that they form a frame around the edge (fig. 6).

Complete the bottom layer by filling in the gaps in the middle of the plot. Choose flat stones shaped to slot neatly into place and lie side by side but do not compact them—they need to be able to move slightly under the shifting pressures of the wall above (fig. 7).

Lay further layers of stone in the same way until you are nearly level with the ground. Then run a long straightedge across the top of the hole to check that the top layer of stones is level with the surrounding ground along its length.

Building the wall

Before you start building, construct a pair of 'batter frames' to act as a guide to the correct placement of the outer stones. Make each of these from four pieces of lightweight timber—

5 *Then compact any loose earth in the bottom of the plot by trampling all over the area or tamping it with a length of timber*

9 *Then nail two smaller timber battens across the uprights so that the frame is shaped like a cross-section of the wall*

13 *Pack the centre of the wall with small infill stones as you build upwards and insert a number of large throughs at random intervals*

6 *Lay the foundations, first by lining the outside of the plot with a number of large, rectangular-shaped stones placed side by side*

7 *Then, as you build upwards, fill the gaps in the middle with small, loosely-packed stones. Choose shapes which slot neatly into place*

8 *With the foundations completed, build a pair of batter frames to act as guides. Sharpen the bottom end of each of the uprights*

10 *Push the batter frames into the ground at each end of the foundations and check carefully that they are secure and upright*

11 *Then tie pieces of string to the uprights. Extend them along both sides of the foundations, about 50mm above ground level*

12 *Use these strings as guides for the correct placement of the outer edging stones and move them up as the wall progresses*

14 *Place throughs along and across the wall as you approach the end of each section to leave a neat, flat vertical face*

15 *Complete the wall by laying a course of throughs along the top. Select large, flat stones slightly longer than the wall span*

16 *On top of the throughs lay a course of round-topped coping stones, set on edge and all leaning gently in the same direction*

two side and two crosspieces—shaped like a cross-section of the wall.

Position the two outer timbers so that they slope gently inwards towards the top of the proposed wall at an angle of roughly 10° and sharpen the bottom ends so that you can drive them into the ground (fig. 8). Then nail the other two pieces across the side pieces to complete the frame (fig. 9). Check that both frames are tall enough to accommodate the wall you want to build, and that their batter is correct, before continuing.

Push the frames into the ground at either end of your foundations and tie pieces of string between them, on both sides, about 50mm from the ground (fig. 10). These will serve as a guide for the bottom course of stones and can be moved to a higher point as you build upwards (fig. C).

Lay the bottom course 50mm in from the sides of the foundations using medium-sized edging stones. Make sure that their outer edges just touch the guiding strings and check that each stone is as level as possible by wedging small stones underneath.

Once the bottom course is in position, fill the gap down the centre with small infill stones. As before, pack these loosely so they can move and take the weight of the wall above.

Next, move the guiding strings upwards and start work on the second course. On this, make sure that each stone spans two others directly beneath it—rather like brick-work. This offset pattern—which should be continued all the way up the wall—gives a neat finish and prevents weak vertical cracks from developing across the face of the wall (fig. B).

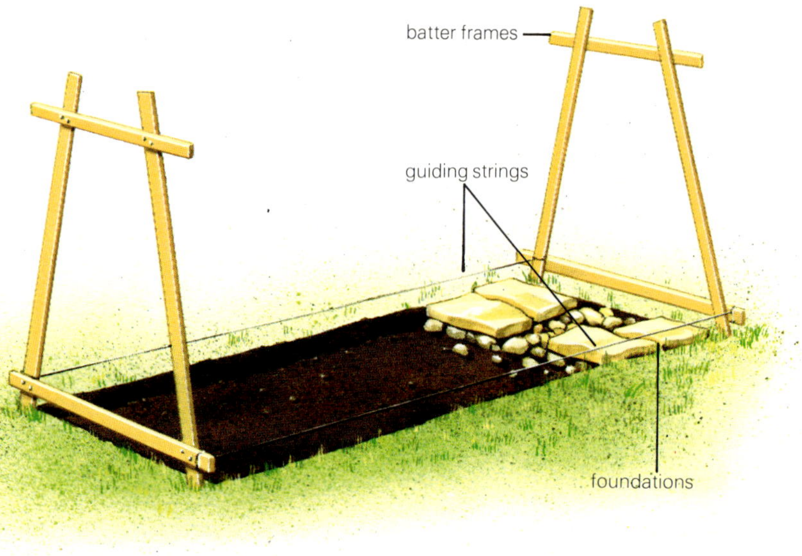

C. Above: *Specially constructed batter frames placed at each end of the foundations match the cross section of the wall and hold the building lines*

D. Above: *The techniques used to erect a free-standing wall can be adapted to build other structures like this simple banked terrace*

On each course from the second upwards, insert a number of large 'throughs' at random intervals. Select these carefully so that they are just long enough to finish level with both sides of the wall. Try to make sure that the end of each section of wall ends in a neat, flat, vertical face. Place throughs in alternate layers along the length of the wall and across its width (fig. 14).

Lay courses of stone until you reach a position about 500mm lower than where you want the wall to end. You should then add a double course of finishing stones.

Topping the wall

Finish the wall with a complete course of throughs capped by a row of rounded coping stones set on edge.

Select throughs of equal size, slightly longer than the width of the wall directly below and lay them side by side along the top. The overhang which this creates will allow rain-water to fall straight to the ground rather than seep into the stonework below (fig. 15).

On top of the throughs, at both ends of the wall, place two medium-sized edging stones to act as 'stops'. Then select flat, round-topped stones and lay them on edge so that they all lean gently in the same direction (fig. 16). The coping stones are given this slant to help them adjust to any minor shifts in the wall; if they were placed vertically, on edge, they would either drop off the wall altogether or fall haphazardly to one side.

Drystone retaining walls

A raised terrace in a garden always looks spectacular and helps to show off plants and bushes to their best advantage. A retaining wall to finish off the terrace is built in the same way as a free-standing wall except that it has only one face.

Clear the site—including the flower bed—and an area about 50mm in front of the retaining wall. Dig out the foundations to a depth of 150mm and fill these with two or three layers of flat stones (see above).

Use large throughs and occasional edging stones to construct the retain-ing wall. As you lay each course, shovel earth back into the bed to the same level. Once the wall is finished—usually about three courses—pile the earth high above it to form a rounded bed. Smaller retaining walls can be added half way up the bed to add to the decorative effect and create a second terrace (fig. D).

Build a drystone planter

You can add a special feature to any drystone wall by building a small section of the top as a planter for flowers and border plants. The wall shown in the picture and in the plans also has a large bay at the end to form a pier flanking an entrance way.

Construct the wall using techniques described on pages 218 to 222, up to the level of the top course of through stones. Then, instead of finishing off with coping stones, continue along each face with two courses of edging stones set in mortar, leaving a bay in the middle.

Fill the centre with well-packed soil to create a raised planting bed. You can also pack earth into small gaps left lower down the wall and train alpine plants or ivy to grow in them and up the wall.

The pier at the end of the wall is built in the same way, following the desired outline. The large bay in the centre can be filled out with rubble.

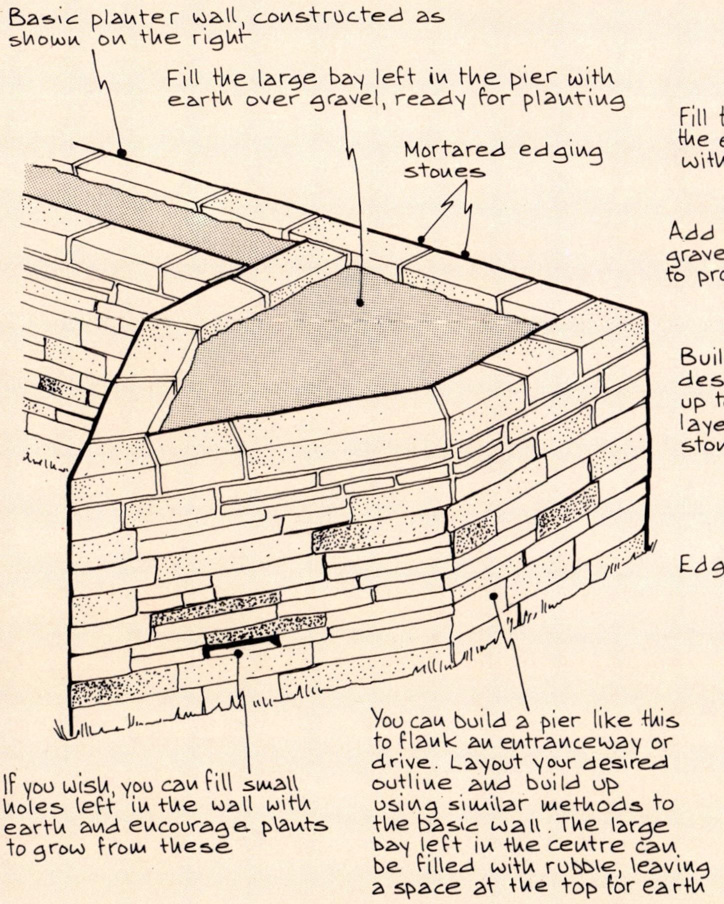

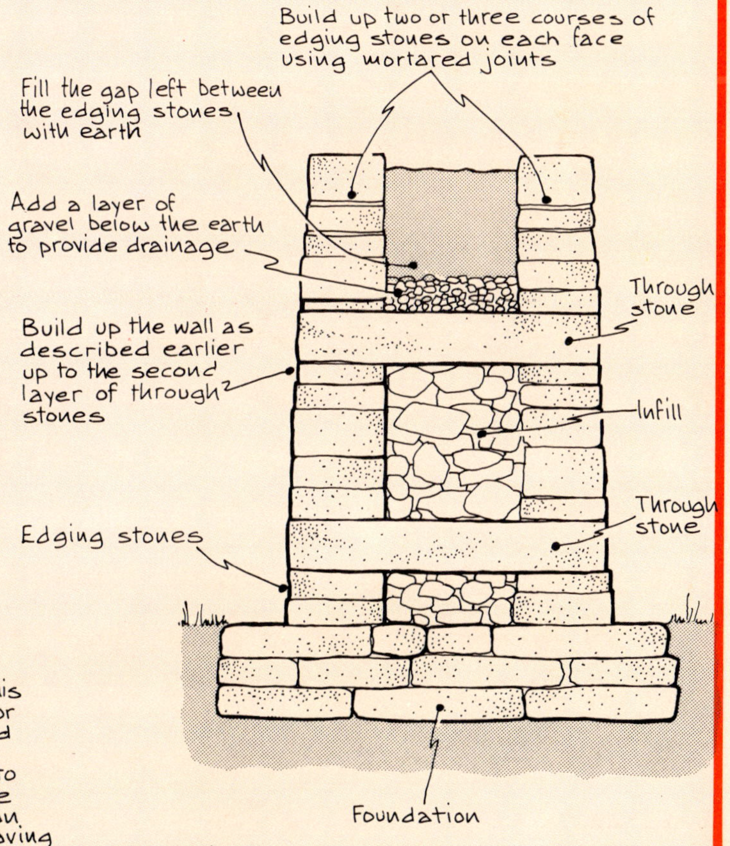

Cross-section of basic wall construction

Chapter 6
GARDEN CONSTRUCTION
Greenhouses and conservatories

A conservatory is one of the most delightful ways of adding more space to your home. In the picture **below** a space for casual dining has been attached to the exterior of the house. Access is through the living room, but, to make the serving of food convenient, the window has been turned into an open hatch giving a very pleasant view from either side.

Hanging plants and the light coloured cane furnishings add to the bright, cheery atmosphere. In a conservatory it is best to choose light colours to keep the room from becoming dreary on rainy days. Select furniture that can easily be moved from outdoors to indoors. A slate floor (or you could use tiles instead) gives an outdoor feeling to the room and is very resistant to water. Other types of flooring may be spoiled when watering plants or if an overhead panel

breaks during a rainstorm.

The serious plant lover may find in time that the addition of a greenhouse in the back garden is the best place for putting a growing collection of house plants. In the picture **below** tender, flowering potted plants that include pelargoniums and fuchsias give a splash of colour to the garden throughout many months of the year. In the summer you can place them outdoors or bring them inside the house for special occasions.

Perhaps the smallest practical greenhouse is one that is built as an extension to your kitchen window, such as the one in the picture **right.** An array of colourful flowering plants, especially in the winter months, gives you something pleasant to focus on when you are doing the washing up. A small kitchen greenhouse is the ideal spot for growing herbs that will not only add a decorative touch to the kitchen but will provide a convenient means for getting the right ingredients to cook good food.

Exterior walls at right-angles are an

ideal area to add a conservatory to your house. In the picture at **left** a patio has been converted into a conservatory, but it still retains the feeling of being outdoors.

The warmth created by sunshine, however, means that the patio can be enjoyed for a longer time of the year. It means also that outside walls in the home receive extra insulation especially when, as in the picture, there are several French windows which would otherwise be a source of draughts.

Wrought iron supports are a lovely decorative touch—they were widely used in Victorian times which is when conservatories became common.

The beautiful arched and stained glass windows in the picture **right** give this conservatory its very special quality, and it is greatly enhanced by the row of plants that extend the width of the wall.

Your plants need not take up precious room space in the conservatory. The addition of shelving may be all that is needed for grouping your plants.

In a conservatory with glazed ceiling panels, protection is often required during periods of the day when there is strong sunlight—otherwise plants could scorch and the room would become unbearably hot. A roller blind such as the one in the

picture **below** will diffuse light coming into the room; bamboo blinds also keep out some sunlight. For a really good screening your best bet is an inexpensive blind of pinoleum—very fine wood strips woven with cotton.

Whether you are thinking of attaching a conservatory to your house or building a greenhouse in your garden, you need not limit yourself to the usual traditional designs. In the picture **left** a very charming greenhouse has been constructed to look like a Victorian gazebo. A number of prefabricated greenhouses exist, which when installed in your garden, will not only be functional but add to its overall appearance. The small greenhouse in the picture left also provides a pretty and tranquil place for sitting and relaxing.

But the important thing to consider when choosing a particular design of greenhouse—or conservatory for that matter—is that it fits in with its surroundings. In this picture natural wood and a geometric shape complement the straight lines of the paving stones and the flower beds. But this formality is well balanced by the more informal layout of the rockery and flowering shrubs.

Building a garden shed

● The advantages of building your own garden shed ● Designing the shed ● Siting the foundations ● Constructing the floor ● Making the wall frames ● Adding the roof ● Cladding ● Doors and windows

A. Above: *A garden shed is a highly practical and attractive addition to any house. This design, although not cheap, is extremely flexible*

A garden shed is a versatile supplement to any home, serving the multiple purposes of storeroom, planthouse and garden feature. As a storeroom, it is ideal for bulky items such as bicycles, deckchairs, lawnmowers, and decorating equipment – things that would be out of place inside the house. As a workroom, it offers a space to store poisonous chemicals and dangerous tools – though in this case the door should have a secure lock – and an area where messy or noisy projects can be undertaken without disturbing the rest of the household.

Whatever your requirements, there are two ways to acquire a shed that will meet them. You can either build one from your own design and to suit your pocket, or else purchase a prefabricated kit which can be fitted together on a prepared site.

Prefabricated kits are available at prices that are competitive with the price you would pay for the raw materials, and in a wide range of sizes and styles. Designs vary but – despite their obvious advantages – these types of shed will not offer you the versatility, or the satisfaction, that would come from designing and building your own. However, they are light and easy to assemble and are supplied with all the fittings – such as bolts, hinges, brackets and roofing felt – as well as suggestions for the type of foundation to use. If your time is limited, it is well worth examining this possibility. Even if you decide against it, studying prefabricated kits will suggest features you may not have previously considered.

Designing your own

Designing your own shed is a way of ensuring that you get what you want, and you can adapt it to the purposes for which you intend to use it. If you need it only for storage, consider the size and amount of equipment, and how best to arrange it. If you want a work area, consider the nature and position of the window. Bear in mind that a work bench would benefit from direct light but that the window should be at least 150mm above the work surface to avoid damage. For germinating or growing more sensitive plants, such as tomatoes or peppers, large windows which face the sun or a roof light would be an advantage.

The shed shown in fig. A is a good working model to base your design upon. It is a functional but sturdy and attractive shed intended for storage and general DIY projects. It is constructed in six sections: the floor on to which the four walls are screwed; the four wall frames which bolt together at the corners; and the roof. The size and position of its 50mm × 50mm vertical and horizontal members make them ideal for bearing shelves or as lateral supports for a work surface.

Additional horizontal members on the walls at appropriate heights provide support for tool-holders made from dowelling. These are simple and handy fixtures for supporting long handled tools such as rakes, hoes and brushes. Incorporate them in positions which will not interfere with work surfaces or shelves. When the shed is completed, use a 9mm wood bit to drill holes 25mm deep at 75mm centres on the horizontal member. Cut a length of 9mm dowelling into 75mm or 100mm lengths and smear a small amount of PVA woodworking adhesive on the end of each of them. Insert these into the holes, tapping them into position with a mallet. To avoid wastage, use a tenon saw to cut 12mm down the diameter of the dowel before you apply the adhesive. This will retain the adhesive rather than squeezing it out of the hole.

1 *Having levelled the ground below the shed, lay the completed base frame in position and check that it is square by measuring both diagonals*

2 *The joists must be well preserved, preferably by soaking them in bags of preservative. Use chocks to ensure that the frame is in fact level*

3 *Next screw the sheets of flooring grade chipboard to the frame, countersinking all the screws and overlapping the sheets over the joists*

4 *The walls are constructed using only halving joints and stopped housing joints. First assemble the frame 'dry' and check that it is properly square*

5 *Then glue and screw each of the outside corners, using two screws at each to prevent the frame from moving diagonally and distorting*

6 *The angle of the roof slope in this design is 13° from the vertical. To start with set this angle on a sliding bevel using a protractor*

The door is the only prefabricated element in the design. This is a 1.8m × 750mm boarded framed door, wide enough to allow a heavy lawn mower to be moved easily in and out of the shed. Though you could make a matching door by nailing shiplap cladding to ledges and braces, reasonably priced standard components are readily available. Use these to cut down the amount of work wherever it is feasible to do so. A further possibility is to purchase prefabricated windows. This would eliminate the really time consuming work, especially if you decide that you need openable windows.

Buy all these ready-made components before you begin work so that you can design and build the walls with openings of the correct dimensions.

When deciding on the size of a shed, consider the headroom you will need. Bear in mind that a ridged roof entails more work and careful thought, but will provide more headroom. A simpler alternative would be a single pitch roof sloping away from the wall in which the window is fitted.

Siting the foundations

Prepare a site for the shed in a position that is unobtrusive yet accessible. Corners are ideal because they are the least used part of the garden. Try to minimize the amount of space that the shed encroaches upon by siting it in an otherwise dead area.

Prepare the site by levelling the ground and clearing obstructions. Excavate the topsoil to a depth of 150mm over an area 200mm larger than the area of the shed. Insert shuttering boards so that you can lay a concrete raft in the normal way but so that the edges extend 50mm beyond the area that the shed will occupy. Lay 75mm of hardcore in the trench, leaving a gap around the edges. Pack this down and cover it with a polyethylene sheet which will act as a damp proof course. Lay 75mm of concrete membrane on top of this in the normal way and thoroughly tamp down the surface, especially at the edges. This will provide a raft foundation that is thicker at the edges (where it supports the walls) than it is in the centre.

A different method for providing a base is to lay paving slabs as you would if you were laying them for a patio or path. Make sure the surface is truly level so that it gives as much support to the floor joists as possible. Alternatively, lay 200mm deep concrete foundations at the two short ends of the shed and one at its centre. Make these appropriate to the width of the shed and at least 200mm wide. When it has set, lay a damp proof

Building a garden shed

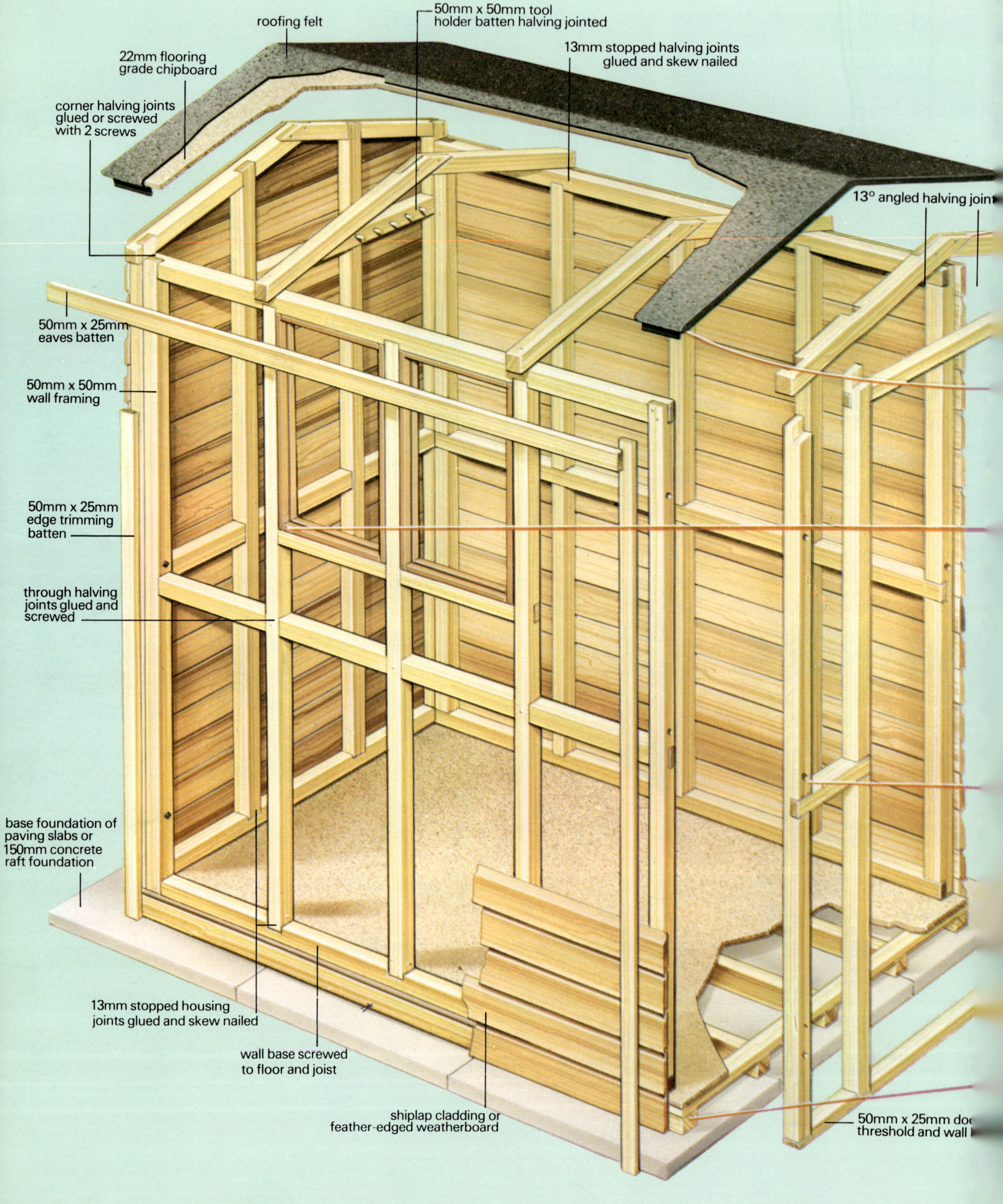

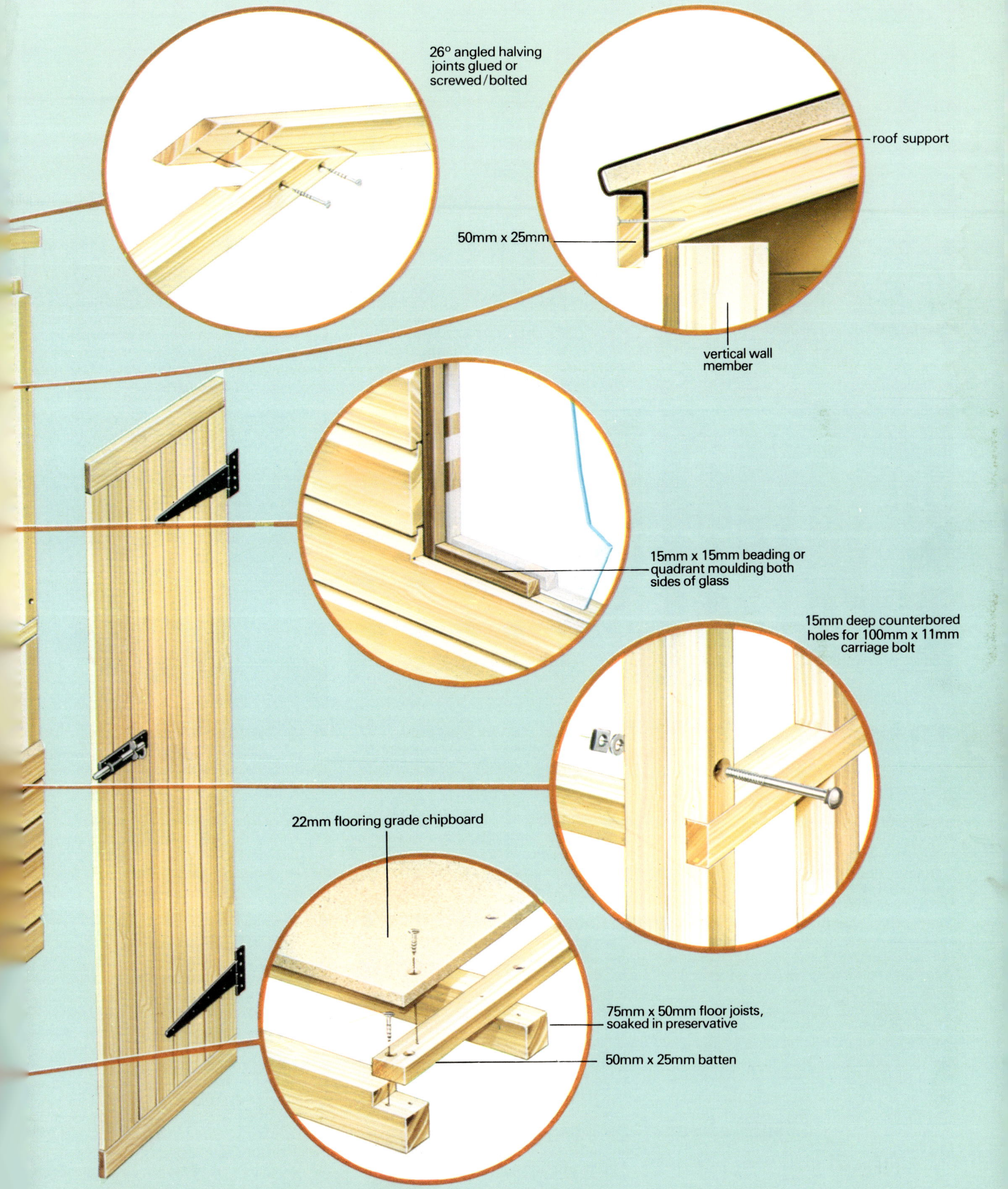
26° angled halving joints glued or screwed/bolted
roof support
50mm x 25mm
vertical wall member
15mm x 15mm beading or quadrant moulding both sides of glass
15mm deep counterbored holes for 100mm x 11mm carriage bolt
22mm flooring grade chipboard
75mm x 50mm floor joists, soaked in preservative
50mm x 25mm batten

7 *Mark the vertical wall members with the sliding bevel and cut all of them out at the same time. Then trim the joints with a chisel*

8 *The gable end roof supports are joined with a halving joint. The correct angle is 26° and all should be cut at the same time with an overlap*

9 *Glue the joint then fix the support timbers together with three screws, having drilled and countersunk the holes and then cut off the horns*

13 *Make absolutely sure that the walls follow the floor exactly then insert a carriage bolt, secure it loosely, then repeat this at each corner*

14 *Once all corners have been bolted loosely, insert the rest of the bolts and tighten up. Screw the walls to the floor frame with 90mm screws*

15 *Position the edge trimming batten accurately, using a piece of the shiplap cladding as a guide, then nail it securely in place*

membrane over the concrete and screw or bolt 75mm by 50mm timber bearers – liberally soaked in preservative – to the concrete, using wall plugs to hold it in position. Rag bolts or steel strips set into the concrete before it dries provide an alternative method of securing the timber bearers. However, you must make careful calculations if you are to ensure that the bolts will correspond to their positions on the bearers.

Yet another alternative – one also supplied by manufacturers of pre-fabricated kits – is to use concrete bearers, either on independent foundations like those above, or on brick piers. This is a particularly useful method for installing a shed on very uneven ground because it allows you to extend above the unevenness.

In all three methods, make sure the base is flat and level. Ensure that the bearers are correctly positioned by checking them with a spirit level, if necessary using a long length of straight batten to stretch from one pier to the next.

The floor

With the foundation or base for the shed prepared, construct the floor, making sure that the size corresponds to the external dimensions of the wall frames.

Use 50mm × 75mm timber for the floor joists. Cut these to length and notch each end of the joists to accept a 50mm × 25mm batten. This will help to keep the floor square and the joists in their correct position while you position the floor covering. It also offers a support to the edges of the end floorboards where they span the joists.

Aim to provide joists at 300mm centres to ensure that the floor will be able to bear the weight of any heavy garden equipment. Before joining the joists to the batten, soak all the timbers in a strong preservative such as creosote, paying particular attention to the end grains. Try to soak as much as possible of the timber in the preservative for at least 24 hours.

With the timber prepared, screw the batten in position on the joists, checking the diagonal measurements to make sure that the frame is square and true. Place the frame on to the foundations using a spirit level to ensure that it lies level on its supports. If necessary, pack up low sections with spare pieces of timber, again soaked in preservative.

When using piers or strip foundations that contain bearers, screw the joists to the bearers. L-brackets at the four

10 *It is most important that the joints are finished smooth and flush to allow the roofing sheets to fit flush, so trim them with a smoothing plane*

11 *Mark the position of the vertical members directly on to the roof support, then cut out the through halving joints and dry assemble*

12 *Hold two adjacent frames exactly in position with clamps, then drill and countersink holes for the fixing bolts*

16 *Next thread a length of twine tautly between the two gable ends to guide the positioning of the intermediate roof supports*

17 *With the roof supports in place fix the chipboard covering, allowing eaves and ends to overlap. Mitre the abutting edges to fit*

18 *Next position the first sheet of roofing felt over the chipboard, allowing a 180mm edge overlap, and fix it with galvanized flat heads*

corners will be sufficient to prevent any possible movement.

Use 100mm × 19mm tongued-and-grooved floorboards to cover the joists, or the cheaper and quicker flooring grade sheets of chipboard. If you use tongued-and-grooved floorboards, nail the first board in position, then cramp the subsequent boards – in threes or fours – tightly together against the first. Use two 50mm oval or floorboard nails to secure each board to each floor joist.

To cramp the boards tight, use sash cramps (bar clamps) or folding wedges. To use wedges for this purpose, nail the first board in position then place three subsequent boards alongside it. Cut four wedges from some spare 50mm × 50mm timber and nail a length of scrap timber alongside the loose floorboards, parallel to them but less than 100mm away from the last one. Insert the two pairs of wedges between the scrap timber and the loose floorboards, tapping them with a hammer or mallet. The wedges will cramp the floorboards together against the first one. Use 50mm oval nails or floor brads to secure the floorboards before you remove the folding wedges, then remove the wedges and the scrap timber. Continue in this way – cramping three boards at a time – until the floor is complete. Punch the nail heads below the surface of the boards.

When using chipboard as a surface drill and countersink the holes at 200mm intervals along each joist. Use 33mm or 50mm countersunk screws to secure the chipboard to the joists. Bear in mind that only standard size sheets are available and that you may have to cut the sheets to size in order to cover the floor completely. If this is the case, butt joint the sheets above a joist so that each sheet is adequately supported.

The wall frames

With the floor complete and in position, construct the wall frames. Make each frame separately using 50mm × 50mm timber throughout, and halving joists or stopped housing joists rather than butt joints; this allows you to dry assemble the structure as you proceed, and in this way you can keep a continuing check on the sizes and dimensions.

When each frame is complete, dry assemble it, checking it along the length of its diagonal measurements to make sure that it is square. Both diagonal measurements should be equal.

To ensure that the frame maintains its shape while you assemble the rest of the structure, glue and screw the corner joints first, using two screws for each corner. Tap home the intermediate vertical members, gluing and skew nailing (toe nailing) them to the top and base plates of the walls. Aim to provide vertical members at 400mm centres but adjust the positions to suit the dimensions of your shed.

A horizontal member at a point 900mm from the floor may seem unnecessary, but it will provide a very positive lateral support to the vertical members as well as offering a support for a work surface or bench. Incorporate such a timber into all four walls as you assemble them, again using halving joints.

Similar horizontal members for supporting shelves or tool-holders should also be incorporated at this stage. If you mark up all the joints at once, using a marking gauge and try square, chopping them out systematically with a chisel and mallet will save a great deal of time.

The shed shown in fig. A is designed so that the two short walls have integral gable ends. All four of the roof bearers—the two gable ends and the two intermediate roof bearers—are constructed at the same time to ensure a uniformity of angle. Each joist contains a 26° angled halving joint at the ridge, while the vertical bearers which support the roof are cut with 13° angled halving joints.

An alternative is to make all four walls rectangular, adding the ridge and gable ends separately. If you choose to adopt this method make all four walls the same height and add roof braces and the roof itself after all the walls are in position.

With all four wall frames complete, including openings for the door and windows, place two adjoining walls in position with the help of an assistant. Adjust them until they correspond to the edges of the floor, then use a G-cramp (C-clamp) to hold them temporarily.

Join the frames at each corner with three 100mm M9 coach bolts and countersink the heads (fig. 12). Do the same at all four corners then, with the frame erect, use 75mm or 100mm screws to screw the base plates of each wall to the floor. This will complete the shell of the shed on to which the cladding can be nailed.

Alternatively, nail the cladding—feather-edged weatherboard or shiplap cladding—to the frames before you erect them. Bear in mind, though, that each wall section will be much heavier and that you will need to bolt through the cladding as well as through the corner sections. In most cases, this will mean using longer bolts. In addition, temporarily clamping the clad sections together will demand the attention of at least two people whereas the skeletal

19 *Secure the second sheet of roofing felt as before, nailing at 150mm centres, then fit a smaller capping piece across the apex of the roof*

20 *Having clad the framework with the shiplap panelling, cut the length below the roof to the correct size and cut it to fit the supports*

23 *Similarly, having cut the gable end trimming pieces to size, nail them in place, sandwiching the felt behind to create a waterproof join*

24 *Nail the window beading in place around the frame then glaze the windows using a putty bed and fixing the glass in place with beading*

frames can be easily manipulated by one person. With either method, you will be able to dismantle each wall section as a complete unit simply by unscrewing the coach bolts from the inside.

The roof

The shed shown in fig. A is designed so that the end walls determine the pitch of the roof. The gable ends are integral to the end walls, with two corresponding intermediate roof bearers screwed to the top of the long walls. If you use this method, use a string line stretched between the end walls to determine the correct position of the intermediate bearers (fig. 16). Flooring grade chipboard, cut to size with an allowance for a 50mm overlap at the eaves and gables, then covered with roofing felt, completes the roof.

If you construct rectangular walls of equal height you will need to erect a ridge with a roof bearing framework to support the roofing material.

A single-pitch roof presents fewer problems but has the disadvantage of a much less attractive appearance and, generally, less head room. Simply build one side wall—preferably a wall containing a window—higher than its opposite counterpart. Run roof joists from one wall to the other, either screwing through them into the tops of the wall, or cutting birdsmouth joints. Alternatively, use simple steel twist brackets screwed to the joist and to the wall frame.

Whichever roof you choose, use chipboard as a covering, leaving an overlap of 50mm beyond the ends of the roof supports. This 50mm overlap can accommodate a 50mm × 25mm fascia which

21 *Cut the felt at the corners and fold and tack both pieces around the roofing sheets in order to prevent water from running over the timber*

22 *Having cut the eaves board to size nail it to the ends of the roof support timbers, sandwiching the roof felt against the cladding*

25 *Screw the sliding door bolt in place on the door, then, having determined the position of the receiving part, screw it in position on the frame*

26 *Attach the T-hinges to the door then screw the hinge to the shed, making sure that the screws are long enough to penetrate the frame*

gives an attractive finish to both gutter and eave level as well as protecting the edge of the roofing felt (fig. 22). Screw the chipboard to the roof frame with 33mm countersunk screws at 200mm centres and cover the whole with at least two layers of roofing felt. Use flat-headed galvanized nails to secure the felt to the chipboard and give added protection to the ridge of the roof by adding a narrow strip of felt as a capping section.

Cladding

Certain grades of exterior hardboard sheets can be used as a cladding for a garden shed but this is not the most attractive material for this purpose. A far more common choice is either feather-edged weatherboard (wedge-shaped in section), or interlocking shiplap cladding.

Weatherboard is popular in shed construction because it weathers well and has a sturdy rustic appearance. When in position, each board overlaps the one beneath it by 25mm to 35mm to form a sheltered joint free from capillary action. Secure each board to the frame separately so that each board can expand and contract without cracking. Use 33mm or 50mm oval nails.

The corners—and the end grains of the boards are protected by edge trimming battens which are nailed into position before the boards are nailed to the frames. The edge trimming battens should be thicker than the boards and positioned so that they extend beyond the face of both boards (fig. 15). Shiplap cladding is protected at the corners in a similar way. However, methods for fixing these two types of boards differ. Shiplap cladding comprises softwood boards milled and rebated to interlock. They provide a weatherproof and attractive exterior that can be treated with varnish, preservative or paint to create the desired effect. With edge trimming battens in position, fitting them to the framework is simply a matter of cutting them to length and slotting them together. Use galvanized nails to secure each board separately to the 50mm × 50mm wall frames, placing the nails 12mm above the joint between boards.

Doors and windows

If you use prefabricated door and window frames, screw the frames to the walls before you fit the cladding. The frames themselves can then act as trims against which you can butt the cladding, obviating the need for edge trimming battens at these points. If you do not use prefabricated units, nail 75mm × 25mm linings to the door and window openings to frame them and to act as edge trimmers for the cladding.

Use two or three gate hinges for the outward-opening door of the shed, incorporating a thin batten on the closing side of the frame as a door stop. Quadrant moulding pinned to the reveals of the window openings is adequate as a rebate for the window panes. Bed the panes on a thin bed of putty to prevent them from rattling and use quadrant moulding on the external side of the pane too, again bedding the glass on a thin layer of putty.

Openable windows demand more care when you come to fit them You will need to build a casement for the panes, but you can hinge this at the top, bottom or sides according to your tastes.

Weatherproofing

The floor and lower parts of the frame are the most susceptible to damp and the weather, so make sure that you apply a liberal coat of preservative to the floor. The joists should also be soaked.

The most versatile and effective wood preservative is pentaclorophenol. You can paint or varnish over it whereas creosote stains the wood much darker and does not permit painting. Use an old paint brush to apply it to all the exposed surfaces of the wood, adding another coat 24 hours later. Pay particular attention to joints and endgrains making sure that the preservative coats as much and as liberally as possible. Be very careful when using any kind of preservative and make sure that you read the manufacturers advice—especially on safety.

If you decide to paint the shed, apply at least two coats of waterproof paint after priming and undercoating the timber. Spread the paint liberally along all the joints in the shed.

Building a greenhouse

● The advantages of building a greenhouse from scratch ● Basic considerations to bear in mind ● Design and construction of basic lean-to assemblies—one clad with PVC corrugated roofing sheets, and one glazed

A. **Above:** *A lean-to greenhouse is a pot planter's paradise and an asset to any home. In it you can be 'outside' and relax even when the weather is bad—and it is far cheaper than an extension*

In temperate climates, the growing season for many plants in the open is short, and this is bound to restrict your choice of plants and flowers. But a greenhouse can alter the situation completely, enabling plants of many kinds to be grown all the year round. In colder climates, an even greater variety of plants can be propagated and grown if the greenhouse is heated, as this will allow you to grow exotic examples from warmer regions around the world.

Building your own greenhouse is not a very complicated job, and it permits you to design and tailor the building to suit your individual needs, the requirements of the site, and the plants that you wish to grow. It can also be surprisingly cheap.

Basic considerations

One of the first things to decide is the type of crop to be grown, noting any special requirements; for example, indoor carnations grow best in tall greenhouses, and need more ventilation than most crops. If you are uncertain about the most suitable greenhouse for your needs consult a nursery or an experienced gardener. However, for average purposes, it is usually a matter of selecting a convenient and sunny spot, either making use of an existing wall to build a lean-to greenhouse, or alternatively siting it apart from other buildings as a free-standing unit.

The size and type of greenhouse best suited to your needs are partly governed by the space available, the site itself, the crops and the final cost.

The lean-to type, best sited on an east-west axis in the sun, is usually cheaper to make, to heat (because of its better insulation), and to maintain than a free-standing model of similar size and construction. The mini greenhouse variation can be either a lean-to or free-standing type (see below).

Available space may be further restricted by planning regulations. Structures in front of the building line between the house and the road are normally prohibited in the UK. On the other hand small greenhouses which are less than 3m high and which do not occupy more than half the garden area are not usually subject to planning consent. Unless you are absolutely certain of the planning regulations in your area, you should consult the local council before starting work.

Design and construction

All buildings have a number of important design and construction requirements, and in the case of a greenhouse there are six main considerations.

● **Appearance:** This is influenced by the design and also by the construction materials—usually wood and glass.

● **Strength and durability:** A greenhouse should be capable of withstanding the worst possible conditions of wind, sun, storms, frost and snow. Timber glazing bars, for example, should ideally not be less than 20mm deep for a 1m span, and the depth should be increased by 12mm for each additional 500mm of span.

● **Light:** Maximum light is of course necessary all the year round so avoid narrowly spaced glazing bars, aiming for intervals of between 450mm and 750mm.

● **Ventilation:** This is critical, and trials have shown that the total ventilator area should ideally not be less than 15 percent or one-sixth of the floor space.

● **Ease of construction:** It is very important that a greenhouse project does not demand great expense on tools and materials, and in this respect a timber frame is a good choice.

● **Low maintenance:** Costs need to be kept in mind, and simplicity of design, combined with sound construction techniques are of great importance.

Comparison with kits

When deciding whether to erect a proprietary kit greenhouse, or to build a home made unit, the acid test for most people boils down to cost; but to make a valid comparison you have to take into account many factors, including quality, design, construction and durability. Often the kit price excludes such items as the base, the glass and delivery, so the comparison must be made on the cost of the different greenhouses erected on site complete. This way you can make a fair assessment of relative costs.

The materials for a typical built-from-scratch greenhouse are no more than half of the price of a similar kit. And, given that you can take satisfaction from your own labour, making a greenhouse is still an economically worthwhile proposition.

Nature and scope of the models

Although this article describes how to build two lean-to types of greenhouse, a free-standing span or apex type with a high central ridge or a mini greenhouse can also be made with certain modifications.

Timber is excellent for the main structure because it is versatile and easy to work with, and presents few problems with either glazing or cladding. Also, less condensation forms on wooden frames than on metal ones because they retain a more even temperature. Given the occasional treatment with paint or preservative, timber structures can last 20 to 30 years and more.

Softwood should be treated with a horticultural grade of preservative containing copper napthanate (in the UK, a suitable choice would be Cuprinol). Special attention should be paid to joints and those parts of the building which are in contact with the ground. These should be soaked for a few hours in a container of the solution. Long timbers such as bottom plates can be laid on a long sheet of polyethylene gathered along the corners and edges to form a receptacle or bag into which preservative is poured.

Although it costs about 50 percent more, cedar wood is a timber which requires little treatment or maintenance because it has a natural oil which resists decay and is ideal for outdoor use.

Both the lean-to greenhouse designs are made up of four sections—two ends, the front and the roof. The designs as shown are adequate for a greenhouse with an eaves height of 1.52m, a ridge height of 2.13m and a width of 2.33m. This should allow considerable freedom of movement, but the measurements can easily be adapted to your own requirements, especially the length. However, if and when altering sizes, keep in mind the standard sizes of cladding materials: this avoids needless cutting and subsequent waste. Also, when building larger structures, heavier timbers and bracing are necessary for extra strength.

The four frames of the greenhouse can be assembled in one or two ways. The frames can be made up separately, then bolted together and screwed to the wall. Alternatively, the wall timbers or studs can be screwed to the wall first, and the framework then constructed in situ. The frame can later be glazed or clad with PVC corrugated roofing sheet (such as Novolux in the UK). Standard 4mm thick glass is adequate for glazing and this should be installed in 'modules' as nearly square as possible. This means in effect that the glass is panelled. For instance, on the roof, each run of glass between timbers consists of three panes of overlapping glass. This avoids the use of large panes of glass which are both vulnerable and difficult to instal.

When planning the greenhouse, remember to allow extra for the width of glass or PVC sheeting 'lost' in channelling grooves or housings.

1 First prepare the site, providing an even bed of hardcore which should be well tamped down, and paint the back wall with a weatherproof agent

2 Having cut the back horizontal and vertical timbers and applied a timber preservative, fix the horizontal wall plate with long coach bolts

3 Once the loadbearing wall plate has been fixed the vertical back frame can be secured to the wall using masonry nails

4 Lay a single course of lightweight building blocks then mortar treated posts into the hollow corner blocks. Make sure that the posts are vertical

5 *In order to save much wasteful trimming of the cladding material, it makes sense to use it as a guide when actually building the structure*

6 *The bottom plate of the front frame is a structural component and so it should be firmly fixed to the building blocks with wall anchors*

7 *At this stage apply a liberal amount of timber preservative to the bottom plate, making quite certain that you treat all cuts and end grain*

Making the four frames is very simple. The essence of the separate parts is that they are self-bracing, in other words they have an intrinsic strength in their unassembled state. The following is only a guide however, and you should feel free to modify the construction if you want to change the dimensions.

End frame: Using planed softwood timber, cut the base, top, back and front to size then make half-lap angle joints at the ends using a tenon saw and chisel. Make T-halving joints to take the upright and horizontal timbers; these in turn are then cut to size with half-lap joints at the ends. The joints in the top rail must of course be cut to the appropriate angle.

In all cases, paint the prepared cuts with preservative before putting them together. Drill and countersink two screw holes at each joint to take the appropriate screws. Do, however, avoid drilling too deep or the screws will have an insufficient grip. Finally assemble the timber sections and screw them together, making sure that the bottom corners are perfectly square.

End frame with door: Preparation and assembly of the parts is the same as for the first end frame, but with three differences. The lower horizontal timber cross rail from the front stops at the centre upright instead of running through to the back. This allows for the door. Also necessary is a projecting vertical door stop fixed behind the centre upright and aligned with the door.

The door itself is made from two uprights, fixed to three cross pieces with half-lap joints at the ends and T-halving joints in the centre. Drill and countersink the appropriate screws as before. Then fix three 150mm 'T' hinges to the cross members of the door. The door should not actually be hung until the end frames are fastened to the wall, but check that the door fits the frame before erecting the structure and adjust as necessary.

Front frame: Cut the four upright timbers to the correct length, making T-halving joints in the centres. Then cut the top, centre and base members, with half-lap end joints, plus two evenly spaced T-halving joints on each. Paint all joints with preservative and allow this to dry before drilling and countersinking to take two screws at each joint. Finally, assemble and screw the timbers together, making sure that the corners are square and that the bottom plate is laid flat side down like those of the end frames. If you decide to put a door in the front frame, follow the instructions given above. As before, do not hang the door until the structure is complete, but do make sure that it fits the frame before moving on to assemble the greenhouse.

8 *Once the preservative is dry, set the bottom plate on the building blocks. Make sure that it is flat then render the building block course*

9 *The PVC roofing sheets can be secured to the structure either with battens or in grooves—the latter being easy to make with a circular saw*

11 *Where thin section timbers are butt or halving jointed it is best to secure them with a screw. Always drill holes to avoid splitting the wood*

Roof: Repeat as for the front frame, with the addition of a ventilator seating. Cut the ventilator seating timber with half-lap joints at each end and screw this securely into the extended half-lap joints of the two centre timbers. Because of the sloping roof it is necessary to chamfer the back timber by about 7°, just sufficiently to allow it to butt squarely against the wall when fixed to the wall plate. Make the ventilator frame in the same way as the door, with the necessary size adjustments. Fix two 150mm strap hinges to the roof frame for the ventilator and make sure that it is a good weatherproof fit.

Foundations

The base of the greenhouse must be raised above the ground level, to keep it clear of surface water.

10 *The essence of the greenhouse structure is that the frame is self-bracing. The front top plate is thus nailed to the front corner posts*

If you are building on soil then you will have to dig a foundation to provide a base, the top of which should be at least 25mm above ground level.

It may be that there will be an existing foundation of sorts, in the form of a driveway, path or patio. Providing this consists of paving slabs or concrete laid over a hardcore base it will be adequate, although the level will still have to be raised to the proper height.

One way of doing this is to fit a formwork of 25mm × 25mm battening around the base and fill it with concrete. If you use this method, you must ensure that the new concrete bonds well to the existing surface by coating the latter with a solution of PVA bonding agent.

An alternative is to 'build' the base by laying paving slabs or a layer of bricks – with mortared joints in between them – on the top of the existing surface.

Whichever method you choose, the finished surface must be painted with a proprietary waterproof sealing compound (such as Aquaseal 40 Heavy Duty) to damp-proof it.

The base must be absolutely level when finished otherwise the wooden frames of the greenhouse will be at staggered heights when you come to assemble them and therefore they will not fit.

A far simpler method of isolating the timber frame from the ground is to build a single course of lightweight building blocks on top of a shallow 150mm concrete foundation, then lay the bottom plates on the frames. Using this method, the two front corner posts, suitably preserved, may be anchored into hollow blocks, and the rest of the structure constructed about these (fig. 4). If the course is continued around the floor area, there will be a step at the base of the door.

12 *Housing joints are normally skew-nailed, but a galvanized steel angle bracket screwed under the joint provides added strength*

13 *Alternatively, screw through joints after drilling and plugging the end grain of the longitudinal timber to avoid splitting it with the screw*

If you feel that this is a disadvantage, the blocks and bottom plate can be constructed with a cutout for the door. However, without the step it will be very difficult to both keep the door away from the rot-inducing soil, and to make the greenhouse draughtproof.

The receiving wall

The wall to which the greenhouse is attached should, ideally, be absolutely vertical. Unfortunately few walls are. If the wall is less than 12mm out of plumb, the gap can be filled with a bricklaying mortar. But, if it is over 12mm or you do not want a wedge-shaped mortar gap, then you will have to shape three lengths of 50mm × 50mm timber (two vertical battens support the two end frames, and the horizontal batten – the wall plate – supports the roof) so that they form a vertical surface to which the greenhouse frame will be attached. Shape the timber to fit the wedge-shaped gaps, then, having laid a thick layer of sealing mastic or compound along the wall and the timber where the surfaces will meet, screw the timber firmly to the wall with wall plugs or large bolts.

Construction

All the joints should be both glued and screwed, using a waterproof adhesive such as urea formaldehyde and either brass, galvanized or japanned screws. The glass or PVC sheeting can be housed either between narrow wooden battens or in glazing grooves cut with a plough plane, router or power saw.

Assembly

Drill the back plate of one end frame and fix it to the vertical timber attached to the wall, then do the same at the other end frame. Move the front frame into place, drilling and fixing the base to the bolts (which are set in concrete). Drill and screw the ends of the front frame to the respective front timbers of the end frames. The shell of the greenhouse is then ready to receive the roof frame. This should be drilled and fixed to the end and front frames as well as to the wall plate, and when fitting it, you should make quite sure that the frame is flush with the wall to avoid distortion.

PVC

To clad the frame first lay one sheet of PVC roofing on the ventilator (if fitted), bedding it down on foam eaves filler and fixing it with nails and washers. Then fix the casement stay and hinges. Carefully position and secure the remainder of the PVC sheets to the roof, using eaves filler, and securing them with screws and washers.

angled T-halving joint
angled butt joint
angled T-halving joint
glazing groove
glazing batten
flashing
glazing groove
mastic
glass
angled ha
overlapping glas
angled T-halving joint
glazing batten
angled bridle joint
ngued-and-grooved panelling
support batten
housing joint
bridle joint

Alternative constructions

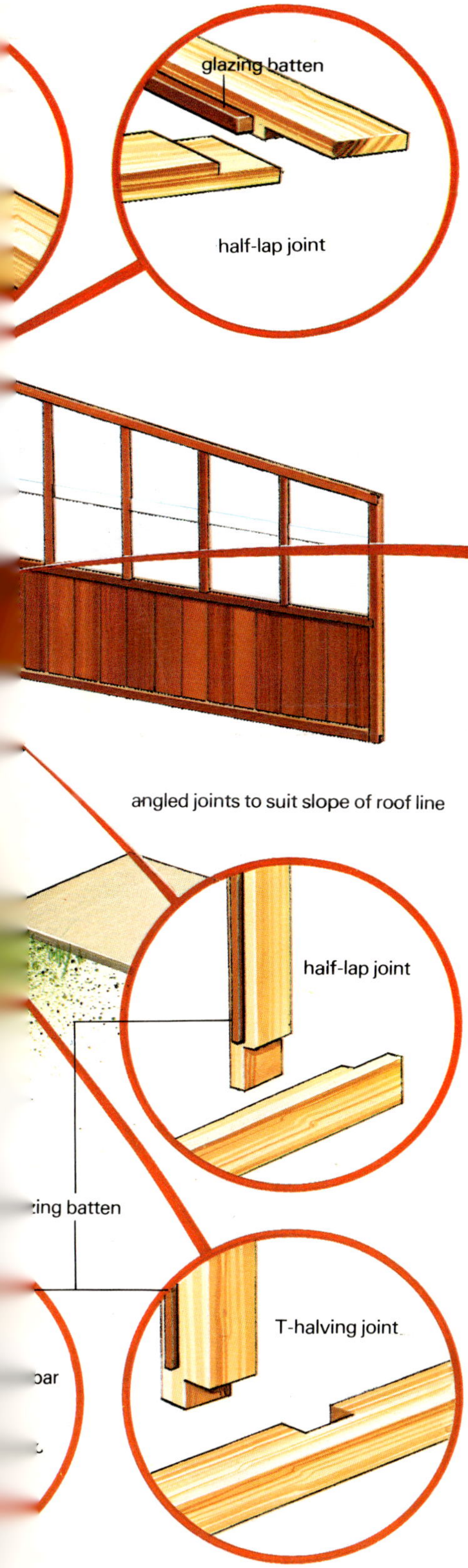

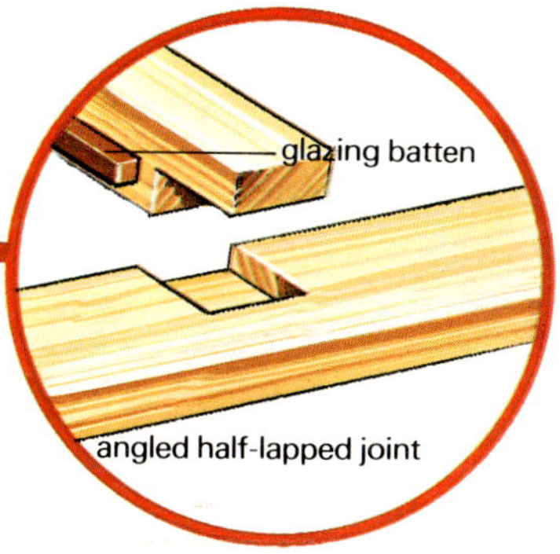

The glazed and boarded greenhouse **(left)** has been designed as simply as possible so that it can be constructed with a minimum of time and effort. The generous eaves height of 1520mm and a ridge height of 2130mm ensures adequate headroom, especially around the edges at bench or staging level where plants are sited. And the width of 2330mm allows considerable freedom of movement.

The timber section for the standard sized greenhouse should be at least 50mm × 50mm for all structural components and 75mm × 50mm for the door posts. The door battens should be 25mm × 25mm and the glazing beading should be 16mm × 16mm.

The measurements can be adapted according to your requirements, especially the length. If the design is extended in this way some extra reinforcing will be necessary mid-way along the roof and side. A glazing bar can be replaced by a 75mm × 50mm timber and a cross bar at the side would add rigidity and strength. A similar stout piece of timber should be inserted mid-way along the side section.

Throughout the design two main glass widths—460mm and 610mm—are used. The window and roof glass, it must be noted, is installed in 'modules' as nearly square as possible. This means in effect that the glass is panelled. For instance, on the roof each run of glass between timbers consists of four panes of overlapping glass.

In the case of a PVC sheet clad greenhouse (below) the timber section should be at least 50mm × 50mm. The hardwood corner posts should be 75mm × 75mm, but you can get away with 50mm × 25mm for the wall plate and vertical wall timbers.

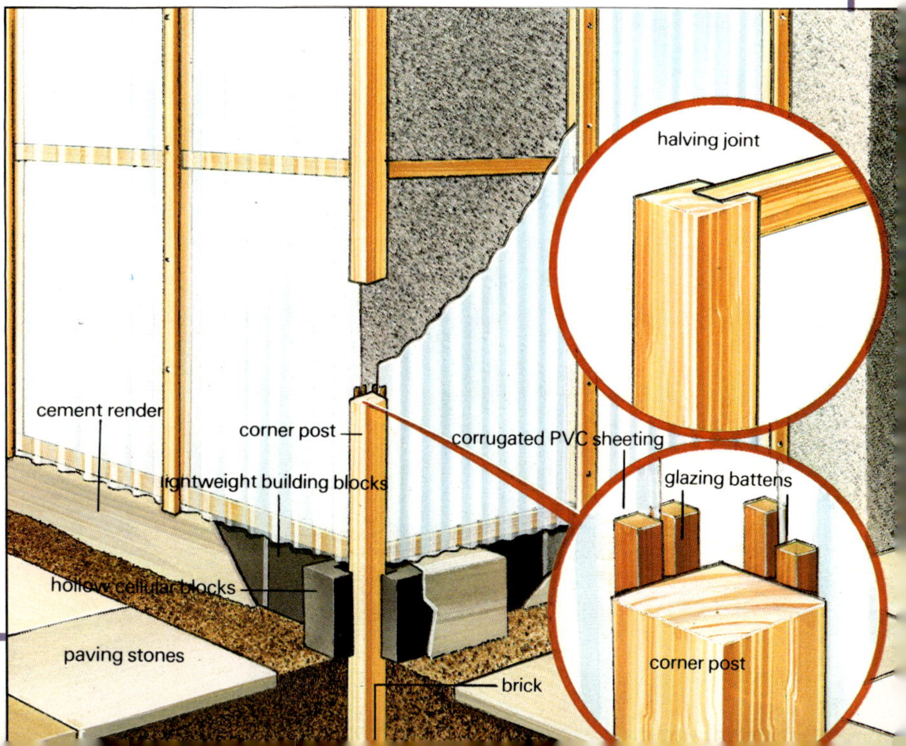

14 *The PVC sheet can be cut using an abrasive disc fitted to a circular saw or saw attachment. Use a stout length of timber as a fence*

15 *When fixing the PVC cladding, support the sheets from below and from behind then drill through them and into the supporting timber*

16 *Use pre-formed polystyrene eaves filler strips when fitting the roof to provide rigidity and also to draughtproof the greenhouse*

Fix PVC sheeting to the door frame in the same way as to the ventilator, then fix the door in place, making sure that it opens and closes freely. When covering the ends, it is necessary to measure carefully then cut the PVC sheet to shape using a fine toothed saw.

Glazing

The method of overlapping glass panes is quite simple. First press a bed of putty along the glazing beading shelf, then press the bottom pane of glass into the putty. Now hold the next higher pane where it will be fixed, and mark the sides of the structure where the bottom of the pane will be located.

Put the pane aside for the time being and drive a 25mm nail into each side of the woodwork immediately next to the lower pane, level with the marks, until just about 6mm of the head is still protruding. You now have two metal stops on which the next pane can rest while it is puttied in position. The process is repeated for successive panes. There are several types of proprietary clips that are made for joining overlapping glass sheets, but they all suffer from the same disadvantage – the final pane often has to be cut to fit. The nail method, on the other hand, allows you as little or as much overlap as you need.

Where a structure abuts against a wall you must provide a run-off for rain water at the junction point. This flash could be zinc, lead or copper chased into the mortar, but a simpler alternative is to use self-adhesive flashing.

Door catches, handles and the ventilator stay add the finishing touches, along with weatherboarding, which should be nailed over the roof ends and treated with preservative.

17 *The window sill is fixed above the bottom cladding to provide a weather seal. All metal fittings must be of a type suitable for outdoor use*

18 *One great advantage of cladding the greenhouse with PVC roof sheeting is that it can be stretched or squashed to take up minor adjustments*

Variations on the basic theme

Mini greenhouse: A smaller version of the lean-to greenhouse, this is tended from the outside and has one or more opening doors at the front. Usually, this type of greenhouse is essentially a modified lean-to in which similar methods of construction to the basic design are used, with twin doors placed centrally and no end door.

The internal height should be at least 1500mm so that shelving can be fitted to double the effective area, allowing 700mm headroom for plants on each level.

Apex or span: This is a free-standing model which rises to a central ridge and it can be constructed along the lines of two lean-tos placed back to back.

The necessary modifications include a central ridge with capping, a central door in one end, and side and end bracing to provide rigidity.

19 *With the end of the roof butted against the backing wall, the joint can be made weathertight with a timber batten, mastic and self-adhesive flashing*

Build a carport

This attractive carport forms a practical alternative to a full garage, being both simple and cheap to build. It includes an enclosed outhouse in which you can store bicycles, tools and garden implements

Most car owners have to fight a constant battle to keep the car's body work from deteriorating due to rust caused by exposure to the elements. One way to minimize this is to keep your car under cover. But garages are expensive and complicated to build, and you need a fair amount of space. An alternative, which avoids most of the problems, is to build a carport.

And this design includes a practical outhouse which will provide secure cover for bicycles or tools.

Before you begin work, think about siting carefully. You must, of course, have access for the car, but also, if it is near the house, beware of cutting out light to the windows, or of blocking access to the garden. If there are trees nearby, think about whether it will be difficult to clear fallen leaves from the roof. Think too about access to the shed with wheelbarrows or bicycles. If there is a fence, you may be able to incorporate it into one of the sides. You must have a slight slope on the roof, so that rainwater will drain, so think about which way it is best for the water to run off.

Construction is simple if you set out carefully. Treat all timber with wood preservative before use. Install the uprights, then pave or concrete the base. Fit the cross beams and rafters, then add the roofing. Board in the shed and the side as required. Door height depends on which way the roof slopes (the larger is given).

Every two years retreat the timber with wood preservative. Clear fallen leaves from the roof and make sure no weeds grow around the timbers.

Workplan

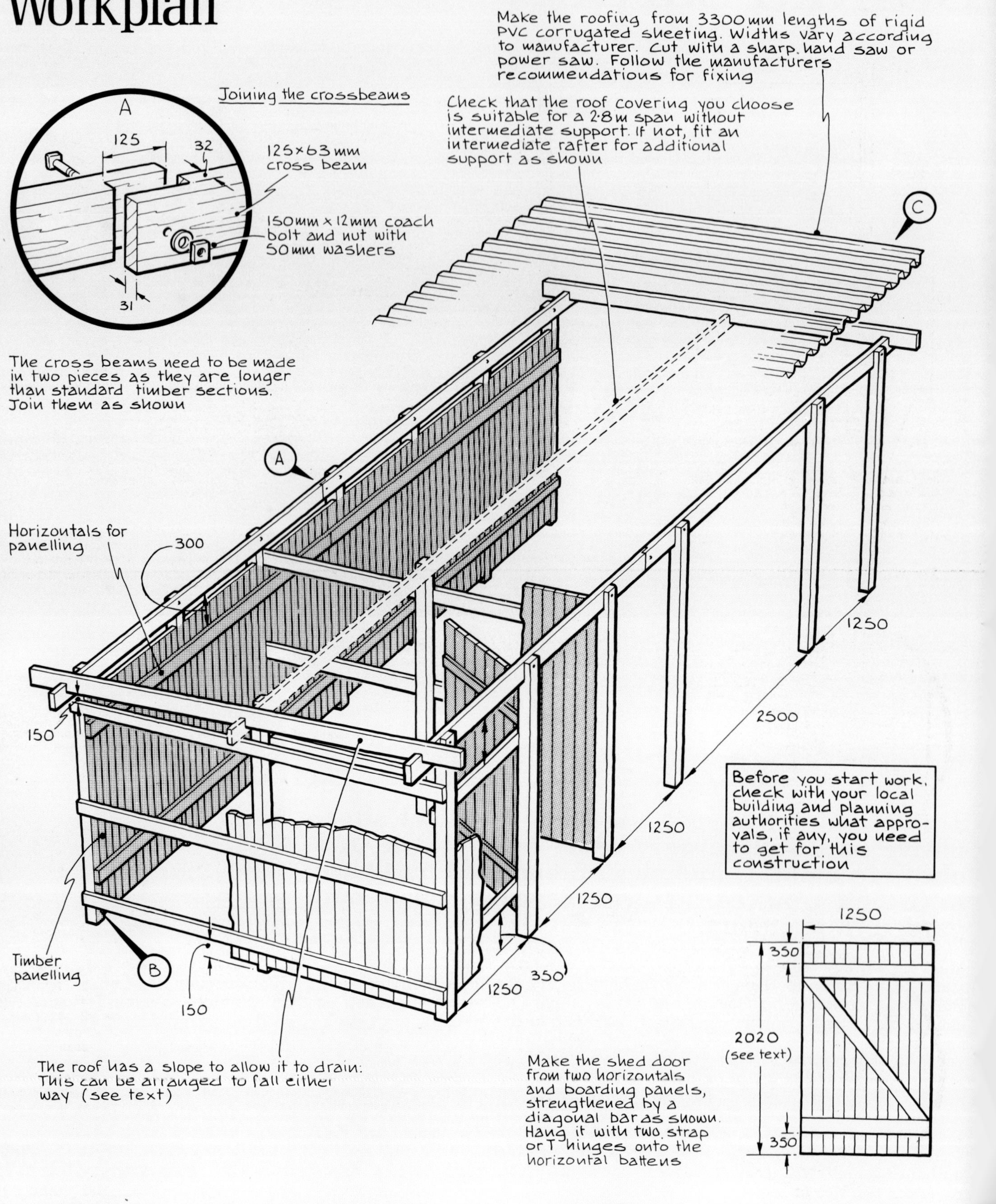
Make the roofing from 3300mm lengths of rigid PVC corrugated sheeting. Widths vary according to manufacturer. Cut with a sharp hand saw or power saw. Follow the manufacturers recommendations for fixing
Joining the crossbeams
A
125
32
125×63mm cross beam
150mm×12mm coach bolt and nut with 50mm washers
31
Check that the roof covering you choose is suitable for a 2·8m span without intermediate support. If not, fit an intermediate rafter for additional support as shown
C
The cross beams need to be made in two pieces as they are longer than standard timber sections. Join them as shown
A
Horizontals for panelling
300
150
1250
2500
1250
1250
350
1250
Before you start work, check with your local building and planning authorities what approvals, if any, you need to get for this construction
Timber panelling
B
150
1250
350
2020 (see text)
350
The roof has a slope to allow it to drain: This can be arranged to fall either way (see text)
Make the shed door from two horizontals and boarding panels, strengthened by a diagonal bar as shown. Hang it with two strap or T hinges onto the horizontal battens

Cross section of shed

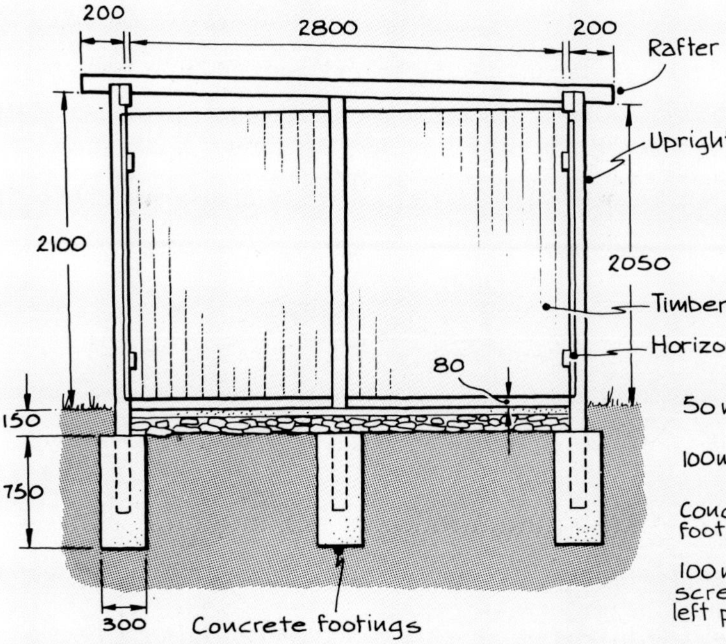

Laying the base slabs and setting the posts

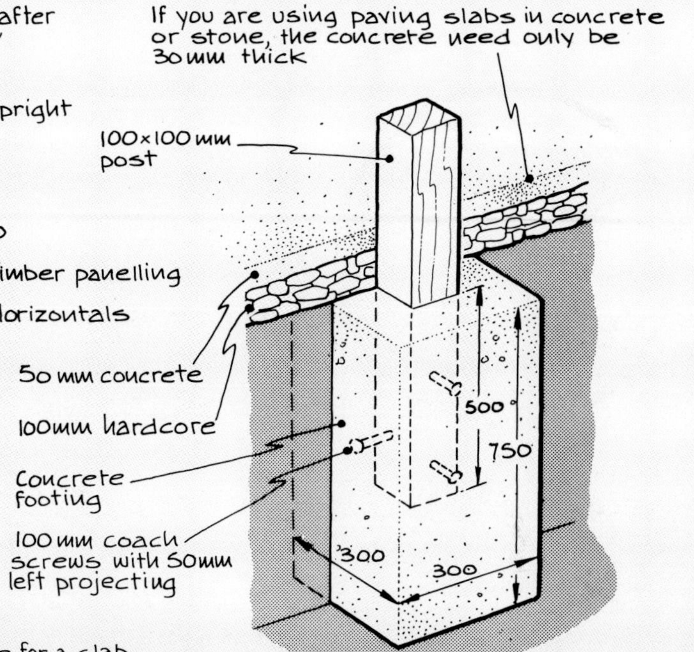

In Canada, check your local building codes to find out what depth of footings and base slabs you need for your region

Prepare the base for a slab consisting of 100mm of hardcore and 50mm of concrete. Set out positions of posts and excavate holes approximately 1 metre deep for the footings. Soak the sunken ends of the posts thoroughly in preservative, and concrete in position before laying the rest of the concrete slab. Remember that the posts are longer on one side to allow the roof to slope

Fitting the panelling

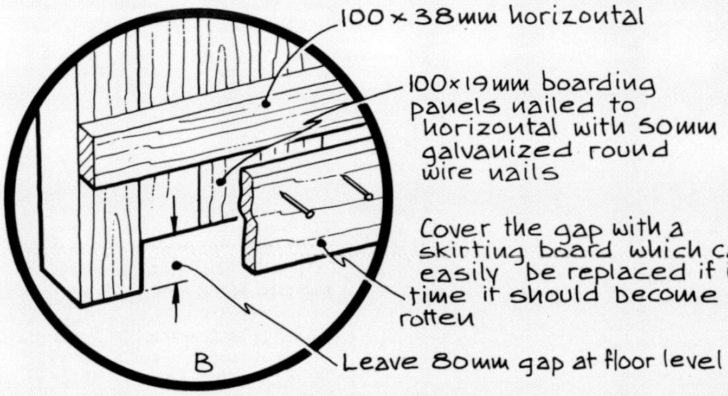

Join and fix the roofing panels using only the manufacturers recommended fixings which are designed for corrugated PVC roofing. Nails are not suitable because it is not possible to control the tightness with which they are hammered home, and there is risk of shattering the sheet. Also the nail head is not large enough to give a firm fixing.

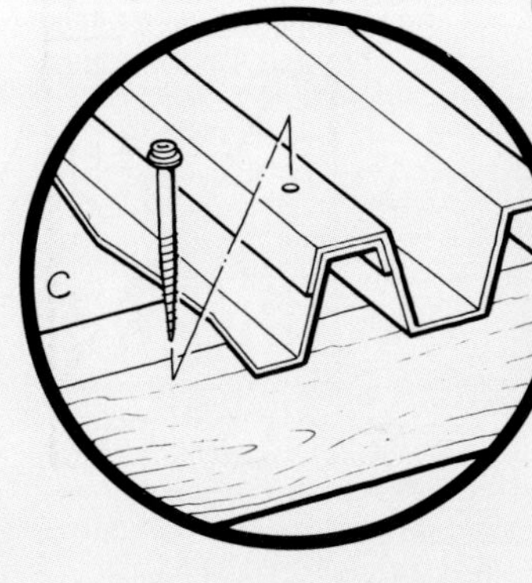

Drill all holes using a normal metal working twist drill bit

Cutting list
All sizes are in millimetres. Timber is sawn. The list is for the full basic carport including the outhouse. Omit parts as necessary for alternative versions.

Part	Materials	No.	Size
uprights	100mm × 100mm sawn softwood	15	3000mm
crossbeams	125mm × 63mm sawn softwood	4	4200mm
(joined to make two beams 8200mm long)			
rafters	100mm × 38mm sawn softwood	2	3300mm
intermediate beam	125mm × 63mm sawn softwood	2	4200mm
(joined to make one 8200mm length. This is only needed where roofing will not span 2800mm)			
horizontals (shed)	100mm × 38mm sawn softwood	6	3000mm
horizontals (shed)	100mm × 38mm sawn softwood	2	2700mm
horizontals (shed)	100mm × 38mm sawn softwood	1	3600mm
horizontal (carport)	100mm × 38mm sawn softwood	2	3900mm
(joined to make one long beam)			
boarding (shed)	100mm × 19mm sawn softwood	26	3900mm
		or 52	1920mm
boarding (carport)	100mm × 19mm sawn softwood	44	3600mm
		or 88	1800mm

Roofing: Rigid PVC corrugated sheeting in 3300mm lengths. Width varies according to manufacturer. Recommended fixings, sealing tape or mastic.
Additional materials: 18 No. 170mm × 12mm coach (carriage) bolts and 50mm washers, 100mm galvanized wire (common) nails. 55mm galvanized wire nails, hinges and door lock, sand, cement, hardcore, aggregate.
Finish: Timber preservative.

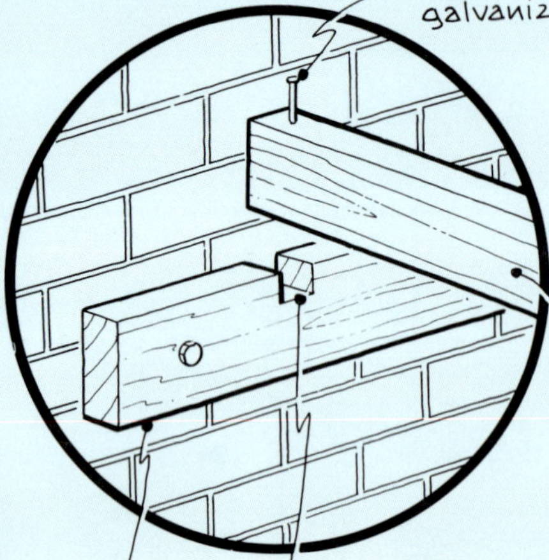

Making a lean-to carport

Construction is similar to the carport with shed, but only uses 4 uprights, and has open sides. You could easily panel in the side if preferred. The higher cross beam is bolted to the house wall and so the rafters and the roof do not overhang on this side but butt up to the wall. The width of this carport is slightly greater, so you can cut your timbers to the same lengths already given

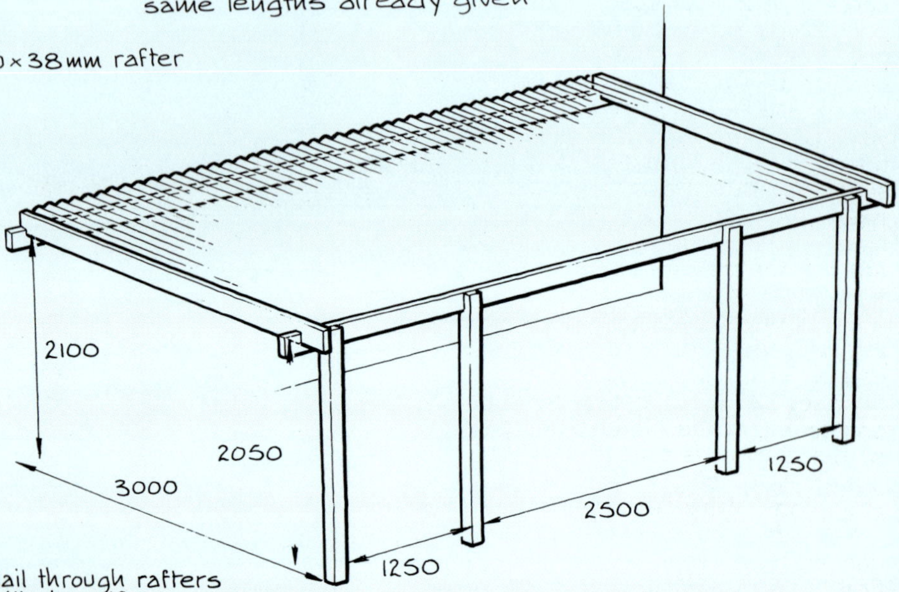

Joining the rafters

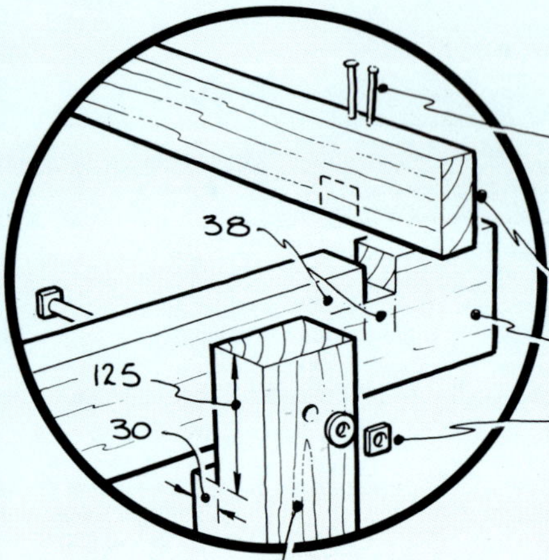

Free standing version without shed

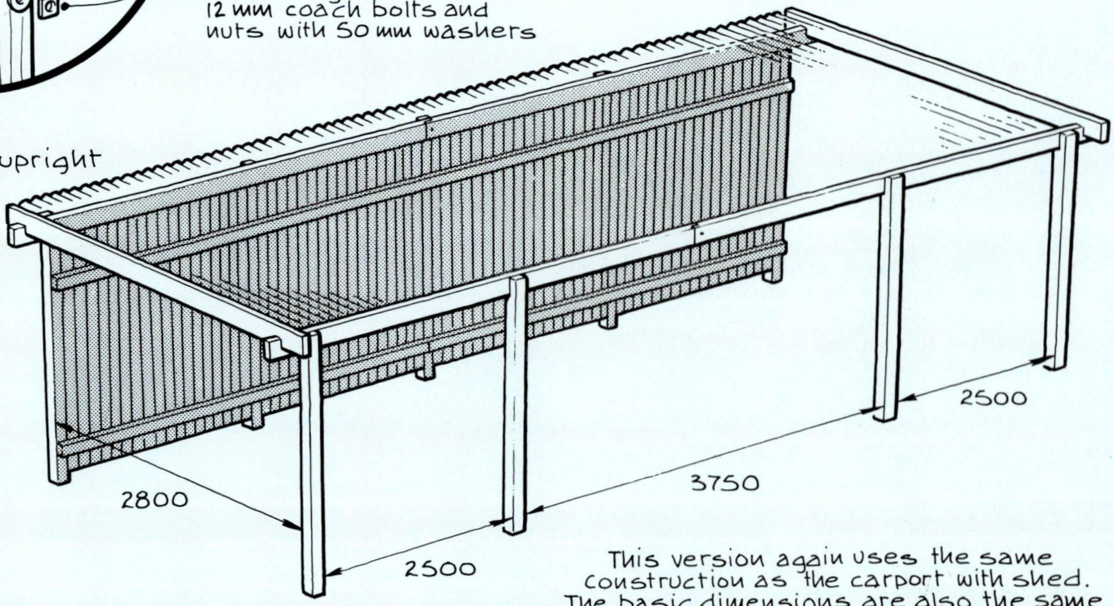

This version again uses the same construction as the carport with shed. The basic dimensions are also the same, though only four uprights are used on the open side. The panelling is optional and could be omitted

Alternative ideas

The design on page 243 shows how you can build a carport complete with an outhouse in which to store bicycles or garden implements. But you can easily adapt the basic design if you would prefer a simple carport, or if your space is limited.

These pictures show two of the possibilities. On the right, the carport is built as a lean-to on the house wall. This is ideal if you only have a limited space at the side of the house, and it also saves on materials, since you only need the timber supports on one side. In this design, you must arrange for the roof to slope down from the house.

Below, the illustration shows another idea for a free-standing carport. This is similar to the one on page 243 but omits the shed enclosure. In the picture, one side of the carport is fenced in. If you prefer, you can leave this out, or enclose both sides with cladding.

You can build both of these designs with very little modification to the basic construction. Where they do vary substantially, details are given on page 246.

Octagonal greenhouse

This small octagonal greenhouse has overtones of the Victorian garden gazebo about it. Yet its clean lines and small size make it ideal for any setting.

You can make this greenhouse out of almost any type of timber. If you use softwood, make sure it has been well treated with preservative (preferably pressure-impregnated) and liberally treat all joints with preservative as you cut them. Remember that this treatment may affect the type of finish you can give the timber—ask your timber merchant before buying. To prevent rusting, use galvanized nails and brass screws throughout the construction.

After marking out the perimeter of the octagon on your base, start by making the four opposed main frameworks. Hold these in position on the base (you will need helpers) and nail the top and bottom tie rails to them—these rails effectively complete the octagon shape. Fit the window sills and clad the lower portions of the walls. Then make the conical roof structure. Take great care in cutting out the compound angles in the rafters. Dry-assemble the rafters on the ground, making sure they fit together neatly. A template may help you with the shape of the 'birds mouth' cut which fits over the framework top rails.

The octagonal capping piece strengthen the roof structure and hel keep water out of the joint at th crown. Cut them out from hardwood planing them to a conical shape wit a block plane. Screw them into pos ition after fitting all the rafters.

Some ventilation is important, s make a couple of simple window frame to fit two of the main frameworks. Fi a standard narrow door to a thir framework. Use standard or horti cultural 3mm glass in all the opening —measure each one individuall before buying the glass. All the glazing is held in position with wooden glazing beads and bedded in on putty o mastic. Finish the greenhouse with paint or stain to improve both appearance and durability.

Workplan

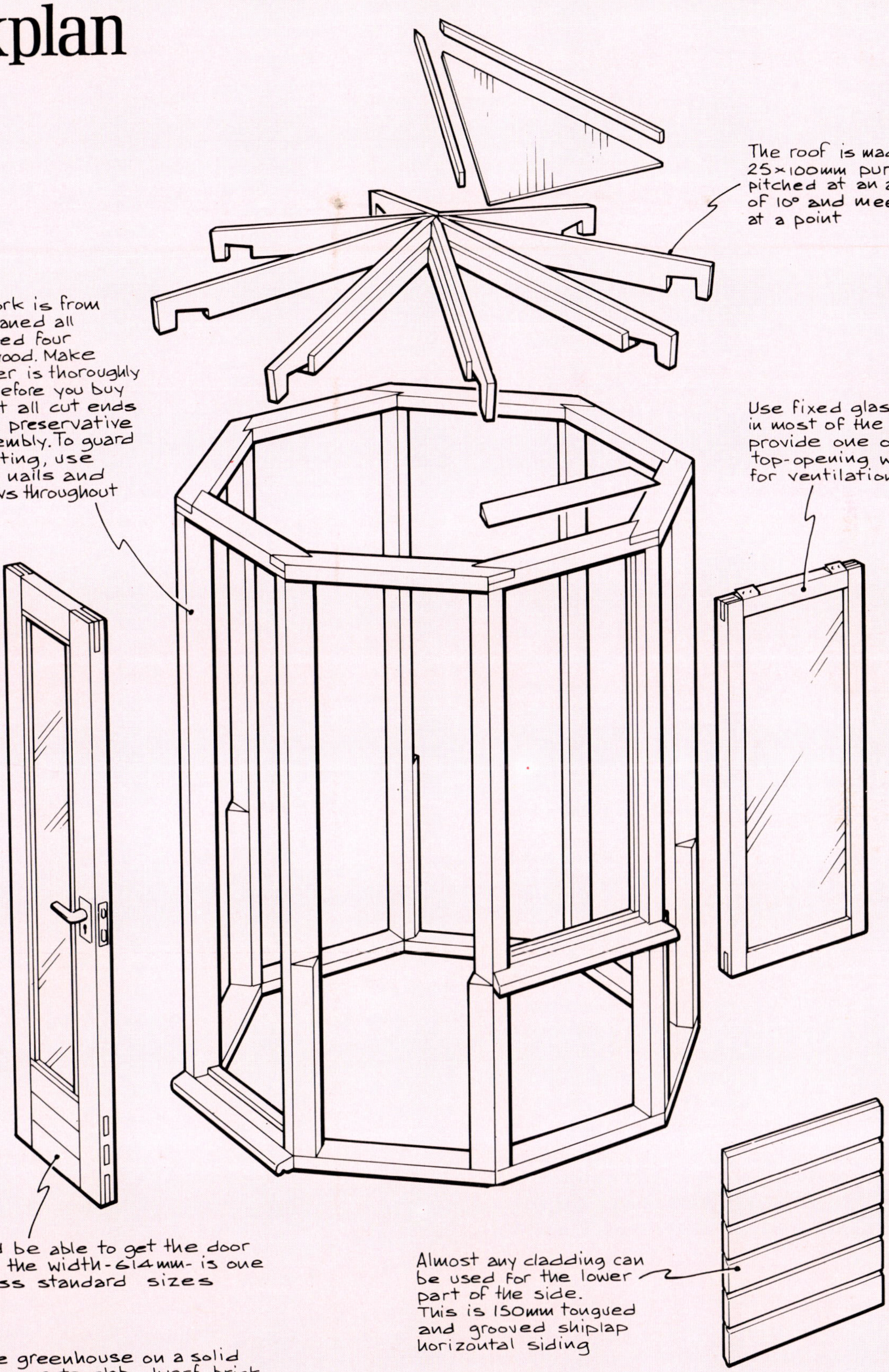
The roof is made from 25×100mm purlins, pitched at an angle of 10° and meeting at a point
The framework is from 50×100mm planed all round (dressed four sides) softwood. Make sure all timber is thoroughly preserved before you buy it, and treat all cut ends liberally with preservative during assembly. To guard against rusting, use galvanized nails and brass screws throughout
Use fixed glass panes in most of the sides, but provide one or two top-opening windows, for ventilation
You should be able to get the door to fit, but the width - 614mm - is one of the less standard sizes
Almost any cladding can be used for the lower part of the side. This is 150mm tongued and grooved shiplap horizontal siding
Stand the greenhouse on a solid base - a concrete slab, dwarf brick wall, or well-laid paving slabs

Setting out :-

1. Start by drawing, on your foundations, a regular cross with each arm at 90° to its neighbour and 933mm long. Use chalked lines or string and pegs, depending on your foundations. Take care orientating the cross - the ends of the arms are at the corners of the octagon

2. Draw a line joining up the ends of two adjacent arms. Run a new arm 933mm long from the centre of the cross through the middle of the joining line. Repeat for the other three pairs of arms

3. The ends of the eight arms form the corners of the octagon. Join them up to mark out the actual sides of the greenhouse (each 706mm long)

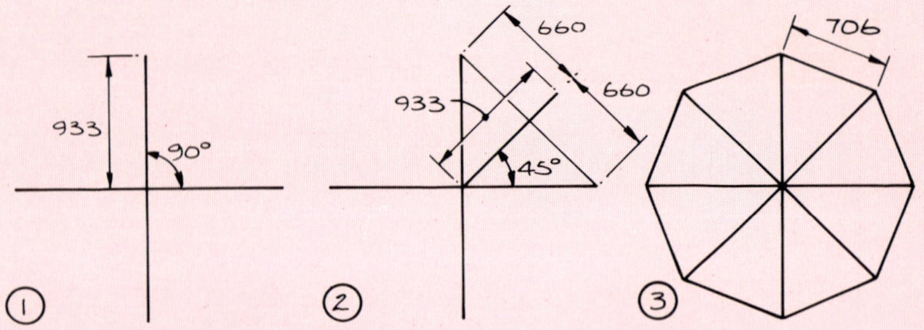

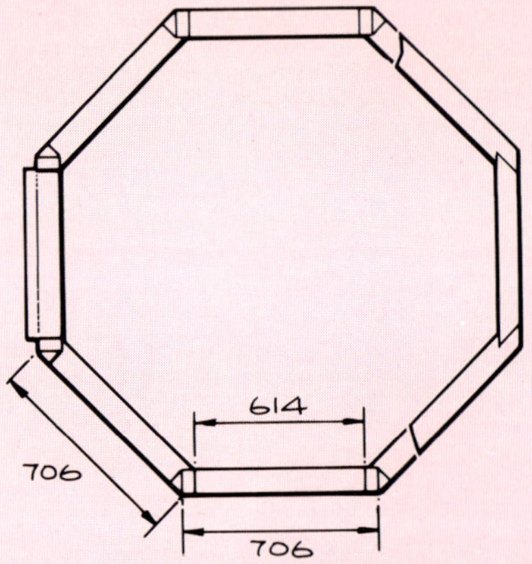

Part section - Part plan

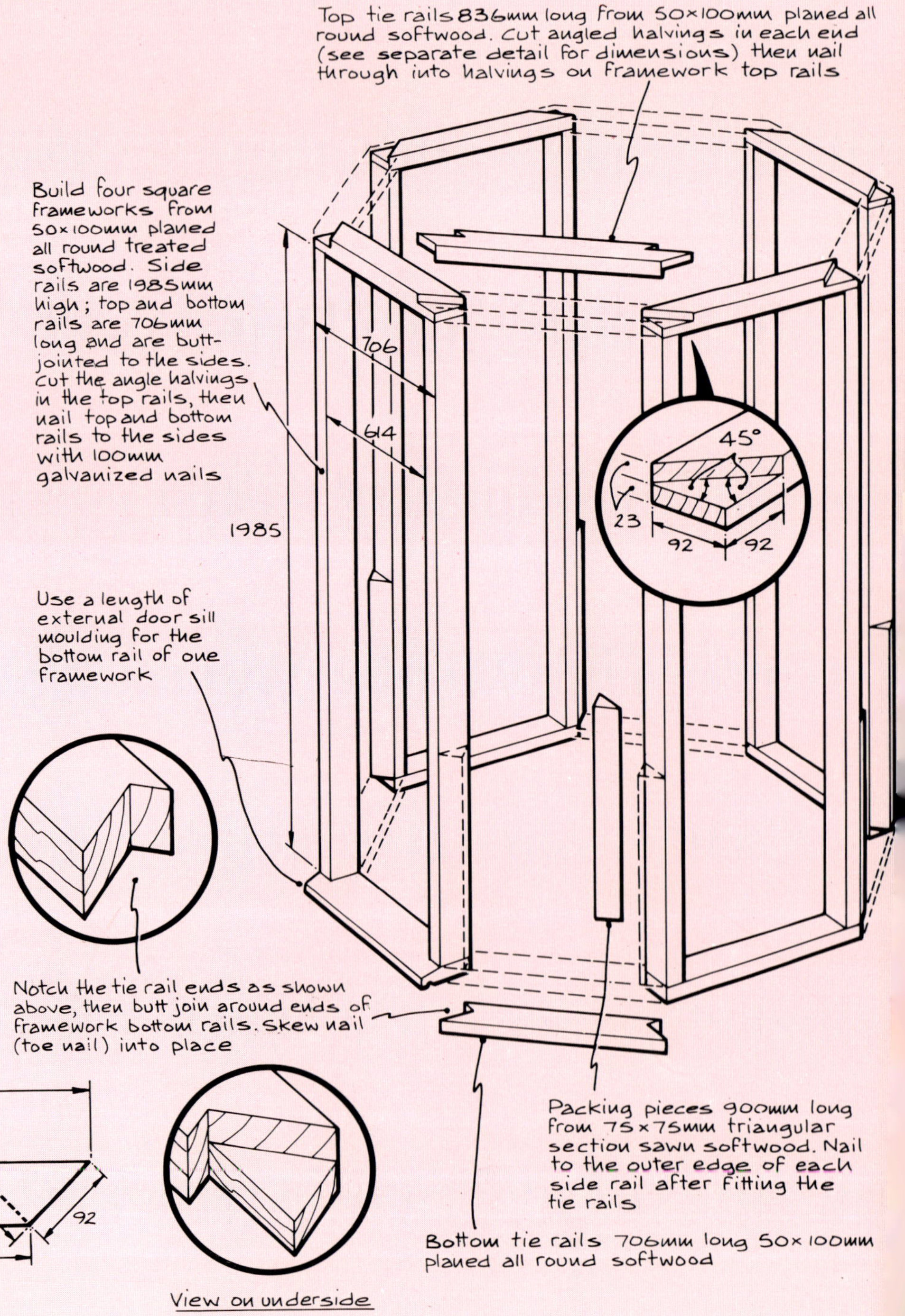

Bottom tie rail detail

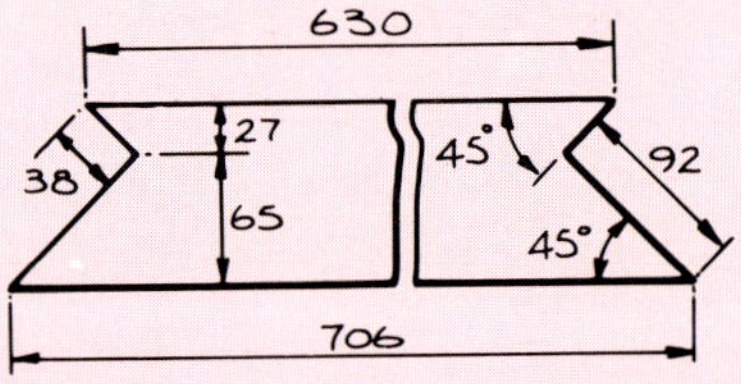

Top tie rail detail

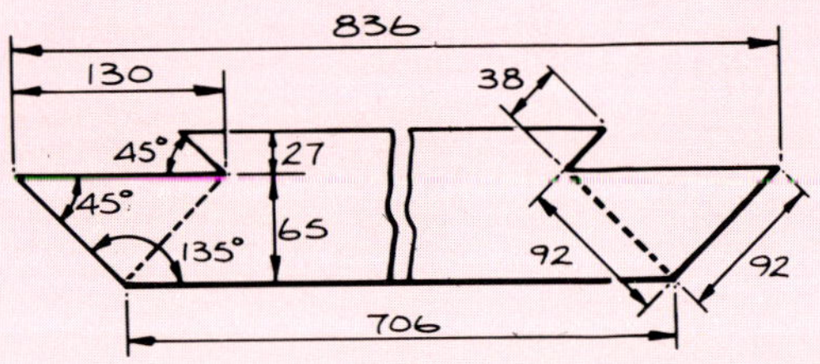

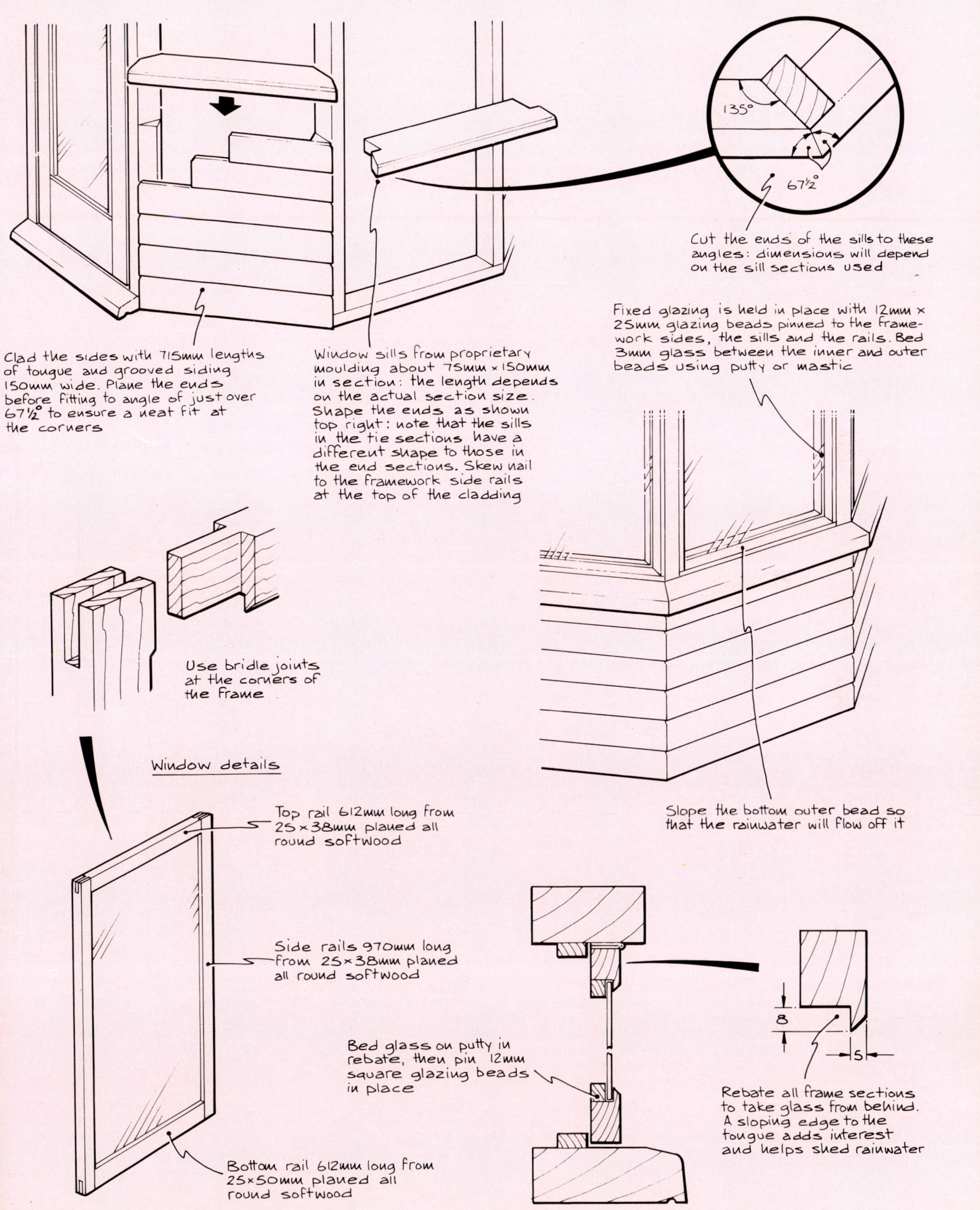
135°
67½°
Cut the ends of the sills to these angles: dimensions will depend on the sill sections used
Clad the sides with 715mm lengths of tongue and grooved siding 150mm wide. Plane the ends before fitting to angle of just over 67½° to ensure a neat fit at the corners
Window sills from proprietary moulding about 75mm × 150mm in section: the length depends on the actual section size. Shape the ends as shown top right: note that the sills in the tie sections have a different shape to those in the end sections. Skew nail to the framework side rails at the top of the cladding
Fixed glazing is held in place with 12mm × 25mm glazing beads pinned to the framework sides, the sills and the rails. Bed 3mm glass between the inner and outer beads using putty or mastic
Use bridle joints at the corners of the frame
Window details
Top rail 612mm long from 25 × 38mm planed all round softwood
Side rails 970mm long from 25×38mm planed all round softwood
Bottom rail 612mm long from 25×50mm planed all round softwood
Slope the bottom outer bead so that the rainwater will flow off it
Bed glass on putty in rebate, then pin 12mm square glazing beads in place
8
5
Rebate all frame sections to take glass from behind. A sloping edge to the tongue adds interest and helps shed rainwater

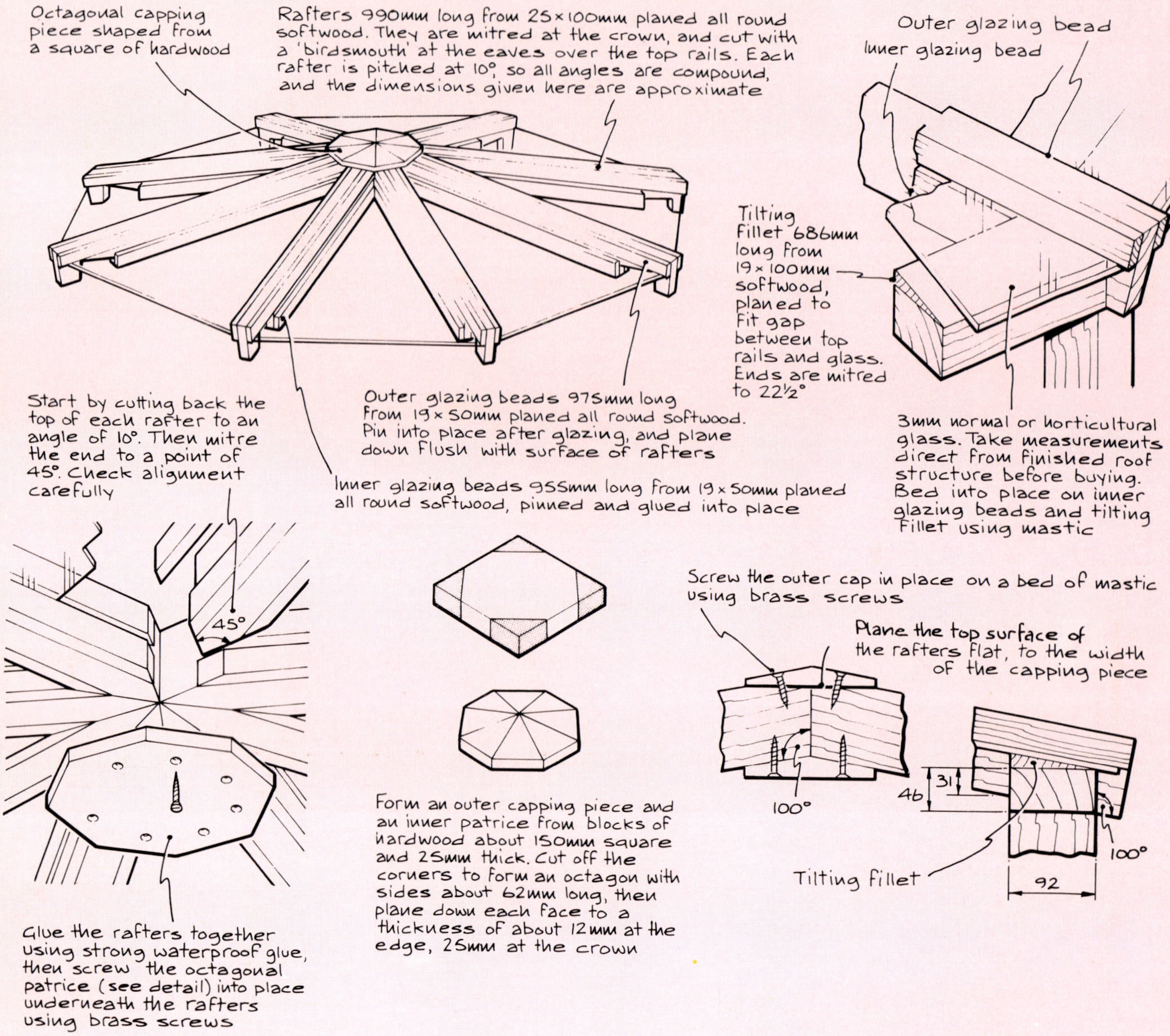

Cutting list

All sizes are in millimetres. All timber is planed all round, PAR (dressed four sides, D4S).

Part	Material	No.	Size
side rails	50 × 100mm softwood	8	1985mm
top rails	50 × 100mm softwood	4	706mm
top tie rails	50 × 100mm softwood	4	842mm
bottom rails	50 × 100mm softwood	3	706mm
bottom tie rails	50 × 100mm softwood	4	706mm
door sills	standard moulding	1	706mm
packing pieces	75 × 75mm triangular sawn section	8	900mm
window sills	standard moulding	7	810mm (1)
cladding	150mm T & G siding	42	715mm
rafters	25 × 100mm softwood	8	990mm
outer glazing bars	19 × 50mm softwood	16	975mm
inner glazing bars	19 × 50mm softwood	16	955mm
tilting fillets	19 × 100mm sawn softwood	8	686mm
outer capping	25mm hardwood	1	150 × 150mm
inner patrice	25mm hardwood	1	150 × 150mm

window frame			
top rail	25 × 38mm softwood	1 (2)	612mm
side rails	25 × 38mm softwood	2 (2)	970mm
bottom rail	25 × 50mm softwood	1 (2)	612mm
glazing beads	12 × 12mm softwood	1 (2)	2.9m
fixed window glazing bead	12 × 25mm softwood	1 (3)	6.4m
door	standard size	1	1981 × 614mm
glass	3mm	–	8 sq m in total (1)

Additional materials: Urea formaldehyde adhesive, galvanized round wire (common) nails; brass woodscrews.

Finish: Paint or stain.

Notes

(1) Approximate quantities.
(2) You need these quantities for each opening window.
(3) You need these quantities for each fixed window.

A garden pergola

Dress up your back garden or patio with a shady, plant-covered pergola. This project includes designs for several types of timber frame and a version with stone columns.

A pergola can add interest to all kinds of garden design, whether it encloses a small patio-type back garden or covers a walkway in a large landscaped area. The choice of site can quite radically effect the construction, so you should consider this carefully first.

For example, a pergola over a patio attached to the house may best be built as a lean-to supported on one side by the house wall. A pergola covering a walkway between two areas of the garden will be free-standing, but if it is along the edge of the plot you need to incorporate fencing along one side. If the ground is uneven, you can either set the tops of the posts level or keep them the same length and have the pergola following the undulations of the ground.

Few points of the design, which is essentially an open skeleton are critical: simply pick those features which best suit the pergola you have in mind and the materials you have available. But in general, you should work to the height and width indicated so that you provide an adequate walkway when the structure is covered with plants.

Most of the materials specified are sawn softwood. This should be well treated with timber preservative before use since it is difficult to re-proof without disturbing the plants. If available, oak will provide the most durable timber structure, or you can use larch poles for a rustic look. Stone or brick piers are ideal for a really long lasting structure.

Set all the uprights in concrete, then add the beams. Several different beam arrangements are detailed. For extra support for climbing plants, add trellis or plastic coated wire mesh frames to the uprights.

Many kinds of plant are suitable – you can plant climbers such as vines or rambling roses at the base of the uprights and border plants in between. Remember that the structure will look bare in winter unless you include some evergreens.

Workplan

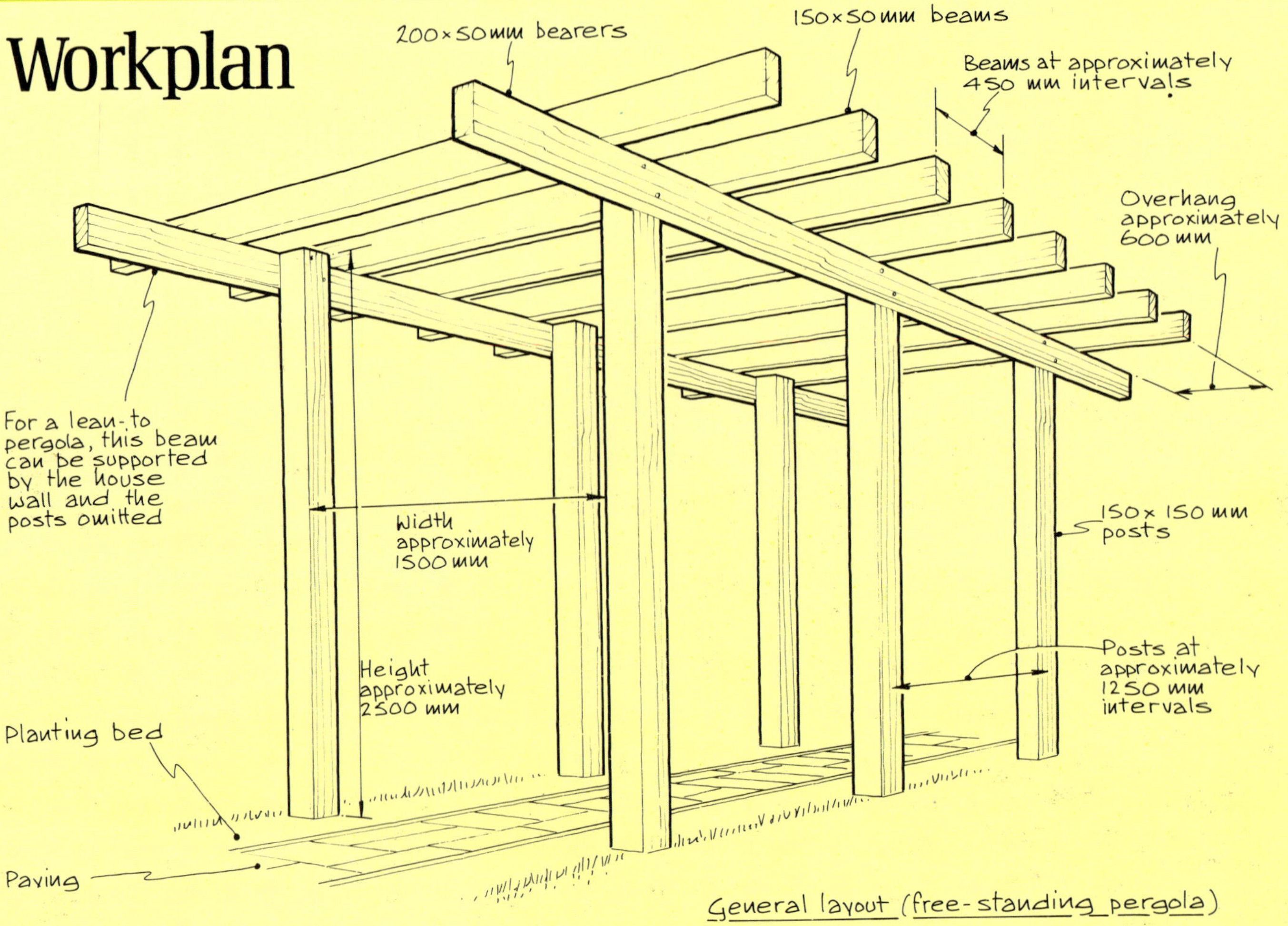

General layout (free-standing pergola)

All timber must be thoroughly treated with timber preservative, paying particular attention to the end grain. See text for further details

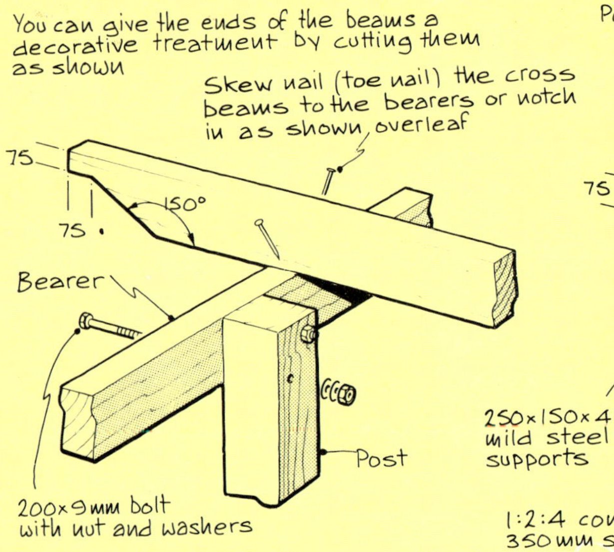

Beam fixing detail

Paving and post fixing details

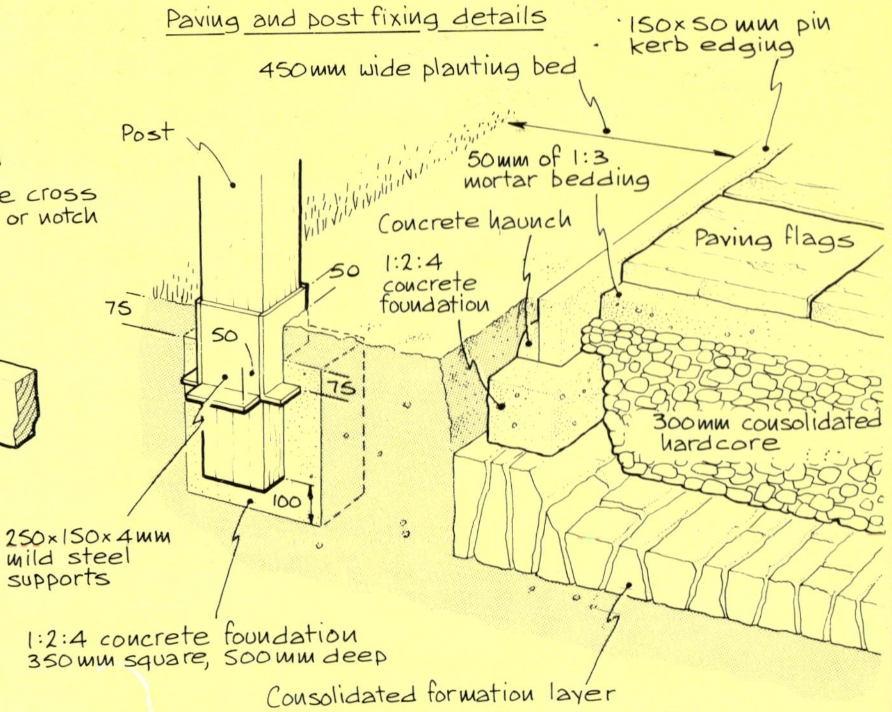

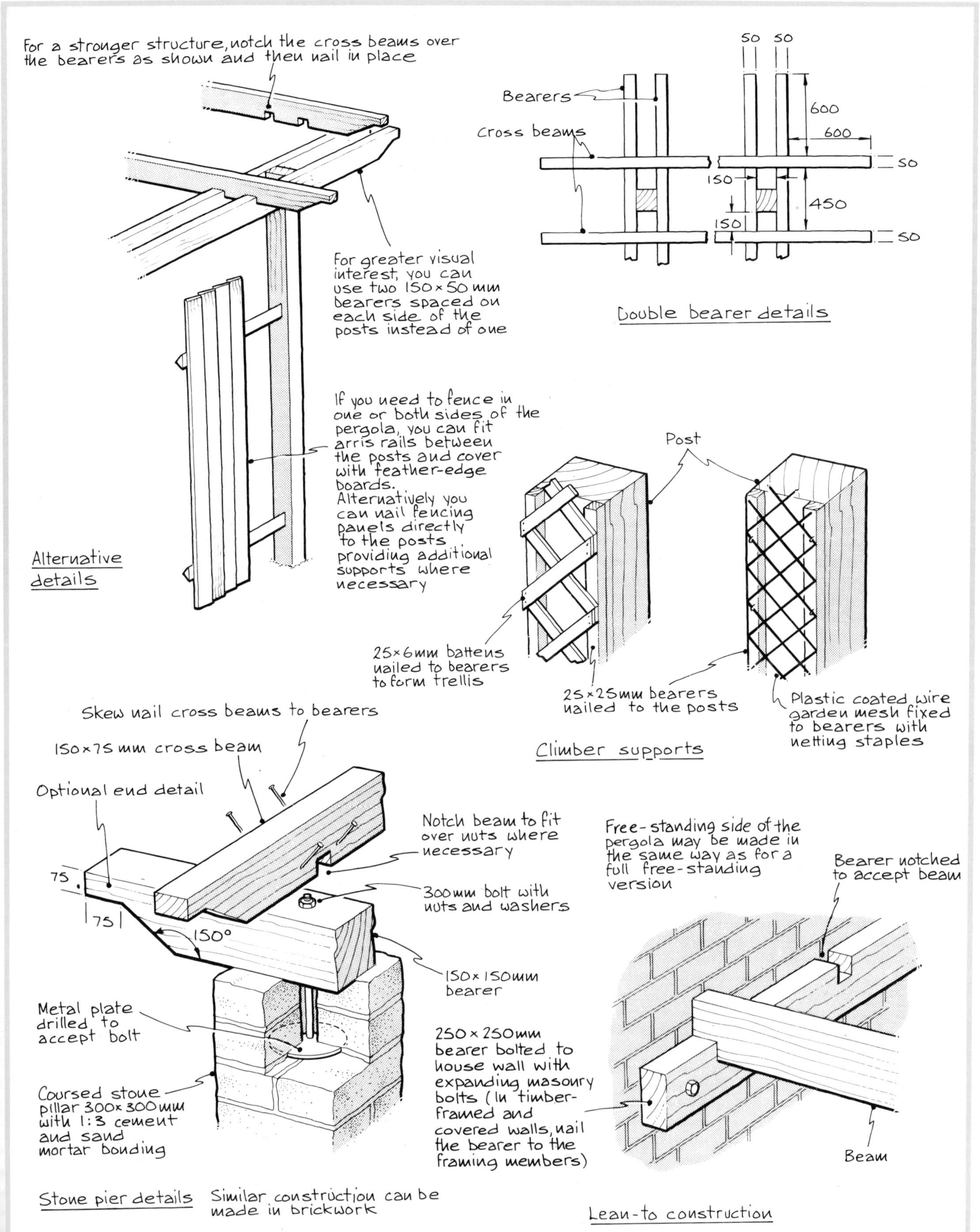
For a stronger structure, notch the cross beams over the bearers as shown and then nail in place
For greater visual interest, you can use two 150 × 50 mm bearers spaced on each side of the posts instead of one
If you need to fence in one or both sides of the pergola, you can fit arris rails between the posts and cover with feather-edge boards. Alternatively you can nail fencing panels directly to the posts providing additional supports where necessary
Alternative details
50
50
Bearers
Cross beams
600
600
50
150
450
150
50
Double bearer details
Post
25 × 6 mm battens nailed to bearers to form trellis
25 × 25 mm bearers nailed to the posts
Plastic coated wire garden mesh fixed to bearers with netting staples
Climber supports
Skew nail cross beams to bearers
150 × 75 mm cross beam
Optional end detail
Notch beam to fit over nuts where necessary
75
75
150°
300 mm bolt with nuts and washers
150 × 150 mm bearer
Metal plate drilled to accept bolt
Coursed stone pillar 300 × 300 mm with 1:3 cement and sand mortar bonding
Stone pier details
Similar construction can be made in brickwork
Free-standing side of the pergola may be made in the same way as for a full free-standing version
Bearer notched to accept beam
250 × 250 mm bearer bolted to house wall with expanding masonry bolts (In timber-framed and covered walls, nail the bearer to the framing members)
Beam
Lean-to construction

Index

All-purpose garden 9-10
Alpine plants 20
Apple trees 8
Assault course for children 92
Awnings 36-7, 38, 39, 40
Azaleas 9

Bamboos 10
Barbecues 12-13, 44, 67, 71, 113, 116
Barrels 71, 116
Bay trees 71
Beech hedges 180
Benches 13, 115
Berberis hedges 180
Bird table, building a 187
Blinds, *see* Awnings; Sunshades
Blockbuilding 211-12, 213-15
Box hedges 180
Brick
  bonds 136-7
  foundations 138
  matching the house 6
  paths 10, 13
  patios 70
  quoins 138-41
  screens 14
  steps, 79, 82
  terminology 136-7
  terraces 10
  terraced planter 144-5
  types 140

Canada
  additives to concrete 120
  brick paths 78
  creosote 188
  masonry cement 138
Carnations 236
Carport, building a 243-7
Cement, storing 122; *see also* Concrete
Ceramic tiles for patios 70
Chairs, garden 110-11, 114, 116
Cherry blossom 8
Cladding, stone 66
Clay soil 56
Clematis 7, 70, 178
Climate 6
Climbing frames
  children's 69, 90-1, 98-102
  rustic 72-3
Climbing plants 9, 66
Cobble stones for patios 70
Compacting machines (plate tampers) 125-6
Concrete
  adding colour 120
  additives 120
  blocks, making 211
  breaking up 124-5
  buying 121-2
  mixes (table) 120-1
  mixes for swimming pools 156
  mixing 119-23
  paths, repairing 83-6
  paving stones 10, 123
  quantities 120-1, 130
  raft foundations 132-4
  slabs for patios 70
  terraces 10
  tools for 124-9
  walls 10
Concrete mixers 126-7, 129
Conifers 26, 30, 66, 180
Conservatories 34, 224-7
Containers for vegetables 14
Cotoneasters 66, 180
Cottage gardens 9, 10
Courgettes 72
Cracks in paths 83-5
Crazy paving 13, 134-5
Creepers 7, 11, 14, 66
Creosote for fences 188
Crops, storing 30
Cucumbers 72
Currants 8, 14
Cypress 180

Deckchair covers 117
Downlighters 42
Downpipes 61
Drainage 30, 56-61, 80
Drains 58-60, 90
Drives 43, 61, 85-6
Drystone planter 223
Drystone walls 21, 27
  building 220-2
  components 218-19
  planning 220
  retaining 222
Dustbins 7, 204-5

Electricity
  cables for 49
  extension leads 51
  for detached garages and greenhouses 46
  installing overhead cables 47
  installing underground cables 48
  supply and connections 49
Espaliers 8

Fairy lights 50, 51
Fences
  chain link (mesh) 206-10
  close boarded (feather) 182, 183, 190, 198-205
  gravel boards 190-1, 201, 203
  interwoven panelled (lapped) 183, 191
  masonry plinths 203-4
  palings 183, 184
  palisade (picket) 184, 191-2
  post and rail 184
  preserving 188-9
  repairing 188-92
  rustic 184
  sloped 202-3
  trellis 184
  wood for 10
  wooden posts 192, 199-200
Ferns 71
Field drains 58
Flagstone paths, repairing 87
floodlights 42
Fountains 15, 16, 19, 51
Front gardens 7, 171-6, 184
Fruit trees 14
Furniture, garden 31, 69-70, 71-2, 108-12, 113, 114-5
Fuchsias 180, 225

Garden sheds, *see* Sheds
  Gates 184-6
  faulty gate posts 194-5
  faulty hinges 196
  lights for 50
  play area 89
  repairing 193-7
  types 195
  wooden 186, 195, 197
  wrought iron 185-6, 195, 196
Gooseberries 8, 14
Granite (grit), *see also* Concrete
  drives, repairing 87
  flower beds 12-13
  rockeries 21, 24
Greenhouses 8, 225-7, 236-41, 248-52
Grow bags 14

Hammocks 116
Hawthorn 180
Heathers 26
Hedges 8, 9, 10, 178, 180, 181
Herb gardens 7, 8, 14
Herbaceous borders 9
Holly
  danger to children 89
  hedges 180
Honeysuckle 7, 180
Hornbeam 180
Hoses, storing 34

Ivy 7, 11, 63, 71, 72

Lanterns 42
Laurels 71
Lavender 72, 89, 180, 181
Lawns 6, 7, 9, 12, 52-5
Layout, garden 7
Leisure garden 8-9
Lettuce 72
Lighting, *see also* Electricity
  positioning 43
  restrictions in Canada 42, 46
  underwater 42
  wiring for 42-3, 49-50
Lilacs 9, 180
Lonicera 66, 180
L-shaped gardens 9

Mortar, *see also* Concrete
  for bricks 137
  for building blocks 212
  for swimming pools 156
  mixes 120-1, 122
  plasticizers 138

Narrow gardens 29

Orchids 8
Organic solvents for preserving fences 188-9
Ornaments for pools 19
Outlet holes in walls, 59, 60-1; *see also* Weep holes
  Oxygenating plants in pools 15

Paddling pools 9, 69, 89, 91
Painting walls 62, 64-5
Paths 8, 74-7
  brick 74, 78-82, 85
  curved 82
  draining for 61
  materials for 13
  mosaic 76
  patterns 78, 81
  paving for 75
  pebbles for 76
  preparation 80
  repairing 83-7
  sloped 28
  stone 76-7
  unusual 86-7
  wooden 75, 76
Patios 12, 29, 38, 67-73; *see also* Terraces
  lighting for 42, 44, 45
  materials for 70
  planning 69
  position 67
  quarry tiled 70
  sites for 80
  sunshades and awnings for 40-1
Paves areas 12
Paving 7, 9, 10: *see also* Crazy paving
Paving stones, making 123
Pear trees 8
Pelargoniums 225
Peonies 9
Pergolas 8, 9, 14
  building 253
  for patios 70
  lighting for 44
Philodendrons 72
Planning gardens 10, 11
Plant pots 6
Planters 13, 14, 59, 67
  brick terrace 142-5
  drainage for 57
  drystone 223
  for front garden 171-6
  on patios 72
  stepped 176
Play areas 7, 9, 31, 69, 88-97
Plum trees (Prunus) 8, 180, 181
Ponds 7, 10, 13, 15, 20, 30, 42, 44
Porches as garden sheds 34
Privet hedges 66, 180
Pyracantha 180

Raft foundations, concrete 130-4
Reeds 15, 16
Returfing 52-5
Rhododendrons 9
Rock gardens 7, 13, 27, 28
  constructing 24-5
  designing 20-3
  do's and don'ts 23
  plants for 20
  size and shape 21-2
  stones for 22, 24-5
Roses 7, 9, 70
Rustic work
  chairs 110-11
  fences 184
  stools 109
  tables 112

Sandpits 7, 9, 69, 88, 91, 94-7
Screens 64, 70, 211, 216-17
Shade 14, 20
Sheds, garden 8, 30, 32-3, 34, 228-35
Shrubs 7, 14
Slides, children's 69
Slopes 20, 26-30, 56-7
Small gardens 11, 12
Soakaways 56-7, 59-60, 61
Soil 6, 56
Spotlamps 42, 43, 44
Square gardens 10
Statues 70
Steps 13, 28, 29
Stone 10, 14, 17, 22
Stool, making a rustic 109
Storage 31-6, 41
Strawberries 8, 14
Streams 15
Subsidence in paths 84
Summerhouses 33
Sundecks (lounges) 31, 115
Sun lounger, making a 118
Sunshades 37, 39-40
Swimming pools
  backfilling 158
  blockwork 154
  checklist 151
  choosing 147-8
  concrete and mortar mixes 156
  construction 152-9
  disinfecting 165
  electricity for 164
  equipment list 165
  excavating 151
  filters 161
  filtration 159-64
  fittings 158
  flooring 154-5
  heating 166-70
  installation programme 157
  ladders 162-3
  lights for 42
  liners 155-7
  marking out 150-1
  panel type 153
  planning 146-51
  plant room 162-4
  render coating 157-8
  services 150
  tools and plant 158
  types 146-7
  water turnover 165
Swing seats 116
Swings 69, 90-1, 103-7

Tables 112, 114
Tamarisk hedges 180
Tarmac drives, repairing 85-6
Terraces 6, 7, 29; *see also* Patios
  brick planter 142-5
  draining for 57
  drystone retaining walls 222
  materials for 10
  sunshades and awnings 40-1
Tomatoes 14, 72
Tree house 89, 92
Trellises 8, 14, 40, 66
  as fencing 184
  for patios 70-1
  in the front garden 171
Tubes for children 90-1
Turf and returfing 52-5

Underwater lights 42

Valerian 178
Vegetable garden 7, 8, 9, 10, 14
Vegetable rack, making a 34-5
Vines 8, 12, 14, 40
Virginia creepers 7

Wall lamps 42
Walls 9, 14
  concrete for 10
  drystone 218
  flintstone 177
  foundations for 179
  improving 62
  materials for 179
  open bond 140-1
  retaining 29-30, 57, 59
  screen 216-17
  stone slab 179

Water butts 15
Water gardens 15-19, 30
Water lilies 15, 18, 19
Water tables 56
Waterfalls 15, 16, 17, 19, 30
Weep holes in walls 30, 59, 142, 145
Wendy houses 90
Wigwam for children 92-3
Wiring for outside lights 42-3, 45
Wisteria 62

Yew
  danger for children 89
  hedges 180